ORGANISATIONAL STRUCTURE OF HEALTH CARE SYSTEM AND HOSPITAL ADMINISTRATION

ORGANIZATIONAL STRUCTURE OF HEALTH CARE SYSTEM

ORGANISATIONAL STRUCTURE OF HEALTH CARE SYSTEM AND HOSPITAL ADMINISTRATION

HEALTH CARE SYSTEM AND HOSPITAL ADMINISTRATION—I

DR. S.L. GOEL

Professor of Public Administration (Retd.),
Panjab University, Chandigarh
Editor, Indian Journal of Public Administration, IIPA, New Delhi
Former Member, UGC, Former Member Distance Education Council
Former Member All India Board of Management, AICTE
Member, Executive Council, IIPA, New Delhi.
Former Vice-President, IIPA, New Delhi.
Emeritus Fellow, University Grants Commission
Former Director, State Bank of India (Local Board) Chandigarh
Former Director, National Horticulture Board, Ministry of Agriculture,
Government of India, New Delhi.

DEEP & DEEP PUBLICATIONS PVT. LTD.

F-159, Rajouri Garden, New Delhi-110027

Organisational Structure of Health Care System and Hospital Administration
(Health Care System and Hospital Administration—1)

ISBN 978-81-8450-191-9

Typeset by S.S. COMPOSERS
3190, Mohindra Park, Shakur Basti, Delhi-110034.

Printed in India at MAYUR ENTERPRISES
WZ Plot No. 3, Gujjar Market, Tihar Village, New Delhi-110018.

Published by DEEP & DEEP PUBLICATIONS PVT. LTD.
F-159, Rajouri Garden, New Delhi-110027.
Phones: 25435369, 25440916
E-mail: ddpbooks@yahoo.co.in • ddpubs@gmail.com
Showroom:
2/13, Ansari Road, Daryaganj, New Delhi-110002 • Telefax: 23245122

Contents

Contents

Preface

Eleventh Five Year Plan observes that "the health of a nation is an essential component of development, vital to the nation's economic growth and internal stability."

The Tribune editorial dated 17.1.2009 deplores about the miserable conditions of health in India. In the editorial "Mother and Child Health Care must reach the vulnerable", it is observed that the governments, both Central and State, have been proclaiming time and again that health and education are their top priority. But the latest UNICEF State of the World Children report once again proves that India faces a major challenge in healthcare. Its record in treating mothers and children, the most vulnerable section of the populations, seems most disheartening. According to the report, India loses nearly one million neonates annually.

Since the institutional delivery rate in India is rather poor, undisputedly there is an urgent need to step up institutional deliveries. There is also an equally pressing requirement to train midwives to ensure safe deliveries at home. The health programmes have to lay emphasis on recognizing mother and child as a single entity that deserves care. Only a healthy mother can give birth to a healthy baby. Contributory factors like poor education, low socio-economic status and malnutrition too need to be addressed. In a nation that has begun to boast of medical tourism, ironically health care for all, especially the rural poor still remains a distant dream. All these problems must be taken care of at all levels of health and hospital administration.

Assuring a minimal level of health care of the population is a critical constituent of the development process. Since independence India has built-up a vast health infrastructure and health personnel at primary, secondary, and tertiary care in public, voluntary, and private sectors. For producing skilled human resources, a number of medical and paramedical institutions including Ayurveda, Yoga and Naturopathy, Unani, Siddha, and Homeopathy (AYUSH) institutions have been set-up.

The concern for better Public Health Care is universal. At the G-8 Summit in Japan (July 2000) major powers pledged to improve health care system of the developing, underdeveloped and poor countries. The leaders vowed to reduce by the year 2010 the number of HIV-infected people by 25 per cent, tuberculosis deaths by 50 per cent, the burden of diseases associated with malaria by 50 per cent. AIDS will leave 44 million orphans in the next decade. The goal is to encourage initiatives to properly manage the Public Health Care system to solve the myraid problems.

Promotion of health is basic to national progress. Nothing could be of greater significance than the health of the people in terms of resources of socio-economic development. In spite of this realisation, the people living in the developing world and especially 70 per cent of them who live in rural areas have little or no access to modern medicine and health care. Inevitably this results in morbidity and high rate of mortality from preventable diseases. This state of hopelessness and frustration among the people is not because of the lack of professional knowledge or competence but due to poor administration of health services at all levels. Administration can provide the means whereby the most effective use can be made of the knowledge and skills of the personnel responsible for the health care delivery system. The benefits of modern science and technology can reach the people only if such services are properly planned and effectively implemented.

The design of an administrative system is a basic aid to the achievement of its primary objectives; if the design is unsound, the achievement of objectives is likely to fall short of expectations. This requires the capabilities to design and manage the health care administration. Though there has been great expansion of health services, primary health centres, dispensaries, hospitals and hospital beds, and community health centres and also at secondary and tertiary health care level, the functioning of Health Care system is not upto desired expectations. Even the Ninth Five Year Plan (1997-2000) has admitted it and enlisted a number of factors responsible for inefficient functioning:

- Persistent gaps in manpower and infrastructure especially at the primary health care level.
- Sub-optimal functioning of the infrastructure; poor referral services.
- Plethora of hospitals not having appropriate manpower, diagnostic and therapeutic services and drugs, in Government, voluntary and private sector.
- Massive inter-state/inter-district differences in performance as assessed by health and demography indices; availability and utilisation of services are poorest in the most needy states/ districts.
- Sub-optimal inter-sectoral coordination.
- Increasing dual disease burden of communicable and non-communicable diseases because of ongoing demographic lifestyle and environmental transitions.
- Technological advances which widen the spectrum of possible interventions.

- Increasing awareness and expectations of the population regarding health care services.
- Escalating costs of health care, ever widening gaps between what is possible and what the individual or the country can afford.

The World Health Report 2000 rightly describes that health systems consist of all the people and actions whose primary purpose is to improve health. They may be integrated and centrally directed, but often they are not. Having remained small-scale, largely private or charitable and mostly ineffectual entities for centuries, the health systems have grown explosively in this century, knowledge has been gained and applied. They have contributed enormously to better health, but their contribution could be greater still, especially for the poor. Failure to achieve this potential is more due to systems failings than to technical limitations. It is therefore, urgent to assess current performance and to judge how health systems can reach their potential.

During the Eleventh Five Year Plan period, the following will receive priority:

- Establishment of Hospital Development Committees in all government hospitals.
- Improvements of infrastructure and facilities in district hospitals.
- Provision of high-quality secondary health care services for every block in the country.
- Creation of state-of-the-art medical education research, and care institutions in all disciplines of medicine.
- Creation of new institutions and upgradation of existing tertiary care hospitals.
- Mainstreaming of AYUSH systems to actively supplement the efforts of the allopathic system

This volume deals with levels of health care administration supported by a chapter on World Health Organisation as this International Specialized Agency has played a pioneering role in the genesis, development, growth and diversification of health care. This volume has been divided into 11 chapters supplemented by tables, charts and graphs to make the reading interesting and illustrative. Besides, chapters are supported by case studies. The contents reflect the coverage in this volume.

The understanding of functions, responsibilities and activities of each level is essential to make model health plans with a real thrust on implementation.

Eleventh Five Year Plan, 2007-12, Vol. II observes that for Strengthening Existing Health System, there is need to shift to decentralization of functions to hospital units/health centres and local bodies. The States need to move away from the narrow focus on the implementation of budgeted programmes and vertical schemes. They need to develop systems that comprehensively address the health needs of all citizens. Thus, in order to improve the health care services in the country, the Eleventh Five Year Plan will insist on Integrated District Health Plans and Block Specific Health Plans. It will mandate involvement of all health related sectors and emphasize partnership with PRIs, local bodies, communities, NGOs, Voluntary and Civil Society Organizations.

This work would be useful for all those dealing with health care management—Doctors, Nurses, Paramedical Staff as well as for Policy-makers and Planners for Health. It would also be of relevance to trainees, teachers and students of health management. Health Development is not possible without the Philosophy, Science and Practice of Health Administration and Management.

The implementation of the suggestions made in various chapters would ensure physical, mental, social and spiritual health to all, as enshrined in the constitution of World Health Organisation. Besides, this would help the academicians, national health officials, public health administrators, medical research workers and the policy-makers and planners in the proper understanding of the problems and their possible solutions in the area of health care delivery system. These will be of great interest to students and teachers engaged in medical education, research, training and consultancy. The author will consider his labour well rewarded if the findings of the study are translated to provide decent health care to millions of people living in rural areas, urban slums and tribal areas. The slogan of new millennium is not merely to live longer but live healthier as well.

"Happiness, happiness, happiness
It may be of different origin on this earth
But the happiness of being healthy
Is the real happiness".

Chandigarh S.L. GOEL

International Health Care Administration

Role of the World Health Organisation (WHO)

"The International Cooperation which is implicit in the very concept of the World Health Organisation is the alchemy which has translated the goodwill and good sense of nations into actions directed to making this world a healthier and more decent place for all mankind."

The present Director General Dr. Margaret Chan has observed about WHO as: Some of the work done by WHO is visible and familiar; the response teams sent to contain outbreaks, the emergency assistance to people affected by disasters, or the mass immunization campaigns that protects the world's children from killer diseases. Other work is visible because the diseases being addressed—HIV/AIDS, tuberculosis, and malaria—have such a high profile for global health.

The work of WHO is also visible in statistics, as we chart changing trends and sound the alarm when needed. As one example, we need to be concerned about the sharp rise of chronic diseases. Long thought to be the companions of affluent societies, diseases such as heart disease, cancer, and diabetes are now occurring in larger numbers and at an earlier age throughout the developing world.

Some activities undertaken by WHO are largely invisible quietly protecting the health of every person on this planet, every day. By assigning a single international name to drugs, WHO helps ensure that a prescription filled abroad is what the doctor ordered back home. Our standards help protect the safety of everyone's food and the quality of medicines and vaccines. When pollution in air or water reaches a dangerous level, it is WHO, standards that are used as the measure.

Our greatest concern must always rest with disadvantages and vulnerable groups. These groups are often hidden, living in remote rural areas of shantytowns and having little political voice.

WHO works to make these people—and their unmet health needs—

more visible and thus worthy of our priority concern. In addressing the needs of these populations, we work together with governments and a host of agencies, foundations, non-governmental organisations, and representatives of the private sector and civil society.

One statistic from these vulnerable groups stands out as especially tragic; more than 500,000 women die each year from complications of pregnancy. To reverse this trend, WHO and its partners must address complex problems that have their roots in social and economic conditions and the failure of health services tò reach the poor. These same problems account for many other needless deaths.

All of our efforts—and their prospectus for success—are greatly aided by today's unprecendented interest in health as a route to development, accompanied by equally unprecedented energy, initiatives, and funds.

This brochure provides some highlights from our broad range of activities—both high-profile and behind the scenes—that are working to improve world health.[1]

According to "Working for Health: An Introduction to the World Health Organisation" The World Health Organisation (WHO) is the directing and coordinating authority on international health within the United Nation's system. WHO experts produce health guidelines and standards, and help countries to address public health issues. WHO also supports and promotes health research. Through WHO, governments can jointly tackle global health problems and improve people's well-being.

Last but not least, WHO is people. Over 8000 public health experts including doctors, epidemiologists, scientists, managers, administrators and other professionals from all over the world work for WHO in 147 country offices, six regional offices and at the headquarters in Geneva, Switzerland.[2]

A. EVOLUTION AND OBJECTIVES OF THE WHO

Introduction

In the post-war period, a very significant development has been the establishment of a pivotal international organisation concerned with the problems of world peace and human welfare, This organisation is commonly known as United Nations. Since its birth it has been playing an increasingly vital role in easing the world tensions and conflicts which can erupt into a world conflagration as well as in alleviating the widespread hunger, poverty, ignorance, want, disease and allied problems. This organisation has been supplemented by the establishment of closely allied specialized agencies which deal with each of these stupendous problems more specifically.

When the UN Charter was being framed attention was initially focused on the problems of peace and security in the world. But at the instance of the USA, at the Yalta Conference, it was decided to create an Economic and Social Council as an integral part of the new international organisation (UN) to deal with the rapidly emerging economic and social problems.[3] The ECOSOC is to study the problems of human and social well-being as well as to formulate appropriate policies and direct their implementation in this connection. The UN system is thus founded upon the sound idea that no peace can be stable unless it is based upon nations whose citizens are substantially free from distress. privation and frustration.[4] The realisation that removal of poverty and improvement of economic conditions all around would be potent factors for peace prompted the expansion of the UN system. The United Nations Development System comprises the UN itself, five regional Economic Commissions and other major programmes and organs. Besides, there are separate inter-governmental specialised agencies.

In this monograph, we are concerned only with the important agency influencing directly or indirectly the promotion of health. The specialised agency responsible for international health is WHO. But there are other organs of UN (e.g. United Nations Development Programme, UNICEF, World Food Programme, etc.) and specialized agencies (e.g., FAO, ILO., etc.) which also influence the promotion of health. Thus, there is a need of coordinated effort by the UN system to produce the desired output. Coordination may be achieved through collaboration in working for the same cause, or cooperation—the sharing of a joint task by two or more parties; often it includes both modes of action. If, for instance, food shortage emerges as a top priority issue at a given time or in a particular area. The combined facilities and efforts of several agencies may be required to alleviate the distress: the technical advice and help of the FAO in increasing output, the assistance of the WHO in highlighting nutritional needs or in combating malaria and thereby releasing additional manpower for productive employment, the help of UNESCO and ILO in the field of training, the provision of emergency supply by the UNICEF, and the support of other agencies in the development of transport facilities or community organisation. In this chapter, we shall discuss the organisation and functioning of WHO with special reference to the South-East Asia Regional office.

Health and disease have no political or geographical boundaries. Disease in any part of the world is a potential danger to other parts. "Nothing on earth is more international than disease," said Paul Russel. The problems of international health is more pressing today as the world has become smaller. In his inaugural address to the 31st Session of the South East Regional Committee of WHO at Ulan Bator (22-28 Aug., 1978), T. Ragcha, First Vice-Chairman of the Council of Ministers, Mongolian People's Republic, said, "In our age, the age of communication boom and of increased intercourse among nations the problem of protection of human health transcends national boundaries and becomes a common concern of the international community. A failure in one country in the field of disease prevention may affect any other country. Therefore, it becomes increasingly imperative for national governments to coordinate the internal efforts in the field of health protection to develop closer cooperation between themselves and to participate actively in the work of the World Health Organisation."[5] In order to protect against the spread of the disease from one country to another many attempts were made. A brief account of those efforts which existed before the WHO came into existence is mentioned below:

1. Sanitary Conferences and Conventions

The International Public Health had its origin in the sanitary conference which opened in Paris on 23rd July, 1851. Five International Sanitary Conferences were held in 34 years after 1851. They failed to produce an agreed international sanitary convention. After this three sanitary conferences on cholera and the fourth on plague were held. They were consolidated into a single International Sanitary Convention in 1903.

2. Pan American Sanitary Bureau (PASB)

The bureau was created by the Second International Conference of American States held in Mexico city from 12 October, 1901 to 31 Jan. 1902. In 1947, the bureau became the general secretariat of an overall organisation, the Pan American Health Organisation. With the establishment of the WHO, the bureau became the WHO Regional Office for the Americas.

3. Office or International O'Hygiene Publique (OIHP/OFFICE) (1907)

It was created in 1907 to disseminate information on communicable diseases and to supervise international quarantine. The office continued to exist until 1950 when its responsibilities were taken over by the WHO.

4. The Health Organisation of the League of Nations

The creation of the League Organisation at the end of World War I called for an examination of the means for international collaboration in all fields, including health. There were many reasons for establishing a separate health organisation in addition to the already existing Paris Office (OIHP). First, since the creation of the Paris Office in 1907, other health questions beside quarantine had arisen which seemed to call for international action. Secondly, the advanced nations recognised the obligation to help improve the health of the backward nations. Finally; the menace of the typhus epidemics ranging in 1919-20 and the scale and urgency of post-war health problems loomed large. The modest resources of the office could not cope with it.

At the outbreak of World War II in 1939, international health work came almost to a standstill but was not abandoned. The League transferred its remaining functions, including those of health to the UN in April 1946. On October 16 of the same year, the functions and personnel of the League Health Organisation were formally transferred to the WHO.[6] The League of Nations Health Organisation had a great impact upon the functioning of the WHO as it left to the World Health Organisation a valuable legacy of recorded experience and in addition, certain statutory obligations for epidemiological services and publications.[7]

5. United Nations Relief and Rehabilitation Administration (UNRRA)

With the end of the Second World War emerged the urgent need to help the war devastated countries, to combat epidemics and restore their health services. It had been foreseen that no existing international health services organisation would be able to undertake this massive task. At the first session of UNRRA's council in 1943, it was agreed that health work would be one of its primary responsibilities.[8]

In June 1945, UNRRA provided 450 teams, including 380 doctors and 435 nurses, to care for the health of the millions of displaced persons who wanted to return to their countries. At the end of 1946, UNRRA, designed as a temporary organisation to deal with an emergency, terminated its official existence and its health activities were taken over by the WHO Interim Commission. It suffered from the defects associated with a large and temporary "international organisation created towards the end of a World War. Nevertheless, it carried out, by far, the largest international health, programme ever executed. It played a major part in the prevention of post-war epidemics and in the reconstruction of health services. Its residual funds were of immense value to its successor agencies, particularly in the health field.

6. Birth of WHO

Delegates of 50 nations in the UN Conference on International Organisation held in San Francisco from 25 April to 26 June, 1945 approved a proposal put by the delegations of Brazil and China that an international conference should be held to establish an international health organisation. The constitution was drawn up at this conference in 1946. An Interim Commission was set-up to carry on the work for the new organisation which held five sessions. On 7 April, 1948, the 26 of the 61 member governments ratified the constitution and the WHO was born as a specialised agency of the United Nations. The First Health Assembly opened in Geneva on 24 June 1948 with delegations from 50 of the 55 governments.

Thus, the creation of the WHO after World War II as a specialised agency of the United Nations marked a considerable advance in the Evolution of the International Health Organisation. It presents a culmination of efforts at international health cooperation initiated a century ago. It absorbed and unified all the existing organisations for the time being transforming it into single, world-wide inter-governmental body.

The 'Magna Carta' of Health

The Constitution of the World Health Organisation has been called the 'Magna Carta' of health. In its final form, it constitutes one of the most powerful instruments for international collaboration to enable man to improve his condition of life.

Concept of 'Health' in the Bill of Human Rights

The United Nations Commission on Human Rights, which met in Geneva in December 1947, incorporated in the Charter of Human Rights the following article:

> "Everyone, without distinction as to economic and social conditions, has the right to the preservation of his health through the highest standards of food, clothing, housing and medical care which the resources of the State and community can provide. The responsibility of the State and community for the health and safety of its people can be fulfilled only by provision of adequate health and social measures."[9]

Objectives

The main objective of the WHO is "the attainment by all peoples of the highest level of health" which is set out in the Preamble of the Constitution. The Preamble of the Constitution states: "Health is a state of complete physical, mental and social well-being and not merely the absence of disease or infirmity. The enjoyment of the highest attainable standard of health is one of the fundamental rights of every human being without distinction of race, religion, political belief, economic and social condition. The health of all peoples is fundamental to the attainment of people and security and is dependent upon the fullest cooperation of individuals and states.

The achievement of any state in the promotion and protection of health is of value to all. Unequal development in different countries in the promotion of health and control of disease, especially communicable disease, is a common danger. Healthy development of the child is of basic importance; the ability to live harmoniously in a changing total environment is essential to such development.

The extension to all people of the benefits of medical, psychological and related knowledge is essential to the fullest attainment of health. Informed opinion and active cooperation on the part of the public are of the utmost importance in the improvement of the health of the people. Governments have a responsibility for the health of their peoples which can be fulfilled only by the provision of adequate health and social measures.

Thus, WHO's work covers a wide spectrum of activities, ranging from the fight against most of the world's diseases to the award of fellowships, from the monitoring of environmental conditions detrimental to health to the collection of international statistics; from the training of health personnel to multilateral research endeavours.

Functions

In order to achieve its objectives, the functions of the WHO are:

(a) to act as the directing and coordinating authority on international health work;

(b) to establish and maintain effective collaboration with the United Nations, specialised agencies, governmental health administrations, professional groups, and such other organisations as may be deemed appropriate;
(c) to assist governments, upon request, in strengthening health;
(d) to furnish appropriate technical assistance and in emergencies, necessary aid upon the request or acceptance of governments;
(e) to provide or assist in providing, upon the request of the UN Health Services and facilities to special groups, such as the peoples of Trust territories;
(f) to establish and maintain such administrative and technical services as may be required including epidemiological and statistical services;
(g) to stimulate and advance work to eradicate epidemic, endemic and other diseases;
(h) to promote, in cooperation with other specialised agencies where necessary, the prevention of accidental injuries;
(i) to promote, in cooperation with other specialised agencies where necessary, the improvement of nutrition, housing, sanitation, recreation, economic or working conditions and other aspects of environmental hygiene;
(j) to promote cooperation among scientific and professional groups which contribute to the advancement of health;
(k) to propose conventions, agreements and regulations, and make recommendations with respect to international health matters and to perform such duties as may be assigned thereby to the organisation and are consistent with its objectives;
(l) to promote maternal and child health and welfare and to foster the ability to live harmoniously in a changing total environment;
(m) to foster activities in the field of mental health, especially those affecting the harmony of human relations;
(n) to promote and conduct research in the field of health;
(o) to promote improved standards of teaching and training in the health, medical and related professions;
(p) to study and report on, in cooperation with other specialised agencies where necessary, administrative and social techniques affecting public health and medical care from preventive and curative point of view, including hospital services and social security;
(q) to provide information, counsel and assistance in the field of health;
(r) to assist in developing an informed public opinion among all peoples on matters of health;
(s) to establish and revise as necessary international nomenclature practices;
(t) to standardise diagnostic procedures as and when necessary;

(u) to develop establish and promote international standards with respect to food, biological, pharmaceutical and similar products; and

(v) generally to take all necessary action to attain the objective of the organisation.

Activities

The forms of assistance which may be provided include:

(a) expert personnel to provide advisory, executive and operational services;

(b) fellowships, training courses and seminars; and

(c) equipment and supplies.

The WHO assisted projects fall in the following broad categories:

(a) Control of Communicable Diseases

Control of communicable diseases (e.g., parasitic, bacterial, viral), eradication or control programmes, laboratory facilities and vaccine production.

(b) Education, Training and HRD

Education and training of professional, technical and auxiliary staff, grant of fellowships, study tours and conferences, manpower development.

(c) Coordination of Medical Research and Supporting Services

Collaborative research, reference centres, research grants for training and exchange and scientific groups.

(d) Development of Public Health Services

Public Health Administration, organisation of medical care, hospitals, laboratories and nursing services, environmental sanitation, cancer and cardiovascular diseases, drug control and vital health statistics.

(e) Development of Primary Health Care Services

We should keep in mind that WHO is in no sense of the term a World Health Service; it helps governments at their request and in accordance with the policy laid down by the Health Assembly.

B. ORGANISATIONAL STRUCTURE AND FUNCTIONS

The basic structure of the WHO comprises three organs:

(1) The World Health Assembly (Health Assembly).

(2) The Executive Board (Board).

(3) The Secretariat headed by the Director-General.

(I) Health Assembly

It is the supreme policy-making body of the Organisation. The first World Health Assembly met in the Palais des Nations, Geneva, Switzerland, from 24 June-24 July 1948. It was attended by representatives of 52 of the then 54 Member States and by observes from 14 non-Member States and 10 international non-governmental organisations.[10] It is the only organ in which all members enjoy direct representation. As of 1 January, 2007, it consisted of 193 members and two Associate members. Each Assembly elects a President and five vice-presidents, who hold office until their successors are elected. The work of the Assembly is conducted by two main Committees: Committee A to deal predominantly with programme and budget matters, and Committee B to deal predominantly with administrative, financial and legal matters.

Decisions are taken through the adoption of resolutions which may be tabled by any Member. There must be a two-thirds majority of the members present and voting for important questions such as the adoption of conventions or agreements and fixing the amount of the effective working budget. Decisions on other questions require a simple majority. Its functions are enumerated in the Constitution. Most important of these being:

(a) to determine the policy of the Organisation;
(b) to name the members entitled to designate a person to serve on the Board;
(c) to appoint the Director-General;
(d) to review and report activities of the Board and of the Director-General and to instruct the Board in regard to matters upon which action study, investigation or report may be considered desirable; and
(e) to supervise the financial policies of the Organisation and to review and approve the budget.

The Health Assembly has been passing resolutions affecting the health of the world as a whole. Professor E. Aujaleu (France), President of the 21st World Health Assembly, 1968, and the Chairman of the 24th and 25th Sessions of the Executive Board, 1959-60, offered the following comments on the Assembly's role:

The Assembly has shown considerable dignity in its discussions. It has handled extremely delicate subjects—the refugees in the Middle-East, assistance to Portugal, the health situation in Vietnam with particular care to avoid offence and even with a certain all-round imperturbability. I believe that the Assembly has reached almost complete maturity. Its maturity will be truly complete when we refuse to divert a single hour to the raising of political problems with which we are neither competent nor qualified to deal. The moment may not be far off; at least sincerely hope so.[11]

Most major policy decisions have been taken by the 31st Health Assembly without dissenting voices. It was remarked by Professor Julie

Sulianti Saroso, President of the 25th Health Assembly that no Health Assembly has passed without decisions being taken which marked a new milestone in mankind's continual struggle against disease. The Sixteenth World Health Assembly was held in Geneva from 14 to 23 May 2007. The Assembly elected Ms J. Halton (Australia) as President. From the South-East Asia Region, Mr. Kye Chun Yong from DPR Korea was elected as one of the five Vice-Presidents. Dr. A.A. Yoosuf from Maldives was the Vice-Chairman, Committee B. The Health Assembly also elected Thailand for membership to the General Committee on Credentials and Indonesia and Sri S.A. Khan Lanka to the Committee on Nominations.[12]

The First World Health Assembly in 1948 decided that World Health Day should be celebrated every year on 22 July in commemoration of the signing of the WHO Commission on that date in 1946 by 61 governments at the International Health Conference in New York. The Second World Health Assembly, however, considered that schools and other educational institutions worldwide could and should act as important focal points for the observance of this day. Since schools in most countries were having vacations in July, they could not observe the occasion. The Assembly, therefore, chose 7 April, the day the WHO Constitution came into force, as a suitable alternative. The Assembly resolved that, beginning 1950 and each year thereafter, World Health Day should appropriately be celebrated on 7 April by all Member States.

(2) Executive Board

It consists of 34 members technically qualified in the field of health. The Board meets at least twice a year. Its first session is generally held at the beginning of the calendar year at which it sorts out the budget and programme estimates of the Director-General. The second session follows the annual meeting of the Assembly in winter. One-third of the members retire every year. Dr. S.L. Molapo the then Chairman of the Executive Board reviewed the role and functions of the Board. He said, "The Board has indeed performed its task efficiently, with sincerity and integrity. Achievements are exacting but the faith which was the forerunner and continues to be the moving spirit of achievements is of even greater importance."[13]

The 120th and the 121st sessions of the Executive Board were held in Geneva from 22 to 30 January 2007 and 24 to 26 May 2007, respectively. During the 120th session, resolutions were adopted on: poliomyelitis; tuberculosis control; health systems; oral health; integrating gender analysis and actions into the work of WHO; avian and pandemic influenza; smallpox eradication; rational use of medicines; better medicines for children; health promotion; WHO's role and responsibilities in health research; prevention and control of non-communicable diseases; and health technologies.[14]

(3) The Secretariat

Secretariat is the staff of WHO headed by the Director-General who is the Chief Technical and Administrative officer of the organisation. He is assisted by Assistant Director-Generals and other staff in carrying out his duties and responsibilities. He appoints the staff in accordance with the staff regulations prescribed by the Assembly, submits the budget to the Executive Board and to the Assembly.

This year, i.e. 2008 marks the 60th anniversary of WHO. This special occasion presents WHO with an opportunity to celebrate achievements in global public health over the last 60 years, demonstrate the impact of WHO's work and address challenges for the future.

The World Health Report 2007—A safer future: global public health security in the 21st Century marks a turning point in the history of public health, and signals what could be one of the biggest advances in health security in half a century. It shows how the world is at increasing risk of disease outbreaks, epidemics, industrial accidents, natural disasters and other health emergencies which can rapidly become threats to global public health security. The report explains how the revised International Health Regulations (2005), which came into force this year, helps countries to work together to identify risks and act to contain and control them. The regulations are needed because of single country, regardless of capability or wealth, can protect itself from outbreaks and other hazards without the cooperation of others. The report says the prospect of a safer future is within reach—and that this is both a collective aspiration and a mutual responsibility.

(4) Regionalisation

Regionalisation connotes the geographical arrangements used by the WHO to establish decentralisation. Much of the effectiveness of the WHO has often been attributed to its decentralised structure, which enables it to come to grips as directly as possible with local and regional realities. There are six regions of the WHO, which are as follows:

Region	*Headquorter*
1. South-East Asia	New Delhi (India)
2. Africa	Brazzaville (Congo)
3. The Americas	Washington D.C. (USA)
4. Europe	Copenhagen (Denmark)
5. Eastern Mediterranean	Alexandria (Egypt)
6. Western Pacific	Manila (Philippines)

Each Regional Organisation consists of a deliberative organisation (Regional Committee), a Chief Executive called the Regional Director and an Administrative Office called the Regional Office.

Let us now discuss the structure, personnel, finances and role of the

Soulh-East Asia Regional Office of the WHO in the promotion of health among the people of this region. South-East Asia regional office was the first to be set-up by the WHO. It is located in New Delhi and its Regional Committee consists of eleven member-states. (See Organisational Chart No. 1.1). The names of the member-states are mentioned below (with the date of joining the Region).

1. Bangladesh	19th May, 1972
2. Bhutan	8th March, 1982
3. Democratic Peoples' Republic of Korea	8th March, 1982
4. India	12th January, 1948
5. Indonesia	23rd May, 1950
6. Maldive Islands	5th November, 1965
7. Mayanmar	July, 1948
8. Nepal	2nd September, 1953
9. Sri Lanka	7th July, 1948
10. Thailand	26th September, 1947
11. Timor test	2002

The committee holds at least one session every year. The head of Regional Office is the Regional Director. He is appointed by the Board in agreement with the Regional Committee for a fixed period of five years. In the performance of his technical duties; he is assisted Deputy Regional Director, Programme Managers, WHO Programme Coordinators, Public Information Unit and a Director Support programme. (See Graph 1.1)

As of 30 June 2007, the total staff strength of the Region was 509, consisting of 132 international professionals (Ps), 35 national professional officers (NPOs) and 342 general service staff. The SEA Region has a diverse professional workforce, with 40 nationalities; 61 of professional staff come from this Region. The staffing strength of the Region has grown gradually over the last three years, as illustrated in (Graphs 1.1 and 1.2) the female personnel conserted of 43.34 per cent as on June 2006, and 40.30 per cent as on June 2007. (See Chart 1.2)

As part of the continuing efforts to strengthen country presence, maintain technical excellence in the field and manage increased activities due to decentralization at the country level, 13 new professional and NPO posts were established with extra budgetary resources during the year 2006-07. In addition, the services of 104 temporary staff (68 professionals, 4 consultants, and 32 NPOs) were provided to technical programmes. Strong human resources support was provided to major projects like Polio Eradication, Tuberculosis and HIV/AIDS through special services agreements (SSAs). By the end of June 2007, 1622 SSA holders were engaged to support national health projects in Member-Countries.

In order to provide enhanced support to country offices, staff development and learning (SDL) activities were focused on six priority areas: (1) management and leadership; (2) building core competencies;

GRAPH 1.1

Professional Staff Gender Distribution in the SEA Region (June 30, 2006 vs. 30 June, 2007

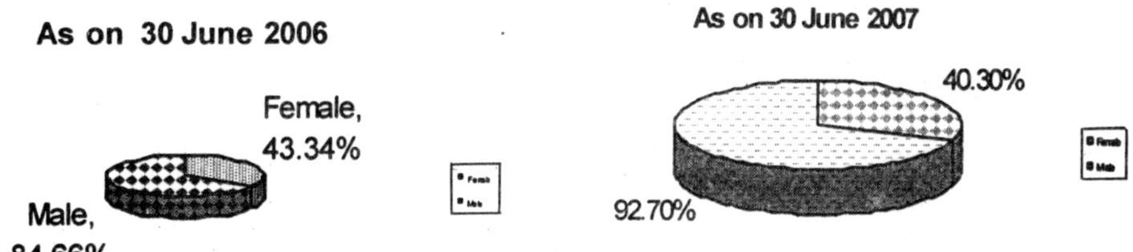

GRAPH 1.2

Staff Strength of SEARO in the Last Three Years

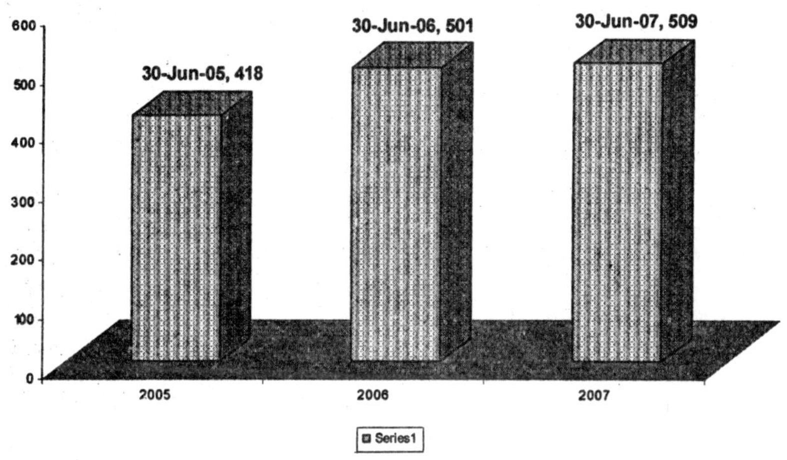

Source: WHO: SEARO: 1st July, 2001-30June,. 2007.

(3) technical skills development; (4) managerial and administrative skills and competence; (5) induction of new staff; and (6) improving learning excellence. A regional SDL Plan is being implemented in this regard.

In order to improve operational efficiency, strengthen results-based management and effectively decentralize authority and responsibilities, a global management system (GSM) is being developed. While the Regional Office's HR team contributed regional inputs and perspectives into the development of GSM, efforts were continued to enhance the utility of existing systems in order to streamline and simplify HR processes and procedures.[15]

The professional staff is recruited on the basis of international selections. The staff members belong to different nationalities. There are a number of problems in the recruitment of experts from the international market because of the adherence of the principle of geographical distribution and other procedural difficulties. The delegates to the Regional

CHART 1.1

Organisational Structure of WHO

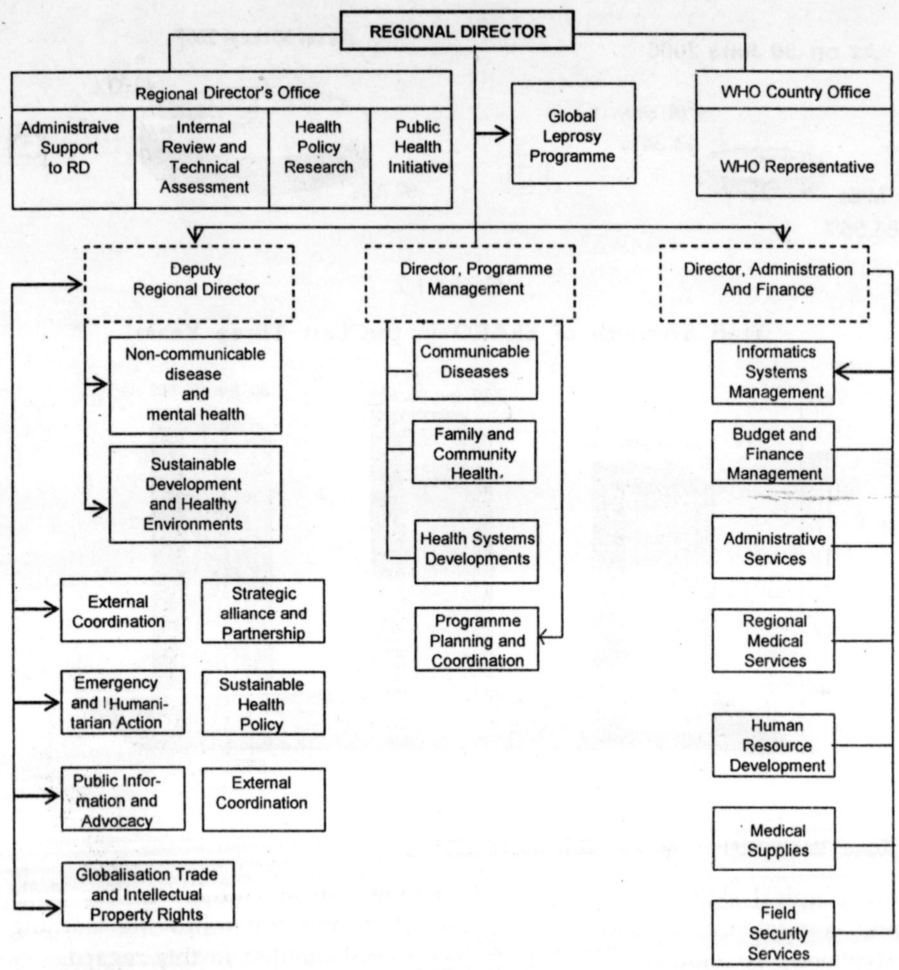

Source: WHO: SEARO (1st July 2006 to 30 June 2007).

Committee wanted posts not be to allowed to remain vacant since the programme schedule would otherwise be affected adversely. To overcome the quantitative shortage relating to internationally recruited staff, the following facts and suggestions may be taken into consideration:

(a) Local talent within the region may be mobilised whenever available.

(b) A purely mathematical or quota approach based on the principle of geographical distribution would prove to be too rigid for attracting talent. A delicate compromise would therefore be advisable between overall efficiency and the principle of geographical distribution.

(c) The field staff may be given higher emoluments in order to attract first-rate health experts.

(d) A suitable balance between internal promotion and recruitment of fresh talent from outside may be worked out.

(e) Utilisation of the services of experts on a long-term basis in different regions would require greater emphasis on long-term planning and better communication between the headquarters and the regional office.

Finances

The source of income of this organisation comprises contributions received from members in accordance with a scale determined annually by the World Health Assembly. The headquarter organisation distributes the funds among the six regions of the WHO after meeting its own expenditure and the expenditure to be incurred on global and inter-regional health activities.

Most of the delegates were of the view that the region should get at least 18-20 per cent of the total regular budget of the WHO and not 12-15 as had been the practice. Though the budget appears to be large, in concrete terms it comes to virtually nothing. It is inadequate in the context of the health problems and health needs of the member-states. Anyhow, even the limited scope of the operation made possible, by the mobilization of the finances has created a new consciousness among member-states about the health needs.

What is the role of the technical resources channeled through this office of WHO in the promotion of public health? Most of the delegates who came to attend the Regional Committee meetings were of the opinion that the resources, though very modest in relation to the total flow of external assistance into a member-state were of great value and were difficult to obtain from alternative sources. Moreover, it strengthens universal cooperation in regard to developmental tasks confronting many nations. After all, it represents a partnership, not an international charity. It may, however, by emphasized here that as the technical assistance provided through this office is quantitatively small, in relative and absolute terms, its contribution should be utilized strategically within the framework of all available inputs, whether these are to be provided from a country's internal resources or from outside assistance including bilateral programmes.

The Regular Budget (RB) working allocation for the 2006-07 biennium is US$ 97.46 million for the Region, which compares favourably with the 2004-05 allocation of US$ 93.15 million. The current working allocation represents 98.1% of the approved Regular Budget for 2006-07, with the Director-General withholding 1.9% (US$ 2.3 million) to provide for the inability of some Member States to pay their assessments. The increase in the budgetary allocation was distributed as per the criteria agreed upon during the Fifty-eighth session of the Regional Committee held in Colombo, Sri S.A. Khan Lanka in 2005 to ensure preferential treatment for countries in the greatest need, while also ensuring that each country in the Region got some additional funding. The ratio of distribution of RB funds between countries and the Regional Office was maintained at 75% to 25%, respectively. Compared to other regions, the SEA Region allocates the highest proportion of its RB funds to countries. (See Graph 1.3)

GRAPH 1.3

Trends in RB and EB Funding

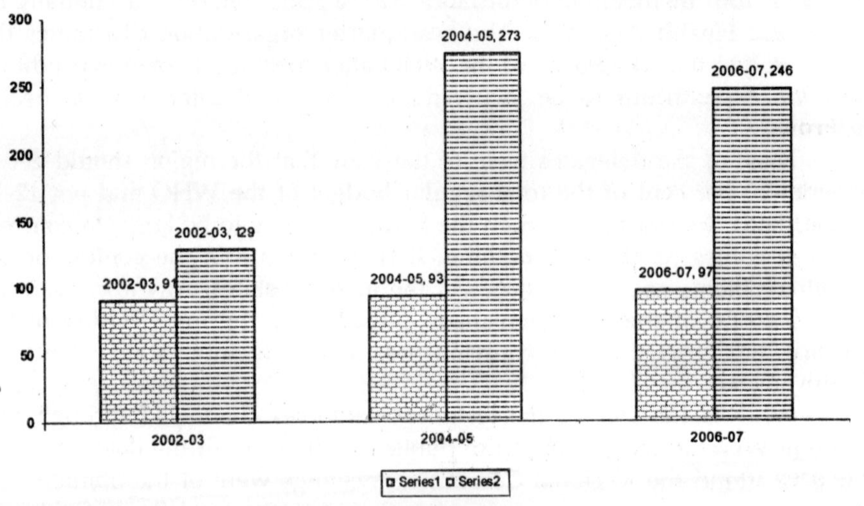

Source: The Work of WHO: SEARO—(1st July 2006 to 30 June 2007.

The Fifty-eighth World Health Assembly in May 2005 approved changes to the financial regulations effective 1 January 2006 that have a significant effect with regard to recording of income and expenditure. The income can now be recorded when the donor agreement is signed, thus enabling immediate programme implementation without waiting for actual receipt of funds. For recording of expenditure, the new financial regulations now follow the delivery principle, i.e. obligations due to be delivered within the biennium will be treated as expenditures. These changes apply to all funds. Special attention is being paid to ensure that the work completed and delivered on time.

Extra budgetary funding (EB) to the Region has grown steadily and now stands at US$ 246 million. This figure is likely to increase further by the end of the biennium.[16] (See Anneures 1.1, 1.2, 1.3)

Working of WHO

The Regional Office has been helping the member-states in almost all fields of public health promotion. Its role continues to be of great importance: Some 50 years ago, South-East Asia had the dubious distinction of being the world's reservoir of cholera and smallpox. Malaria claimed 100 million victims a year, with about one million deaths. Tuberculosis posed a major problem in both urban and rural areas. In some of the worst affected areas in Burma, Sri Lanka and India, about 80 percent of the people suffered from filariasis; Yaws claimed about 12 million patients in Thailand and Indonesia; leprosy, malaria and trachoma affected millions. The death rate of infants under five was as high as 50 per cent. We shall discuss the role of the Regional Office under the following heads:

1. Provision of Expertise.
2. Fellowships.
3. Equipment.
4. Headquarter Support to Regional Organisations.

1. Provision of Expertise

The Regional office attempts to provide useful know-how through experts to member-states to improve the general health conditions in most of the field.

2. Fellowships

Opportunities of advanced studies abroad in the fields in which a developing country is deficient are widely recognised as an effective way of developing its human capital without which no enduring social and economic development is possible. One of the WHOs principle methods of helping governments to train technical personnel for their health services has been to provide fellowships for advanced studies abroad. The improved training thus acquired by such persons must be reflected in renewed impetus and administrative practices in the field of public health. It should be kept in mind that a WHO fellowship is awarded not primarily with a view to the personal advancement of the recipient but as a means of strengthening the health services of his country.

The training activities in SEARO have been classified into two main categories: (a) fellowships, and (b) study tours, for the administration and management of which clearcut guidelines have been further developed.

In order that Member-Countries had more and better trained health personnel, WHO launched a comprehensive system of WHO fellowships as early as 1948. The fellowships grants were for study in various fields: health services, control of communicable diseases, clinical and basic medical sciences and medical and nursing education. Fellowships accounted for about 20 per cent of the WHO regular budget. Since 1948, the number of WHO fellowships has steadily increased.[17]

3. Equipment

The WHO also provides equipments and supplies. The policy of the WHO in regard to supply is that supplies are provided to meet emergency needs and the specific needs for accomplishing WHO projects, but at the same time to assist member-countries to become eventually independent of foreign and even international aid wherever it is feasible.

4. Headquarter's Support to Regional Organisations

WHOs headquarters provides central technical services which form the backbone of international health work. These may be classified into 5 main heads:

(a) Epidemiological Surveillance of Communicable Diseases

Information is collected through the Weekly Epidemiological Record, and daily telex information system.

(b) International Health Regulations

The aim of International Health Regulations is to ensure maximum security against international spread of diseases with a minimum interference with world traffic.

(c) Health Statistics

It would help to bring uniformity in the notification of diseases and causes of deaths. In this way, it would be possible to compare and define health problems more accurately.

(d) International Standardisation

To ensure and define uniform standards for the strength and purity of medical substances.

(e) Publication and Documentation

Besides the above functions, the headquarters appoints Expert Committees and scientific groups which keep the governments posted with up-to-date information on advances in the various fields of health. The experts who come together constitute a hallmark of eminence in a particular subject. Moreover, a large corpus of agreed thinking by the leading experts in any field is collected and kept up-to-date. The members of these committees did not represent their governments but acted in an entirely personal capacity. The report of these committees generally appear in the technical Report Series.

Study groups supplement the more formal expert groups. Their functions are exploratory. The reports are also published in the Technical Report Series.

The WHO headquarters publications of particular value to health workers are: the WHO Bulletin containing original scientific articles and monograph series. Then there are public health papers which usually contribute to the study of a particular health question. Lastly, there are Technical Report Series containing the published reports of the WHO Expert Committees and Study Groups. The WHO also publishes valuable reference books especially Health situation in the world.

Performance of Regionalization

It may be pertinent here to mention that the higher executives and several delegates from the member-states have highly commended the effectiveness of the regional pattern of administration in the WHO. Dr. Candlu, Director-General of the WHO, addressed the Regional Committee of SEA in 1953. Appreciating the impact of regionalisation on the organisations functioning, he said:

> "I have worked for an almost equal time at headquarters and in one of the regions. For my part, I am convinced that but for regionalisation, most of the results for which it can be credited could not have been achieved. To my mind regionalisation is much more than a mechanical division of assignments between headquarters and the six regional offices. . . . For me regionalisation is essentially a recognition of the fact that promotion of health on a world basis must be a truly two-way cooperation between independent and equal partners.
> In may own limited experience, I have seen many times that the mere transfer of techniques, skills and supplies from one country to another is meaningless unless it is accompanied by a thorough appreciation of the local problems. We must do everything in our power to encourage all efforts to bring about genuine cooperation between the nations of the world, however, small."[18]

Dr. P.K. Ratnasingham, Deputy Director of Health Services (PHS), Colombo, addressing the SEARO anniversary session, remarked:

> "Now after twenty years, we can say with confidence that this was a wise decision as health problems of South-East Asia have to be discussed and solutions found by the sons of the soil who feel for their own people and who will know their needs, customs and habits.[19]

Dr. Chellappah. the Ceylon representative at the First World Health Assembly in 1948 referred to the slogan of the Health Services. know your area. know your people.[20]

Dr. C. Mani, who was very active since inception of the WHO and remained as the Regional Director for 20 years remarked: For the first time in Public Health history, an International Health Organisation and the national health departments were brought together so closely and so effectively. I have no doubt that popularity and success of WHO today is in a large measure due to this effective system of decentralization. Through this system, health officials of Government and of WHO are continuously thinking together. WHO is not a far off organisation to be approached for technical assistance through long range paper artillery. The organisation is situated on the governments very doorstep, in fact immediately inside their doors available for consultation and assistance.[21]

Dr. L. Bernard, Assistant Director-General of the WHO stated:

> The WHO has had nearly a quarter of century of practical experience of regionalisation. It may be fitting to acknowledge that the expenditure has been rewarding. We trust that it will enable the organisation, in the future, to contribute positively to international endeavours towards the developing more rational and efficient approaches to cooperation.[22]

The same is true about other regions, for example, Dr. K. Camara. Guinea. said about the African Region: One of the happiest decisions of our agency was to set-up regional organisations. The regionalisations of WHOs activities has made it possible to establish services better adapted to their requirements in the member-states of the African region while at the same time giving more responsibility to the national health authorities with their greater awareness of local conditions.[23]

The fifty-first session of the Regional Committee including apart from the Director-General of WHO, Ministers of Health of Bhutan, DPR Korea, India, Indonesia, Myanmar, Nepal and Sri Lanka participated. They felicitated WHO on its achievements in the promotion of health, prevention and control of diseases and for its continued technical support and cooperation to the member-states. The former Director-General Dr. Gro Herlem Brundtland, in her address, asserted WHOs continued role as the centre of excellence for providing norms and standards, supporting national capacity building and innovative approaches for health development.[24]

C. WHO AND INDIA

A number of health projects are being implemented in India with assistance form WHO in the form of experts, and supplies and equipment.

In the field of Health and Family Welfare, India has various ongoing and proposed programmes of cooperation with international agencies like WHO, UNDP, ILO, UNICEF, UNFPA, World Bank, as also with a number of foreign agencies like SIDA (Sweden), DANIDA (Denmark), NORAD (Norway), ODA (U.K.) and USAID (USA), World Bank.

World Health Organisation (WHO) is collaborating with this country in providing and developing health care facilities. India makes regular annual contribution to WHO.

The contribution is paid to WHO in four instalments. Druing the current biennium 2006-07, Government of India have to pay a total of US$ 33,63,020 after availing all the credits given by WHO, an amount of US$ 16,81,510 as 1st and 2nd instalments have been paid to the WHO up to June 2006 and the rest two instalments of US$ 8,40,755 each may have to be paid. The current biennium 2004-05 will end on 31st December, 2007.

Activities under WHO are funded through two sources-the country budget which comes out of contributions made by member-countries and Extra Budgetary Resources which comes from (a) donations from various sources for general or specific aspects of health; and (b) funds routed through the WHO to countries by other member-countries or institute agencies. India is the largest beneficiary of the country budget. The budget is operated on a biennium basis, calendar year wise funding under the country budget during the current biennium, i.e. 2006-07 is US $ 8,985,000. WHO funding is available for taking services of the experts on contractual basis on specific terms and references; training within and outside the country; holding of workshops, seminars and meetings for raising awareness or exchange of information and medical supplies of equipment, viz: (i) Contract Service Agreement; (ii) Fellowship; (iii) Agreement for Performance of Work; (iv) Local Cost Subsidy; and (v) Supplies and Equipment, etc.

Monitoring the activities for timely and effective utilization of funds and their proper accounting is one of the main tasks. Some of the important activities taken up during the current biennium are: (i) Essential medicines; drugs kits supplied at PHC as well as district level Hospitals, (ii) Oral Health activities through Premiere Institute, school, etc., (iii) Health Promotion activities introduced and implemented through different Hospitals, (iv) Health Policy and enhancing health system performance, (v) Research proposal, (vi) Tobacco free initiative, (vii) Indian System of Medicine and Homeopathy strengthened, (viii) Strengthening of primary health care of tribal people, (ix) Guinea worm eradication, (x) Control of communicable diseases, (xi) Health education for empowerment of poor, (xii) promotion of health education for adolescents, (xiii) Malaria control, and (xiv) Vaccine preventable diseases, etc.

The areas of work financed by WHO, *inter-alia* cover HIV/AIDS, communicable and non-communicable diseases, mental health, drug abuse, environment, food safety, maternal and child health besides health policy, health financing and social protection as well as emergency preparedness and response. WHO has also switched over to the system of Direct Financial Cooperation (DFC) from the earlier system of Local Cost Subsidies (LCS). The new procedure envisages completion of various stages and reporting the progress to WHO before further financing the activities. WHO Fellowships: Under WHO Fellowships programme, 145 and 405 nominations have been made for abroad and within the country fellowship courses respectively, in more than 100 different field.[25]

The WHO provides assistance to member-states on a biennium basis for supplies and equipment, training/fellowships, study tours, short-term consultants, subsidy for Group Educational Activities (Seminars/ Workshops/Meetings/Conferences/Studies, etc.) and for participation of Indian experts in various symposia, workshops and seminars organised by the WHO and other international organisations in India and abroad.

D. ASSESSMENT OF THE FUNCTIONING OF THE WHO

Many member-states appear to be satisfied with the working of the Regional Office. They have made known their feeling during several sessions of the Regional Committee. To give a few examples, S. W.R.D. Bandaranaike, the then Prime Minister of Sri Lanka, (erstwhile Ceylon) while addressing the 12th session of the Regional Committee said:

> "I cannot help feeling that amongst the various specialized agencies of the UN that are all, one way or another, doing useful and valuable work, the WHO takes the pre-eminent place in actual practical achievements. Various health problems of the world have been dealt with in an unobtrusive manner that does not hit the frontlines of the world press. In our region of SEA, these problems are naturally more serious and more numerous than in some other regions. But I can speak from my own personal experience of the immensely valuable work that has been done in Ceylon."[26]

Kurt Waldheim, UN Secretary General said, WHO has clearly demonstrated the catalytic role open to an international organisation with precise objectives, a clear conception of its own part and consistency in its activities, however, limited the resources may be at anyone time in relation to the needs. ...The WHO has always fought for the cause of social development and can claim credit for the greater awareness which now exists for the social aspects of the development process.

Bisnuram Medhi, the then Governor of Madras while addressing the 14th Session of the Regional Committee said. The WHO can take credit for the control of major communicable diseases and for the improvement of medical education and promotion of vital health statistics and health education in collaboration with the Government in the region with a view to improving national health services.[27]

UNU the former Prime Minister of Burma said, The WHO has during the ten years of its existence amply justified its establishment. It has assisted member-countries in strengthening public health administration, in improving and developing maternal and child health and nursing services and in solving urgent health problem . . . All this has been done without WHOs becoming a supranational health administration.[28]

K.K. Shah, the then Union Minister for Health. Family Planning, works, Housing and Urban Development, Government of India in his address to the 23rd Session of the Regional Committee, praised the WHOs performance thus, Suffice it to say that WHO has stood like a tower of strength in a global war against diseases and sickness.[29]

Dr. P. Dolgor, Director, Ministry of Public Health Ulan Bator, said, WHOs activities and its achievements made in this region make us sure of the bright future ahead of this organisation.[30] Dr. Nyom Osor, Ministry of Public Health, Mongolia said recently, "WHO has become for these decades a highly prestigious international organisation. Playing an increasingly active role in strengthening universal peace and in promoting the noble and human cause of the health cause of the health and welfare of man."[31]

Besides, most of the academic writers have been appreciating the functional role of the WHO. Stephen S. Goodspeed has said, "The work of the WHO on such problem as malaria, tuberculosis, venereal diseases and the promotion of maternal and child welfare has been outstanding. Its contribution to the welfare of mankind cannot be measured accurately enough to portray the overall usefulness of the agency, but it can be said that the work of WHO has been an unmitigated blessing."[32]

Future Assistance Policy of WHO in the South-East Asia Region

The aim of the WHO, as stated in its Constitution, is an exalted one-the attainment by all peoples of the highest possible level of health. Some striking advances have been made, but the international community still faces many health hazards and problems. The burden of preventable communicable diseases is still with us to consume a large portion of national as well as international resources. A major part of the world is still without safe water supply and minimum standards of sanitation and housing.

Hence the SEARO would have to go a long way to enable the countries of Asia to achieve the standards of health defined in the WHO Constitution. Most of these standards have already been attained by the advanced countries. It would be better if in order to become more effective, the SEARO maintains a continuous review of the scope of its programmes and its organisational capacity to implement the programme. In all the programmes assisted by WHO, Health Education plays an important part which needs be intensified. (See Chart 1.2)

In order to solve these present and emerging problems. WHO's programmes must be dynamic and suited to the needs of the member-states. In a message, the Director-General of WHO, Dr. Mahler, stated:

> "Who's mission is firmly rooted in its constitution. The constitution does not change, but, in response to new challenges, the programme based upon it must move forward in a state of perpetual evolution. This evolution is not only continual but also geared to the real needs of the countries for which WHO was created to serve."[33]

Thus. the SEARO would have to expand its operations to provide technical assistance to the member-states to find solutions to the existing and also the emerging problems of public health. This would involve much larger mobilisation of financial resources from member-states and

CHART 1.2

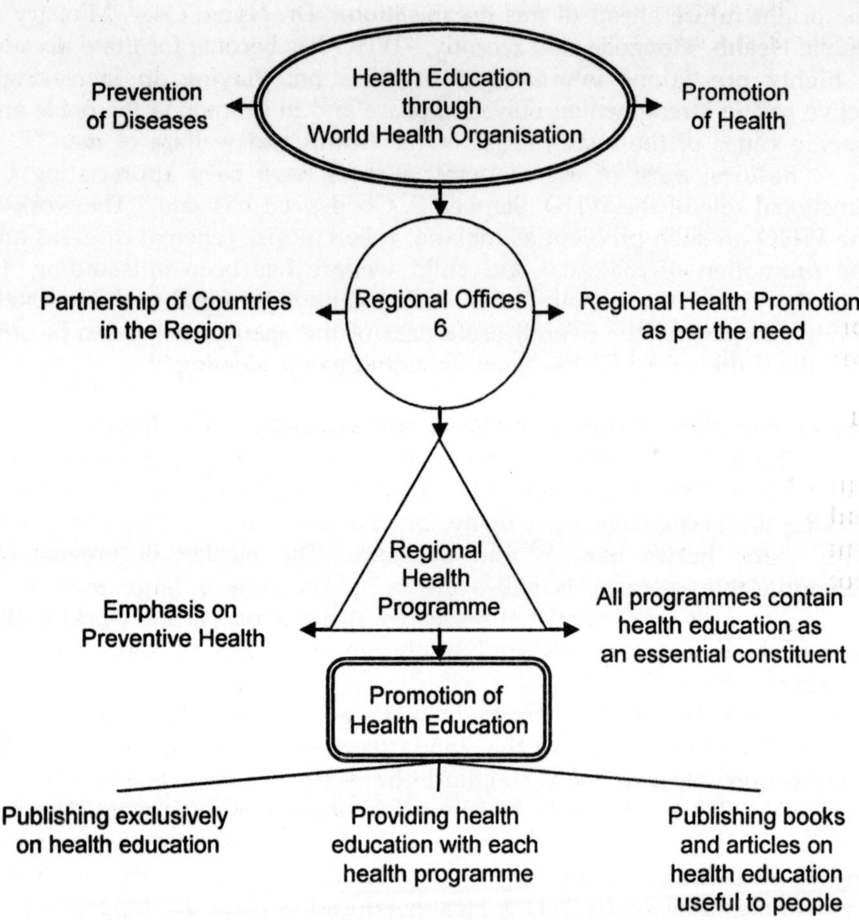

continuous review of the administrative capacity and advance personnel and programme planning by the SEARO as well as meaningful cooperation of the member-states. We need the services of WHO more than before.

Dr. Uton Muchar Rafei, Former Regional Director South-East Asia Region said: The Fourth International Conference on "Health Promotion: New Players for a New Era—Leading Health Promotion into the 21st Century", was held in Jakarta in July 1997. It was the first such conference to be held in a developing country, and the first to involve the private sector in supporting health promotion. It provided an opportunity to reflect on what has been learned about effective health promotion, to re-examine the determinants of health, and to identify the directions and strategies that must be adopted to address the challenges of promoting health in the 21st

Century. The Conference adopted, "The Jakarta Declaration on leading Health Promotion into the 21st Century."

The Declaration include the following priorities for health promotion in the 21st Century:

- Promote social responsibility for health,
- Increase investments for health developments,
- Consolidate and expand partnerships for health,
- Increase community capacity and empower the individual, and
- Secure an infrastructure for health promotion.

The participants also endorsed the formation of a global health promotion alliance to advance the priorities for action in health promotion set out in the Declaration.

A World without WHO

Dr. Gro Harlen Brundtland. the Fifth Director-General of WHO emphatically states that the value of the World Health Organisation can be judged by looking at its achievements over the past five decades and by imagining what the world would look like today if WHO had never been born. In a world without WHO:

- there would be no global forum for reaching consensus on the sensitive health and human rights issues raised by the AIDS epidemic,
- there would be no independent honest broker to match the funding needs of developing countries in the field of health with the resources potentially available from financing agencies and donor countries,
- national health officials would not be able to count on global moral support in the battle against tobacco addiction,
- there would be no politically neutral body to monitor the health effects of radiation fallout after nuclear accidents, and
- there would be no unifying moral and technical force to galvanize, guide and support countries in achieving health for all.[34]

She further adds that over the 50 years WHO has been the torch bearer for global health. While giant strides are being made, the new millennium will bring its own challenges. These have to be met boldly. WHO will continue to strive with its member-countries to ensure better health for all.[35]

Notes and References

1. WHO: Working for Health, An Introduction to the World Health Organisation, pp. 1-2.

2. WHO: Working for Health, An introduction to WHO, p. 1.
3. E. Settinius. The Yalta Conference, p. 25.
4. Norman Hill, International Organisation, New York, 1952, p. 48.
5. WHO, SEARO: SEA/RL31/2.
6. Report of the Interim Commission to the First World Health Assembly, Part 1, p. 10.
7. WHO, The First Ten Years in the WHO, pp. 30-31.
8. WHO, SEARO, Twenty Years in South-East Asia, 1948-67, p. 13.
9. WHO: Fifty Years of WHO in South-East Asia Highlights: 1948-98, pp. 11-12.
10. WHO: Fifty Years of WHO in South-East Asia Highlights: 1948-98, p. 15.
11. *WHO Chronicle*, Vol. 22, No. 7, July 1968, p. 296.
12. WHO: The Work of WHO in South-East Asia Region, 1 July 2006-3 June 2007, Report of the Regional Director, p. 75.
13. WHO: *WHO Chronicle,* Vol. 27, July-Aug. 1973, 1st July 2006, p. 283.
14. WHO: The Work of WHO in South-East Asia Region, Report of the Regional Director, p. 76.
15. The World of WHO: July 31st, 2006, pp. 88-89.
16. The Work of WHO: July 31, 2006, in South-East Asia Region, Report of the Regional Director, p. 89.
17. WHO: Fifty Years of WHO in South-East Asia Highlights, New Delhi: 1948-98, p. 25.
18. Sixth Session of the WHO Regional Committee for South-East Asia, (New Delhi, 1953), p. 12.
19. WHO, SEARO Anniversary, Commemorative Meeting (New Delhi, October, 1968), p. 21.
20. *Ibid.*
21. *Ibid.,* p. 55.
22. WHO: 23rd Session of the WHO Regional Committee for South-East Asia (New Delhi. October, 1970), p. 64.
23. WHO: *WHO Chronicle.* Vol. 27. Nos. 7-8, p. 283.
24. National Rural Health Mission, Annual Report 2006-07, pp. 285-86
25. Annual Report of the Ministry of Health and Family Welfare, 2006-07, pp. 285-96.
26. 12th Session of the WHO Regional Committee for South-East Asia, (New Delhi, 1959). Min. I. Rev. I Annex. 2. (Text of Address of Shri S. W.R.D. Bandaranaike, Prime Minister of Ceylon.
27. 14th Session of the WHO Regional Committee for South-East Asia (New Delhi, 1961), Min. I, Annex. (Text of Address of Shri Bisnuram, Medhi, Governor of Madras.
28. 10th Session of the WHO Regional Committee for South-East Asia, (New Delhi, 1957), Min. I, Annex. I (Text of Address of the Prime Minister of Burma).
29. 23rd Session of the WHO Regional Committee for South-East Asia, (New Delhi, 1970), p. 64 (Text of Address of Mr. K.K. Shah, Union Minister for Health, Family Planning, Works, Housing and Urban Development, Government of India).
30. WHO: SEARO Anniversary (Commemorative Meeting: Sept. 72), Text of Address of P. Dolgor, Director, Department of International Affairs, Ministry Public Health, Ulan Bator.
31. SEA/R/C, 31, p. 57.
32. Stephen, S. Goodspeed, The Nature and Functions of International Organisation, New York, 1967, p. 632.
33. 27th Session of the WHO Regional Committee for South-East Asia, New Delhi, October, 1974.
34. WHO: SEARO, Fifty Years of WHO in South-East Asia, New Delhi, 1999, p. 106.
35. *Ibid.*

ANNEXURE 1.1

Budgetary Implementation, 2006-07
by Country/Intercountry/Regional Office (Activities)
Regular Budget
(as of 30 June 2007)

(Expressed in US $)

Member-State	Allotted*	Committed: Disbursement	Committed: Unliquidated Obligations	Committed: Total	%	Uncommitted	%
Bangladesh	6 480 000	2 662 684	1 444 709	4 107 393	63	2 372 607	37
Bhutan	1 949 900	1 436 395	164 174	1 600 569	82	349 331	18
DPR Korea	2 985 200	1 626 925	370 970	1 997 895	67	987 305	33
India	9 791 400	4 148 593	3 476 109	7 624 702	78	2 166 698	22
Indonesia	3 646 500	1 993 579	548 516	2 542 095	70	1 104 405	30
Maldives	1 338 800	792 778	212 948	1 005 726	75	333 074	25
Myanmar	5 163 900	3 202 214	967 139	4 169 353	81	994 547	19
Nepal	4 719 500	3 441 749	796 975	4 238 724	90	480 776	10
Sri Lanka	2 655 600	1 318 272	689 954	2 008 226	76	647 374	24
Thailand	3 336 920	1 744 068	1 345 440	3 089 508	93	247 412	7
Timor-Leste	571 500	274 940	73 671	348 611	61	222 889	39
Country Total	42 639 220	22 642 197	10 090 605	32 732 802	77	9 906 418	23
Intercountry/ Regional Office	1 600 000	610 749	147 873	758 622	47	841 378	53
SEAR Total	44 239 220	23 252 946	10 238 478	33 491 424	76	10 747 796	24

*After HQ budget withholding.

ANNEXURE 1.2

Budgetary Implementation, 2006-07 by Country/Intercountry/Regional Office
Extrabudgetary Funds
(as of 30 June 2007)

(Expressed in US $)

Member-State	*Allotted**	*Committed*			%	*Uncommitted*	%
		Disbursement	*Unliquidated Obligations*	*Total*			
Bangladesh	20 499 651	10 220 416	3 317 89	13 391 605	65	7 108 046	35
Bhutan	233 552	90 346	34 288	124 634	53	108 918	47
DPR Korea	10 159 246	6 210 864	1 412 887	7 623 751	75	2 535 495	25
India	67 219 031	40 856 118	11 381 309	52 237 427	78	14 981 604	22
Indonesia	52 292 165	31 158 566	6 535 312	37 693 878	72	14 598 287	28
Maldives	690 920	539 246	17 224	556 470	81	134 450	19
Myanmar	14 127 430	6 905 419	2 465 419	9 370 838	66	4 756 592	34
Nepal	10 321 714	5 781 740	1 869 759	7 651 499	74	2 670 215	26
Sri Lanka	3 687 496	2 243 497	457 057	2 700 554	73	986 942	27
Thailand	2 360 942	1 327 220	211 284	1 538 504	65	822 438	35
Timor-Leste	641 267	459 166	49 831	508 997	79	132 270	21
Country Total	182 233 414	105 792 598	27 605 559	133 398 157	73	48 835 257	27
Intercountry/ Regional Office	64 103 176	24 823 752	10 950 213	35 773 965	56	28 329 211	44
SEAR Total	246 336 590	130 616 350	38 555 772	169 172 122	69	77 164 468	31

*After HQ budget withholding.

ANNEXURE 1.3

Budgetary Implementation, 2006-07
by Area of Work (in descending order)
All Sources of Funds
(as of 30 June 2007)

Areas of work	*Committed*						*Total*		
	Regular budget			*Other sources*					
	Disbursement	*Unliquidated obligations*	*Total*	*Disbursement*	*Unliquidated obligations*	*Total*	*Disbursement*	*Unliquidated obligations*	*Total*
1	*2*	*3*	*4*	*5*	*6*	*7*	*8*	*9*	*10*
Immunization and vaccine development	691 909	267 946	959 855	65 144 589	13 065 678	78 210 267	65 836 498	13 333 624	79 170 122
Tuberculosis	711 827	221 815	933 642	16 915 356	8 578 720	25 494 076	17 627 183	8 800 535	26 427 718
Emergency preparedness and response	439 796	131 208	571 004	16 004 501	2 358 353	18 362 854	16 444 297	2 489 561	18 933 858
Epidemic alert and response	1 072 547	629 930	1 702 477	9 556 309	4 757 075	14 313 384	10 628 856	5 387 005	16 015 861
HIV/AIDS	808 988	389 607	1 198 595	10 960 497	3 286 171	14 246 668	11 769 485	3 675 778	15 545 263
Communicable disease prevention and control	800 612	183 366	983 978	3 192 428	1 236 603	4 429 031	3 993 040	1 419 969	5 413 009
Health system policies and service delivery	2 453 301	1 453 712	3 907 013	309 141	267 563	576 704	2 762 442	1 721 275	4 483 717
Malaria	738 110	222 572	960 682	2 147 625	1 348 247	1 495 872	2 885 735	1 570 819	4 456 554
Human resource for health	2 371 236	1 184 751	3 555 987	404 378	115 097	519 475	2 775 614	1 299 848	4 075 462
Surveillance, prevention and management of chronic, non-communicable diseases	1 855 701	932 582	2 788 283	600	60 752	61 332	1 856 301	993 314	2 849 615
Child and adolescent health	1 053 523	383 479	1 437 002	802 888	585 213	1 388 101	1 856 411	968 692	2 825 103
Making pregnancy safer	1 146 871	534 210	1 681 081	681 706	288 552	970 258	1 828 577	822 762	2 651 339

(Contd.)

Annexure I.3

1	2	3	4	5	6	7	8	9	10
Health and environment	1 087 991	472 220	1 560 211	331 693	191 138	522 831	1 419 684	663 358	2 083 042
Tobacco	596 273	307 206	903 479	565 656	571 683	1 137 339	1 161 929	878 889	2 040 818
Essential medicines	1 053 776	470 830	1 524 606	511 716	102 942	414 658	1 365 492	573 772	1 939 264
Health information, evidence and research policy	987 520	339 313	1 326 833	423 249	86 523	509 772	1 410 769	425 836	1 836 605
Health promotion	644 495	160 923	1 005 328	85 872	190 126	275 948	730 227	551 049	1 281 276
Reproductive health	203 676	107 201	310 879	681 934	235 236	917 170	885 610	342 439	1 228 049
WHO's core presence in countries	—	—	—	813 572	327 032	1 140 604	813 572	327 032	1 140 604
Knowledge management and information technology	782 899	196 116	979 015	102 254	47 259	149 513	885 153	243 375	1 128 528
Mental health and substance abuse	402 616	310 214	712 830	144 627	240 315	384 942	547 243	550 529	1 097 772
Policy-making for health in development	608 938	218 323	826 961	26 355	82 217	108 572	634 993	300 540	935 533
Essential health technology	525 285	92 166	617 451	226 660	67 147	293 807	751 945	159 313	911 258
Nutrition	411 562	110 521	522 083	110 648	50 449	161 097	522 210	160 970	683 180
Violence, injuries and disabilities	350 078	143 113	491 191	111 743	68 219	179 962	461 821	211 332	673 153
Food safety	369 458	178 983	548 441	77 457	33 972	111 429	446 915	212 955	659 870
Health financing and social protection	270 663	151 096	421 759	56 062	94 582	150 644	326 725	245 678	572 403
Human resources management	6 616	3 263	9 879	380 610	139 110	519 720	387 226	142 373	529 599
Direction	292 153	81 760	373 913	—	—	—	292 153	81 760	373 913
Communicable disease research	205 309	83 308	288 617	43 923	13 616	57 539	249 232	96 924	346 156
Gender equality, women and health	69 335	45 655	114 990	12 416	60 608	73 024	81 751	106 263	188 014
Governing bodies	129 765	71 855	148 620	—	—	—	126 765	21 855	148 620
Infrastructure and logistics	113 507	9 232	122 739	(10 065)	5 594	(4 471)	103 442	14 826	118 268
Total	21 252 946	10 238 478	33 491 424	130 616 35038	555 772	169 172	122 153 869	29648 794 250	202 663 546

*Activity only.

Health Administration at the Union Level

Organisation and Working of Ministry of Health and Family Welfare

Health and Human development form integral components of overall socio-economic development of a nation. Amartya Sen in his keynote address to the Fifty Second World Health Assembly, Geneva (18th May, 1999) made strong plea for promoting health to ensure development. To quote him, "How does health relate to development? The first point to note is that the enhancement of health is a constitutive part of the development. Those who ask the question whether better health is a good "instrument" for development may be overlooking the most basic diagnostic point that good health is an integral part of good development; the case of the health care does not have to be established instrumentally by trying to show that good health may also help to contribute to the increase in economic growth.

Second, given other things, good health and economic prosperity tend to support each other. Healthy people can more easily earn an income, and people with higher income can more easily seek medical care, have better nutrition, and have the freedom to lead healthier lives.

Third "other things" are not given, and the enhancement of good health can be helped by a variety of actions, including public policies (such as the provision of epidemiological services and medical care). While there seems to be a good general connection between economic progress and health achievement, the connection is weakened by several policy factors. Much depends on how the extra income generated by economic growth is used, in particular whether it is used to expand public services adequately and to reduce the burden of poverty. Growth mediated enhancement of health achievement goes well beyond mere expansion of the rate of economic growth.

Fourth even when an economy is poor, major health improvements can be achieved through using the available resources in a socially productive way. It is extremely important, in this context. to pay attention to the economic considerations involving the relative costs of medical treatment and the delivery of health care. Since health care is a very labour-intensive process, low-wage economic have a relative advantage in putting more—not less-focus on health care.

Finally, the issue of social allocation of economic resources cannot be separated from the role of participatory politics and the reach of informed public discussion. Financial conservatism should be the nightmare of the militarist, not of the doctor, or the school teacher. or the hospital nurse. If it is the doctor or the school teacher or the nurse who feels more threatened by resource considerations than the military leaders, then the blame must lie partly on us, the public, for letting the militarist get away with these odd priorities.

Ultimately, there is nothing as important as informed public discussion and the participation of the people in pressing for change that can protect our lives and liberties. The public has to see itself not merely as a patient. but also as an agent of change. The penalty of inaction and apathy can be illness and death.[1]

Chart 2.1 depicts the synoptic view of Health Care Administration in the country from top to bottom.

ROLE OF THE UNION GOVERNMENT

In view of the federal nature of the Constitution areas of operation have been divided between Union Government and State Governments. Seventh Schedule of Constitution describes three exhaustive lists of items, namely, Union List, State List and Concurrent List. Though some items like Public health, hospitals, sanitation, etc., fall in the state list, the items having wider ramification at the national land like population control and family welfare, medical education, prevention of food adulteration, quality control in manufacturing of drugs, etc. have been included in the Concurrent List.

According to the Constitution, the Central Government is concerned only with international health matters, assisting and coordinating State activities, establishing standards and promoting research and professional education. Most other health matters are thus reserved for the States and their health departments, though a few, such as mental health, food adulteration, drugs and vital statistics are on the Concurrent list. The 42nd Amendment to the Constitution has made "Population Control and Family Planning" a Concurrent subject and this provision has been made effective from January 1977. The two Health Survey Committees (Bhore and Mudaliar) reporting in 1946 and 1961, did not recommend an amendment to the Constitution although it was stressed that the Central Government should have greater powers to coordinate the activities of the State authorities dealing with health. Many persons from time to time have stressed that the Ministry of Health should be given more powers to deal with health matters.[2]

CHART 2.1

Synoptic View of Health System in India

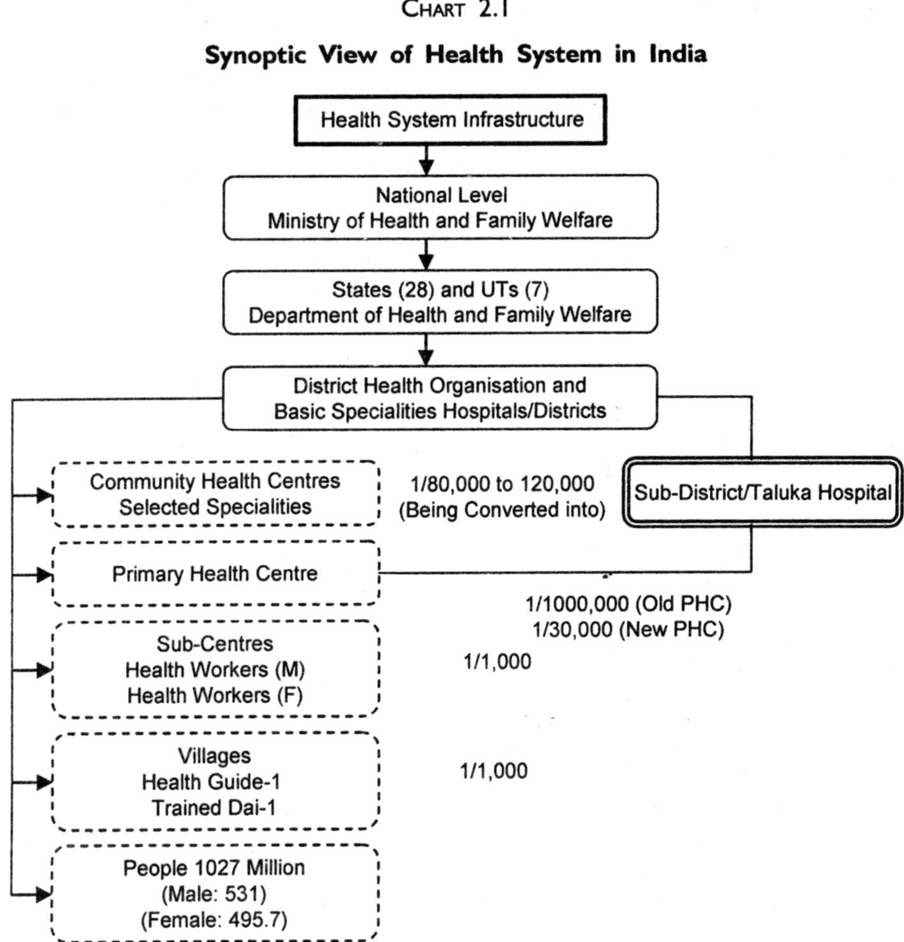

The Union Ministry of Health and Family Welfare is instrumental and responsible for implementation of various programmes on a national scale in the areas of Health and Family Welfare, prevention and control of major communicable disease and promotion of traditional and indigenous systems of medicines. Apart from these, the Ministry also assists states in preventing and controlling the spread of seasonal disease outbreaks and epidemics through technical assistance.

Ministry of Health and Family Welfare incurs expenditure either directly under Central Schemes through its two departments, including the attached offices of DGHS and its various subordinate offices, or by way of grants in aids to the autonomous/statutory bodies, etc. and NGOs. In addition to the 100% centrally sponsored family welfare programme, the Ministry is implementing several World Bank assisted programmes for control of AIDS, Malaria, Leprosy, and Tuberculosis and Blindness in designated areas. Besides, State Health Systems Development Projects with

World Bank assistance are under implementation in various states. The projects are implemented by the respective state governments and the Department of Health and Family Welfare only facilitates the States in availing of external assistance. All these schemes aim at fulfilling the national commitment to improve access to Primary Health Care facilities keeping in view the needs of rural areas and where the incidence of disease is high.[3]

"The Indian Constitution does not list health as a fundamental right. The recommendatory Directive Principles of State Policy enjoin the state to raise nutrition level and improve public health (Article 47). But many court rulings have interpreted the fundamental right of protection of life and liberty (Article 21) as inclusive of the right to health, implying state obligation to protect citizens from medical negligence.

Pt. Jawaharlal Nehru said:

> "The Central Health Ministry is the pivot round which all the major schemes for improving the standards of health of the nation revolve. All major schemes have necessarily to be sponsored and encouraged by the Central Ministry."

Speaking about the role of the Central Health Ministry, Raj Kumari Amrit Kaur, Minister of Health (1947-57) observed:

> "Health in India is a state subject and the Union Government has mainly as advisory and coordinating function to discharge. The Central Ministry of Health in pursuit of its objective, health for all, has had to initiate countrywide programmes and to coordinate the activities of the various participating States and to see that no State lags behind for lack of Central aid whether in the matter of material or human resources or of technical know-how. In doing this the centre has not arrogated to itself any power of overall control but has maintained the coordinating and advisory function through the Central Council of Health."[4]

The Ministry of Health and Family Welfare plays a vital role in the national efforts to enable the citizens to lead a healthy and happy life. Under the Indian Constitution, the items of public health, sanitation, hospitals and dispensaries fall in the State List. Items like population control and family planning, medical education, adulteration of foodstuffs and other goods, drugs and poisons, medical professions, vital statistics including registration of births and deaths and lunacy and mental deficiency find a place in the Concurrent List.

The Ministry of Health and Family Welfare at the Centre is responsible for implementation of numerous programmes of national importance like family welfare, primary health care, prevention and control of major diseases, etc. which form the main plank of our development efforts. The Ministry has several Centrally sponsored schemes which are implemented through the States. At the same time, it also implements various Central Sector Schemes. All these schemes aim at fulfilling our national commitment to attain the goal of Health for All by 2000 AD in accordance with Alma-Ata Declaration of September 1978 to which India is also a signatory.

Realising the need for establishing comprehensive and integrated primary health care services and family welfare services to reach the people's doorsteps even in the remote and far-flung rural areas, an integrated health care delivery system with the maximum community participation has been developed and is being implemented. The administration and implementation of all these programmes is organised through an integrated structure of health and family welfare services in the country.

STRUCTURAL GROWTH AND EXISTING SET-UP

Before 1947, the medical and health services at the Centre were administered by two separate departments, one under the Director-General of IMS and the other under the Commissioner of Public Health. After independence, these two offices were amalgamated under the Director-General of Health Services and the Post of Commissioner of Public Health was abolished. The Union Ministry of Health was vested with several additional responsibilities, namely, Family Planning, Works and Housing and Urban Development. The functions of Works and Housing and Urban Development were transferred from this ministry. Family Planning was raised to the status of a full-fledged department in 1966, and the Ministry was designated as the Ministry of Health and Family Planning. It is known at present as "Ministry of Health and Family Welfare."

The Union Ministry of Health and Family Welfare is headed by a Cabinet Minister with a Minister of State to assist him: The Union Minister of Health and Family Welfare comprises of the following departments each of which is headed by a Secretary to the Government.

The Union Ministry of Health and Family Welfare comprises the following departments, each of which is headed by a Secretary to the Government of India:

Department of Health and Family Welfare

I. Function of Department of Health and Family Welfare:

1. Maintenance of standards through National Health making and setting up institutions of National Importance.
2. Monitoring progress to ensure compliance of standards.
3. Collecting Health intelligence to ask the states to take immediate action if the disease situation demands it.

4. Promote inter-sectoral goals to ensure good impact.
5. Manpower Development through the establishment of Medical Education institutes of Excellence.
6. Promoting Health research to improve health care system.
7. Promotion of Family Welfare and RCH Activities.

The main aim of the Department of Health and Family Welfare is to determine standards, coordinate state activities and help the state in providing decent care.

The functions of the Family Welfare Department are:

(a) To organize family welfare programmes through family welfare centres throughout the country.
(b) To create an atmosphere of social acceptance of the programme and to support all voluntary organisations interested in the programme.
(c) To educate every individual to develop a conviction that a small family size is valuable for him or her, and to popularise every known, appropriate and acceptable method of family planning and to leave the choice of method to the individual couple.
(d) To disseminate the knowledge on the practice of family planning as widely as possible through all available publicity and educational measures, and to provide service agencies nearest to the community.
(e) To organise basic research of human fertility, genetics and population dynamics and on the evolution of easy and more reliable method of contraception.
(f) To study the social factors that affect fertility and to take such steps as will reduce the number of children in a family, e.g., raising the age of marriage, education and employment of women, etc.
(g) To coordinate the family planning programme with the child welfare and maternal health services throughout the country.
(h) To organise production of contraceptive devices in adequate quantities to maintain the supply at all levels preferably free or at a minimum cost.
(i) India system of medicine and Homeopathy helps to promote IISM in the country through training, research and use.

Let us now discuss important activities of the Ministry affecting Community/Primary Health Care at the local level.

Organisation of Department of Health and Family Welfare and Department of AYUSH

Directorate General of Health Services (Dte. GHS) is an attached office of the Department of Health and Family Welfare and has subordinate offices spread all over the country. The DGHS renders technical advice on all medical and public health matters and is involved in the implementation of various health schemes. In order to implement the policies and programmes of the Ministry in an effective manner, there are three subordinate offices viz., Family Welfare Training and Research Centre, Mumbai; Homoeopathic Pharmacopia Laboratory, Ghaziabad and Pharmacopia Laboratory for Indian Medicine, Ghaziabad which function directly under the Ministry. Besides, there are 34 autonomous statutory bodies and three Public Sector Undertakings under the Administrative control of the Ministry.

2. The Department of Indian Systems of Medicine and Homeopathy

It was established in March 1995 and had continued to make steady progress. Emphasis was on implementation of the various schemes introduced around the thrust areas identified by the Department. The thrust areas are education, standardisation of drugs, enhancement of availability of raw materials, research and development, information, education and communication and involvement of ISM & H in National Health Care.

ADMINISTRATION

In order to achieve the commitment of the Government to provide better health care facilities, the Department of Health and Family Welfare has enforced discipline and accountability amongst its officers and staff. Necessary steps and new initiatives have been taken to ensure that the Government policies and programmes are implemented in efficient and in a time-bound manner. The Department has also taken initiatives and made vigorous efforts to ensure and improve effectiveness of different National Programmes and Schemes.

With a view to provide responsive administration and streamline system for redressal of staff grievances, Deputy Secretary (Administration) is attending to the service-related grievances of the staff in the Department of Health and Family Welfare who is available for personal hearing of the staff on every Tuesday between 10.30 A.M. to 1.00 P.M. Secretary, Department of Health and Family Welfare also gives personal hearing to the staff grievances on first Monday of every month. For redressal of public grievances, Joint Secretary in the Department of Health and Family Welfare is functioning as nodal Officer for Public grievances relating to the Department to gear and take steps for quick disposal of the grievances. He is assisted by Director (Welfare and PG) for timely redressal of grievances of the Public.

FUNCTIONS

Most of the functions of this ministry are implemented through an autonomous organisation called Director-General of Health Services (See Chart 1.1). The functions of the Union Ministry of Health and Family

Welfare in terms of specific responsibilities are:

(a) Maintenance of international health relations, administration of port health and quarantine laws.
(b) Administration of Central Health Institutions, training colleges, laboratories and hospitals.
(c) Promotion and maintenance of appropriate standards of education in medicine, nursing, dental, pharmaceutical and of ancillary health personnel through statutory bodies and coordination and collaboration with various national associations in health programmes.
(d) Promotion of medical and public health researches through the Indian Council of Medical Research and other research institutions and bodies.
(e) Regulation and development of medical, dental, nursing and pharmaceutical professions in consultation with the State governments.
(f) Establishment and maintenance of drug standards (including antibiotics) and of control over the manufacture and sale of drugs and biological products.
(g) Collection of information regarding development in the medical and health services in India and abroad to be made available to all State Governments through the Central Bureau of Health Intelligence.
(h) Maintenance of a Central Medical Library.
(i) Promotion and coordination of health activities through the Central Council of Health.
(j) Establishment of close contact with other Ministries in respect of health measures, e.g., Employees State Insurance Scheme, Factories Act, etc.
(k) Coordination of various activities through consultative committees of the Parliament, statutory bodies, committees and associations.
(l) Negotiations with International bilateral agencies.
(m) Planning and organisation of health activities throughout the country in collaboration with the State Governments and the Planning Commission.
(n) Evaluation of health schemes organised in the country.
(o) Assessment of health conditions in the country through health and morbidity surveys and by regular collection of vital and health statistics and spreading of the information throughout the country.
(p) Promulgations of Central enactments on health matters as may be provided by the Constitution of India.
(q) Organisation of health measures as are required for: (i) the control of inter-State spread of communicable diseases, (ii) the

sanitary control of inter-State traffic, and (iii) control of food, drugs in the inter-State commerce.

(r) Organisation and maintenance of a Central Health Service.

(s) Establishment of total medical care programmes for the Central Government Employees (Central Government Health Scheme).

(t) Carrying out of the functions of health services in the centrally administered areas.

(u) Power to lay down and enforce minimum standards of health administration for these services which are within the immediate control of other departments, e.g., Railways, Prisons, Labour, etc.

Les us now discuss important activities of the Ministry affecting Community/Primary Health Care at the local level.

1. National Health Programmes (See Chart 2.2)

There are certain health problems which need the attention of Central Government as the diseases know no barriers. Besides, these involve a huge expenditure beyond the capacity of the States. The Central Government plays a very important part in planning, guiding and coordinating all the national health programmes in the country. The implementation of these programmes is done at the State level, The following important health programmes are being implemented:

2. National Vector Board Disease Control Programme

The National Vector Borne Disease Control Programme (NVBDCP) is one of the most comprehensive and multi-faceted public health activities in the country and concerned with prevention and control of vector borne diseases, namely, Malaria, Filariasis, Kala-azar, Dengue and Japanese Encephalitis (JE). The Directorate of NVBDCP is the nodal agency for planning, policy-making and technical guidance and monitoring and evaluation of programme implementation in respect of prevention and control of these vector borne diseases. The States are responsible for planning, implementation and supervision of the programme. The vector borne diseases namely Malaria, Filaria, Japanese Encephalitis, Dengue and Kala-azar are major public health problems in India. Chikungunya fever, that re-emerged as an epidemic outbreak after more than three decades, has added to the problem. The vector borne diseases are complex; since their presence and transmission depends on interaction of numerous ecological, biological, social and economic factors. Increasing travel within and across countries is also responsible for spread of vector borne diseases.[5]

Out of the six vector borne diseases, malaria, filariasis, Japanese Encephalitis, dengue and chikungunya are transmitted by different kinds of vector mosquitoes, while Kala-azar by sand flies. The transmission of vector borne diseases in any area is dependent on frequency of man-vector contact, which is further influenced by various actors including vector density,

CHART 2.2

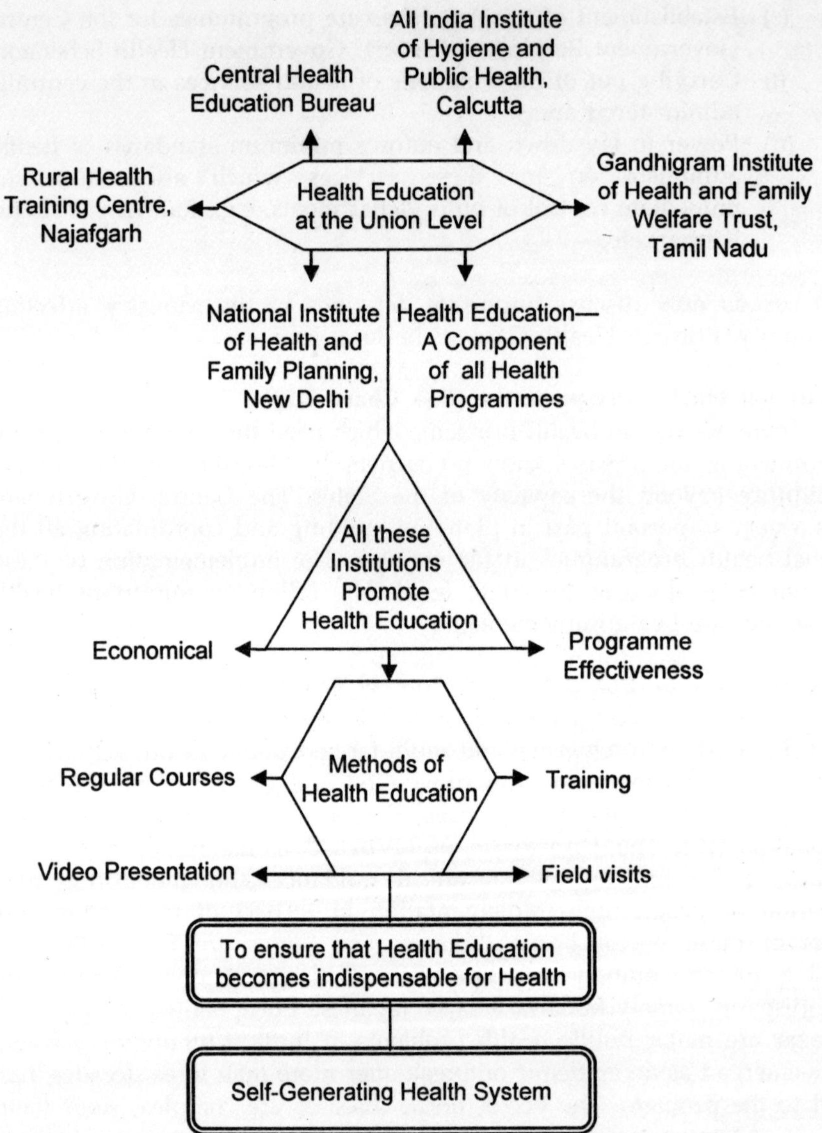

biting time, etc. mosquito density is directly related with water collection—clean or polluted, i.e. it is dependent on availability of suitable larval habitats.[6]

Under NVBDCP, the three pronged strategy for prevention and control of VBDs are: (i) Disease Management including early case detection and complete treatment, strengthening of referral services, epidemic preparedness and rapid response, (ii) Integrated Vector Management (For Transmission Risk Reduction) including Indoor Residual Spraying in selected high risk areas, use of Insecticide treated bed nets, use of larvivorous fish, anti-larval measures in urban areas, source reduction and minor environmental engineering, (iii) Supportive Interventions including Behaviour Change Communication (BCC), Public Private Partnership and Inter-sectoral convergence, Human Resource Development through capacity building, Operational research including studies on drug resistance and insecticide susceptibility, Monitoring and evaluation through periodic reviews/field visits and web based Management Information System.[7]

The other National Health Programme are:

1. National Leprosy Eradication Programme.
2. National TB Control Programme.
3. National Programme for control of Blindness.
4. National Iodine deficiency disorders control Programme.
5. National Cancer Control Programme.
6. National AIDS Control Programme in India.
7. National Mental Health Programme.
8. Guinea Worm Eradication Programme (GWEP) in India.
9. Yaws Eradication Programme in India (YEP).
10. Integrated Disease Surveillance Project (IDSP).
11. Dry De-Addiction Prgramme.
12. Up-Gradation and Strengthening of Emergency Facilities of State Hospitals Located on National Highways.
13. National Programme for Prevention and Control of Diabetes, Cardiovascular diseases and Stroke.
14. Public Health Foundation of India.

3. Prevention of Food Adulteration (PFA)

The Prevention of Food Adulteration Act has been in vogue since June 1955. It was amended by Parliament in its February 1976 Session and later in 1986 with a view to plugging the various Loopholes which had come to the surface during the implementation of the act.

The subject of the Prevention of Food Adulteration (PFA) is in the Concurrent list of the constitution. However, in general, the Enforcement of the Act is done by the State/UTs governments. The Central Government primarily plays an advisory role in its implementation besides carrying out various statutory functions duties assigned to it under the various provisions of the Act. Four Central Food Laboratories have been established under the Act, which work as appellate laboratories for the purpose of the Analysis of appeal samples of food lifted by the Food Inspectors of the States/UTs and Local bodies. There are 72 food Laboratories under the administrative control of various state/union territories governments and Local Bodies.

Since the signing of SPS and TBT agreements under the WTO, the issue of international trade in food has become very important. Food standards at the international level are set by the Codex Alimentarius Commission. India has participated in the meetings of this Commission and has effectively advocated the stand of the developing countries regarding the process of standard setting so that their interests are not compromised.

An attempt is being made to harmonise to the extent possible the Standards under the PFA Rules with Codex standards.

4. Control of Drugs Standards

The Drug Control Organisation functions under the Drug controller. It is responsible for enforcing the provisions of the Drugs and Cosmetics Act, 1940. Drug Standard Control is a social measure intended to ensure that the community is provided with drugs of Standard quality. The main objectives of the organisation are:

(a) Controlling the quality of imported drugs and drugs moving in inter-State commerce;

(b) Coordinating the activities of the States and advising them on matters relating to uniform administration;

(c) Laying down regulatory measures and standards of drugs; and

(d) Granting approval of 'new drugs' proposed to be imported into or manufactured in the country. It has been conducting training programmes for the training of Drugs Inspectors and Drug Analysts concerned with drug standard control.

There is a Drug Technical Adivsory Board and Drug Consultative Committee constituted under the Drugs and Cosmetics Act. 1940 to advise the Central and State Governments and the Drug Technical Advisory Board on matters tending to secure uniformity in the administration of the Drugs and Cosmetics Act. It consists of representatives of the State and Central Governments.

5. Medical Education

The Centre has set-up regulatory bodies for monitoring the standards of medical education, promoting training and research activities. This is being done with a view to sustain the production of medical and para-medical manpower to meet requirements of the health care delivery system at the primary, secondary and tertiary levels in the country. To achieve the objective, medical council of India has been set-up.

The Medical Council of India was established as a statutory body under the provisions of the Indian Medical Council Act. 1933 which was later repealed by the Indian Medical Council Act, 1956 with minor amendments in 1958 (36 of 1958) and 1964 (24 of 1964). A major amendment in the Indian Medical Council Act, 1956 was made in 1993 to stop the mushroom growth of medical colleges, increase of seats and starting of new courses without prior approval of the Central Government in the Ministry of Health and Family Welfare. The main functions of the council are:

(i) Maintenance of uniform standards of medical education at under-graduate and post-graduate level;
(ii) Maintenance of Indian Medical Register;
(iii) Reciprocity with foreign countries in the matter of mutual recognition of medical qualifications; and
(iv) Provisional/permanent registration of doctors with recognized medical qualifications, registration of additional qualifications and issue of Good Standing Certificate for doctors going abroad to commonwealth countries.

Indian Nursing Council set-up under the INC Act, 1947, Dental Council of India set-up under Act 1948, Pharmacy Council of India, Act, 1948 were set-up.

6. Medical Research

Medical Research is coordinated through Indian Council of Medical Research (ICMR), It has a network of 21 permanent research institutes and six regional medical research centres distributed throughout the country. During 1997-98 the Council continued research on a wide spectrum of subjects through intramural and extramural projects including various multi-centric collaborative projects.

The Council is administered by a Governing Body chaired by the Minister for Health and Family Welfare. The Council receives grant-in-aid from the ministry under Plan and Non-plan for meeting its normal expenditure as well as for plan activities.

7. Health Intelligence

The Central Bureau of Health Intelligence, established in 1961, is the agency at the national level, for collection, compilation, analysis, evaluation and dissemination of health statistics. It also disseminates epidemic intelligence to States/Union Territories informing against spread of epidemic diseases and provides Necessary intelligence on quarantinable diseases to the World Health organisation, according to the International Sanitary Regulations. The Bureau maintains liaison with research institutions in India and abroad and promotes research in health statistics. The Bureau has been giving technical assistance in respect of health statistics to different states.

The Bureau is activity engaged in the monitoring and evaluation of a strategy of 'Health for all by 2000 A.D.' in India. In compliance with the resolution of the World Health Assembly, the Ministry of Health and Family Welfare (MOHFW) has been periodically conducting exercises for monitoring and evaluating the goal of 'Health For All' (HFA). The earlier rounds of monitoring work were carried out in 1982, 1988 and 1994 while the evaluations were undertaken in 1985, 1991 and 1997.

The Bureau has the following objectives: .

(a) To centralise collection, compilation, analysis, evaluation, synthesis and dissemination of all information on health statistics for the nation as a whole,
(b) To work out uniform and standard returns so as to get uniform information for efficient interpretation.
(c) To disseminate epidemic intelligence to States and international bodies.
(d) To organise training programmes for personnel in Medical Health statistics in order to meet the expanding needs in the field.
(e) To promote research in health statistics through cooperation with national and international bodies.
(f) To prepare annual report for DGHS and Ministry of Health and Family Welfare.
(g) To publish special issues on different medical and public health problems in the country.

8. National Medical Library

The National Medical Library (NML) under the aegis of Directorate General of Health Services provides wide and efficient access to information to all Health Science Professionals in the country.

9. Facilities for Scheduled Castes and Scheduled Tribes

India is a signatory to the Alma-Ata Declaration, 1978 and is committed to achieve the goal "Health for All by the year 2000 A.D." The National Health Policy (1983) accordingly envisages high priority to provide health services to those residing in the tribal, hilly and backward areas as well as to endemic disease affected population and vulnerable sections of the society.

Accordingly, the strategy adopted for meeting the Health care needs of Scheduled Tribes and Scheduled Castes envisages the provision of preventive, promotive and curative services through a network of Primary Health Centres, Rural Dispensaries and at village level through Health Guides and Trained Dais supported by implementation of programme for control of communicable diseases, undertaking of research in diseases to which Scheduled Tribes/Scheduled Castes are generally prone. The mobile dispensaries and camps catering to their needs, at their door-steps are being organised, wherever feasible.

10. Central Government Health Scheme

The Central Government Health Scheme was started in Delhi in 1954 to provide comprehensive care to the Central Government employees stationed at Delhi. The scope of the scheme has been gradually extended over the years to cover cities outside Delhi, Bombay, Allahabad, Meerut, Kanpur, Patna, Calcutta, Nagpur, Madras, Hyderabad, Bangalore, Jabalpur, Jaipur, Pune, Lucknow, Ahmedabad, as well as other sectors of population, such as the employees of the autonomous organisations, retired Central Government pensioners, existing and ex-MPs, ex-Governors and retired Judges of Supreme Court and High Courts. The services provided are now comprehensive and include:

(1) Laboratory investigations,
(2) Outdoor treatment,
(3) In-patient treatment,
(4) Specialist care,
(5) Emergency services,
(6) Domiciliary services,
(7) Supply of medicines,
(8) Ambulance services,
(9) Ante-natal confinement and Postnatal care,
(10) Optical and dental care, and
(11) Family Welfare Services.

11. International Cooperation for Health and Family Welfare

Various international organisations and the United Nations Agencies provide significant technical and material assistance for many Health and Family Welfare Programmes in the country.

World Health Organisation

"The World Health Organisation (WHO) is collaborating with this country in providing and developing health care facilities. India makes regular annual contribution to WHO. The WHO provides assistance to Member States on a biennium basis for supplies and equipment, training/fellowship/study tours, short-term consultants, subsidy for Group Educational Activities (Seminar/Workshops/Meetings/Conferences/Studies, etc.) and for participation of Indian experts in various symposia, workshops and seminars organised by the WHO and other international organisations in India and abroad.

World Bank

State Health System Development Projects are being implemented in the following States with World Bank Assistance:

(i) Andhra Pradesh (from 1995 for 6 years) 608 crore;
(ii) Karnataka (1996 for 5 years) 546 crore;
(iii) West Bengal (1996 for 6 years) 698 crore;
(iv) Punjab (1996 for 5 years) 425 crore; and
(v) Orissa (1998 for 5 years) 415.58 crore.

The state of Maharashtra has also been cleared by the Bank Board on 8th December, 1998. Besides, small help is rendered by many counties.

CRITICAL APPRAISAL

Ministry of Health and Family Welfare has been striving to improve the status of health of the people in the country. Planned development of over five and a half decades has resulted in improved health facilities. (See Table 1.1 for latest statistics). It has been playing an effective role in co-ordinating the efforts of the State governments and has been supplementing their efforts through national programmes and centrally sponsored schemes. Besides, this Ministry has been providing guidance to the State Health Institutions and Administration. It has also set-up autonomous institutions to guide the Union and States in the formulation of health policies in their respective fields. Over the years it has become so unwieldy that it is difficult to manage its operations efficiently. These national institutes have become a burden on the exchequer. For example, the Estimates Committee was critical of the performance of AIIMS. It remarked that 19 years after the setting up of the institute—a depressing picture is revealed in the field of medical education in India. Why is it so? Is it because of the fact that the persons working in these institutions have been living in ivory towers forgetting about the needs of a common man? Is the common man paying taxes to perpetuate this class of people? The Ministry find answers to these questions and make its structure relevant to the needs of the society. Dr. Mahler, Director-General of the WHO, while addressing the senior doctors at the PGI Chandigarh said that it was a pity that a country like India with its rich intellectual background had still to grapple with basic health problems even 30 years after independence.[8]

According to Tarlok Singh:

> "Whatever the shortcomings of the past two decades and more, and the unbolt rigidities and injustices of our social institutions and modes of thought and behaviour, India possesses resources of unusual richness. We see this on all sides—in the endowments of nature, in economic and technological capacities, in potentials for growth, in the quality and wealth of manpower, in the institutions for research and training, in the available pool of talent and experience. Presently, these resources and energies are being somewhat frittered away for lack of a sense of fundamental directives and failure to build up a shared national effort. The appraisal of the record of constructive endeavour since independence undertaken in this country supports the belief that it is within India's grasp to eliminate swiftly the worst forms of poverty and, over a period of years, to create a cohesive social order and classless society based on the values of equality, welfare and mutual cooperation."[9]

There is a need of bold attempt and innovations to set the whole structure in order to subserve the needs of the society. Let us now discuss some facts and suggestions which can help in the improvement of the functioning of this Ministry.

1. Inadequate Facilities

Health facilities in India face many operational difficulties, these include inadequate funding for drugs, supplies and other consumables, shortages of diagnostic facilities and laboratory equipment, and a general deterioration of physical infrastructure

These major constraints lead to a low quality of care and inefficient functioning of the system at first referral units in the district health system. Some innovations have been initiated, based on the concept of community participation (cost-sharing) and through a system of matching grants.[10]

Sirilaksana Khoman in his article, "Rural Health Care Financing in Thailand" clearly observed that health care financing has become as issue of global interest and socialist countries grapple with rising costs, dwindling resources, poor-quality care, inefficient resource use, and unequal distribution of services. Transition economies in Indochina, Eastern Europe, and China, as well as capitalistic strongholds like the United States, face formidable challenges in determining who should pay for health care and how it should be managed.

In developing countries rural areas are of particular concern because regional disparities in income put rural populations at a disadvantages in term of living standrards and access to health care. Moreover, limited administrative capacity in rural areas makes it harder to manage whatever financing scheme is implemented, especially in areas where large portions of the populations are engaged in subsistence activities, cut-off from the formal sector.[11]

2. Poor Accessibility for Disadvantaged Groups

Modern medicine today is not within the reach of common man, which is a great cause of concern. Policy-makers in the government and especially in the Ministry of Health and Family Welfare need to redefine health policy to ensure priority of health care to disadvantaged sections of the society. Dr. Hiroshi Nakajima, Director-General of World Health Organisation, while inaugurating the meeting on "Policy-Oriented Monitoring of Equity in Health and Health Care," convened from 29 September to 3 October 1997 at WHO headquarters in Geneva stated that the overall gains in health that have occurred around the world are being overshadowed by increasing disparities between rich and poor. Such inequalities are both unnecessary and unjust. To quote him: "Equity is a value that governments subscribe to, but do not always make explicit in their policies. The importance of emphasizing this value is that it is often overlooked in today's attempts to tackle the financial problems of health care. Health systems are in turmoil, partly because of severe economic difficulties in some parts of the world. Ministries in rich and poor countries alike have responded to the current pressure by introducing health sector reforms that are market-friendly and encourage competition. Such mechanisms may generate revenue for health, but may increase inequities. The overall gains in health that have occurred around the world are being overshadowed by increasing disparities between rich and poor. The number of people living in absolute poverty now comprises one-fifth of the global population or 1.3 billion people. In health and health care, the gap is widening between rural and urban areas, with resources concentrated in the cities. Within the same country, life expectancy and infant mortality rates may vary enormously between regions and often over 80% of public health expenditures benefit less than 40% of the population."[12]

The Government of India must ensure health care to all otherwise, the well off population may also be affected in the long-run as President Roosevelt rightly stated that "poverty anywhere is a danger to prosperity everywhere." In the new-millennium our policy measures should go in favour of the poor to ensure equality which involves equity in provision and use of health facilities irrespective of income levels.

3. Fragmentation of Sectoral Responsibilities at National Level

Health affects and is affected by other socio-economic factors. There is little coordination between the Ministry of Health and Family Welfare and other ministries to ensure sustained development. Besides, there is no attempt to educate, empower people to ensure equity. To quote World Health Organisation:

There are numerous obstacles to the creation of health-supporting environments, not least of which is the fragmentation of sectoral responsibilities at national level. In many countries, health remains the concern of a single ministry rather than a goal to which each sector or ministry contributes in a conscious and coordinated manner. Similarly, traditional boundaries between government and non-governmental organisations, and between the public and the private sectors, hinder the development of strategies and policies informed by an awareness of health and health needs. This fragmentation can reduce the impact of health-promoting activities, particularly those undertaken at the local level. It is of only very limited benefit.[13]

Participation and empowerment are also the key to reducing the gaps between the "haves" and the "havenots." This inequality not only results in disparities in health status but also prevents groups such as women, elderly people, children and indigenous people from playing a full role in creating health-supporting environments. Ensuring that our surroundings are conducive to good health thus means directing effort at all levels, within and between all sectors of society. By doing so we can make the healthier choice, the easier choice and lay the foundation for true social and economic development. In the new millennium, we have to empower the people in the real sense, i.e. controlling the system and not merely participating theoretically.

4. Research Bears no Relevance to Practical Problems

There has been a lack of cooperation and coordination among the institutions engaged in teaching and research. This resulted in disjointed, isolated and rank duplication of scientific research in several national laboratories resulting in waste of scarce resources. The Public Accounts Committee in its 40th Report of the 5th Lok Sabha (1971-72) emphasized the importance of collaboration and coordination among various agencies engaged in medical research with ICMR taking lead and suggested that energetic steps may be taken to enlarge the scope of collaboration to avoid repetitive research.

Besides, over the years, for a variety of reasons the medical research programmes in the country could not follow the path of problem-oriented medical research in priority areas such as nutritional disorders, control of communicable diseases, operational research for providing health care to all, research in medical education, health manpower planning, utilisation of health personnel, research in indigenous system of medicine, etc. The Sixth Draft Plan (1978-83) was also critical of the research policy pursued so far. It was stated that:

> "Medical research in the past had, by and large, failed to lay emphasis on problems of immediate practical importance. Efforts were mostly towards collection of disjointed and isolated research work by individuals/agencies in the country."

The Estimate Committee in its 102nd Report pointed out that "the purpose of medical research is to bring about results of practical utility in the fight against disease with the maximum expedition possible and that little purpose will be served unless the results of research can find immediate application in the field. . . . It is unfortunate that resources and time and talent of the medical community of the country have not been meaningfully utilized over the years according to well thought out priorities.'[14] Thus, there is a need of costing of research projects in terms of time and money likely to be required for their completion. The aim of the research should be to solve health problems of the social significance to the country.

The foreign sponsorship of research projects has not been examined properly before accepting the proposals. The Public Accounts Committee in their 167th and 200th Reports have been very critical of the research projects conducted in collaboration with foreign organisations, e.g. Genetic Control of Mosquitoes Unit Projects, the Bird Migration and Arbovirus studies, the ultra low volume spray experiments, the Pantnagar Microbial Pesticides project and some of the research projects undertaken in West Bengal and Narangwal in collaboration with the John Hopkins University. The Committees are not unwilling to concede the importance of research efforts, the projects examined revealed a rather casual attitude and indifference on the part of the authorities concerned towards foreign supported research in India. The Committee reiterated the imperative need for the utmost care, caution and critical scrutiny before approving foreign sponsorship of research projects undertaken in India, particularly when such projects have military or quasi-military implications of an almost incalculable character. Such researches must be got conducted by the Indian scientists. If the foreign collaboration is indispensable, Research ventures should ensure the following:

(a) that such ventures are not only of potential value for the country but are of immediate productive utility;
(b) that the objectives of the projects are clearly spelt out and the research plans are notified in advance so as to avoid any ambiguity;
(c) that the collaborating Indian agency or institution has personnel with the requisite qualification and equipment to concurrently evaluate and monitor the progress of the research;
(d) that the technical and administrative control of the projects and determination of policies vest only with the Indian agencies and personnel concerned;
(e) that all data and materials collected are shared with the Indian collaborators;
(f) that any kind of secrecy in the conduct of research is eschewed and that the results of the research are made public; and
(g) that all research is conducted in accordance not only with the country's own environmental standards but the international environmental standards as well.[15]

In the new millennium, research must also be encouraged in the areas of equity, quality, telemedicine, etc. to benefit the poor people.

5. Unsuitable System of Medical Education

The objective of a good medical education should be to produce general practitioners, specialists, teachers and research workers. The factors governing this are the curriculum, medium of instruction, duration of course admission qualifications, the examination system, teacher-students' relationship, prospects of teachers and students, etc. Besides, it may be mentioned that the medical education should fit in with the needs of the country and the conditions prevailing there. For instance, seventy per cent of the population of India live in rural areas. The training given to the doctor should enable and motivate him to carry on his work among the vast masses in the villages. We have been designing our under-graduate and post-graduate medical education which can fulfil this basic aim. There has been a big gap between aims and fulfilment. J. Gallagher, Regional Officer for education and training, WHO Regional Office for Europe has expressed concern about inadequate communication between educational system for health personnel and the health administrations that use the products of these systems. There is very little understanding of how the manpower training and development needs of health administration can be met in a systematic way.[16]

The Government of India launched Reorientation of Medical Education Scheme in 1977 with the objective of involving the various medical colleges in the country in the direct delivery of health care services to the rural and semi-rural population. Under the scheme, each medical college in the country is to accept in the first instance, the total responsibility for promotive, preventive, curative health services in three Community Development Blocks in the district in which the institution is situated. The objectives of the scheme are:

(i) To expose the Medical faculty, residents, Interns and the students to the Rural Community;
(ii) To train the students, Interns and Residents in Community Organisation and Community Participation; and
(iii) To render comprehensive health care to the villages in collaboration with the local Primary Health Centres.

It has been expressed in the Fifth Plan document that teaching in medical colleges still requires a radical change for its orientation towards the need for community care. Medical education over the years, has been urban biased. It is hoped that it would be possible to produce medical graduates who are aware of the health problems of the community, who have a sense of compassion and motivation to serve the public and who have ability to effectively meet the urgent needs of the health care problems of the rural masses and the urban-poor.

According to the Estimates Committee:

> "The National Policy should indicate in unmistakable terms the goals to be achieved and the method of accomplishment.
> Such a policy especially in the context of health being a State subject will help in maintenance of the requisite standards of medical education throughout the country in keeping with the needs of the people."[17]

The Government of India has announced the National Medical Education Policy. In the new millennium, there is a need to set-up a Health Care Medical Service Commission responsible for planning of medical manpower, medical education, research, training of all para-medical personnel. This commission when appointed should use Health and Medical Educational Planning as a means of rationalizing the education of health manpower. Besides, the Commission may encourage the health administrator to provide the policy and planning background required for this purpose.

6. Lifestyle Causing many Health Problems

Lifestyles in many countries are also changing radically. Today, more and more people are employed in sedentary occupations in offices and factories, a considerable change from the outdoor labour of earlier times. This has contributed to an increase in morbidity and mortality from heart disease and stroke, the two conditions which are responsible for the majority of premature deaths occurring in the Region. Changes in dietary habits from traditional diets rich in fibre and low in fat, to convenience foods rich in salt, fat and calories and low in fibre, have contributed to the proliferation of these diseases. Such dietary habits are also associated with cancers of the breast, rectum and prostrate.

7. Implications of Privatisation and Globalisation for Better Health Services

It is important to note, however, that the implications of globalization for public health are not all negative. The diffusion of modern technologies and ideas between countries presents promising opportunities for improving global health in the future. Recent advances in telecommunications technology, for example, have resulted in global communication links which are unprecedented in world history. Communications technology can be exploited for health purposes, which includes telemedicine, interactive health networks, disease surveillance systems, communications links between health workers, human resource development and continuing education and distance learning.

In summary, a strong case can be made that the globalization of public health represents an important trend for the 21st century. Although some transnational health problems have historical precedents, many new issues are emerging which are unique to our time. The 1997 Kyoto conference on climate change underscored the fragility of the world's ecosystem, and showed how interdependent the health of all of humanity has become. Shared global problems transcending state borders call into question conventional paradigms which divide countries into North and South or developed and developing.[18]

Administrative and financial devolution by the states to The PRIs especially in the area of health and education remains an areas of major concern. The Constitution has placed onerous responsibilities on PRIs. They require financial resources to discharge the tasks assigned to them and emerge as viable institutions of self-government. Financial devolution is also desirable as the control of Investment decisions by local communities leads to better Utilization of scarce resources. Panchayats would need greater Powers of taxation and avenues non-tax revenue. States Could provide matching grants to panchayats to take up Specific projects. Apart from, the funds that flow to Panchayats for centrally sponsored and state sector schemes, Unites grants could also provided to the PRIs. The PRIs Need to raise resources from the local community and end Their dependence on government funds. The functional domain the PRIs can be enlarged only if they pay adequate attention to their resource-base.

TABLE 2.1

India and Comparable Countries

	India	*Sri Lanka*	*China*	*Vietnam*
Infant mortality (per 1000 live births)	60 (2003)	13 (2003)	30 (2003)	19 (2003)
One year olds fully immunized for measls (%)	58 (2002-04)	99 (2003)	84 (2003)	93 (2003)
Population with sustainable access to improved sanitation (%)	30 (2002)	91 (2002)	44 (2002)	41 (2002)
Under five mortality (per 1000 live births)	87 (2003)	15 (2003)	37 (2003)	23 (2002)
Births attended by skilled birth attendants (%)	47.6 (2002-04)	97 (1995-2003)	97 (1995-2003)	85 (1995-2003)
Maternal mortality (per 10,0000 deliveries)	407 (adjusted 2000)	92 (adjusted 2000)	56 (adjusted 2000)	130 (adjusted 2000)

Source: Towards Faste and More Inclusive Growth—An approach to the 11th Five Year Plan, GOI, Planning Commission, Dec. 2006.

The onus for devolving functions, functionaries and financial sources to the PRIs rests with the state governments. Though the state have, slowly, transferred functions and financial to the PRIs, these institutions are hampered by lack of administrative support. PRIs have to be adequately staffed and the functionaries must be trained in planning, budgeting and accounting tasks. An elaborate system for auditing of panchayat finances has to be put in place. At present, adequate safeguards against the misuse of resources by elected functionaries do not exist in many states. These issues need to be tackled on a priority basis. The 74th Constitutional Amendment Act provided for the constitution of District Planning Committees (DPCs). However, the Constitutional provision on DPCs is rather weak as it provides for the preparation of only draft Plans by the DPCs. State governments have not given adequate attention to the DPCs and the Government of India's guidelines on district planning have not been fully operationalised DPCs should be set-up and its functionaries must be trained in the basics of planning. The gram sabha/panchayat should be associated with the preparation of villages development Plans based on the felt needs of the panchayat samiti and district-level plans to make the grass-root planning process a reality in the Tenth Plan period.

The 10th Plan aimed at providing essential primary health care, particularly to the underprivileged and underserved segments of our population. It also sought to devolve responsibilities and funds for health care to PRIs. However, progress towards these objectives has been slow and the targets on MMR and IMR have been missed. Accessibility remains a major issue especially in areas where habitations are scattered and women and children continue to die en route to hospitals. Rural health care in most states is marked by absenteeism of doctors/health providers, low levels of skills, shortage of medicines, inadequate supervision/monitoring and callous attitudes. There are neither rewards for service providers nor punishments for defaulters. As a result, health outcomes in India are adverse compared to bordering countries like Sri Lanka as well as countries of South-East Asia like China and Vietnam.[19]

We have come a long way in promoting better health in 20th century. With the new developments, we should ensure decent health care to all in the new millennium so that people can enjoy good quality of life and not simply adding of years.

Notes and References

1. Amanya Sen, Health in Development, in *Bulletin of the WHO*, Vol. 77, No. 8, 1999, p. 623.
2. Ministry of Health and Family Welfare, Annual Report, 2005-06, p. 11.
3. Ministry of Health and Family Welfare, GOI, Annual Report, 2006-07, p. 2.
4. Borkar, G., Health in Independent India (Revised Edition) 1961, Ministry of Health, New Delhi, p. ix.
5. Employee State Insurance Corporation—A Brochure.
6. Ministry of Health and Family Welfare, Annual Report, 2006-07, pp. 2-3.
7. National Rural Health Mission, Ministry of Health and Family Welfare, GOI, Annual Report, 2006-07, p. 65.
8. *The Tribune*, Chandigarh, February 24, 1979.
9. Tarlok Singh, India's Development Experience, Macmillan India, 1974, Delhi; pp. 453-54.
10. WHO, Health Situation in the South-East Asia Region, 1994-97, p. 186.
11. Innovation in Health Care Financing, Proceedings of a World Bank Conference, March 10-11, 1997, p. 183 (Ed. George Schibel)
12. WHO: Final Report of meeting on Policy Oriented Monitoring of Equity in Health and Health Care, Geneva, 29th and 30th Sept. 1997, p. 2.
13. WHO: *World Health*, 51st Year, No. 2, March-April 1998, pp. 22-23.
14. Lok Sabha Secretariat: Estimates Committee, 102nd Report, (5th Lok Sabha), New Delhi, 1975, pp. 92-94.
15. Lok Sabha Secretariat, Public Accounts Committee: Fifth Lok Sabha, 200th Report, 1976, New Delhi.
16. J. Gallagher: "Educational Planning and Health", in *WHO Chronicle*, 30: 70-71 (1976).
17. Lok Sabha Secretariat: 102nd Report, Estimates Committee, (Fifth Lok Sabha), p. 4.
18. WHO: Globalisation and Public Health: A New Challenge for WHO, *World Health*, March-April, 1998, p. 25.
19. Towards Faster and More Inclusive Growth—An approach to the 11th Five Year Plan, GOI, Planning Commission, Dec. 2006.

Population Policy and Family Planning

The ultimate goal of the world's population policy must be to achieve an equilibrium based on low birth and death rates that can be sustained throughout a distant future for the world and its several parts.

—*F.W. Notestein*

The programme of family welfare and family planning is in the interest of peace and humanity in order to improve the quality of life for families in developing countries particularly in rural areas and in urban disadvantaged poor.

—*Tokyo Declaration of Parliamentarians issued in March, 1978*

ADMINISTRATION OF FAMILY PLANNING PROGRAMME

The growth rate in population absorbs the national income and lowers the standard of living. The world population conference indicated in the population plan of action that population growth and population policy must be viewed not in isolation, but in the context of development. It was mentioned by the Secretary-General that "Current and potential world-wide population trends evidently cannot continue for as long as even one century without causing serious dislocations and crises in many areas.[1]

Myrdal in his book, "Asian Drama" gave a stem warning to the world in regard to population explosion when he said, "Demographers are of the view that if fertility does not decrease, a time will come when mortality will lose its relative independence of levels of living and begin to rise again."[2]

Alexander Kessler[3] in his article, "Family Planning and the role of WHO" in *World Health,* May-June 1994 stated that the success of family planning programmes has led to a considerable decrease in average family size in developing countries, yet actual numbers continue to increase. This poses enormous challenges in terms of providing food water, energy and services, let alone improving the quality of life. Far more emphasis must be placed on the importance of family planning services.

Family planning and health are intimately related. Family planning can promote women's health through the prevention of unwanted pregnancies, limiting number of births, and proper spacing, timing of births and foetal health. Family planning also promotes the health of the child through the reduction of child mortality, and promotion of the child development. Maryellen Fullam stresses the importance of family planning as instrument for the promotion of health. He says:

> "Uncontrolled fertility directly threatens the health of mothers and infants and may undermine the health of other family members. Today, no health programme can be considered complete unless it offers ready access to the appropriate family planning measures for all potential parents."[4]

Rapid population growth leads to social and psychological tensions, and breakdown of a distribution system. Civil amenities such as water and power supply, housing, transport and social utilities like schooling, educational, health and medical services fall much short of demand in spite of their constant expansion. Besides, it leads to political and social corruption and accentuates economic disparities.

The experiences and lessons gained from Indian Planning suggests that effective population control, designed to restore the balance between vital rates by reducing the level of fertility, has a positive influence on the process of economic development and modernization. An eminent scholar has rightly mentioned that "A reduction in fertility would make the process of modernization more rapid and more certain. It would accelerate the growth of income, provide more rapidly the possibility of productive employment of all adults who need jobs, make the attainment of universal education easier and it would have the obvious and immediate effect of providing the women of low income countries some relief from constant pregnancy, prostitution and infant care."[5]

Thus, we can say that the problem of growing population has reached such menacing proportions that it has become a real threat to the socio-economic stability of the country. The excessive growth in population does not affect the stability of the national economy alone, it disturbs the stability of the entire body politic. It poses a colossal threat to our social structure. In our fight against poverty, disease, hunger, malnutrition and unemployment, checking the rapid growth of population is as important as raising production in the farms and factories and provision of social services. Population control is one of the chief issues which the country has to resolve and accord top priority in its march towards social and economic development. The programme of family planning is of vital importance for our country. It is a positive and constructive approach to the betterment of the quality of life of the community. Thus, it is evident to the key to India's economic future based on social justice lies in the immediate and effective implementation of a nation-wide population programme.

MEANING

Family Planning Programme makes a planned and scientific approach to the issues and problems of family life and attempts to solve them to make the family life happier, harmonious and fruitful. Family planning was thought of as a public health problem. It was stated in the First Five Year Plan:

It is apparent that population at a level consistent with the requirement of national economy should be established. This can be secured only by the realisation of the need for family limitation on a wide scale by the people. The main appeal for planning is based on considerations of health and welfare of the family. Family limitation or spacing of the children is necessary and desirable in order to secure better health of the mothers, and better care and upbringing of children. The measures described to this end should, therefore, form part of the public health programme. A distinction must be made between population control and family planning. Population control is influenced and determined by a government policy motivated by socio-economic considerations. Family planning, on the other hand, is a responsibility of the family, who has given various definitions of family planning.

An Expert Committee (1991) of the WHO defined family planning as: "a way of thinking and living that is adopted voluntarily upon the basis of knowledge, attitudes and responsible decisions by individuals and couples, in order to promote the health and welfare of the family group and thus contribute effectively to the social development of the country."[6]

Mr. Ramakrishna Mukherjee has defined family planning in broader and narrower context. In broader context, he says that:

(i) It is not matter of mere biological arrangement between a man and a woman, albeit in the "social" setting of a family.
(ii) It is not exclusively a "cultural" issue: culture defined as an aggregate of what a person or group of persons desires and detests in every-day-life, the aggregate being formed, from the past upto date in the course of socialisation and, thus, provides the person or the group with a matrix of perception of life itself.
(iii) It is a matter of systematic understanding of the human kind with reference to the world as a whole and not merely one of its sectors: The Third World.

In the narrower sense, he says, that family planning is, regarded as a managerial issues particularly relevant to the Third World. It involves the following measures:

(a) Propogation of appropriate slogans for a "small family";
(b) Running family planning centres for sterlisation; and
(c) Distribution of contraceptives and education of the people to use them for their own good.

Another Expert Committee (1971)[7] defined and described family planning as follows: "Family Planning refers to practices that help individuals or couples to attain certain objectives:

(a) to avoid unwanted births;
(b) to bring about wanted births;
(c) to regulate the intervals between pregnancies;
(d) to control the time at which births occur in relation to the age of the parents; and
(e) to determine the number of children in the family."

Dr. H. Mahler, ex-Director General of WHO has rightly said in *World Health* (June 1984) that in all societies, the family in one form or another is the Central nucleus for people, for their lives, their loves, their dreams and their health. So the people must be helped to understand that it is in their own interest to plan their families. And when they want to plan their family, appropriate information and services must be available in a context that provides confidence and security. Clearly what most parents want are healthy children who will grow upto become healthy adults. Today, it is possible for families through the use of technically and culturally appropriate contraceptive means to choose the timing and spacing of their children, and thus to complement other traditionally accepted means of child spacing such as breast-feeding. And quite apart from the positive health effects of family planning, the ability of couples to control their own fertility has opened the way for women to achieve the full and equitable participation in social and economic development that is their due.

In *World Health* (June 1984), it is correctly stated that healthy families do not just happen, they are planned. The birth of a healthy wanted child is a joyous occasion. A child has chance of being born healthy, of surviving the first few years of life and growing well are enchanced if parents plan their children, so that they are born not before the mother is 18 or after she is 35-at least 2 years apart. Family Planning improves the health of women by helping them avoid high-risk pregnancies.

A WHO Expert Committee (1970)[8] has stated that family planning includes in its purview: (1) the proper spacing and limitation of births, (2) advice on sterility, (3) education for parenthood including pre-natal and post-natal care, (4) sex education, (5) screening for pathological conditions related to the reproductive system (e.g. cervical cancer), (6) genetic counselling; (7) pre-marital consultation and examination, (8) carrying out pregnancy tests, (9) marriage counselling, (10) the preparation of couples for the arrival of their first child, (11) providing services for unmarried mothers.

(12) teaching home economics and nutrition, and (13) providing adoption services. These activities vary from country to country according to national objectives and policies with regard to family planning. This is the modern concept of family planning.[9]

STATUS IN INDIA

Population of the country has multiplied by more than four times during the century. It became 84.6 crore in the 1991 census and is 1,027 million as on March 1, 2001 (531 million males and 496 million females from 361 million) at the time of independence. The India's population now is thrice that of USA (For details see Table 5.1). According to United Nations Fund Population Activities (UNFPA) estimates, world population is currently increasing at the rate of about 80 million per year. India alone is contributing to a fifth of the total increase in world population, every year. This is excessive as can also be seen from the fact that India has only 2.4% of the world land area, while its population constitutes 16% of the present world population. The already unusually large pressure of population on land in India, coupled with still continuing large annual increase indicates that the population situation in India is already critical.

Such large and still increasing population has big implications for availability and incidence of unemployment in the society. The pressure of population is also very relevant for the state of environment. The high levels of population on land, in air and in water in large parts of the country indicate that the carrying capacity of land and environment is being exceeded.

NATIONAL POPULATION POLICY

India adopted a comprehensive and holistic National Population Policy (NPP) 2000 with clearly articulated objectives, strategic themes and operational strategies. The Policy enumerates certain socio-demographic goals to be achieved by 2010, which will lead to achieving population stabilization by 2045. The Policy also prescribes an Action Plan for implementing the strategic themes listed in the Policy.

The National Population Policy, 2000 has identified the immediate objectives as meeting the unmet needs for contraception, health care infrastructure and trained health personnel and to provide integrated service delivery, with the following interventions: (i) Strengthen community health centres, primary health centres and sub-centres; (ii) Augment skills of health personnel and health care providers; (iii) Bring about convergence in the implementation of related social sector programme so that the Family Welfare Programme becomes a peoples' programme; (iv) Integrate package of essential services at village and household level through mobile clinics and counselling services; and (v) Explore the possibility of accrediting private medical practitioners and revive the system of licensed medical practitioners, who could provide specified clinical services.

TABLE 3.1

Decadal Variations in Population Growth in India, 1901-2001

*Census year **	*Total population in million*	*Average annual exponential growth rate*	*Progressive growth rate over 1901 in per cent*
1901	238.4	—	—
1911	252.	10.5	65.8
1921	251.3	-0.03	5.4
1931	279.0	1.04	17.0
1941	318.7	1.33	33.7
1951	381.1	1.25	51.5
1961	439.2	1.96	84.3
1971	548.2	2.20	129.9
1981	683.3	2.22	186.6
1991	846.3	2.14	255.0
2001	1027.0	1.93	330.6

* Including Assam and Jammu and Kashmir. The 1981 Census was not held in Assam and the 1991 Census was not held in Jammu and Kashmir due to disturbances. The 1981 and 1991 census data include estimated figures for these two states.

Source: Census of India, 1981, General Population Tables, Series 1, India, Part II-A (I), pp 35-50, 536-37; Census of India, 1991, Final Population Totals: Brief Analysis of Primary census Abstract, Series 1, India, Part 2 of 1992, p 86; Census of India, 2001, Provisional Population Totals, Series 1, India, Paper 1 of 2001, p. 34.

S.P. Singh in his Article, "Problems of Population and Sustainable Development in India" in *PA*, January-March 2003, observed that, with a population of about one billion, India has achieved many dubious distinctions. Now India is a country with largest number of unemployed youth, handicapped people, beggars, slum-dwellers and illiterates in the world. The population of illiterates in India is larger than the total population of any country in the world except for People's Republic of China. Every third illiterate in the world is an Indian. It is irony that in all these areas India, come what may, will lead the world for many more years to come. It is pity indeed that in near future we will be able to achieve a few more dubious demographic distinction.

GENSIS AND GROWTH

Policy-making and Planning for family

Welfare Family Planning as an official programme was adopted in India in 1952. Before this, the Family Planning Association of India was formed in 1949 in Bombay. On 11 April 1951 the Advisory Panel on Health Programmes appointed a sub-committee on Family Planning. The sub-committee strongly recommended that family planning should be recognised as an official programme to protect the health and welfare of mothers and children and to aid the national economy by reducing the birth rate concurrently with the death rate in order to stabilise the population. During the first of Five Year Plans (1951-61) the programme was taken up in a modest way with a clinical approach. During the Second Plan period, 549 urban and 1,100 rural clinics were set-up.

The programme was reorganized in the Third Plan after the publication of the 1961 census result which showed a higher growth rate than anticipated. It was towards the middle of the Third Plan that the emphasis was shifted from the clinical approach to the more vigorous extension educational approach for motivating the people for acceptance of the small family norm and for provision of services.

A full-fledged Department of Family Planning was created in the Ministry of Health and Family Welfare. During the three annual plans (1966-69), the programme which was described as the 'kingpin' of the plan was made time-bound and target-oriented with vastly increased funds. In the Fourth Plan, the programme was accorded the highest priority. More emphasis was given to training, research, publicity, organisation, supplies and evaluation. Medical Termination of Pregnancy Act, 1971, was passed which came into force from 1 April 1972. With this Act, State Governments were empowered to constitute relevant boards to certify the registered doctors who were willing to perform the operations causing termination of pregnancy. Though the MTP Act is mainly a health measure, it also supplements the family welfare programme because a large percentage of women undergoing medical termination of pregnancy readily accept family planning measures to avoid future conceptions.

The experiences gained within the country and outside had amply established that health of women in the reproductive age group and of small children (up to 5 years of age), is of crucial importance for effectively tackling the problem of the growth of population. This perception has led to change in the approach from Family Planning to Family Welfare. Since the Seventh Plan implemented during 1984-89, the FW programmes have evolved with the focus on the health needs of the women in the reproductive age group and of children below the age of 5 years on one hand and on the other hand, to provide contraceptives and spacing services to the desirous people. Thus, the family welfare programme has objectives of stabilising population of the country early and to ensure good reproductive and child health status of the existing population. These objectives are pursued by addressing contraception issues, maternal health issues, child survival issues and by encouraging citizens through IEC to use these services.

Various programmes have led to very substantial improvement in health indicators. The achievements with regard to some prominent health and population indicators is depicted in the Table 3.2

The Approach Paper to the Ninth Plan brought out by the Planning

TABLE 3.2

Achievements of the National Family Welfare Programme

Indicator	Past Level		Current Level	
Crude Birth Rate	41.7	(1951-61)	25.4	(2001)
Crude Death Rate	22.8	(1951-61)	8.4	(2001)
Infant Mortality Rate	146	(1951-61)	66	(2001)
Maternal Morality Rate	437	(1992-93)	4.07	(1998)
Life Expectancy at Birth (years) Est. Male	37.1	(1951)	63.87	(2001)
Female	36.1	(1951)	66.9	(2001)
Effective Couple Protection Rate	10.4	(1970-71)	48.2	(1998-99)
Total Fertility Rate	6	(1951)	3.2	(1999)

(Relevant years in parentheses).

Universal Immunisation was started in 1985-86.

Commission has shown the inadequacy of the investment made for family welfare. This is a severe handicap, particularly when it is noted that in almost all respects, the health care system needs up-gradation and it needs to reach out to many more people for the national goals to be achieved. While there is a steady improvement due to economic development, spread of education/literacy and empowerment of citizens, substantial problems in regard to education/literacy, particularly among the weak performing states and in regard to empowerment particularly of women, remain. It has been now renamed as Reproductive and Child Health (RCH).

Containing population growth was one of the six major objectives of the Eighth Plan Recognizing the fact that reduction in infant and child mortality is an essential pre-requisite for acceptance of small family norm, Government of India has attempted to integrate MCH and Family Planning as part of Family Welfare services at all levels, NDC approved modified Gadgil Mukherjee Formula which for the first time gave equal weigtage to performance in MCH Sector (IMR reduction) and FP sector (CBR reduction) as a part basis for computing central assistance to non-special category States. This initiative ensured that the inter-linkages between Family Welfare Programme and Development was kept in focus in State Plans.

In order to give a new thrust and dynamism to the ongoing Family Welfare Programme the National Development Council set-up a Sub-committee on population to consider the problem of population stabilisation and come up with recommendations to improve performance. The report of the sub-committee was considered and the recommendations were endorsed by the NDC in its meeting in September 1993. The NDC Committee on Population had recommended that Family Welfare Programme should take cognizance of the area specific socio-economic, demographic and health care availability differentials and allow requisite flexibility in programme planning and implementation. For this purpose the NDC Committee recommended that there should be:

(a) Decentralised area specific planning based on the need assessment.
(b) Emphasis on improved access and quality of services to women and children.
(c) Providing special assistance to poorly performing states/ districts to minimise the inter and intra-state differences in performance.
(d) Creation of district level database on quality and coverage and impact indicators for monitoring the programme.

ORGANISATION

The apex body at the centre is a cabinet committee which is presided over by the Union Minister of Health and Family Welfare. It includes Ministers of States for Finance, Human Resource Development, Home Affairs. It also includes a member from the Department of Electronics and Scientific and Industrial Research. This body has the overall responsibility for the formulation of national policies on the family planning and for reviewing the progress in their implementation. (Chart 3.1).

To Co-ordinate the family planning activities among the different States, the Central Family Planning Council has been set-up as an advisory body for policy-making. It includes Health Ministers from all the States and is presided over by the Union Minister of Health and Family Welfare, Vice-President in Union Minister of State. The Union Deputy Minister in the Ministry of Health. Other members are from the Planning Commission, representatives of the Union Territories, representatives of major voluntary organisations, labour organisations, selected members of Parliament, Eminent individuals in their personal capacity and officials from the various ministries. It has representatives from a wider section of interests in family planning, including those that are directly charged with the implementation of the programme.

The Department of Family Welfare (earlier Family Planning) within the ministry is responsible for the implementation of policies. The Secretary to the Government of India in the Ministry of Health and Family Planning is overall in incharge of the Department of Family Welfare. An Additional Secretary assists the Secretary and provides overall direction to programme implementation. He is known as Additional Secretary and Commissioner for Family Welfare. There is a Joint-Secretary who supervises the working of the Technical Wing of the Department which provides technical guidance to the various programme activities, i.e. Sterilisation, IUD, Post-Partum, M.C.H., Training, Mass Education, besides Evaluation and Research. The Additional Secretary's duties include policy formulation, programme planning, supervising the programme implementation and co-ordination of activities of the department with other related ministries and departments of the Government of India.

CHART 3.1

Organisation Chart: Department of Family Planning

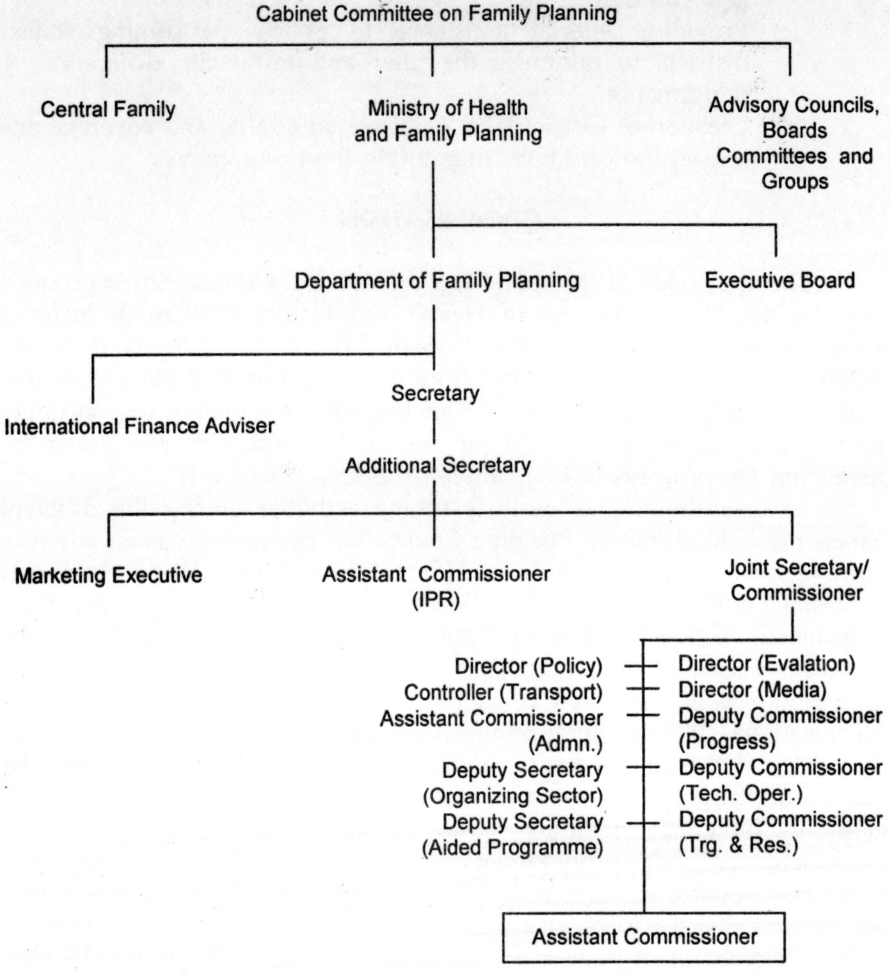

*Adapted from the Ministry of Health and Family Planning, Report: 1974-75 (New Delhi). Government of India Press, (No. date), p. 123.

There are two wings of the department: (A) Administrative Wing (the Secretariat), and (B) Technical Wing with many divisions. On the secretariat side, there is: (i) Policy Division, (ii) an Aided Programme Division, (iii) an organised sector, (iv) Voluntary Organisation's Division, and (v) a Plan Budget Division.

(i) The Policy Division looks after formulation of policies concerning family welfare.

CHART 3.2

Organisation for Family Planning in a State

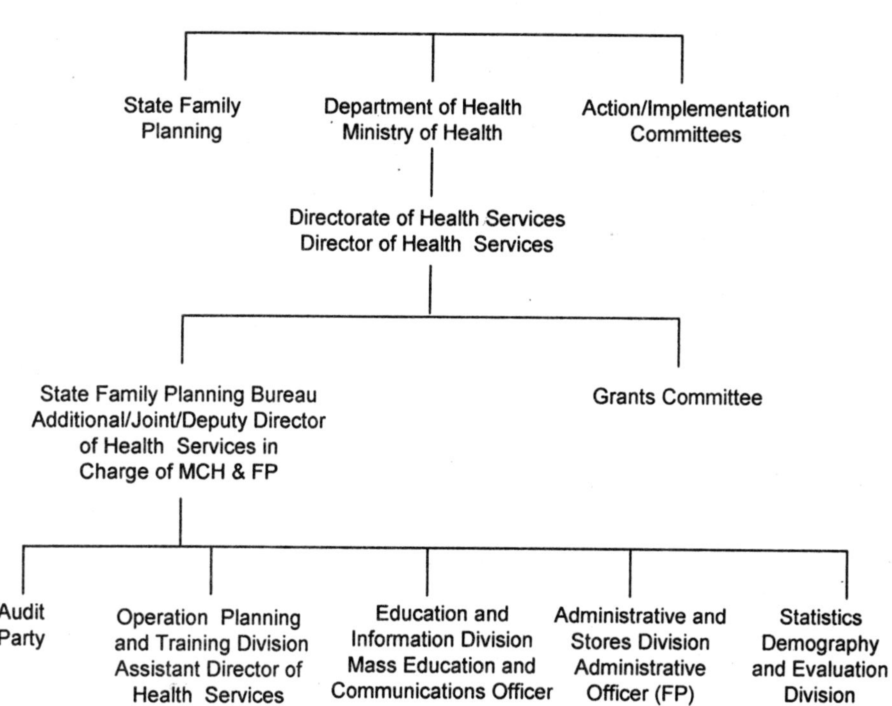

(ii) The Aided Programme Division looks after the activities of organisations which receive extra government assistance and aims at improving upon the scope and quantum of medical and health care services.

(iii) The Organised Sector Division Co-ordinates Departmental Policies and Measures affecting the family planning activities of public bodies and private organisations which are collectively called institutions in the organised sector.

(iv) The Voluntary Organisations Division assigns programmes to voluntary agencies and aims at assessing the efficiency and effectiveness of these agencies.

(v) A Plan Budget Division looks after the finances of the Programme.

On the technical side, the following divisions are functioning. The functions are clear from the names of the divisions:

(i) Programme Appraisal, Co-ordination and Training and Sterilisation (including Research) Division.

CHART 3.3

Organisation for Family Planning in a District

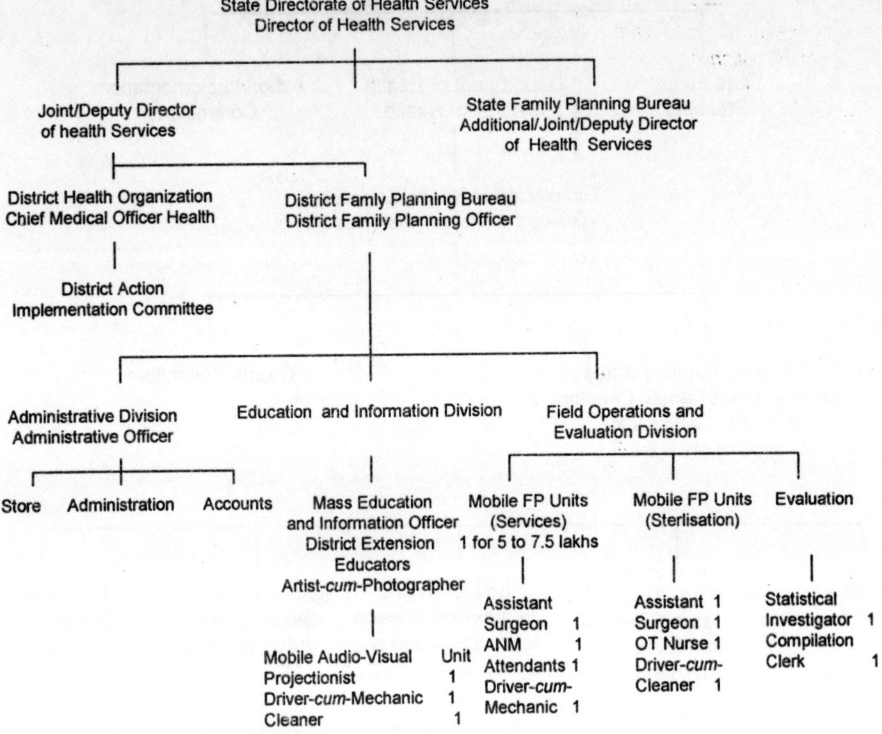

(ii) Technical Operation Division.
(iii) Maternal and Child Health Division.
(iv) Evaluation and Intelligence Division.
(v) Mass Education and Media (including population education) Division.
(vi) Nirodh Marketing Division.
(vii) Transport Division.
(viii) Projects Division (Area Projects).

Organisation at State Level

In order to co-ordinate the family welfare activities between the State Governments and the Central Government, the Directorate of Health and Family Welfare for each State gives adequate support to the State Health and Family Welfare Departments. Organisation at District and block levels. (Charts 3.3 and 3.4) At the district level there is a Distt. Family Planning Bureau while at block level Family Planning has been integrated with health services. Besides, the Primary Health Care complex is responsible at the village level.

CHART 3.4

Organisation for Family Planning in a Block

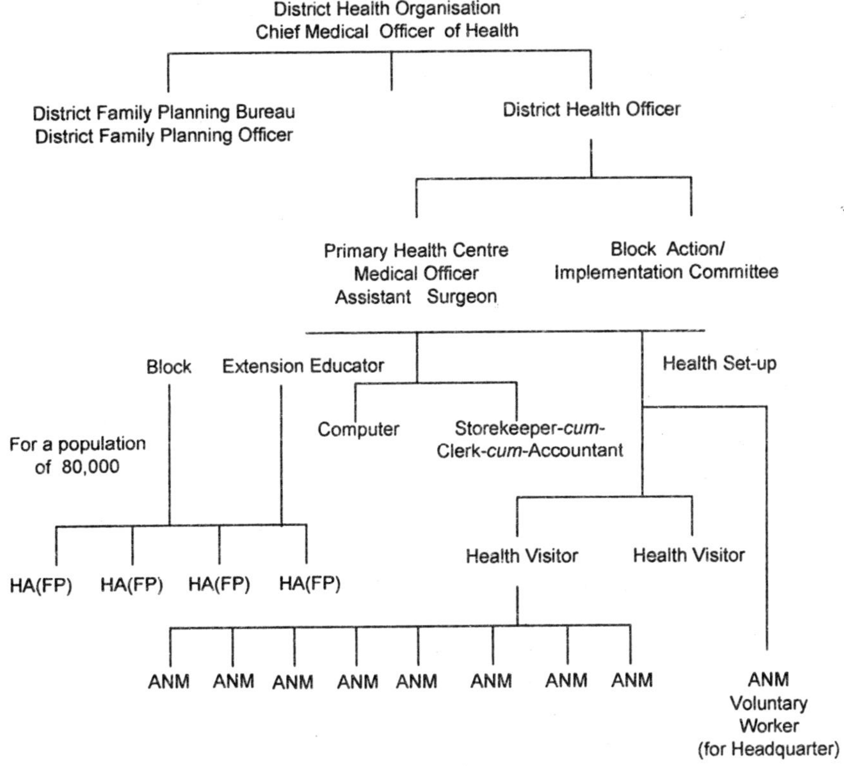

SERVICES

The National Family Welfare Programme provides the following contraceptive services:

- Sterilization as a terminal method.
- Intra-Uterine Devices (IUD) for the spacing births.
- Daily Oral Contraceptive Pill for spacing births.
- Condoms for spacing births.

Emergency Contraceptives Pill (E-Pills)

Department of Family Welfare introduced procurement of Emergency Contraceptive Pills (E-pills) in National Family Welfare Programme during 2002-03. This contraceptive is used within 72 hours of un-protected Sex. Following quantities of E-pills were procured during 2002-03 and 2003-04 for distribution to states. No procurement has been made during 2004-05 and 2005-06 however, procurement of 10.00 lakh packs is proposed during 2006-07.

The acceptance level of the various methods of contraception during the last two years has been as given in Table 3.3

TABLE 3.3

Acceptance of Various Services from 1995-96 to 2005-06 and 2006-07

	1995-96	1996-97	1997-98	1998-99	2002-03	Compare of two years 2005-06	2006-07	% Change from 2005-06 to 2007
Sterilisation	4422319	3870226	4127065	1283402	473100	1.53	1/35	(-)11.8
IUDs	6857882	5680671	6085744	263463	6108000	2.76	2.44	(-)11.6
Oral Pills	5090850	5250179	6249222	5081306	16537000	6.93	7.74	11.7
Condom	172974291	17214327	16730468	12984061	8243000	18.03	17.91	(-)0.7

Source: Annual Report, Ministry of Health and Family Welfare from 1995-96 to 2006-07.

Prevention of Unwanted Pregnancy

The data from National Family Health Survey has shown that awareness regarding contraception is nearly universal. But there is an unmet for contraception, The Family Welfare Programmes will gear itself to meet the unmet need during the Ninth Plan period. Vasectomy is safer than tubectomy and efforts will be made to increase acceptance of vasectomy, so that there is substantial reduction in the morbidity associated with terminal methods of contraception. Quality of contraceptive care will be improved. Couples will be provided with balanced information on all available methods of contraception and the advantage and disadvantage of each of these methods so that they choose the method best suited to their needs. Such a balanced presentation and counselling will in the long-run not only improve acceptance of contraceptive care, but also improve continuation rates of temporary methods of contraception. The quality of services will be improved through appropriate training of service providers at all levels.

MTP Services

Over two decades have elapsed after the enactment of legislation for Medical Termination of Pregnancy (MTP) Act. Over the last two decades the Government of India has taken steps to provide trained manpower and equipment at secondary and primary health care level for safe legal abortion services.

It is obvious that after the initial rise, the reported number of MTPs has remained below 0.6 million for the last 15 years. In 2001, it was 7,66,762. In spite of efforts to improve the availability of, and access to, induced abortions services in the primary health care set-up, safe abortion services are not available to majority of rural population in India. Even today majority of the estimated 7.6 million induced abortions are not carried out in settings recognised for legal abortion and about 8.9% maternal deaths in India are due to septic abortion.

Efforts to improve access to family planning services to reduce the number of unwanted pregnancies and cater to the request for induced abortion will continue to receive intensified attention during the Ninth Plan. In addition, efforts will be made to improve access to safe abortion services by training physicians in MTP and recognising and strengthening institutions which are capable of providing safe abortion services for the first trimester. IEC efforts through appropriate channels of communications to improve awareness among women about availability of safe abortion services at affordable cost through appropriate channels of communication will be intensified. Provision for first trimester abortion will be coupled with appropriate contraceptive care so that these women do not incur the risk of yet another unwanted pregnancy and induced abortion.

RESEARCH AND DEVELOPMENT

The ICMR is the nodal research agency for funding basic, clinical and operational research in contraception and MCH. In addition to ICMR, CSIR, DBT and DST are some of the major agencies funding research pertaining to Family Welfare Programme. The National Committee for Research in Human Reproduction assists the Department of Family Welfare in drawing up priority areas of research and ensuring that there is no unnecessary duplication of research activities. Some of the major institutions carrying out research in this area include the Institute for Research in Reproduction, Bombay, National Institute of Nutrition, Hyderabad, National Institute of Health and Family Welfare, New Delhi, Central Drug Research Institute, Lucknow and the Central Council for Research in Ayurveda and Siddha, Delhi. A network of 18 Population Research Centres conduct studies on different aspects of Family Welfare Programme and undertake demographic surveys."

Bask and Clinical Research

Development and testing of new contraceptives include contraceptives which are considered to be effective in Indian Systems Medicine.

- Research on methods for male fertility regulation,
- Clinical trials on newer non-surgical methods of MTP, and
- Post-marketing surveillance of Centchroman.

Operational Research

- Studies on the ongoing demographic transition and its consequences.

- Studies on continuation rates and use of effectiveness of contraceptives.
- Research on operationalising integrated delivery of RCH services nutrition, education, women and child development, rural development and family welfare services at village level.

MONITORING OF FAMILY WELFARE SERVICES

Monitoring and evaluation form an essential component of FW programme. Indicators used for monitoring and evaluation include process indicators and impact indicators. Process indicators are used to monitor the progress of implementation of the programme through monthly progress reports as compared to the annual targets/Expected Level of Achievements (ELAs).

Training

Training to medical and paramedical health professional is imparted in various training institutes, centres and schools. Basic training is imparted in ANM training schools, LHV training schools and MPWM training schools and selected Health and Family Welfare Training Centres. In-service training is imparted in National Institutes; State Regional Health and Family Welfare Training Centres, HFWTCs and by District Training Teams.

CRITICAL APPRAISAL

To quote S.P. Singh again, What has happened elsewhere can happen in India too provided there is a massive campaign to educate eligible couples, particularly in villages, about the benefits of limiting the size of the family. This point has of course been emphasized innumerable times and at different places but it has never been sincerely implemented. Rural people, steeped in ignorance and obsolete religious relief, still do not know the harm that big family size brings to them and consider every child as a gift of God. This notion must be altered if family planning is to succeed. However, the education campaign must always be backed by easy availability of modern contraceptive measures that can enable people to plan their families. One of the reasons why family planning measures have not yielded the desired results is that it has not been honestly implemented. The unmet need for family planning has been reported to be quite high. According to the National Family Health Survey 2, the current unmet need for family planning is 16 per cent and it is higher in rural areas than in urban areas.

Inspite of the existence of infrastructure and availability of technology to control the growth of population, we have not been achieving the desired results. K.B. Sahay in his article, "Population: Time for Tough Measures", in the *Daily Tribune* (January 28, 2000) has rightly portrayed the present population scene which present a depressing picture. To quote him: "It is very well known that we are adding at least about 1.5 crore "additional" children every year to our population. Thus, the reality is that hardly 10 percent of the "additional" children accruing every year in India are getting (even) enrolment in primary schools and the rest 1.35 crore per year are being left to grow up without any school education. Thus, we need to open at least 60,000 new primary schools per year to meet the constitutional requirement whereas we have been opening only 6000 new primary schools per year. Thus, our "educational rate" is, in fact, declining about 1.4 per cent per year. It is feasible now for the country to open 60,000 new primary schools per year and provide free and compulsory primary education to all the children as required in the constitution without first controlling our population growth? And, again, it is possible to empower women without even primary school education?

It might be recalled that in 1970 Dr. Norman Borlaug, in his speech that he gave on the occasion of receiving the Nobel Prize cautioned that whatever was being done by way of increasing food production would give us a breathing time of not more than 30 years which should be used to tame the population monster. We have now come to the end of that grace period but our population is still increasing by about 1.6 crore per year. Also, according to a recent study report, "Population, Food Production and Nutrition in India", published by UNFPA, India (Oct.1999), "there is an urgent need to reduce population growth so that the demand for foodgrains can be reduced and effectively met."

The question arises as to what is the major problem? It may be mentioned that the main problem in the less developed world including India is that of inadequate and inefficient administration which directly or indirectly impinge on the implementation of family planning programmes. The success of family planning programmes can ensured only through innovative, impartial, honest and efficient administration. There is a need that Family Planning Administration must be modernized, i.e. recreated, renewed and revitalized to achieve the predesigned changes and output. This needs a different trend and magnitude of Administrative Management, culture and capability especially in a challenging area of Family Planning. Let us analyse some of the problems in detail which affect the functioning of family planning programme:

I. Ineffective Environmental Linkages

It is understood that the implication of family planning programme is a quite complex process in which medical, cultural, psychological, social, economic, administrative and even political factors are involved and intermingled. The existing family planning organisations are operating like other government departments and thus their performance is not adequate. A good organisation must respond to and react to the changes in the environment and establish environmental linkages, linkages are points of interactions with the environment. They can be classified into four categories: (a) enabling, (b) functional, (c) diffused, and (d) normative linkages.

(a) Enabling Linkage

It ensures and protects the organisational authority to operate its access to resource and its power to achieve results. One of the most important factors which impinges on the programmes from its formulation to execution is political and its impingement on both the programme and its executors occur at all levels (national, regional, provincial, district) and at the programme input levels (financial allocations, personnel, material resources). The impact of policies and the political processes on the programme is both positive and negative and this insight provides the directions and options available to ensure greater success in programme implementations. Since political constraints are neither permanent nor inseparable, there is urgency in adopting measures designed to optimise the positive contributions of political support as well as minimise and mitigate the harmful effects of partisan interferences. To make Family Planning Programme effective and stronger there is a need of more visible political commitment and commitment for demographic rather than health or welfare reasons.

For Family Planning administrators to operate successfully in this political environment they must acquire not only a deeper insight of the 'political games' as well as the 'political skills' needed to serve and thrive in that environment. An important asset is the capability of programme leaders to seek and maintain support from key political elites both at the national and local levels.

The Family Planning Workers at all levels must keep in touch with political elite to generate favourable public opinion. In this context, there is a great need at the local level where the family planning programmes are being implemented. Here, they must involve the members of Panchayat and other local leaders so that they can help the family planning workers in developing momentum.

(b) Functional Linkage

It is to link the programme with the task environment, i.e. university, research institutes, hospitals, etc. The Family Planning workers must analyse the agencies interested in the developmental activities and then get their support and guidance in their work. Such agencies are existing from national to local levels. For examples, at the Grass-root level, we have teaching institutions, extension offices of many development departments. The need is to develop effective linkages in order to get the benefit of their existing structures and mechanisms. Let us discuss some of them.

(i) Collaboration with Rile Elites

In this connection, it is suggested that there should be effective collaboration between the universities and the family planning programme as the universities can be a sources of strength to the programme from the policy formulation to evaluation. To quote K.P. Bahadur

> "The involvement of intellectuals in the programme has distinct advantages. This was done in Turkey with excellent results. They have the ability and the social position to carry its message to the lower classes and to convince those who are hovering on the fringe of doubt."[10]

At the moment there is a dichotomy between the social scientists and the medical specialists which must fade away as early as possible. In South Korea, one of the reasons ascribed for the success of the programme is the association of the university with the family planning programme.

(ii) Collaboration with the Hospital

The success of family planning programme depends to a great extent on the way the programme can operated through the health services network in the country. The hospital provides a good platform from the educational and motivational point of view. About 200 million people approach the hospitals every year in the country and there the people are most amenable to advice upon any aspect of their personal behaviour including family planning. Maternity wards are special places for such work. Moreover, the hospital is the best place for family planning as it can provide all the services to deal with after effects.

Conventional contraceptives are not being used by the people in India because it requires high motivation and good standard of living, e.g., the sale of Nirodh has touched 50 million mark in India while in USA with half the population, sale is about 6000 million per year, in Japan with of fifth of India's population, the sale is 250 million per year. Therefore, the country should rely on sterilization, IUD, etc. Both of these require supervision of a high order. Hence, we must streamline the administration of the hospitals so that the hospital staff can also take up Family Planning Programme work with more earnestness and seriousness.

(iii) Co-ordination with Voluntary Agencies

Voluntary agencies can play an effective role in mobilizing the public opinion in support of the programme. The Family Planning Association of India and its branches in the States are rendering useful service. In this connection, it may be suggested that to revolutionise the programme, FPAI may take initiative in setting up the "Women's Club" in every village in South Korea. At present, the 'Mother's Club' having a membership of, 20-40 women in each of 19,000 villages has become a multi-purpose basic organ for the nation-wide 'New community movement' since 1971, in Korea. It is significant to note that the family planning programme became integrated into a broader community movement by the Mother's Club at the village level.[11] This experiment has been a great success in South Korea. We can bring these members in the communication network with the help of a four-step strategy mentioned below:

(a) Provide the opinion leaders with the information necessary for a full understanding of the reasons for family planning including its relationships to national and particularly local development,
(b) Invite their suggestions for local activities,
(c) Involve them in the purview of radio and television programmes, and
(d) Invite them to open discussion about family planning in the community whether formally or informally.[12]

Mrs. Helvi Sipila has also stressed that the associations of women organisations will surely help in checking the menace of population explosion.[13] A study of the inter-relationship of the status of women and family planning was conducted in accordance with economic and social council resolution.[14] The report affirmed:

(a) The right to decide freely and responsibly on the number and spacing of their children is a fundamental right of individuals which facilitates the exercise of other human rights especially by women.
(b) Adequate information, education and services enabling individuals to exercise this right are essential prerequisites for ensuring their complete integration in social and economic development at all levels.
(c) Family Planning which should constitute an integrated and essential part of development plan and programme in countries suffering from over-population can only succeed in concert with other measures which also improve the status of women.[15]

It can be said that the best contraceptive in the world is the involvement and the overall improvement of the status of women. Meher C. Nanavatty in his Article, "Organising Communities" has rightly stated that the process of Community Organisation, which is necessary for shouldering this work, has to be generated in developing community education for population control. The development of the nucleus of local leadership, involving the community in the study of the needs and requirements of the programme, the association of existing groups and their leader in the promotion of the programme, the effective use of educational and audio-visual aids with emphasis on creating the climate of change for and acceptance of programme. Their inclusion needs to be ensured by the non-official Organisations which would take upon themselves the responsibility of promoting community education for population control.[16]

(c) Diffused Linkage

"Life enlighten movement" means to reach the clients through mass-media. Organized family planning programme requires a high level of user participation. Any successful family planning effort must be understood and accepted by the people and be based on public trust and confidence. It cannot be solely dictated or legislated. Family planning is such a multifaceted personal and intimate subject that its practice can only occur on an individual, voluntary basis.[17]

The art of developing common understanding among people is vital to bring about change of attitudes and behaviour. Sociologists have classified the diffusion process which leads to a widespread acceptance of the programme into five stages:

- Awareness (the individual's first introduction to a new idea or practice).
- Interest (the stage at which he actually seeks further information and background data).
- Evaluation (the stage of assessment on theoretical grounds).
- Trial (a limited phase of experiment), and finally acceptance or adoption.

Naturally, the duration of the process depends upon personality factors which differs with individuals. Mass-media helps in creating awareness, in providing stimulation and motivation and in giving ready access to information. But at the specific stage of evaluation, trial and adoption, inter-personal, face to face, communication counts for much more and the inability of the mass-media to maintain a two-way dialogue with regular feedback restricts their utility.[18] Therefore, no medium of communication is as effective as one human being talking to another. The UNESCO has rightly stated:

The process of social and economic development is a process of human development for people are the targets as well as the essential variable in development. Communication being a two-way process, provides for participation at whatever stage of enlightenment of the individuals composing a society find themselves. Change agents are key factors in both the communication development processes since they are instruments for getting facts to the people upon which decisions can be based.[19]

The function is to be performed mostly by the field workers. At present, the field workers are not fully equipped to do this interpersonal communication resulting into much mis-informed criticism of the programme. For example, on the personal discussion of the writer with a group of rickshaw-pullers, it was revealed that they were not undergoing family planning operations as they thought that they would not be able to ply their rickshaws afterwards. Similarly, in a discussion with educated people one finds that the adoption of family planning programme would lead to many social and psychological maladjustments. It was found in a survey that multi-purpose workers felt a need for more training to develop skills and techniques to contact, communicate and persuade their clients in their own particular setting and identity of personality. Even the Haryana Government has admitted that training of the workers in the field needs re-orientation and pre-service training of multi-purpose workers is absolutely necessary.[20]

The ultimate test of establishing diffused linkage can be ascertained from the following:

(a) Awareness of the needs and problems of population control;
(b) Knowledge of schemes in operation, their objectives, service, eligibility criteria, agencies and functionaries for the delivery of services;
(c) Community's conviction about the efficacy and usefulness of the services;
(d) Community's clear understanding of its participation and contribution;
(e) Active involvement of the people, their leaders, institutions, organisations; and
(f) Normative Linkage.

There has been little attempt to incorporate the family planning behaviour into the existing value system of the society. Social values act as a hindrance to ready adoption. For example, if people talk about birth control behaviour naturally related to sex, it is traditionally regarded as impolite. Besides, the demand for sons to carry on the family line has been predominant in the Indian society. Not only social values but also religious values often act as a hindrance.[21] Therefore, the mass-media and communication officers and family planning workers must dispel all these false impressions and taboos after a careful survey and research in demography. Mass-media and communication officers may intensify their efforts by organising public meetings of different groups—labourers, farmers, workers, union leaders and extensive use of various media like, cinema, exhibition, radio, TV, etc. may be made. At present, the full use of mass-media is not being made in the real sense inspite of the availability of the arrangements. More attention is to be paid to uneducated rural people and economically depressed classes. Family planning and fertility control behaviour of the client group especially eligible women have been affected by their socio-economic background.

It is found that the higher educated women tend to have a small number of children and the use of contraceptives and induced abortion is more prevalent among them. The socio-economic status as well as the urban-rural diffusion of client groups are clearly pronounced in their family planning behaviour. The Government of India, Ministry of Health, has also admitted that "high fertility rates have been identified as more a function of poverty than of anything else." Therefore, more attention must be paid to groups living under conditions of poverty.

2. Limited Financial Resources and Absence of Cost Consciousness Among Family Planning Personnel.

The most important aspect about the finances for the Family Planning Welfare is its effective utilisation, i.e. to ensure optimization. This can be ascertained from the physical results achieved. V.M. Dandekar in his Article, "Population Front of India's Economic Development" in Economic and Political Weekly, April 23, 1988 has analysed the Family Planning Programmes. He states that the expenditure on family planning increased from Rs. 12.14 per eligible couple in 1980-81 to Rs. 37.7 in 1985-86. There is a great variation in States, the expenditure per eligible couple varied from Rs. 59.59 in Kerala to Rs. 23.47 in Bihar. The cost per birth averted has increased from Rs. 285.63 in 1980-81 to Rs. 590.87 in 1985-86. Study the Deptt. of Family Welfare also found this. Expenditure on Family Welfare per eligible couple is the highest in Punjab.

This analysis clearly indicates that the resources allocated to Family Planning are not being fully utilized. Though, there are no two opinions regarding the urgency of averting birth. To quote Mr. V.M. Dandekar, "Whatever the cost, the Family Planning Programme must be pursued steadily. But, it must perform."

"It has been a matter for concern that there are considerable shortfalls in expenditure and disturbing increase in the cost per acceptor . . . Although expenditure has been mounting since the beginning of the Fourth Five Year Plan, Physical Performance has not been keeping pace with it. Capital expenditure on construction activities and vehicles has grown since 1969-70, but the number of equivalent sterilizations has been going down."[22]

3. Not Enough Use of Modern Management Techniques

In a developing country, such as ours, there is a great urgency to control population growth in the shortest time possible before it becomes too late. It is felt that the scope of experimentation is a costly and slow process. As such, we need to apply the new management technique to accelerate the process of population control. Family Planning functions are so pervasive, diverse and vast, in terms of the range of functions, the number of functionaries, and the areas of operation, that it would be risky to fail to appreciate the need for rationalization of the processes of management.

To quote Dr. Chi-Yuen Wu of the UNDP:

> "To create administrative capabilities, commensurate with requirements, developing countries must be able among other things, to use modern management techniques more effectively than in the case of the industrially advanced countries."

Family Planning and Population Programme involve large, complete and inter-related activities which net to be managed consistently to include the desired social change. Though there are a large number of these techniques like PERT/CPM, Operational Research, Organisational Development, Cost-Benefit Analysis, Management Information System, Work Study, Method Study, Performance Budgeting, etc. which can be used profitably to optimise the family planning activities. But, the management techniques suitable for industrial and commercial enterprises may not help in their pure forms. There is a need to modify and develop these techniques to make them applicable to family planning activities. We generally forget it and the result is frustration.

4. Less Emphasis on Relevant Research

Mr. Prodipto Roy in his Article, "The Uses of a Rapid Survey and Feedback to Accurately Assess Demographic Trends" has emphasized the need of co-ordination between researchers and policy-makers, planners and decision-makers. He states that the dialogue between the research workers, decision-makers and action workers must be maintained. The latter must feel free to ask foolish but sometimes difficult research question and the research machinery must be geared to answer these questions. A continual feeding of problems from high political places or low action places to simple or complex research design and execution must maintain a steady cycling and recycling. It is only when this level of research capability is built flexible, fast and with the capacity to save the entire range of problems that arise, will the population problem be put on an intelligent footing so that the policy can be based squarely on scientific facts.[23]

The researches so far conducted have not devoted sufficient attention to fields of organistional structure and functioning of family planning program and modern methods of administrative management. Evaluation machinery needs strengthening at all levels. Independent evaluation may be undertaken to ensure that qualitative aspects of the programme have not been ignored by the states.

Research is not an end in itself, it is only a means to an end. There has been a lack of co-operation and co-ordination among the institutions engaged in teaching and research. This resulted in disjointed, isolated and rank duplication of scientific research in the institutions engaged in population/Family Planning Research resulting in waste of scarce resources. Thus, there is a need that energetic steps may be taken to enlarge the scope of collaboration to avoid repetitive research. Besides, over the years, for a variety of reasons, the medical and family planning programme in the country could not follow the path of problem-oriented research in priority areas. The Sixth Draft Plan (1978-83) was also critical of the research policy pursued so far. It was stated that medical research in the past had by and large failed to lay emphasis on problems of immediate practical importance. The Estimate Committee in its 102nd Report pointed out that it is unfortunate that resources, time and talent of the medical community of the country have not been meaningfully utilized over the years according to well thought out prioritity.[24]

5. Lack of Area Development Profiles and Programmes

The policy of the Family Planning Programme Organisation in terms of targets are made only for the state or country as a whole. No attempt has been made so far to prepare action plans for each sub-centre/primary health centre or urban centre in terms of money, equipment, personnel, time, physical targets, etc. Such action programme if designed would help in effective implementation and monitoring. Here, we can make use of the new techniques of management-PERT/CPM for proper programme planning and resource deployment.

It is understood that planning covers not only the determination of programme objectives and overall targets but also the detailed specification of activities and projects as well as resources allocation for the achievement of specific project targets during a given period of time. In the case of most Asian countries, planning of FP programmes covers only the official statement of programme objectives in terms of national demographic goals and the determination of the overall targets of FP acceptance. There is no such management planning that is conducive to programme implementation through the provision of guidelines for managers and administrators of FP programmes at every level regarding specific actions to be undertaken in terms of what to do (specification of activity design), how much to do (individual activity targets and budgeting), what is required (standard of performance), how to secure the desired performance (monitoring), how to co-operate (organisation), etc. In most Asian countries, FP programmes are conceptually specified into primary functional categories such as: (1) contraceptive services and supplies (FP delivery), (2) information, education and communication; (IEC) for mass education, (3) training of FP personnels, (4) research and training, (5) administration, etc. According to information revealed in the plan documents of programmes, however, the elaboration of these activities into further specific sub-functional categories is not made and thus managerial strategies for achieving the programme targets are hardly demonstrated. The lack of specification of FP programmes in the planning stage does not help in guiding adequately the administrators' role in management planning, monitoring and evaluation.

6. Lack of Team Work in Family Planning

Besides Planning and Training, we may keep in mind that team-work among different categories of personnel engaged in family planning activities is of vital significance.

Most of the Family Planning workers are working in isolation, i.e. their activities are not co-ordinated properly resulting into lower output of services. According to Antonia Ordonex-Plaja: "Team work requires, among other things, that the members have an image of their team-mates, which coincides as precisely as possible with reality. In addition, each member must have a self-image which adjusts to reality as much as possible and thus coincides with the image the other members have of him."[25]

The team work would develop common practices and shared practices. This would also raise the morale of the personnel working at the grass-root level.

Another important area is of Organisational Communication which can bind and keep united all the Family Planning workers. Effective communication in the Family Planning organisation is very important because:

(i) Unless employees know the organisational objectives, they cannot associate them with their own;
(ii) It is essential to the management of change in the organisation. Without facts, understanding, and acceptance, efforts to change are doomed to failure, without well directed communication, are/is not a chance; and
(iii) Without a communication, sharing of ideas with others will take place.

Let us now mention some other problems:

1. No reliable criteria for evaluation of the impact of family planning programme.
2. Inadequate Management Information System to Monitor Family Planning Programmes to ensure effective policy-making, implementation and evaluation.
3. Lack of dedicated and committed leadership.
4. Inadequacy of personnel planning and development.
5. Lack of effective public responsibility and accountability.
6. Lack of adequate administrative machinery for implementation.
7. Increasing women's status through women empowerment.

CONCLUSION

Joung Wahang has identified some potential areas where administrative reforms and improvements can help in increasing operational efficiency, i.e.

(a) To get F.P. methods (including instruments and services) identified and defined;
(b) To get sufficient amount and reliable quality of F.P. instruments and services available to the clients;
(c) To get F.P. instruments and services available to clients in the most appropriate places;
(d) To get F.P. instruments and services available to clients at the most reasonable price and costs; and

(e) To get F.P. instruments and services available without any psychological embarrassment and disturbance to the privacy of clients.

We should not be pessimistic. We should hope that the present momentum built-up since the Sixth Plan would continue. We should not hesitate to bring about innovative changes to make the programme realistic. We cannot afford to allow the programme to go slow as the programme is a source of strength to all other schemes of socio-economic development, whatever may be their immediate goal. Prime Minister Indira Gandhi, has rightly said on September 30, 1983, at New York while receiving the United Nations Population Award.

The enabling objectives during the Ninth Plan period, therefore will be to reduce population growth rate by:

(a) meeting all the felt needs for contraception, and
(b) reducing the infant and maternal morbidity and mortality so that there is a reduction in the desired level of fertility.

The strategies during the Ninth Plan will:

(a) to assess the needs for reproductive and child health at PHC level and undertake area specific micro-planning, and
(b) to provide need-based, demand-driven high quality, integrated reproductive and child health care.

The programmes will be directed towards:

(a) Bridging the gaps in essential infrastructure and manpower through a flexible approach and improving operational efficiency through investment in social; behaviour and operational research.
(b) Providing additional assistance to poorly performing districts identified on the basis of the 1991 census to fill existing gaps in infrastructure and manpower.
(c) Ensuring uninterrupted supply of essential drugs, vaccines and contraceptives, adequate in quantity and appropriate in quality.
(d) Promoting male participation in the Planned Parenthood movement and increasing the level of acceptance of vasectomy.

Efforts will be intensified to enhance the quality and coverage of family welfare services through:

(a) Increasing participation of general medical practitioners working in voluntary, private, joint sectors and the active cooperation of practitioners of ISM and H.

(b) Involvement of the Panchayat Raj Institutions for ensuring inter-sectoral coordination and community participation in planning, monitoring and management.

(c) Involvement of the industries, organised and unorganized sectors, agriculture workers and labour representatives.

It is said that prosperity is a good contraceptive. But the effects of development submerged unless we bring about a low birth rate. Family Planning is an input for development, an indispensable exercise in human capital formation. Education, better capacity for producing and earning a higher rise in per capita income are possible only when population growth is curbed.

Government of India has enunciated the new Population Policy in February, 2000, Commenting on the New Population Policy Business Standard Editorial, "Sense on Population" dated February 17, 2000 commenting on the New Population Policy Business Standard Editorial, "Sense on Population" dated Feb. 17, 2000, remarked, The new national population policy, 2000, however may have a greater chance of acceptance, it incorporates some of the lessons learnt from recent successes in curbing population growth. While the earlier attempts merely emphasized physical targets and ignored the vital aspects of health and education, especially that of the girl child, which are vitally linked to birth rates, the latest policy seeks to squarely address these issues. Besides, it also makes the right kind of noises about investment in social infrastructure as an essential prerequisite for promoting small family norms.

Success of the new policy will depend largely on the way it is implemented by the laggard states and the pace of socio-economic development (including in the field of health and education) that accompanies it. Measures like freezing the number of seats in the Lok Sabha at the current level are essentially facilitators, dispelling states fears that population control will reduce their quota of MPs. There has to be an adequate political will to achieve the twin, variably inseparable, objectives of reducing family size and improving the quality of life. However, The Tribune Editorial "Gaps in Population Policy" dated February 17, 2000 suggested the gaps in new policy and stressed the need to make up these gaps. Increasing population packs a greater destructive power than what Pakistan can cause by hurling a few nuclear bomb blasts. That is because it is concentrated at the bottom of the social and economic pyramid covering three-fourth of the population. The failure to control the exploding numbers is the most damaging of all failures. What the country needed was a radical review of the old policies, alertness to deploy all available instruments and establish enduring contacts with the target segment in rural India. Sadly these are missing in the New National Population Policy unveiled. The document still pins its hopes on a few tired incentives and shapeless promises to rein in population growth. Such sops will be available only after the event — that is, after individuals or couples take themselves out of the reproduction cycle. Actually, the concentration should have been on goading people to enter the charmed circle.

To quote S.P. Singh again, According to the provisional results of the 2001 Census, India's population stood 1,027 million on March 1, 2001, comprising 531 million males and 496 million females. From 361 million at the time of Independence the population reached one billion in 2001, registering an increase of nearly three times. All this had happened when country is not in a position to guarantee adequate nutrition, health and education to the burgeoning population. At the same time, it is true that all this has happened because of mass poverty in the country. Indifferent government is also partly responsible for the current graphic and health scenario. Every year about 18 million people added to India's population during 1991-2001 as against 16 million during 1981-91 (Table 3.1). In other words, each year India's on Increases by the equivalents of the number of inhabitants of Australia, Mozambique or Saudi Arabia

Notes and References

1. UN: E.F.S. 75, XIII. 4, p. 76.
2. Gunnar Myrdal, "Asian Drama: An Inquiry Into the Poverty of Nation", Vol. III, London, 1968, p. 154.
3. Alexander Kessler, Family Planning and the role of WHO" in *World Health*, May-June, p. 30.
4. Maryellen Fullan, "People—A Journal of the International Planned Parenthood Federation", Vol. 5, Number 4, 1978, p. 27.
5. Ansley, J, Coale, "Population and Economic Development", in Phillip M. Hauser (ed.), *The Population Dilemma*, p. 69.
6. WHO, (1971), Technical Report Series, No. 483.
7. WHO, (1971), Technical Report Series, No. 473.
8. WHO, Technical Report Series, No. 442.
9. The *Daily Tribune*, January 28, 2000.
10. K.P. Bahadur, Population Crisis in India, National, New Delhi, 1977, p. 37.
11. Joung, Whaff, Ph.D., Graduate School of Public Admn., Seoul, National University, Seoul, Korea, Seventh General Assembly and Conference on "Implementation—The Problem of Achieving Results", EROPA, 24-31, October 1973, Tokyo, Japan, pp. 69-106.
12. U.N. F/F/S. 75, XIII, 5, p. 383.
13. Mrs. Hevli Sipila, Assistant Secretary General, "Social Development and Humanities Affairs", UN, June 17, 1975, *Weekly News Letter*, UN Information Centre, New Delhi, Vol. 25, No. 3.
14. UN, 1326, (XLIV).
15. UN, F/C/N/6/5755, Add 13, ECOSOC.
16. Council for Social Development, New Delhi, 1969.
17. UN, Public Administration Division of the Department of Economics and Social Affairs, "Organisation and Administration of Family Planning Programme", UN: F/E/75, XIII, 5, p. 494.
18. UNESCO, Communication Media, Family Planning and Development, No. I, Paris, 1975.
19. UNESCO, Communication in Support of Population, Family Planning and Development, E/F/S.75, XIII, 5, p. 482.

20. State Family Planning Bureau, Haryana: National Population Conference (6th to 8th December, 1974), Population Statement of Haryana State.
21. S.S Kamalai, and C. Parvathemma, "Family Planning and Social Values", *Family Planning News*, March 1970, Vol. XI, No. 3.
22. Fourth Five Year Plan, Mid-Term Appraisal, pp. 223-24.
23. Council for Social Development, Aspects of Population Policy in India, New Delhi, 1969, p. 56.
24. Lok Sabha Secretariate Estimates Committee, 102nd Report (5th Lok Sabha), New Delhi, 1975, pp. 92-94.
25. Antonio Ordonex—Plaja, Teamwork at Ministry-level in Teamwork for *World Health*, (ed.) *op. cit.*, p. 170.

Reproductive and Child Health Programme

I. GENESIS

The Universal Immunisation Programme (UIP) aimed at reduction in mortality and morbidity among infants and younger children due to Vaccine Preventable Diseases, was started in 1985-86. The Oral Dehydration Therapy (ORT) was also started in view of the fact that diarrhoea was a leading cause of deaths among children. Various other programmes under Maternal and Child Health (MCH) were also implemented during the Seventh Plan. The objectives of all these programmes were convergent and aimed at improving the health of the mothers and young children and to provide them facilities for prevention and treatment of major disease conditions. While these programmes did have a beneficial impact, but the separate identity for each programme was causing problems in its effective management and this was also reducing somewhat the outcomes. Therefore, in the Eighth Plan, these programmes were integrated under Child Survival and Safe Motherhood (CSSM) Programme which was implemented from 1992-93. The process of integration of related programmes initiated with the implementation of the CSSM Programme was taken a step further in 1994, when the International Conference on Population and Development in Cairo recommended that the participant countries should implement unified programmes for Reproductive and Child Health (RCH). The RCH approach has been defined as "People have the ability to reproduce and regulate their fertility, women are able to go through pregnancy and child birth safely, the outcome of pregnancies is successful in terms of maternal and infant survival and well-being and couples are able to have sexual relations free of fear of pregnancy and of contacting diseases."

This concept is in keeping with the evolution of an integrated approach to the programmes aimed at improving the health status of young

CHART 4.1

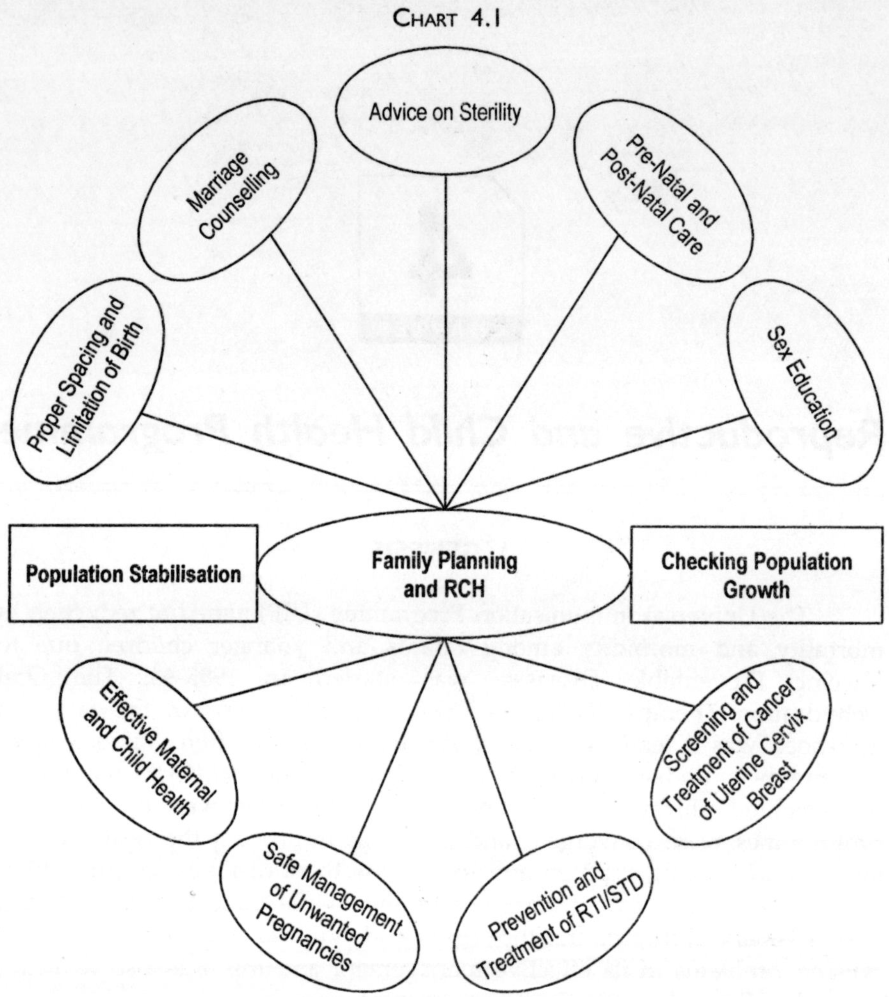

women and children, which has been going on in the country. It is obviously sensible that the integrated RCH Programme would help in reducing the cost of inputs to some extent because overlapping of expenditure would no longer be necessary and integrated implementation would optimise outcomes at the field level. During the Ninth Plan, the RCH Programme, accordingly, has integrated all the related programmes of the Eighth Plan. The concept of RCH is to provide to the beneficiaries need-based, client-centred, demand driven, high quality and integrated RCH services. The RCH Programme is a composite programme incorporating the inputs of the Government of India as well as funding support from external donor agencies including the World Bank and the European Commission.

The RCH programme incorporates the components covered under the Child Survival and Safe Motherhood Programme and includes two additional components, one relating to sexually transmitted diseases (STD) and the other relating to reproductive tract infection (RTI). The main highlights of the RCH Programme are:

(i) The Programme integrates all interventions of fertility regulation, maternal and child health with reproductive health of both men and women.

(ii) The services to be provided will be client-centred, demand-driven, high quality and based on the needs of the community arrived at, through decentralised participatory planning and a target free approach.

(iii) The programme envisages upgradation of the level of facilities for providing various interventions and quality of care. The First Referral Units (FRUs) being set-up at sub-district level will provide comprehensive emergency obstetric and new born care. Similarly, RCH facilities in PHCs will be substantially upgraded.

(iv) The Programme will improve access of the community to various services which are commonly required. It is proposed to provide facilities for MTP at the PHCs, counselling and IUD insertion at SCs in a phased manner.

(v) The Programme aims at improving the outreach of services, particularly for the vulnerable groups of population who have till now substantially been let out of the planning process:
- Special programmes will be taken up for urban slums, tribal population and adolescents.
- Non-Governmental Organisations will be involved in a much larger way to improve out-reach and make it people's programme.
- Skills of practitioners of ISM will be upgraded by training and research and development in ISM will be supported to improve the range of the RCH services.
- Panchayati Raj system will have a greater role in planning, implementation and assessment of client satisfaction.[1]

Ninth Five Year Plan (Draft) has mentioned the following features of RCH Programme:

- Effective maternal and child health care,
- Increased access to contraceptive care,
- Safe management of unwanted pregnancies,
- Nutritional services to vulnerable groups,
- Prevention and treatment of RTI/STD,
- Reproductive health services for adolescents,
- Prevention and treatment of gynecological problems, and
- Screening and treatment of cancers, especially that of uterine cervix and breast.

For over 30 years Family Welfare Programme was known for its rigid, target-based approach in contraceptives. The performance was measured by the reported numbers of the four contraceptive methods Sterilization, Intrauterine device, Oral pills and Condoms. This was widely criticized for being a coercive approach. The 1994 Cairo International Conference on Population and Development (ICPD) formulated a growing International consensus that improving reproductive health and family planning is essential to human welfare and development.

A growing body of evidence and the Cairo consensus suggest "Numerical method specific contraceptive target and monetary incentives" for providers to be replaced by a broader system of "programme performance goals" and measures focussed on a range of reproductive health services. We can say in brief that reproductive and Child Health Services which is equivalent to:

- Family Planning, to focus on fertility regulation,
- Child Survival and Safe Motherhood Programme, and
- Treatment of Reproductive Tract Infections and Sexually Transmitted Infections and prevention of AIDS,

Through

1. Client-Oriented/Mother-Friendly/user-specific, family welfare services, and
2. High quality services.

The specific programmes under Reproductive arid Child Health Services are:

1. Prevention and management of unwanted pregnancies,
2. Maternal care:
   (a) Ante-natal services,
   (b) Natal services,
   (c) Post-natal services,
3. Child Survival, and
4. Treatment of Reproductive Tract Infections (RTl) and Sexually Transmitted Infections (STI).[2] The following definition of reproductive health was approved in April 1994, by the WHO Global Policy Council, provides the basis for action in this field: "Reproductive health implies that people are able to have a responsible, satisfying and safe sex life and that they have the capability to reproduce and the freedom to decide if, when and how often to do so. Implicit in this last condition are the right of men and women to be informed of and to have access to safe, effective, affordable and acceptable methods of fertility regulation of their choice, and the right of access to appropriate

health care services that will enable women to go safely through pregnancy and childbirth and provide couples with the best chance of having a healthy infant."

Reproductive health must address, as its basic elements, sexual behaviour, family planning, maternal care and safe motherhood, abortion, reproductive tract infections (including sexually transmitted diseases and HIV/AIDS, and certain reproductive tract malignancies such as cervical cancer.[3]

II. THE PACKAGE OF REPRODUCTIVE AND CHILD HEALTH SERVICES (See Chart 4.1)

The different services provided under RCH programme are:

1. For the Mothers

- TT Immunization,
- Prevention and treatment of anemia, .
- Ante-natal care and early identification of maternal complications,
- Deliveries by trained personnel,
- Promotion of institutional deliveries,
- Management of Obstetric emergencies, and
- Birth spacing.

2. For the Children

- Essential newborn care,
- Exclusive breast feeding and weaning,
- Immunization,
- Appropriate management of diarrhoea,
- Appropriate management of ARI,
- Vitamin A prophylaxis, and
- Treatment of Anemia.

3. For Eligible Couples

- Prevention of pregnancy, and
- Safe abortion.

4. RTI/STD

- Prevention and treatment of reproductive tract and sexually transmitted diseases.[4]

Principles and Approach

The guiding principles and approach of reproductive health care are to a great extent different than those of the existing dominant approach of MCH and FP programme.[5] A glimpse of the shift in approach and principle can be studied from the Table 4.1. The guiding principles of reproductive health care are those of human rights, ethics, equity, quality of care, universal access, participation, partnership, integration, optimal use of resources and sustainability. Partnerships and sharing of responsibilities between government, governmental organisations and the private sector are important in stimulating new ideas and approaches and ensuring service coverage and quality of care. These principles are the same as the principles of primary health care.

We must keep in mind that reproductive health is a crucial part of general health and, i.e. central to human development. It affects everybody; it involves intimate and highly valued aspects of life. Not only is it a reflection of health in infancy, childhood and adolescence, it also sets the stage for health beyond the reproductive years, for both men and women, and has effects from one generation to another. Reproductive health includes sexual health care, for maintaining and enhancing the functions of the reproductive system, and the prevention and management of RTIs, HIV/AIDS and infertility. Reproductive health care is an integral part of primary health care. The guiding principles and the approaches of reproductive health care are similar to the delivery of primary health care. These are:

- education concerning prevailing health problems and the methods of preventing and controlling them;
- promotion of food supply and proper nutrition;
- an adequate supply of safe water and basic sanitation;
- maternal and child health care, including family planning;
- immunisation against the major infectious diseases;
- appropriate treatment of common diseases and injuries; and
- provision of essential drugs.

Let us now mention the health interventions required for different services at different levels.

ADVANTAGES OF THE SCHEME

RCH can avoid the problems prevalent in earlier family planning programme and can improve the coverage and quality of services provided the RCH programme is implemented as scheduled.

1. Target-free Approach can make the Programme Flexible

The achievements of family planning programmes were judged simply on the completion of targets fixed from above. It was found that the top down approach is not realistic and based on field situations. Thus, the

TABLE 4.1

Principles and Approach of Existing MCH/FP Programme and of RHC Programme

Existing MCH/FP Programmes	*Reproductive Health Programmes*
Target population is primarily women	Target population is both women and men
Vertical programmes	Integrated and inter-sectoral programmes
Top-down planning and Implementation	Bottom-up planning respoding to local reproductive health needs within socio-cultural and economic milieu and decentrallsed implementation
Focus on Individual cases	Public health approach with family and community focus
Pregnancy-based approach	Life cycle approach
Medical approach: health needs identified	Community-based approach: respect women's knowledge and by providers; reliance on medical solutions definition of their health needs; reliance on holistic solutions that take into account the social, biological and psychological factors determining health
Provider centred prescribe fertility control	Client centred: provide information and enable women to methods, choose the methods they wish to adopt
Method specific information provided	Apart from information on all methods of fertility regulation, provide knowledge on sexuality and reproduction
Emphasis on achieving output targets	Emphasis on coverage and quality of services
Services provided in a clinical atmosphere	Provide services in a humane and caring setting
Vague general health rights	Respect specific reproductive health rights

Source: WHO: SEARO, Managing Essential Reproductive Health Care, New Delhi, p. 5.

users' preference is not reflected in the targets. A major feature of the target-free approach in its emphasis on the promotion of modern spacing methods. The approaches intends also to achieve a greater participation of males in the family welfare programme. Moreover, in the absence of method-specific targets, the grass-root level workers including the ANM and the Multi-purpose Health Workers (both male and female) are expected to work closely with the community and arrive at an estimate of the various family welfare activities required in the area population covered by them. The male health workers, in particular, are made responsible for motivation

TABLE 4.2

Principles and Approach of Existing MCH/FP Programme and of RHC Programme

Existing MCH/FP Programmes	*Reproductive Health Programmes*
Target population is primarily women	Target population is both women and men
Vertical programmes	Integrated and inter-sector programmers
Top-down planning and implementation	Bottom-up planning responding to local reproductive health needs with socio-cultuall and economic milieu and decentralized implementation
Focus on individual cases	Public health approach with family and community focus
Pregnancy-based approach	Life cycle approach
Medical approach: health needs identified by providers; reliance on medical solutions	Community-based approach: respect women's knowledge and definition of their health needs; reliance on holistic solutions that take into account the social, biological and psychological factors determining health
Provider centred: prescribe fertility control methods	Client centered: provide information and enable women to choose the methods they wish to adopt
Methods specific information provided	Apart from information on all methods of fertility regulation, provide knowledge on sexuality and reproduction
Emphasis on achieving output targets	Emphasis on coverage and quality of services
Services provided in a clinical atmosphere	Provide services in a humane and caring setting
Vague general health rights	Respect specific reproductive health rights

Source: WHO: SEARO, Managing Essential Reproductive Health Care, New Delhi, p. 5.

for vasectomy and condoms. These activities are expected to result in an improvement in the knowledge of modern temporary methods as well as male methods of contraception; and an improvement in the proportion of spacing as well as male methods in the contraceptive method-mix.

2. Target-free Approach can make the Reporting Honest and Reliable

Field Staff used to do false reporting in order to prove the progress to avoid disciplinary action. This approach has made the reporting realistic and thus can help in effective policy-making and planning.

Earlier, we had malpractices of performing sterilisation/vasecotomy upon ineligible persons. All such cases and practices would be avoided.

TABLE 4.3

Essential Reproductive and Child Health Services at Different Levels of the Health Services System

Health Intervention	*Community Level*	*Sub-centre Level*	*Primary Health Centre Level*	*First referral Unit/District Hospital Level*
1. Prevention and management of unwanted pregnancy	1. Sexuality and gender information education and counselling 2. Community mobilization and Education for adolescence, newly married youth, men and women* 3. Community-based contraceptive** (through panchayats, village health, guides, mahila Swasthya Sanghas, etc. with follow up) 4. Motivating referral for sterilization 5. Social marketing of condoms and oral pills through community sources and G.P. (oral pills to be distributed through health	1. No I as in community level. 2. Providing* oral contraceptives (OCS) and condoms. 3. Providing IUD after screening for contrain-dications. 4. Conselling and early referral for medical termination of pregnancy. 5. Counselling/ management/ referral for side effects, methods-related problems, change of method where indicated. 6. Add other methods to expand choice. 7. Providing treatment for minor ailments and referral for problems. * Social marketing of pills and	Nos. 1-6 and 7. Performing tubal ligation by mililap on fixed dates* 8. Performing vasecotomy 9. Providing first trimester medical termination of pregnancy upto 8 weeks (includes MR) 10. Facilities for Copper "T" insertion to post-natal cases. 11. Treatment facilities for all types of referrals. * PHCs should have facilities for tubal ligation and minilap including OTs and equipments.	Nos. 1 -11 and 12. Providing services for medical termination of pregnancy in the first and second trimester (Upto 20 weeks) where indicated.

	personnel including GPS to women who are starting pills for the first time) 6. Free supplies to health services * to be pioloted ** Panchayats to distribute only condoms	condoms through HW (M & F) may be explored by permitting her to retain the money.		
2. Maternity Care Parental Services		Nos. 1-4 and 5. Three antenatal contacts with women either at the sub-centre or at the outreach village sites during immunization/ M C H sessions. 6. Early detection of high risk factors and maternal complications and prompt referral. 7. Referral of high risk women for institutional delivery. 8. Teatment of malaria (facilities including drugs to be made	Nos. 1-10 and 11. Treatmnent of T.B. 12. Testing of syphilis for high risks group and treatment where necessary including for RTIs	Nos. 1-12 and 13. Diagnosis and treatment of RTI/s STIs 14. Weekly clinics for High risk preganancies.

		available at sub-centre) 9. Treatment for TB and follow-up 10. Preventive measure against all communicable diseases		
Delivery Services	1.Early recognisation of pregnancy and its danger signals. 2. Conducting clean deliveries with delivery kits by trained personnel. 3. Detection of complications referral for hospital delivery 4. Providing transport for referral 5. Referral of new born having difficulty in respiration 6. Management of Neonatal hypotheria	Nos. 1-4 and 5. Superivisng home delivery 6. Prophylaxis and treatment. 7.Routine prophylaxis for gonococci eye infection	Nos. 1-7 and 8. Modified partograph 9. Delivery services 10.Repair of epistiotomy and perennial tears	No. 1- 9 and 10.Treatment of serve sepsis 11.Delivery of referred cases 12.Treatment of high risk cases. 13.Services for obstetrical emergencies anesthesia, ceaserean section, blood transfusion though close relative linkages with blood banks and mobile services
Post-partum Services	1.Breas-feeding support 2. Family	Nos. 1-6 and 1. Referral for complications	Nos. 1-8 and 9. Referral to FRUs for complications	Nos. 1-10 and 11.Management of referred case.

	Planning counselling 3. Nutrition counselling 4. Resuscitation for asphysia of the newborn. 5. Management of neonatal 6. Early recognition of post-patrum sepsis and referral	2. Giving inj. Ergometrine after delivery of placenta	after starting an I.V. line and giving initial dose of antibiotics and ixytocin and indicated.	PHC and FRUs would require additional equipment and training for management of asphyxiated new borns and hypothermia. These include a resuscitation bag and mask and radiant warmers.
Child Survival	1. Health education for breast feeding nutrition immunizations, utilization of services, etc. 2. Detection and referral of high risk cases such as low birth weight, premature babies, babies with asphysix, infections, severe dehydration acute respiratory infections (ARI), etc. 3. Help during Immunization by ANM 4. Help during Vitamin "A"	Nos. 1-6 and 7. Treatment of dehydration and pneumonia and referral of severe cases 8. First aid for injuries 9. Closing watching on the development of child and creating awareness of cheap and nutrition food	Nos. 1-9 and 10. Management of referred cases	Nos. 1-10 and 11. Handling of all paediatric cases including encephalopathy. 12. Identification of certain FRU's to provide specialist services and training.

	supplementation by ANM 5. Detection of pneumonia and seeking, early medical care by community and treatment by ANM 6. Treatment of diarrhea cases and ARI cases			
Management of RTI/STD	1. IEC counselling for awareness and prevention 2. Condom distribution 3. Creating awareness about usages of sanitary pads by women of reproductive period. 4. Creating awareness of about RTI and personal hygiene.	Nos. 1-4 and 5. Identification and referral for vaginal discharge, lower abdominal pain, genital ulcers in women, and urethra discharge, genital ulcers, swelling in scortum or groin in men 6. Diagnosis of RTI and STD by Syndrome Approach 7. Referral of cases not responding to useval treatment 8. Partner notification/ referral.	Nos. 1-8 and 9. Treatment of RTI/STD 10. Syphilis testing in antenatal women.	No. 1-9 and 10. Laboratory diagnosis and treatment of RTIs/STIs. 11. Syndromic approach to detect and treat STD in ante-natal post-natal and at risk groups

Source: Department of Family Welfare, GOI, Reproductive and Child Health, Vol. I, March, 1997, pp. 42-45.

3. New Programme can Infect Forward and Backward Linkages

The RCH programme can promote linkages to make it effective forwards positive health. Since it is not merely a family planning programme, it is a total package covering the total health of women and children, a very positive view.

4. Over-head Cost can be Reduced

Costs incurred in managing programmes in an integrated way can reduce a lot of cost as overhead cost can be reduced.

5. Effective Maternal and Child Health

At the village level, the Auxiliary Nurse Midwife is responsible for rendering maternal and child health services alongwith family welfare services. She is supposed to register pregnant women as assess their health throughout pregnancy, by at least three visits. Regular height and weight checkup, blood pressure test, urine test as well as providing tetanus toxoid injections and iron and folic acid tablets constitute important aspects of any antenatal checkup. Another responsibility of the ANM is to refer pregnant women who have symptoms of abnormal pregnancy or labour, or who have gynaecological problems that are beyond her level of competence, to the Primary Health Centre.

At the instance of the Ministry of Health and Family Welfare, Government of India, New Delhi and as a part of monitoring and evaluation of the performance of the family welfare programme under the new target-free approach, the Population Research Centre, J.S.S. Institute of Economic Research, Dharwad, undertook a rapid survey in the rural area of Belgaum District, Karnataka state during the last two weeks of December 1997 and first two weeks of January 1998. Using a simple and short questionnaire, the survey interviewed a total of 1,000 currently married women aged 15-44, from 50 villages, at the rate of 20 women per village. Apart from several background characteristics of women, the survey collected information on utilization of ante-natal care, place of delivery, and assistance during delivery, child immunizations, knowledge and practice of family planning, visits by the ANM and services received from her; health problems of the women including side-effects of family planning methods, and respondents ratings on various aspects of quality of care provided by the nearest PHC, sub-centre or the ANM.

(a) While the provision of tetanus toxoid injections and iron/folic tablets was better, other components of ante-natal care such as monitoring the weight and blood pressure, and urine tests were not carried out for the majority of women during their pregnancy by multi-member females.

(b) Overall, 51 percent of the deliveries which occurred during the five years preceding the survey took place at home, 30 percent in private hospitals or nursing homes, and little less than one-fifth in government health facilities. Of the births that took place at home, the majority (62 percent) were attended by untrained persons including relatives, friends and neighbours.

(c) Little less than one-quarter of women in the rural areas of Belgaum District have an unmet need for family planning, that is, they are not using contraception even though they do not want any more children or want to wait at least two years before having their next child. The unmet need for spacing (11 percent) is almost the same as that for limiting births (12 percent). If all the women with an unrest need were to use family planning, the contraceptive prevalence rate would increase from 62 percent to 85 percent.

(d) Among the three registers (Eligible Couple register, ANC register, and immunization register) examined, the EB register was found to be relatively more complete and accurate than the other two registers.[6]

In another study a rapid research survey was conducted in rural areas of Dharwad district in Kamataka during February-April, 1997 to check the coverage, quality of services and client satisfaction under the new strategy of 'target-free' approach. The analysis of service statistics for the district showed that removal of targets appears to have made no significant impact on the total number of annual acceptors. However, it had a favourable impact on method mix as sterilizations have come down slightly while acceptors of IUD and Pill have gone up from that of the previous year.

The unmet for contraception was estimated to be 10 percent, 6 percent for limiting and 4 percent for spacing. It was found that immunization levels are yet to become universal. About 70 percent of pregnant women had two doses of Tetanus toxoid vaccination and only half of the children were fully immunized. Measurement of weight and blood pressure, as well as urine tests were reported rarely. Only 40 percent of deliveries were attended by trained persons. On record maintenance, it was observed that EC register was better maintained than ANC and immunization registers. Some of the important policy recommendations emerging from the study are:

1. Improve ANM services, especially make them visit women with unmet need for contraception, and past acceptors of sterilization.
2. As a large number of sterilization acceptors complain about method side effects, a special health campaign for sterilized men and women should be launched by multi-purpose workers female. In order to safeguard future levels of acceptance, past acceptors should be made to feel that they are looked after well by programme functionaries.

3. It should be ensured that sub-centres have adequate supply of drugs, and attempts should be made to reduce waiting time and provide free services at primary health centres. The guilty should be punished.
4. A television set could be placed in PHC waiting room and also cover to disseminate information and messages on health and family welfare and facilities in sub-centres.
5. Concerted attempts should be made to raise immunization levels by workers as they appear to have reached a point of stagnation before acquiring universality.[7]

FACTS AND SUGGESTIONS

1. More Thrust In Weak States

The performance in the implementation of family Welfare programmes in the demographically weak States should be reviewed on a periodical basis with a view to taking remedial measures in consultation and coordination with the concerned State Governments.

2. Reduction of Maternal Mortality and Morbidity

One of the major goals of the Department of Family Welfare is the reduction of maternal mortality and morbidity. The maternal mortality rate of India is 408 per 1,00,000 live births which was projected to be brought down to 200 per 1,00,000 in 2000. The trend in this regard has not changed significantly in the last five years. This is mainly due to the large number of deliveries being conducted at home and by untrained persons.

3. Lack of Adequate Referral Facilities

Lack of adequate referral facilities to provide emergency obstetric care for complicated cases also contributes to high maternal mortality and morbidity. Major causes of maternal death are ante- and post-partum haemorrhage, anaemia, toxaemia, abortions and sepsis. A large number of these causes are preventable through improved maternal care. Promoting safer institutional deliveries and ensuring appropriate treatment of complications can substantially reduce the fatality rate.

4. Major Problems Relating to Menstrual Cycle Need Attention

There are some problems of women like anaemia, mal-nutrition and problems relating to menstrual cycle, etc. which are prevalent in the reproductive age group including the adolescent girls. The women silently suffer these problems due to ignorance, the lack of medical facilities and attention by the concerned authorities. It is high time that the Department of Family Welfare takes note of these problems and takes suitable and remedial steps to identify these women and provide the necessary medical facilities in consultation and coordination with the State Governments and local NGOs.

5. Need of Special Programmes with a Focus on Sections of less Privileged Society

It is pertinent to note that a vicious relationship exists between high birth rates and high infant mortality, contribution to the desire for more children. The highest priority must, therefore, be given to launching special programmes for the improvement of maternal and child health, with a special focus on the less privileged sections of society.

6. Need of Accountable Health Services

It is important to strengthen, energise and make accountable health infrastructure at the village, sub-centre and primary health centre levels, to improve facilities for referral transportation and to encourage and strengthen local initiatives for ambulance services at village and block levels.

The Committee of Parliament on Women Empowerment were informed that the Department has initiated a number of measures to sustain and strengthen interventions started under the Child Survival and Safe Motherhood (CSSM) Programme. The Committee are of the opinion that such programmes need to be decentralised to the maximum possible extent, their delivery, being at the primary level, nearest to the doorsteps of the beneficiaries. While efforts should continue at providing refresher training and orientation to the traditional birth attendants, schemes and programmes should be launched to ensure that progressively, all deliveries are conducted by competently trained persons, so that complicated cases receive timely and expert attention.

7. Need of Rendering Outreach Services

The outreach of the Family Planning Services should be increased by involvement of NGOs, Health Volunteers and through Community-based distribution of contraceptives there should be proper emphasis on programmes for training and skill development of both the Medical Officers and Health workers of both Government and voluntary agencies involved in the delivery of family welfare services, with respect to special procedures such as IUD insertions, sterilisation and also administering of oral contraceptives.

8. Upgrading Primary Health Centres

The Committee during its Study tours to some States have observed the condition of the Primary Health Centres and their poor maintenance. Some of these are set-up in dilapidated buildings with no infrastructure, like electricity, beds, furniture and telephone facilities. They lack the necessary hygiene. At some centres there is no separate ward for female patients and only one doctor is posted on rotation basis to attend to all the patients. Also there is acute shortage of essential drugs and other material. The result is that these Centres are unable to meet the basic health service needs of the community. It is, therefore, necessary that the SC, PHC and

Community Health Centres should be fully operationalised by providing necessary facilities including buildings and residential quarters, filling-up of all vacant posts and ensuring supply of essential drugs, dressings and other consumables.

9. Need of Promotional Services

There is a need for Government to further enhance the annual budgets for Family Welfare Programmes. Prevention and promotion services such as ante-natal, post-natal care for women, immunisation of children, availability of contraceptives, etc., should be given priority in allocation of funds.

10. Need of Training

There is an urgent need for capacity building of the existing staff. The Planning Commission and the Ministry of Finance should also consider the need for a special grant in this connection so as to enable to the Department of Family Welfare to recruit and train health personnel.

11. Increasing of Ante-natal Services

In order to improve the efficiency and effectiveness of the family planning programme, and to achieve better health for both the mother and the child, 100% ante-natal registration should be made mandatory. This should form the basis of identifying high risk pregnancies and the eligible couples for permanent sterilisation.

12. Need of Effective Health Services

Malnutrition, improper/inadequate health care facilities provided/ available to women during pregnancy leads to children being born with physical and mental deficiencies. This aspect needs special attention. Women ought to be made aware of the importance of proper nutrition for pregnant women especially in rural/semi-urban areas.

Soon after the ICPD, UNFPA commissioned a study conducted by 'MODE' Research, 1995, on the changes in people's perceptions on population and development. Conducted in Madhya Pradesh, Rajasthan, Tamil Nadu and West Bengal, the study found heartening changes in perception, it also indicated how far the country still has to travel.

- The small family norm has been accepted, signifying the success of the 50 years of effort at creating an acceptance for fewer children.
- Visible improvement in women's conditions like less purdah, more respect, greater mobility.
- Better communication between husband and wife admitted as a sign of better times.
- Clear bias for sons continues.
- Resistance to delaying first child after marriage very strong.

- Importance of girls' education recognised
- Education as route to empowerment and independence admitted.
- Yet, eventually, marriage and child-bearing seen as only role of women. Productive role is unnoticed.
- There is awareness of FP methods. Competent knowledge of spacing methods lacking.

The study showed that there is still a large unfinished agenda in the areas of reproductive and child health, particularly in the states of Bihar, Madhya Pradesh, Rajasthan and Uttar Pradesh. Over 40% of Indians live in these four states and all exhibit unfavourable demographic trends compared with the rest of India. The goal of population stabilization is achieved only when child survival issues, maternal health issues and contraception issues are addressed simultaneously and effectively. Actual success in containing the growth of population would however, depend upon: Publicly stated support by the community leaders; Resources available for the Family Welfare Programme; Efficiency and accountability in the State Health System for ensuring effective delivery of services to citizens; as also women's education and status in the family. All these inputs have so far not been uniformly available to the required extent for the Family Welfare Programme, thereby not allowing the optimal and potential/best possible benefits to be reaped from the same.

The agenda for population stabilization is multi-sectoral which necessitates decentralization and convergence across sectors. In cooperation with State Governments, the Department of Family Welfare, is bringing about a convergence between the NGOs, the Self-Help Groups (run by the Departmental of Rural Development), the Zila Saksharta Samitis (run by the Department of Education), the social marketing organisations (overseen by Department of Family Welfare) and the panchayati raj institutions, to improve integrated service delivery at community and household levels.

The RCH programme should take care of following factors before formulation, implementation and evaluation strategy:

(a) according to the topography of the District,
(b) according to the priority needs of the people,
(c) linked properly with the objectives and goals of District planning,
(d) fitted into the overall economic and social development of the country,
(e) properly linked with projects in the allied area, and
(f) able to achieve useful and permanent results.

Let us now analysis the factors which impede the effective functioning of RCH programme. It is based on authors' study in Punjab and Karnataka. We have also given suggestions to improve RCH programme.

CHART 4.2

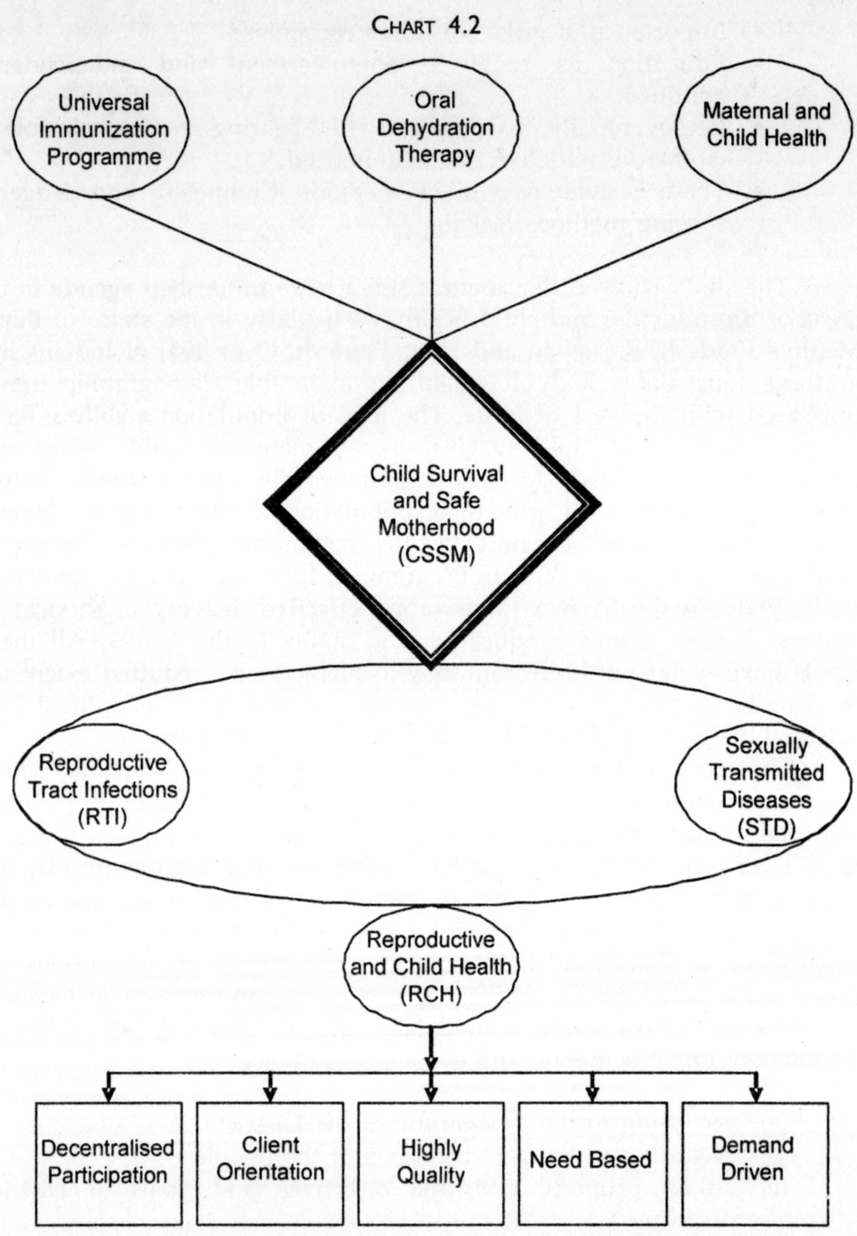

Let us mention the schedule of operation of RCH programme in Punjab and Karnataka (Tables 4.4 and 4.5). We may also mention the facilities required in A, B and C categories of Districts. The project has not so far been implemented fully. However, we discuss our observations and findings on the basis of the experiments done so far. Though it is desirable that the entire package of services indicated above is made available to all those who need it, it will not be possible to immediately implement such a comprehensive package on a nation-wide basis. Hence, it is envisaged that improvement in quality and coverage of services over and above the existing level will be attempted in all states in an incremental manner so that maternal and child health indices improve.

After consultation with experts a package of essential reproductive health services for nation-wide implementation at various levels of health care has been identified. Essential components recommended for nation-wide implementation include:

TABLE 4.4

Punjab—Year-wise Category of Districts

Category	*Year I*	*Year II*	*Year III*
A			
B	Hoshiarpur	Jalandhar	Faridkot
	Patiala	Ludhiana	Rupnagar
	Moga	Kapurthala	Bathinda
		Gurdaspur	Muktsar
		Amritsar	Nawanshahar
		Sangrur	
C	Firozepur	Mansa	
	Fatehgarh Sahib		

Most of the services are already included in the Family Welfare Programme. However, there are wide variations in the quality and coverage of services not only between states but also between various districts in the same state. The focus is therefore on the improvement in the quality and coverage of the services. A project preparation workshop held in September 1995 discussed the issues and problems in implementation of essential RCH package and recommended reproductive and child health services that should be made available at community, sub-centre, PHC and FRU/ District Hospital.

Implementation schedule of Punjab and Karnataka is given in Tables 4.4 and 4.5. The Ministry of Health and Family Welfare has got the research conducted on the impact of RCH programme in the districts. Analysis of the reports indicate that:

(a) Infrastructure facilities non-existent.
(b) Personnel responsible for RCH lack motivation.
(c) Lack of effective supervision.
(d) Slackness in work.
(e) Non-availability of funds.
(f) Lack of team work.
(g) Not following the work as schedules.

TABLE 4.5

Karnataka Year-wise Category of Districts

Category	Year I	Year II	Year III
A	Dakshin Kannada Kadagu (Coorg)		
	Mandya		
B	Uttar Kannada	Hassan	Shimoga
	Chikmaglur	Bangalore (R)	Chitradurga
	Dharwad	Tumkur	
	Mysore		
	Belgaum		
C	Bijapur	Bellary	
	Bidar	Raichur	
	Gulbarga		
	Bangalore		

- Prevention and management of unwanted pregnancy.
- Services to promote safe motherhood.
- Services to promote child survival.
- Prevention and treatment of RTI/STD.

The study in Punjab in some districts revealed not impact of the new RCH programme. The personnel responsible lack motivation and interest. Because of financial crisis, normal functioning of the health department is at a stand still. Besides, there is no supervision, resulting into a absentism and irregularity.

I. Lack of Adequate Facilities in the Institutions Responsible for the Provision of RCH Services

After the project is formulated, the project manager must ensure the availability of necessary inputs. It has been generally observed that the projects are delayed because of the absence of timely availability of all the inputs simultaneously. In one of the projects, the health personnel had no work to do because of the non-availability of vaccine. Obtaining resources is a process that takes place periodically throughout the life of the project. It was revealed that failure to obtain resources simultaneously in time is the most common cause of delay in implementation. The project manager must begin the process of procuring resources immediately after the formulation stage. Sometimes, the process may be started quite early if the resources are scarce and not easily available. The absence of one resource would inflate the cost of the project as the other resources would remain idle. The project manager must take the following steps:

(a) Working with the relative administrative units in preparing a time-table of administrative steps to be taken to obtain the planned resources.

(b) Monitoring this time-table to ensure that the administrative steps are being completed in time.
(c) Taking corrective action as and when necessary.

Inspire of all these precautions, there is a possibility of not reaching the resources in time. What can be done under such critical situation? Most of the experts indicated that the whole project staff remains idle for months together. This is very serious in big projects. It is suggested that project officers may be delegated powers to purchase the inputs locally or employ persons, if not available from the agency as planned. This would ensure that the project is one schedule.

2. Lack of Clarity among the Person Responsible for Implementation of RCH Programme

There is a dichotomy between the personnel responsible for the formulation and the personnel responsible for the implementation of the RCH project. The latter are not clear about the implications of the project. Because of lack of identity, they develop low morale resulting into the poor management. It was mentioned by a number of persons working on some projects that, "they are thrown into the fields to operate the RCH project without proper briefing about the project and its rationale in the total system. Besides, the supervisors, at the head-quarters, never guide them about their role in the projects."

3. Poor Linkages among the Allied Projects

In a particular geographical or functional area, a number of projects are being implemented to improve the standard of living of the people. Most of the projects are complementary and supplementary. Because of the poor co-ordination among the various departments, at the state level, the projects are implemented in the area without developing linkages with each other. For example, a project for the agriculture development to grow more food can be beautifully linked with the health projects on nutrition. Population control has many dimensions and needs the co-operation of many agencies. Thus, there is a need of area planning and developing an integrated area approach where different projects may develop linkages to have optimum benefit.

4. Absence of the Full Involvement of the Beneficiaries in the Formulation and Implementation of Projects

The success or failure of the RCH project ultimately depends upon the acceptance of these projects by the people. If the people are not taken into confidence during the formulation and implementation of RCH projects, these would be less successful. People's participation would provide extra nuclear energy to the success of the RCH projects. Most of the beneficiaries contacted by the writer were of the view that they are not treated as equal partners in the process of formulation and implementation of projects. The failure of the scheme is because of the absence of identity of the people with the programmes. It is essential for the experts to motivate and encourage the people to participate in the formulation and implementation of projects. Although people's participation in affairs governing their lives dates back to the beginning of human society, the concept has taken a new dimension as societies have grown in size and complexity. This is partly because the management has become more and more a specialized enterprise, an area for technocrats and trained general administrators and political leaders.

Although they officially advocate and preach people's involvement, in practice, they bring them into picture only after the major decisions have been made. Hence, they often leave the ordinary citizens to follow their pre-determined paths. Peter Druker agrees with this contention when he says that "the overwhelming majority of these people have little or no opportunity to influence policy, and their perspectives on the situation are systematically ignored by almost all theorists. For them the problem of development is one of the everyday life."

5. Local Communities are Treated as Passive Participants in Improvement and Bettering of their Lives

Most of the project personnel working in the villages return to the cities after their duty hours. The villagers cannot make their views known to them in cities. The result is lack of communication among them. When the project fails, it is intentionally ascribed to the obstinacy, fatalism, illiteracy or apparent irrationality of the poor people. The potential for community involvement has been seriously underestimated. We must encourage people's participation through all methods to promote development.

6. Absence of any Satisfactory Monitoring System to Measure the Regulated Performance during Implementation

Project control is the managerial function that helps the managers to keep the project functioning as scheduled. It is possible only if the realistic advance targets of output are fixed before implementation. This is not being done as is evident from the perusal of most of the projects studied. Monitoring if properly designed, projects can help the managers in keeping the process of implementation as scheduled. The project performance is compared at different intervals of time with the control indicators. Whenever deviations are located, causes of deviations are examined, solutions are found to correct the deviations. The following are the general causes of deviation:

(1) Excessive optimism on the part of the project planners, resulting in unrealistic estimates in respect to:
- the time, funds, manpower or other resources required to do an activity, and.
- the passability of achieving the expected results.

(2) Unfrozen resistance from or changes in the environment of the project (natural disaster, political changes, etc.).
(3) Decisions at higher, managerial levels to change the planned resources inputs of the project (change of a staff member).
(4) Inefficient administrative procedures.

If there is any unavoidable deviation beyond the control of the project authorities, we can think of alternative proposals immediately without wasting the future resources. If such timely action is taken, the developing countries can be sure of the success of the projects. More safely designing the control system means specifying who reports what to whom and when.

7. Unscientific Manpower Planning and Insufficient Utilisation of Project Personnel

The success of the project depends upon the quality and quantity of personnel associated with it. It was observed that in many projects, the projects personnel have their utilisation time as low as 20 per cent. This is highly serious as the resources are being consumed by the establishment rather than invested in the RCH programme. Because of the absence of manpower planning, personnel of the project utilize very little time. People in the area remarked about the workers appointed to motivate people to adopt family planning norm: "They are not available at all. They rarely devote any time for this work. They remain away from their work." It is essential to see through proper manpower planning that only needed persons are appointed and they are utilised to increase in the overall cost-productivity, efficiency and effectiveness. The projects should be so administered as to lead to overall improvement in its performance.

8. Lack of Clarification of Authority, Responsibility and Relationships

In the developing world, the persons responsible for implementation of the project do not work as a team as there is no clarification of authority, responsibility and relationships amongst them, i.e. the roles of the various participants are not often mutually understood. This result into friction among these persons. Most of the time of these persons are spent in their mutual disputes. It becomes very difficult for them to devote their whole attention to the project.

9. Private Sector Engaged in Merely Curative Services

Ninth Plan suggested the Private Sector participation in RCH. It is estimated that the private sector accounts for more than three quarters of all health care expenditure in India. Private sector provides MCH and family planning services also but to a lesser extent. It is increasingly recognised that the private sector represents an untapped potential for increasing the coverage and improving the quality of reproductive and child health services in the country. The challenge is to find ways and means to optimally utilise their potential. The major limitations in the private sector include the following:

(a) the focus has till now been mainly on curative services,
(b) the quality of services is often variable, and
(c) as the users have to pay for the services, the poorer sections of population cannot afford these services.

Some of the initiatives could be through collaboration between public and private sector in providing health care to the poorer segments of population who cannot afford to pay for health services. While organising the involvement of private medical practitioners in RCH care, it is essential to provide orientation training to all and ensure utilization of their services is a cost-effective and sustainable basis.

Private/voluntary organisations providing health care to women are relatively small in number but they could play an effective role in the delivery of reproductive and child health care services at affordable cost, especially in certain specific locations such as urban slums. Giving the private sector and voluntary organisations appropriate incentives to broaden the range of activities and improve the quality of reproductive and child health-related services they offer are other avenues that require exploration. Continued collaboration, training and technical assistance by governmental agencies to private medical practitioners and private/voluntary organisations may help in strengthening reproductive and child health services in remote or under-served areas.

10. Previous Implementation Experience of the Completed Project not Referred to

It was a great surprise to learn that there are no records of past experiences in relation to project implementation. One can always learn from the mistakes of others. Some of the project personnel remarks that "they do not know anything about the difficulties encountered by the project personnel and the causes of the failure of the project undertaken earlier. It is beneficial to examine how major projects have been managed in the past. It would also be better to identify those approaches which have been most successful. We can keep a record of good and bad points of the past project and this cumulative experience may be passed on to the present project managers. In this way, many of the difficulties likely to be encountered would vanish.

Frank A. Wilson in his article, "Planning for Project Management" in the *Journal of Administration Overseas* (July 1979) has rightly mentioned that, "Disappointing and inefficient project performance is a fact of life. Ex-post evaluation of existing projects can be the means by which we can systematically seek to analyse the potential for improving project management. Evaluation studies give the opportunity for developing greater understanding of the way projects are managed and implemented."

11. Faulty and Cumbersome Administrative Procedures

Whenever a project is formulated, we do not pay much attention to the problems of communication, co-ordination, headquarters field relationship, supervision, etc. The purpose of these procedures is to help in the smooth functioning of the project. Without proper procedures developed most of the project personnel remain engrossed in preparing unnecessary reports. These procedure should be clarified in the initial stages of project management, so that no confusion arises later on. If there are already set procedures in a particular organisation, these may be adopted otherwise new procedures may be adopted and made known to the project personnel. It must be clear that administrative procedures are an aid to help the efficient functioning of the project. The meticulous applications of these procedures may result into red-tapism and inefficiency .

CONCLUSION

The new RCH programme has been designed scientifically keeping in view the minor details meticulously. The programme is certainly better than the earlier Family Planning maternal and child health programmes aimed at specific activity. The RCH programme is operative in the whole of the country.

However, with the overall policy made by the Ministry of Health and Family Welfare, each district should design its own programme keeping in view the needs, resources, topography, quality of the peoples, facilities and infrastructure available as well as plan implementation and evaluation to inject flexibility as situations difference from district to district.

Radhakrishna Rao in his Article, "Towards controlling the Numbers" in *The Daily Tribune* (31st January, 2000) rightly suggests that a target free approach has now become a part of the population control drive. To what extent this approach will contribute to the success of population control, no one is sure as yet. Sociologists, however, are clear in their perception that when literacy, health, hygiene and economic, improvements at high priority, family planning stands a better chance of success.

The document prepared for the International Conference on Population and Development has recognised in its programme of action that "the main message for improving individual well-being comprises two elements: to provide contraceptive methods within the broader reproductive health services and to advance women's equal participation in education, health and economic opportunities."

The RCH II is the flagship programme of the Government of India on Reproductive, child and maternal health under National Health Rural Mission. This programme has been re-oriented and revitalized to give it to a pro-outcome and pro-poor focus. A paradigm RCH is envisaged in the manner in which the RCH Program has been conceptualized and implemented based upon key learning's from the first phase of the programme to make it consistent with the requirements of the National Rural Health Mission.

The key characteristics of the RCH II programme include:

- Adoption of Sector wise approach
- Rationalization of existing budget heads and creation of a flexible funding pool.
- Donor convergence.
- State ownership and Decentralized planning and progam implementation.
- Institutional Strengthening at District, State and Central levels for effective programme implementation.
- Results framework and monitoring.
- Public Private Partnership.
- Program Funding—The programme would receive funding from three sources: the government of India: pooled funding from DFID/World Bank/UNFPA and funding from other development partners (including EC, USAID, UNIEF and UNFPA)

Current Status

The Ministry appraised and approved the State Program Implementation Plan (PIPs) for the RCH II program during the year 2005-06 and 2006-07. The funds approved, during the year 2005-06 statewise are given in Table 4.6.

The Ministry in partnership with Development Partners and states conducted a Joint Review Mission and reviewed the progress of the RCH-II program. The progress of the program has been found satisfactory.

TABLE 4.6

State-wise Funds Approved for the RCH-II Program during 2005-06 and 2006-07

Sl. No.	*Name of States/UTs*	*Approved amount for the program during 2005-06*	*Approved amount for the progam during 2006-07*
1	*2*	*3*	*4*
1.	Andhra Pradesh	90.50	135.48
2.	Goa	1.50	1.92
3.	Gujarat	60.50	81.41
4.	Haryana	25.00	33.44
5.	Himachal Pradesh	7.50	10.62
6.	Jammu and Kashmir	12.00	15.34
7.	Karnataka	63.00	88.37
8.	Kerala	38.00	49.61
9.	Maharashtra	115.50	115.40

10.	Punjab	29.00	36.12
11.	Tamilnadu	74.00	106.56
12.	West Bengal	95.50	117.33
13.	A & N Islands	0.50	0.82
14.	Chandigarh	1.00	1.23
15.	D & N Haveli	0.50	0.70
16.	Daman and Diu	0.50	0.72
17.	Delhi	16.50	19.34
18.	Lakshdweep	0.50	0.62
19.	Pondicherry	1.00	1.93
	Sub-Total	632.50	855.94
	EAG States	—	—
20.	Bihar	128.50	140.99
21.	Jharkhand	42.00	49.09
22.	Madhya Pradesh	93.50	121.86
23.	Chhattisgarh	32.50	42.53
24.	Orissa	57.00	71.40
25.	Rajasthan	87.50	107.99
26.	Uttar Pradesh	257.50	299.73
27.	Uttaranchal	13.00	16.19
	Sub-Total	711.50	849.98
	NE States	—	—
28.	Arunachal Pradesh	7.35	5.25
29.	Assam	116.05	110.70
30.	Manipur	11.93	10.46
31.	Meghalaya	9.00	9.98
32.	Mizoram	13.57	4.66
33.	Nagaland	10.36	8.86
34.	Sikkim	1.82	2.46
35.	Tripura	9.67	13.56
	Sub-Total	178.75	165.75
	Grand-Total	1523.75	1871.67

Source: Ministry of Health and Family Welfare, Govt. of India, Annual Report, 2006-07, p. 65.

Notes and References

1. Annual Report, Ministry of Health and Family Welfare, 1998-99, pp. 7-9.
2. State Family Welfare Bureau, DH & FWS, Reproductive and Child Health, Bangalore, July 1988, p. 1.
3. WHO, May-June 1994, p. 30
4. State Family Welfare Bureau, Bangalore, *op. cit.*, pp. 19-20.
5. WHO, SEARO: Managing Essential Reproductive Health Care. New Delhi, p. 5.
6. B.M Ramesh, S.B. Ganiger and D.C. Satihal, "Family Welfare Programme under Target Free Approach: A Rapid Survey in Belgaum District, Karnataka, 1998. Population Research Centre, J.S.S. Institute of Economic Research, Dharwad.
7. P.N. Marl Bhat, Target Free Approach to Family Planning Programme: A Rapid Survey in Dharwad District in Karnataka, Population Research Centre, J.S.S. Institute of Economic Research, Dharwad, pp. i-iii

ANNEXURE 4.1

STATEMENT V

Guidelines to Prepare State Implementation Plan Under World Bank Supported Reproductive and Child Health Project

The categorisation of State have already been intimated to all the States. States are also aware that interventions under the proposed RCH project will be provided as per differential approach finalised with all States.

However, during the State Secretaries' meeting held in September, 1996, some States requested that these interventions may be provided as per categorisation of Districts instead of States, as the districts in States can also be classified as Cat. A, B or C. Separately the problem of States under State Health Systems (SHS) project of World Bank also had to be resolved. Some of the parameters earlier used for classification of States are not available district-wise from 1991 census data. Keeping in view differing needs and availability of reliable data at State and District levels as also available demographic parameters like CBR and female literacy rate district-wise (for major States only), the districts have been classified after computation of weightage and the same may be seen in enclosed Statement A. For some States/UTs where District-wise data is not available the State data has been used for classification. Interventions have, generally, been provided for on District data except when it became necessary to restrict grouping under State Health Systems or under original classification of States. In some cases strengths available due to inputs under Social Safety Net Scheme for 90 demographically weak Districts have been taken into account.

2. Many interventions under the RCH Project will be made available to all States without any differentiation. These are:

Orientation Workshops on RCH

- Facilitation for operationalisation of Target Free Approach.
- Institutional Development.
- Preparation of Annual State and District Training (integrated training as per the plan and requirements of the RCH interventions), Logistics and implementation plans.
- Modified Management information system.
- Additional IEC activities under RCH on Team-Building and Community Sensitisation.
- Urban and Tribal Areas RCH as per the needs of the States based on the pilot studies. (Details to be intimated later).
- Local capacity enhancement, as per the projects submitted separately.
- Setting up of RTI/STI Clinics at left out District Hospitals at places where STD Clinic under AIDS/STD Programme has not yet been provided. The cost of drugs and equipment per unit will be Rs. 75,000.

3. There are some interventions which will be provided to the States on the basis of classification of the Districts and States mentioned at para 1 above. The facilities/interventions which are being considered for the different category of Districts are given below:

Facilities to be Provided in Category "A" Districts

- Provision of RTI/STI drugs at FRUs (*) (Not in the SHS Project States).
- Minor civil work/repairs/maintenance provisions of requisite inputs at FRU/PHC/SCs otherwise being covered under RCH Project @ upto Rs. 10.00 lakh per District for the project period.
- MTP equipments to all FRUs/CHCs not provided earlier will be given.
- MTP equipments in phased manner to all PHCs.
- Upto 2 Lab Teach. for FRUs on contract basis per District for operationalising RTI/STI screening and diagnostic interventions.
- Consultant doctor at PHC as per phasing on fixed day visit basis twice per month @ Rs. 500 per visit. (Government doctors can also be used for this purpose and paid an honorarium on the same term). The expected work of the Consultants during visit will be provided safe abortion services. This facility will be provided upto 75% of PHC only in the initial years with declining phasing as it is assumed that trained doctors are available at other facilities. By the end of 5 years, it is expected that with intensive training, the requirement of Consultant doctors will be reduced to 25% from 75%. Work load norms will be atleast 5 surgical interventions or assisted deliveries out of cases referred from periphery. Minimum of atleast 20 referred cases should be attended by the visiting doctor or each visit. Adequate advance IEC on expected date of visit of doctor should be announced.

Facilities to be Provided in Category "B" Districts

- Provision of RTI and EOC drugs at 1 FJ(U each) (*) (Not in the SHS Project States).
- Minor civil work/repairs/maintenance provisions of requisite inputs at FRU/PHC/SCS otherwise being covered under RCH Project @ upto Rs. 10.00 lakh per District for the project period.
- Two Lab. Tech. at the FRU on contract basis for Lab. Diagnosis of STI/RTI apart from other work.
- All PHCs to get MTP equipments in phased manner.
- Consultant doctor preferably lady at PHC on fixed day visit basis twice per month @ Rs. 500 per visit. (Government doctors

can also be used for this purpose and paid an honorarium on the same term) as per the phasing of MTP equipment and availability of appropriate facility. The expected work of the Consultants during visit is to provide safe abortion services MTP, ANC, PNC and other Family Planning and Family Welfare Services. This facility will be provided upto 75% of PHC only for the initial years with declining phasing as it is assumed that trained doctors are available at other facilities. By the end of 5 years, it is expected that with intensive training, the requirement of consultant doctors will be reduced to 25% from 75%. Work load norms will be atleast 5 surgical interventions or assisted deliveries out of cases referred from periphery. Minimum of atleast 20 referred cases should be attended by the visiting doctor of each visit. Adequate advance IEO on expected date of visit of doctor should be announced.

- SHS Project States viz. A.P., Karnataka, Punjab and West Bengal have already been 'strengthened upto Sub-District level'. The average institutional deliveries in the districts in these states range around 50% as such, for the PHOs with low institutional deliveries (expected around 50%), the facility of the services of PHN/Staff Nurse will be provided in 50% PHOs to improve institutional delivery, ANC/PHC and screening and referral for RTI. This facility will be limited to the 30 identified Category B Districts in these States. They will be staying at the place of posting for round the clock services. Rental for residence @ upto Rs. 5000 per annum will be provided.
- PHC drug kit for management of essential obstetric care will also be provided to the PHOs where PNH/Staff Nurse have been appointed and are providing round the clock services.

Facilities to be Provided in Category "C" Districts

- Provision of EOC drugs at FRUs (*) (Not in the SHS Project States).
- Minor civil work/repairs/maintenance of FRU/PHC/SCs at Rs. 10.00 lakh per District for the project period.
- MTP equipments to all FRUs/CHOs not provided earlier.
- MTP equipments in phased manner to all PHOs.
- Two Lab. Tech. for selected FRUs on contract basis per District.
- Provision of PAN/Staff Nurse on contract basis in all the PHOs (for 30,000 population) in the 90 Social Safety Net Districts for providing institutional delivery, ANC/PHC, Family Planning and Family Welfare. They will be staying at the place of posting for round the clock services and get rental for residence @ upto Rs. 5000 per annum. Under Social Safety Net Scheme provision was made for providing appropriate infrastructure for such

PHCs where this was missing. While a perfect machine may not be feasible, it is expected that 35-40; PHCs in these districts would be having facilities which could not be used with provision of PHN/Staff Nurse for providing essential obstetric care.

- In other Districts, where delivery room and residential quarters have been built under various projects but remain unutilised, a PHN/Staff Nurse on contract basis will be provided at PHC (for 30,000 population). As per available information only about 25% PHCs in Category C Districts can avail this facility.
- Additional ANMs in a phased manner upto 3000 of 50s @ Rs. 3600.00 p.m. will be provided to augment the ability to provide focused attention to safe motherhood in the less developed areas/blocks of these districts in 'C' category. This facility is being restricted to remote and for flung sub-centres in C category Districts of the 8 states originally identified as C category States, i.e. Assam, Bihar, Haryana, Madhya Pradesh, Nagaland, Orissa, Rajasthan and Uttar Pradesh.
- Nominal rental to facilitate the stay of these additional ANMs will be provided.
- A Pilot will be launched for assessing long-term feasibility of referral transport for pregnant women from below poverty line category for their obstetric emergencies to be carried out in 2-3 Cat. C Districts in the 8 States (originally identified as C States) with high infant and maternal mortality.
- All PHOs to get MTP equipments in phased manner.
- Consultant doctor (preferably lady) at PHC on fixed day visit basis twice per month @ Rs. 500 per visit. (Government doctors can also be used for this purpose and paid an honorarium on the same term) as per the phasing of MTP equipment and availability of appropriate facility. The expected work of the Consultants during visit will be provided safe abortion services, MTP, ANC, PNC and other Family Planning and Family Welfare Services. This facility will be provided upto 75% of PHC only, as it is assumed that trained doctors are available at other facilities. By the end of 5 years, it is expected that with intensive training, the requirement of consultant doctors will be reduced to 25% from 75%. Work load norms will be atleast surgical interventions or assisted deliveries out of cases referred from periphery. Minimum of atleast 20 referred cases should be attended by the visiting doctor of each visit. Adequate advance IEC on expected date of visit of doctor should be announced.
- PHC drug kit for management of essential obstetric care will also be provided to the PHCs where PHN/Staff Nurse have been appointed and are providing round the clock services.

- Identification of two FRUs per District is left to the States. However, it is advisable that these facilities CFRUs) be chosen (a) where availability of manpower is assured; (b) equipment kits were provided under CSSM or where these can be shifted from other facilities; (c) infrastructure is already available and Cesarian Section is being carried out; and (d) have good geographic advantage and have defined catchment area to provide referral services.

4. For proper implementation of some of the interventions, it is proposed to phase the interventions by selecting Districts under the Project, taking only those Districts for the interventions, which are prepared to receive the interventions. In the first year of the project, only those Districts should be selected which are able to start the proposed activity positively in the second half of the year of the project. All the pre-requisite activities like training, gaps in infrastructure, manpower, etc., should have been attended to under State MNP where relevant e.g., infrastructure. The phasing of the Districts for some of the major interventions are given at Statement "A-I" and total number of Districts proposed under phasing is given at Statement "C".

5. While preparing the interventions for the States, assumptions used by this Ministry described in pre-paragraphs and below may also be kept in mind by States while preparing the State Implementation Plan and phasing of various interventions and districts over the five year project period .

Source: Department of Family Welfare, Government of India, Reproduction and Child Health, Vol. I, New Delhi, March 1997.

5

CHAPTER

Department of AYUSH, Ministry of Health and Family Welfare*

INTRODUCTION

Inspite of the spectacular advances made by the system of modern/allopathic medicines, the alternative or traditional systems of medicine currently serve the health care needs of a large population in the world. In India, this Indigenous medicinal system comprises of different components, namely, Ayurveda, Yoga and Naturopathy, Unani and Siddha systems. These ancient systems of medicine which are a treasure house of knowledge for both preventive and curative health care are embedded in Indian culture well before the advent of Allopathic System of medicines and have continued to be an integral and significant part of our society. They are officially recognized, codified and well documented. However, its growth and development has not been as encouraging as it should be various problems/constraints affecting the growth of Indian systems of medicine are: neglect by Government, Individualized and inhibitive behaviours, lesser adaptability, lack of quality parameters, abuse of system by unscrupulous practitioners, *ad-hoc* growth, poor resources and allocation and neglect of basic research.

With a view to have a focussed development of the Indian System of Medicine and Homeopathy and to address the health care delivery services through these systems the Government of India (GOI) in 1995 established an Independent department of Indian Systems of Medicine and Homeopathy (ISM&H) under the Ministry of Health and Family Welfare. Government have also formulated and approved a National Policy on ISM&H in 2002 which, *inter-alia*, reiterated that Ayurveda, Unani,

* See Appendix 5.I by Secretary, AYUSH, Appendix II: For Central Council of Indian Medicine; Appendix III: For Central Council of Homeopathy Medicine.

CHART 5.1

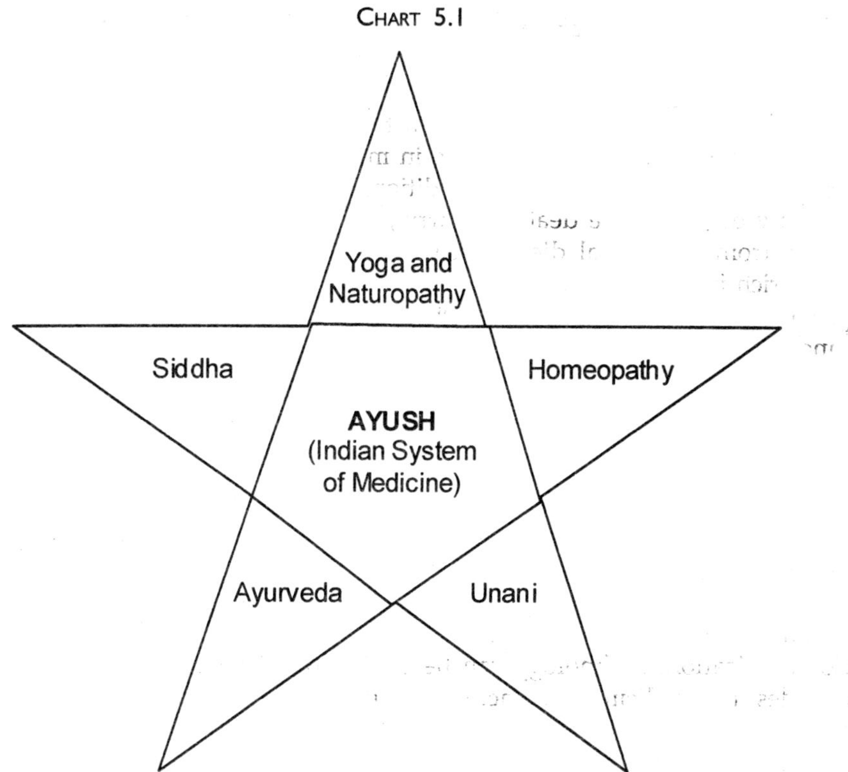

Homeopathy, and Yoga offered a wide range of preventive, promotive and curative treatments and renamed the Department of ISM & H as the Department of Ayurveda, Yoga and Naturopathy, Unani, Siddha and Homeopathy (AYUSH) in November 2003. The major objectives of Department of AYUSH were to promote good health and expand the outreach of health are; to improve the quality of teachers and clinicians; to ensure affordable AYUSH services and drugs which are safe and efficacious; to facilitate availability of raw drugs which are authentic and contain essential components; to integrate AYUSH in health care delivery system and National Programmes; to re-orient and prioritize research in AYUSH; to create awareness about the strengths of these systems in India and abroad and sensitize other stakeholders and providers of heath; and to provide full opportunity for the growth and development of these systems.

ORGANISATIONAL SET-UP

To address the health care delivery services through the Indian System of Medicine and Homeopathy. Government of India (GOI) in 1995 established an independent department of Indian Systems of Medicine and Homeopathy (ISM&H) under the Ministry of Health and Family Welfare.

Thereafter, the Government approved a separate National Policy on ISM&H in 2002 which, *inter-alia*, reiterated that Ayurveda, Unani, Homeopathy, and Yoga offered a wide range of preventive, promotive and curative treatments and renamed the Department of ISM&H as the Department of Ayurveda, Yoga and Naturopathy, Unani, Siddha and Homeopathy (AYUSH) in November 2003. The Department of AYUSH headed by the Secretary to Government in the Ministry of Health and Family Welfare is the nodal agency for overall direction, coordination, budgetary control and policy interventions for implementation of the policy. Two Joint Secretary and 5 Directors/Deputy Secretaries and 4 advisors assist the Secretary (two for Ayurveda and one each for Unani and Homeopathy of the staff through both medical and non-medical in AYUSH Deptt. is 268. Out of the 35 States/UTs, 21 States have established a separate Directorate to coordinate and implement AYUSH-related programmes. As of March 2003, an infrastructure comprising of 3845 hospitals with 65159 beds, 23630 dispensaries, 6.91 lakh registered practitioners, 439 and 96 under-graduate and post-graduate colleges with admission capacity of 23555 and 1888 students respectively and 9226 licensed pharmacies, had been created in the country.

The major objectives of Department of AYUSH are: (i) to promote good health and expand the outreach of public health care; (ii) to improve the quality of teachers and clinicians; (iii) to ensure affordable AYUSH services and drugs which are safe and efficacious; (iv) to facilitate availability of raw drugs which are authentic and contain essential components; (v) to integrate AYUSH in health care delivery system and national programmes; (iv) to re-orient and prioritize research in AYUSH; (vii) to create awareness about the strengths of these systems in India and abroad and sensitize other stakeholders and providers of health; and (viii) to provide full opportunity for the growth and development of these systems.

The National Health Policy, 1983 referred to our rich heritage of medicinal knowledge and suggested that it was necessary to initiate measures to enable India's rich medicinal heritage to develop in accordance with its genius. It took note the fact that vast infrastructure is available in Indian Systems of Medicine and Homeopathy and that it should be integrated at the appropriate level, within specified areas of responsibility and functioning in the overall health care delivery systems, specifically in regard to the preventive, promotive and public health objectives.

The Central Council for Health and Family Welfare in 1999 also recommended, *inter-alia*, that at least one physician from the Indian Systems of Medicine and Homeopathy should be available in every Primary Health Center and that vacancies caused by non-availability of allopathic personnel should be filled by ISM&H physicians. The Council also resolved that specialist ISM&H treatment centres should be introduced in rural hospitals and a wing should be created in existing state and district level government hospitals for extending the health care to the public.

The concern for preservation and scientific development of our rich heritage of medicinal knowledge reflected in National Health Policy, 1983 led to the National Policy on Indian Systems of Medicine and Homeopathy, 2002 which outlined following basic objectives:

(a) To promote good health and expand the outreach of health care to our people, particularly those not provided with health cover, through preventive, promotive and curative interventions through ISM&H.
(b) To improve the quality of teachers and clinicians by revising curricula to contemporary relevance by creating model institutions and Centres of Excellence and extending assistance for creating infrastructural facilities.
(c) To ensure affordable ISM&H services and drugs which are safe and efficacious.
(d) To facilitate availability of raw drugs which are authentic and contain essential, components as required under pharmacopoeial standards to help improve quality of drugs, for domestic consumption and export.
(e) To integrate ISM&H in the health care delivery system and National Programmes and ensure optimal use of the infrastructure of hospitals, dispensaries and physicians.
(f) To re-orient and prioritize research in ISM&H to gradually validate therapy and drugs to address in particular the chronic and new lifestyle-related emerging diseases.
(g) To create awareness about the strengths of these systems in India and abroad and sensitize other stakeholders and providers of health.
(h) To provide full opportunity for the growth and development of these systems and utilization of their potential, strength and revival of their glory.

Policy pronouncements contained in the National Policy on AYUSH-2002 could not be effectively implemented due to poor budgetary support, inadequate monitoring, evaluation and lack of coordination between various implementing agencies and the Ministry. The share of AYUSH in the total health Plan at the Central level was static at 2 per cent during 2000-05 though the policy pronouncement envisaged raising of AYUSH share to 10 per cent with designed growth of 5 per cent in every Five Year Plan. The programme also suffered from absence of an effective system of transfer of funds to the implementing agencies. Out of Rs. 30.90 crore released to 12 State Governments under Centrally Sponsored Schemes during 2002-05, Rs. 16.94 crore were not released to the implementing agencies with delays even upto 36 months.

Let us talk about Indigenous systems of Medicines briefly, i.e. AYUSH.

The term AYUSH covers Ayurveda, Yoga and Naturopathy, Unani,

Siddha and Homeopathy. These systems originated in India as well as outside but got adopted here in the course of time. These systems are popular in a large number of states in the country. There are separate Directorate of ISM & H in 18 states. Though Ayurveda is popular in all these states, it is more prevalent in the States of Kerala, Himachal Pradesh, Gujarat, Karnataka, A.P., Madhya Pradesh, Rajasthan, Uttar Pradesh, Uttaranchal and Orissa. The Unani System is particularly popular in Andhra Pradesh, Karnataka, Bihar, Madhya Pradesh, Uttar Pradesh, and Delhi and Rajasthan. Homeopathy is more popular in Uttar Pradesh, Kerala, West Bengal, Orissa, Andhra Pradesh, Delhi, Bihar and North-Eastern States.[1]

INDIA the land of a highly rich culture history and heritage had the distinction of excelling in the field of the 'Science of Life' at a time when most of the mankind, the world over, was still in the process of evolving itself from its aboriginal moorings. The environment-based efficacious medication practised by saints and sages of repute heavily depended on the organic extracts of herbs and shrubs, seeds and saplings, fruits and flowers. With this sound medicinal knowledge of controlling diseases and physical disorders that passed down the generations, the practitioners of medicine were always open to adopting the medicinal philosophies of other advanced civilizations such as Greece, Egypt and China. This quick assimilation of new therapies gave a fillip to the medical practices and procedures while further broadening the horizons of treatment. It is this confluence of treatment techniques that came to be called the indigenous system of medicine.

Over the last few decades, these traditional systems of medicine have been catching the fancy of the common man and the elite, both within and outside the country. This revival of faith and the consequent growing demand for indigenous system of medicine has revitalized the age-old streams of effective medication. A brief synopsis of some of these popular systems of medicine prevalent in India as a part of its medical services on a selective basis is given below for a better understanding of these therapies.

AYURVEDIC SYSTEM OF MEDICINE

Ayurveda means "Science of Life." It finds a detailed mention in Vedas (5000 B.C.). Around 1000 B.C., it was comprehensively documented in 'Charak Samhita' and 'Sushruta Samhita' according to which health is considered a pre-requisite for achieving the three goals of life—Dharma, Artha, Kama and Moksha. Thus, Ayurveda takes an integrated view of the physical, mental, spiritual and social aspects of the health of human beings, each impinging on others.

The philosophy of Ayurveda is based on the theory of Panchmahabhutas (five elements) of which all the objects and living bodies are composed of. In the human body these elements are represented in the form of Tridoshas or three physiological dispositions—Vata (Ether + Air), Pitta (Fire) and Kaph (Water+Earth). Further, the mental, spiritual attributes are also described in terms of Satva, Rajas and Tamas. Thus, Ayurveda considers the human being as a combination of three 'Doshas', five elements (Panchamahabhutas), seven body tissues (Sapta-dhatu), five senses (Panch-indriyas) with sensory and motor functions, mind (Mansas), intellect (Budhi) and soul (Atman). The doctrine of Ayurveda aims to keep these structural and functional entities in a state of equilibrium which signifies good health (Swasthya). Any imbalance due to internal or external factors causes disease and resorting the equilibrium through various techniques, procedures, regimes, diet and medicine constitute the treatment.

In Ayurveda, diagnosis includes questioning and eight examinations, viz., pulse, urine, faces, tongue, eyes, visual/sensual examinations and inference. It considers the human being as a microcosm (Yatha pinde tatha brahmande), replica of macrocosm Universe. The treatment in Ayurveda system is individualized. While prescribing medicines to a person, one has to consider various factors like the condition of body and mind, temperament (Parakriti), sex, age, metabolic fire (Agni), work-rest pattern, sleep pattern and diet. Treatment in Ayurveda has two components: (a) preventive measures, and (b) curative measures. Preventive aspect of Ayurveda is called Svasth-Vritt and includes personal hygiene, regular daily routine, appropriate social behaviour and Rasayana Sevana, i.e. use of rejuvenative materials/food and rasayans drugs. The curative treatment consists of three major categories of procedures: (i) Aushadhi (drugs); (ii) Anna (diets); and (iii) Vihara (exercises and general mode of life).

Our indigenous health traditions, enshrined in the Ayurvedic, Unani and Siddha systems of health care, need greater attention. We have 6000 years of leadership in Ayurveda. The basic approach to health care in the Ayurvedic system is a holistic one, ranging from attention to diet and lifestyle to the use of plant-based drugs and therapeutic exercises. We should bring about blends of traditional health care practices and modern medicine. Without an extensive revitalization of our time-tested health traditions, the goal of "health for all" cannot be achieved.[2]

HOMEOPATHY

Homeopathy is a system of medicine which believes in a specialized method of curing diseases by administration of potentised drugs which have been experimentally proved to possess the power of producing similar artificial symptoms on healthy human beings.

Down the tradition of Homeopathy, what physicians from the time of Hippocrats (400 B.C.) believed, the 17th century German physician Dr. Christian Frederic S. Hahnemaan concluded – that any substance capable of producing artificial symptom on healthy individuals could cure the same symptoms in a natural disease. This forms the basis of the theory of Homeopathy 'Simila Simlibus Curentur' or let like be treated by like.

Homeopathy is based on the following four cardinal principles: (i) The laws of similars; (ii) The law of direction of cure; (iii) The principle of single remedy; (iv) The theory of minimum doses; and (v) The theory of chronic diseases. The law of similar states that a medicine which can produce artificial symptoms on healthy human beings can cure the similar set of symptoms of natural diseases. The method adopted in experimenting this theory on human beings is now known as Human Drug Pathogenicity (HDP) test. Homeopathy generally uses only a single medicine which has a true similarity of symptoms with that of the remedy. The physician adopts a detailed case study by exploring the physical, psychological and biomedical constitution of the individual. The doses applied are the minimum possible, just sufficient to correct the diseased state.

Homeopathy attaches significance to the nomenclature of diseases to the extent of choosing the auxiliary mode of treatment, prevention, and clinical management, prognosis, etc., not in selection of the remedy. The concept is that the physical, mental and spiritual expression of the sick from the totality of the disease.

Homeopathy has effective treatment for individuals with chronic diseases such as diabetes, arthritis, bronchial asthma, allergic and immunological disorders, behavioural disorders, mental diseases, etc.

UNANI SYSTEM OF MEDICINE

Originating in Greece (4-5th Century B.C.), developed in Egypt, Arabia, Iran, Syria and China, and imported to India during the Mughal period, the Unani System of medicine became native to India due to its mass appeal and continuous use by the people.

The Unani system emphasizes the use of naturally occurring, herbal medicines, though it also used ingredients of animal and marine origin. It has been documented in Al. Qannon, a medical Bible, by Sheikh Bu-Ali Sina (Avicena), (980-1037 A.D.) and in Al. Havi by Razi (850-923 A.D.). The Hakim Ajmal Khan discovered (Asrol) Rawolfia serpentine which established its efficacy in the treatment of high blood pressure.

This system is based on humoural theory, i.e. presence of blood, phlegm, yellow bile and black bile. The temperament of a person is accordingly expressed as sanguine, phlegmatic, chloric and melancholic. According to the Unani theory, the humours and medicinal plants have a direct bearing on the temperament. It also advocates diagnosis of a disease by feeling the pulse, observation of urine, stool, colour of skin and gait, etc.

The treatment comprises three components, namely, preventive, promotive and curative. Speciality in Unani system of medicine is on rheumatic arthritis, jaundice, filariasis, eczema, sinusitis and bronchial asthma. Its efficacy in the treatment and management of cardiac diseases is being researched.

SIDDHA SYSTEM OF MEDICINE

Siddha System is one of the oldest systems of medicine in India. The term 'Siddha' implies miraculous achievements by saintly practitioners in the realm of medicine. Largely therapeutic in nature, it is practiced mostly in Tamil speaking territory, home and abroad.

Under the Siddha system of medicine, diagnosis of disease involves identifying its causes through examination of pulse, eyes, voice, body colour, tongue and digestive system besides a detailed procedure of urine analysis. This system emphasizes that medical treatment is oriented not merely to disease and symptoms but has to take into account the patient, environment, the metrological consideration, age, sex, race, habits, mental frame, habitat, diet, appetite, physical condition, physiological constitution, etc. It is therefore, both individualistic and holistic.

The Siddha medicine which contains mercury, silver, arsenic, lead and sulphur have been effective in treating chronic liver disorder, skin diseases especially 'Psoriasis' rheumatism, anemia, prostate enlargement, piles, peptic ulcer, venereal diseases and even AIDS.

YOGA

Yoga is primarily a way of life propounded by Patanjali in a systematic form. It consists of eight components, namely, Yama (restraint), Niyama (austerity), Asana (physical postures), Pranayama (breathing exercises), Pratyahara (restraining of sense organs), Dharna (contemplation), Dhyana (meditation) and Samadhi (superconsciousness). These steps in the practice of Yoga facilitate better circulation of oxygenated blood in the body resulting improvement in physical health and restrain sense organs inducing tranquility and serenity of mind.

The Yoga Sutras prescribes a number of physical postures which are required to be chosen judiciously and practiced the right way to derive desired benefits. Meditation, when practiced systematically and regularly, reduces metabolic process to the minimum and thereby liberates the mind to more fruitful spiritual pursuits.

Recent studies have revealed that modern age, more than anything else, requires Yoga and meditation not only to prevent diseases and cure illness but also to cumbat stress and strain and other psychosomatic disorders and lead a life of health, happiness and peace.

NATUROPATHY

Naturopathy is not just a drugless therapy; it is also a way of life. Mainly based on the ancient practice of application of the simple laws of nature, it pays particular attending to eating and living habits, fasting, hydrotherapy, cold packs, mud packs, massages, etc.

In AYUSH, training is give at the following place:

1. National Institute of Ayurveda (NIA), Jaipur
2. National Institute of Siddha (NIS), Chennai
3. National Institute of Homeopathy, Kolkata
4. National Institute of Naturopathy, Pune
5. National Institute of Unani Medicine, Bangalore
6. Institute of Post Graduate Teaching and Research in Ayurveda, Jamnagar
7. Rashtriya Ayurved Vidyapeeth, New Delhi
8. Morarji Desai National Institute of Yoga, New Delhi

Standard of Education

The regulatory Councils responsible for prescribing minimum standards of infrastructure in medical institutions, maintaining a centralized database of medical practitioners and monitoring the prescribed standards of medical education had failed in checking the growth of substandard institutions. Most of the 444 colleges of Ayurveda, Unani and Homeopathy in the country lacked minimum required faculty, attached hospitals and teaching facilities. The central register of practitioners had either not been maintained or had not been updated and revised for very long periods. The independence and autonomy of the regulatory bodies had also been diluted.

Research

The four Research Councils, viz. (i) Central Council for Research in Ayurveda and Siddha (CCRAS); (ii) Central Council for Research in Unani Medicine (CCRUM), (iii) Central Council for Research in Homeopathy (CCRH); and (iv) Central Council for Research in Yoga and Naturopathy (CCRYN), continued to initiate and guide, develop and coordinate scientific research in different aspects of respective systems, both fundamental and allied. These councils are the Apex bodies for research in the concerned systems of medicine and are fully financed by the Govt. of India. Their research activities have been reviewed to ensure that Councils undertake meaningful research under fixed parameters within specified period and disseminate research findings for the benefit of educationists, researchers, physicians, manufacturers and common man.

Research activities were not undertaken under fixed parameters within specified time period and their results had not been disseminated for the benefit of educationists, researchers, manufacturers and the common man. During the last 25 years, the Councils had obtained patents for only three Ayurveda drugs and did not contribute concrete research findings in the core area of family planning/contraceptive measures.

Pharmacopoeial Committees did not finalise standards in respect of any of the compound formulations in Ayurveda and Unani even after 40 years of their establishment, though the National Policy-2002 had envisaged completion of this work by 2005.

The National Medicinal Plant Board, set-up as a nodal agency to oversee policies for conservation and development of medicinal plants at the National and State levels did not have an authentic database on demand and supply of medicinal plants and failed to monitor and evaluate the progress of 1077 projects funded by it at a cost of Rs. 62.16 crore during 2001-04.[3]

Availability of Raw Material

Ayurvada, Yoga and Naturopathy, Unani, Siddha and Homeopathy (AYUSH) use various raw materials such as medicinal plants, materials of marine and animal origin, minerals, metals, etc. However, medicinal plants constitute 80% of the raw materials. The effectiveness of these systems mainly depends upon the use of genuine raw materials. According to the report of the world health organisation, over 80% of the world population relies on the traditional systems of medicines, largely plant-based, to meet their primary health care needs. According to another report of the Export Import Bank of India, the value of the medicinal plants related trade in India is of the order of 5.5 billion U.S. dollars and is growing rapidly. The international market of herbal products is estimated to be US dollar 62 billion and poised to grow further.

The Medicinal Plants Board has been set-up as a follow of recommendations of the Task Force on conservation and sustainable utilization of medicinal plants by Planning Commission, vide Cabinet Resolution notified on 24th November, 2000. The apex body of the Board is headed by Union Health and Family Welfare Minister. The main objectives of establishing the Board is to have an agency at National level which would be responsible to co-ordinate all matters relating to development of medicinal plants including drawing up policies and strategies for conservation, proper harvesting, cost-effective cultivation and marketing, etc. of raw material in order to protect, sustain and develop this sector.[4]

Standardisation and Quality Control of ASU and Homeopathy Drugs

Laying down the Pharmacopoeial standards for Ayurveda, Siddha and Unani medicine both for single and compound drugs is an essential item of work. The Ministry had taken up the task of developing pharmacopoeial standards through Pharmacopoeia Committees. Pharmacopoeial standards are important and are mandatory for the implementation of the drug testing provisions under the drugs and Cosmetics Act, 1940 and Rules thereunder. These standards are also essential to check samples of drugs available in the market for their safety and efficacy.

Four different Pharmacopoeia Committees are working for preparing official formularies/pharmacopoeias to evolve uniform standards in preparation of drugs of Ayurveda, Siddha, Unani and Homeopathy and to prescribes working standards for single drugs as well as compound formulations. Recently, the work of the pharmacopoeia committees has been transferred to the respective Councils to ensure expeditious handling.

Scheme on publication of textbooks and acquisition and publication of manuscripts

The scheme aims to prepare and publish good quality text books written by experienced teachers of Ayurveda, Siddha and Unani and also supports acquiring, preserving and publishing manuscripts and out of the print books which are still beyond the reach of the students, teachers and research scholars of Ayurveda, Siddha and Unani. Proposals for Text Book publication received from various Ayurveda, Siddha and Unani Colleges are considered under the scheme.[5]

Implementation of IEC scheme through NGOs

(i) Non-Government Organisations have been involved to promote the strengths of AYUSH systems. One of the activities is the organizing of training workshops for motivating AYUSH practitioners. Health Melas are organized to create awareness among the general public about the efficacy and cost effectiveness of the ISM & H drugs and easy availability of herbs and plants like Tulsi, Haldi, Neem, etc. and about the correct way to grow medicinal plants. Community awareness meetings in cooperation with Mahila Mandals, Yuvak Sanghs, Farmers, Cooperatives, etc. which are already existing at the village level are also organized through NGOs. Yoga classes are conducted in primary and middle schools under the scheme. The Department also helps to organize Seminars and Workshops in AYUSH systems covering various subjects of general interest including medicinal plants.

During 2006-07, Rs. 200 lakhs has been provided to cover new blocks under the NGO scheme. Proposals from 65 organisations covering 95 new blocks have been approved ending October 2006.

(ii) Dissemination of the Information Through Print and Audio-Visual Medium: Education and Communication: In order to disseminate information and educate the general public about the preventive aspects of health care and legal provisions regarding manufacture and sale of AYUSH drugs, the Department printed pamphlets on these subjects which were widely distributed in the Arogya fairs held during the year. The Department also produced six short films on Ayurveda, Siddha, Unani, Yoga and Naturopathy and Homeopathy and films on Home Remedies in Ayurveda and Unani. All these films were shown during the Arogya fairs. VCDs were distributed to the general public on demand.

In order to restore public faith in the efficacy of AYUSH system, it is imperative that quality and safe AYUSH drugs are produced and made available in the market. A Centrally Sponsored Scheme namely—"Quality Control of AYUSH drugs" was launched by Ministry in 2000-01 for ensuring availability of quality AYUSH drugs in conformity with the Drugs and Cosmetics Act, 1940 and eliminating the possibility of production and marketing of sub-standard drugs.

The Department of Ayurveda, Yoga and Naturpathy, Unani, Siddha and Homeopathy (AYUSH) is headed by a Secretary to the Government of India. The Secretary is assisted by two Joint Secretaries and five Directors/ Deputy Secretaries. On the technical side, there are four Advisers (two for Ayurveda and one each for Unani and Homeopathy) and Deputy Advisors. The sanctioned staff strength of the Department in 268, including both secretariat and Technical posts.

Problems

- Ministry's allocation of funding for the programmes under AYUSH was inadequate considering the objectives to be achieved. Ministry allocated 2 per cent of the total Health budget (2000-05) to AYUSH as against 10 per cent envisaged in the National Policy. State Governments did not transfer Rs. 16.94 crore (55 per cent) to implementing agencies for periods up to 36 months.
- Ministry did not maintain any consolidated record of utilisation of grants depriving it of an effective monitoring tool. Thus, Rs. 36.52 crore (72 per cent) remained unutilised with the implementing agencies as of December 2004 out of the grant in aid of Rs. 50.87 crore released to 12 States during 2000-05. Similarly, out of Rs. 4.95 crore released by the Ministry to the states for establishing specialised therapy centres/specialty clinics, ISM&H wings and supply of essential drugs, Rs. 4.90 crore (99 per cent) remained unutilised. An amount of Rs. 53.19 lakh released to the Government of Himachal Pradesh under the Pilot scheme for setting up AYUSH Health Resort Clinics for Tourists also remained unutilised, which defeated the very purpose of attracting tourists.
- None of the 142 colleges whose records Audit test checked, out of total 444 colleges, possessed adequate infrastructural facilities, faculty, attached hospitals with requisite bed strength and OPD/IPD facilities in accordance with the norms laid down by the Regulatory Councils. Five Apex level Institutes set-up by the Ministry as centres of excellence for imparting high quality educational. New Delhi research also lacked infrastructural facilities. Ministry did not ensure that the database of practitioners of AYUSH was updated and revised promptly and regularly. Delays in upgradation ranged between 3 and 22 years in 20 states, which deprived the practitioners of the opportunity of practicing in other states and reduced the outreach of AYUSH Medicare.
- There are neither correlation between the drugs standardised, drugs proved and drugs clinically verified nor any systematic approach to standardisation of drugs as 44 Homoeopathic

drugs were taken up for proving and 47 for clinical verification without having been standardised. Besides, out of 66 project funded at a cost of Rs. 7.13 crore, 59 projects under the scheme 'Extra Mural Research' under 'AYUSH' remained incomplete even after seven years, depriving the people of the benefits accruing out of research.

- Government of India established the Department of Indian Systems of Medicine and Homeopathy (renamed AYUSH from November 2003) in March 1995 with the main objectives of promoting good health, expanding the outreach of AYUSH healthcare through preventive, promotive, mitigating and curative interventions, improving the quality of teachers and clinicians, ensuring affordable and efficacious AYUSH services and drugs and integrating AYUSH in healthcare delivery system and National Health Programmes.
- Policy pronouncements contained in the National Policy on AYUSH-2002 could not be effectively implemented due to poor budgetary support, inadequate monitoring, evaluation and lack of coordination between various implementing agencies and the Ministry. The share of AYUSH in the total Health Plan at the Central level was static at 2 per cent during 2000-05 though the policy pronouncement envisaged raising of AYUSH share to 10 per cent with designed growth of 5 per cent in every Five Year Plan. The programme also suffered from absence of an effective system of transfer of funds to the implementing agencies. Out of Rs. 30.90 crore released to 12 State Governments under Centrally Sponsored Schemes during 2002-05, Rs. 16.94 crore were not released to the implementing agencies with delays even upto 36 months.
- The regulatory Councils responsible for prescribing minimum standards of infrastructure in medical institutions, maintaining a centralized database of medical practitioners and monitoring the prescribed standards of medical education had failed in checking the growth of substandard institutions. Most of the 444 colleges of Ayurveda, Unani and Homeopathy in the country lacked minimum required faculty, attached hospitals and teaching facilities. The central register of practitioners had either not been maintained or had not been updated and revised for very long periods. The independence and autonomy of the regulatory bodies had also been diluted.
- Research activities were not undertaken under fixed parameters within specified time period and their results had not been disseminated for the benefit of educationists, researchers, manufacturers and the common man. During the last 25 years, the Councils had obtained patents for only three Ayurveda drugs and did not contribute concrete research findings in the core area of family planning/contraceptive measures.

- Pharmacopoeial Committees did not finalise standards in respect of any of the compound formulations in Ayurveda and Unani even after 40 years of their establishment, though the National Policy-2002 had envisaged completion of this work by 2005.
- The National Medicinal Plant Board, set-up as a nodal agency to oversee policies for conservation and development of medicinal plants at the National and State levels did not have an authentic database on demand and supply of medicinal plants and failed to monitor and evaluate the progress of 1077 projects funded by it at a cost of Rs. 62.16 crore during 2001-04.

SUGGESTIONS

- Streamline the system and procedures of transfer of funds to States and further allotment by States to implementing agencies by identifying the specific bottlenecks and monitoring the internal procedures closely.
- Introduce a computer-based tracking system for release grants so that their utilisation improves significantly and also insist on obtaining refund of unutilised balances retained by State Governments for over a year which would help avoid blocking of resources when competing sectors face funds crunch.
- Ensure that adequate and identifiable measures are taken to bring in parity in medical education across the country and strengthen the infrastructure in the apex level institutes so as to enable them to function as centres of excellence.
- Ensure that permission to open new colleges, starting PG courses and increasing admission capacity are accorded only after minimum standards of infrastructure prescribed by Regulatory Councils are achieved.
- Ensure autonomy and independence of the Regulatory Councils for promoting transparency and accountability and arrange to get the Central Registers of Practitioners updated covering all the States/Union territories through a time bound programme.
- Draw appropriate guidelines for taking up research activities under fixed parameters in a time bound manner and ensure that research findings relating to all components of each scheme are finalised, patented and disseminated among the stakeholders. The ongoing projects would need to be completed early and findings disseminated to stakeholders such as educationist, researchers, manufacturers and Government Institutions.
- Draw appropriate guidelines for taking up research activities under fixed parameters in a time bound manner and ensure that research findings relating to all components of each scheme are finalised, patented and disseminated among the stockholders.

The ongoing projects would need to be completed early and findings disseminated to stakeholders such as educationist, researchers, manufacturers and Government Institutions.

- Ensure that reasons for slackness in development of pharmachopoeial standards are investigated and specific bottlenecks for ensuring their expeditious publication in the respective pharmacopoeia are identified. Result-oriented supervision would need to be carried out and drug standardisation work done by Research Councils in consultation with the Pharmacopoeia committees monitored by fixing clear areas of responsibility so that efforts are not duplicated and resources not wasted.
- Consider introducing suitable penal measures so that the drug manufacturing units strictly adhere to GMPs.
- Entrust State Medical Plant Boards with clear and direct responsibility of monitoring and evaluating various plantation schemes and preparing an authentic database of prioritized medicinal plants.
- Critically review the status of expansion of outreach of healthcare and introduce appropriate control mechanisms with clearly defined responsibility centres to monitor and ensure optimal utilisation of the existing facilities.
- Set-up of Excellent Universities in Indigenous System of Education to ensure first rate experts in Indian System of Education.

The kind of higher education a university in a developing country provides to its students today, will play a vital role in determining the shape of social, economic, political and industrial development of the country in the years ahead. The function of a university today is not only to enable the students to attain excellence in knowledge, but also to contribute directly to national development, to furnish intellectual and moral leadership to the community at large. Today when our nation is struggling to march towards the establishment of an egalitarian society, based on political and economic justice and social equality, university education can no longer remain a passive spectator. The task of creating a new social order which has assumed paramount importance to day cannot be overlooked by the university community. Thus, the goal of university education has a dual character, firstly, the pursuit of knowledge and the attainment of excellence in different disciplines, and secondly, the development of a sense of ethos which makes the university community conscious of its obligations to the community at large of which it is an important segment. As the report of Education Commission (1964-66) so aptly points out, the university education should have emphasis on internal transformation so as to relate it to the life, needs and aspirations of the nation.

The rapid advances in science and technology have greatly influenced medical science and during the last 50 years the science of medicine has made tremendous advances. Meanwhile, the traditional systems of medicine in different regions of the world have not taken much advantage of the march of science.

University has indeed developed into a model for promoting the concept of health and education. Under the enlightened vision and versatile personality of Hakeem Abdul Hameed Sahib, Chancellor, Jamia Hamdard has succeeded in its long journey towards achieving excellence in learning and healing. Socrates once said that there is nothing stronger than human determination. Hakeem Abdul Hameed Sahib is indeed a man of strong determination, and it is his commitment to the cause of medicine that the Jamia Hamdard has emerged not only an apex institution of Unani Medicine but also of other related sciences. In the pursuit of health-care, the University has developed the well tested effective system of Unani medicine interfaced with modern science and technology. University is making best efforts to make an effective use of herbal and mineral resources through traditional system. University's Majeedia Hospital provides facilities for practicing herbal medicines and facilitating clinical support to our teaching and research wings. The University has produced a comprehensive infrastructure to rejuvenate our traditional system of healing art and certain innovative researches which are being pursued in Unani System here, may be catalyst in making our country free from dangerous diseases.[6]

CONCLUSION

The Department of AYUSH had achieved very little success in achieving the objectives of growth and development, porpogation and promotion of AYUSH health care in the country. Policy pronouncements contained in the National Policy on AYUSH-2002 could not be effectively implemented due to poor budgetary support. Inadequate monitoring, evaluation and lack of coordination between various implementing agencies and the Ministry. The share of AYUSH in the total health Plan at the Central level was static at 2 per cent during 2000-05 though the policy envisaged raising of AYUSH share to 10 per cent with designed growth of 5 percent in every Five Year Plan. The programme also suffered from absence of an effective system of transfer to funds to the implementing agencies. Out of Rs. 30.98 crore released to 12 state governments under Centrally Sponsored Schemes during 2002-05, Rs. 16.94 crores were not released to the implementing agencies with delays even upto 36 months.

Notes and References

1. Ministry of Health and Family Welfare, GOI, Annual Report, 2006-07, p. 337.
2. M.S. Swaminathan, "Shaping India's Health Destiny", *University News*, 45(36), Sept. 0-09, 2007, p. 25.

3. Ministry of Health and Family Welfare, GOI, Annual Report, 2006-07, p. 359.
4. *Ibid.*, p. 373.
5. Ministry of Health and Family Welfare, GOI, Annual Report, 2006-07, pp. 377, 389.
6. Shakeel Ahmad, "Indigenous Health Education in the Universities", *University News*, 36(46), Nov.16, 1998, pp. 15-16.

APPENDIX 5.1

1. Department of Indian Systems of Medicine and Homeopathy (ISM&H) was created in March, 1995 and re-named as Department of Ayurveda, Yoga and Naturopathy, Unani, Siddha and Homeopathy (AYUSH) in November, 2003 with a view to providing focused attention to development of Education and Research in Ayurveda, Yoga and Naturopathy, Unani, Siddha and Homeopathy systems. The Department continued to lay emphasis on upgradation of AYUSH educational standards, quality control and standardization of drugs, improving the availability of medicinal plant material, research and development and awareness generation about the efficacy of the systems domestically and internationally. Department of AYUSH has taken steps in 2006-07 for mainstreaming of AYUSH under the National Rural Health Mission with the objective of optimum utilization of AYUSH infrastructure for meeting the unmet health needs of the Indian population. Pharmacopoeial standards of a large number of single crude drugs have been completed and the work of laying down pharmacopoeial standards for poly-herbal formulations, which are R&D intensive, has been taken in hand. AYUSH industry has also been encouraged to actively assist in this stupendous task. Efforts have been made under the Golden Triangle Partnership project in collaboration with Indian Council of Medical Research (ICMR) and Council of Scientific and Industrial Research (CSIR) for botanical standardization and development of R&D base drugs based on India's traditional medicinal knowledge. The first International Conclave on Traditional Medicine was organized by Department of AYUSH in collaboration with National Institute of Science Communication And Information Resources (NISCAIR), CSIR at New Delhi on 16-17 November, 2006 which was supported by WHO-India Office, World Intellectual Property Organisation (WIPO) and Asia Pacific Centre for Transfer of Technology (APCTT) and was attended by more than 300 delegates from member-countries of SAARC, APTMNET, IBSA and BIMSTEC regional fora and internationally recognized experts on standardization, quality control, safety and efficacy of traditional medicine. The Department of AYUSH made a presentation on Ayurveda before the European Union Medicinal Evaluation Agency, London on 15th May 2006 and as a result of these efforts, a para on Ayurveda was included in the joint Indo-EU Summit statement released in Helsinki by EU-India leaders in October 2006.
2. There has been a quantum jump in the Plan provision of the Department of AYUSH in the last three years of the 10th Plan.

Keeping in view the substantial increase in Plan budget, efforts have been made to productively utilize Plan funds for propagating in-situ conservation and ex-situ cultivation of medicinal plants, upgradation of AYUSH education institutions, mainstreaming of AYUSH in National Health System by providing financial assistance to States to open AYUSH wings district hospitals and speciality IOPD clinics at various levels and assistance to States as well as AYUSH industry for strengthening their standardization and quality control capabilities. During the year 2006-07, Plan and Non-Plan provisions stand at Rs. 383 crores and Rs. 66.29 crores, respectively. Steps are being ensured to fully utilize ten per cent outlay kept for the North-Eastern States and Sikkim by the end of 2006-07.

3. The Department attaches priority to maintain standards of medical education in AYUSH systems. All through the 10th Plan efforts have been made to strengthen the existing national institutes which were set-up to lay down benchmarks for teaching, research and clinical practices of different systems. The Department is actively pursuing the proposal for establishment of an All India Institute of Ayurveda at Sarita Vihar, New Delhi that would be a center of excellence for research and development in Ayurveda. Substantial financial assistance has been provided to Government and Government-aided AYUSH UG/PG colleges for upgrading their infrastructure. It is also proposed to set-up an Institute of Folk Medicine in Arunachal Pradesh during the 11th Plan period as well as the North-Eastern Institute of Ayurveda and Homeopathy at Shillong. It is also proposed to provide financial assistance for development of selected AYUSH UG/PG institutions into Centre of Excellence for AYUSH education in the 11th Plan. The Under Graduate and Post-Graduate regulations 2006 of Central Council of Indian Medicine for Minimum standards of Ayurveda, Siddha and Unani education have been approved. The new regulations aim to improve the basic standards of Medical Education in terms of infrastructure and staffing requirements.
4. The Department continued to emphasise the need to prevent growth of sub-standard colleges and sought active involvement of the regulatory Councils and State Governments to achieve these objectives. The IMCC Act, 1970 and HCC Act, 1973 had recently been amended for making it mandatory to seek prior permission of the Central Government for establishing new colleges; starting new and higher courses and increasing admission capacity in Ayurveda, Siddha, Unani and Homeopathy colleges. The IMCC (Amendment) Act, 2005 and HCC (Amendment) Act, 2005 have been introduced in the

Parliament with a view to bringing about transparency and accountability in the functioning of these Councils as a part of Department's policy to improve standards of graduate and post-graduate education in Ayurveda, Siddha, Unani and Homeopathy. The Indian Medicine and Homeopathy Pharmacy Bill, 2005 has also been introduced in Parliament to establish a Central Pharmacy Council for Indian Medicine and Homeopathy to regulate and standardize pharmacy education.

5. Standardization of drugs and quality control continued to receive focused attention of the Central Government. The Department of AYUSH has assigned the highest priority to the laying down of pharmacopoeial standards for ASU&H drugs. The work of laying down of pharmacopoeial standards of single crude drugs has been more or less completed and it is proposed to lay down pharmacopoeial standards for 300 to 400 most widely used Ayurvedic medicines in the next three years. To keep these objectives in mind the Ayush Research Councils have been declared as the Secretariats for the Pharmacopoeia Committees. An ambitious modernization plan is also under implementation for modernization of Pharmacopoeial Laboratory for Indian Medicine (PLIM), Ghaziabad with a view to expediting laying down of pharmacopoeial standards.
6. In addition, the Department of AYUSH has sensitized all the State Licensing Authorities and State Departments who are responsible for administration of the Indian Drugs and Cosmetics Act, 1940 and Drugs and Cosmetics Rules, 1945 to ensure compliance by all Ayurveda, Siddha and Unani (ASU) drug manufacturing units with the provisions of the Acts and Rules relating to display of all ingredients used in the preparations together with the quantity of each ingredients on the label of the medicine. All the State Ayurveda, Siddha, Unani and Unani Drug Licensing Authorities have also been instructed to take action against the defaulting ASU drug manufacturers for failure to comply with the Good Manufacturing Practices (GMP) notified under Schedule 'T' of the Drugs and Cosmetics Rules, 1945.
7. To address domestic as well as global concerns relating to presence of heavy metals in Ayurveda, Siddha and Unani formulations, the Department of AYUSH has initiated a research project under the Golden Triangle Project in collaboration with the Central Council for Research in Ayurveda and Siddha (CCRAS), Council of Scientific and Industrial Research (CSIR) and Indian Council of Medical Research (ICMR) for physicochemical characterization and safety study of eight most widely used Bhasmas (Herbo-metallic compounds) prepared in accordance with the classical texts. Results of these studies would be shared with the public at large. Secondly, Department

of AYUSH has introduced mandatory testing of heavy metals for Arsenic, Lead, Mercury and Cadmium in all purely herbal Ayurveda, Siddha and Unani drugs for export purposes w.e.f. 1st January 2006 to ensure that before these medicines are exported the manufacturers and exporters should take steps to ensure that these purely herbal medicines should not contain any heavy metal by way of contamination. Mandatory testing for heavy metals could also be introduced for domestic consumption in due course. A Gazette Notification amending the Drugs and Cosmetic Rules with respect to product registration numbers for the manufacture of patent or proprietary Ayurveda, Siddha or Unani drugs and for maintaining of records of raw material used by each licensed manufacturing unit of Ayurveda, Siddha and Unani drugs was issued on 18.10.06.

8. An exercise is also underway to provide financial assistance to ASU drug manufacturing units to acquire essential but costly quality control and R&D equipment in the 11th Five Year Plan by way of 50% subsidy subject to Rs. 50.00 lakh or 50% of the project cost whichever is less. The Department realizes that there is a need to set-up common facilities for AYUSH industry clusters in 15 to 20 major centres of production of ASU drugs.
9. With a view to ensuring sustained availability of quality raw material, National Medicinal Plants Board has been set-up by the Govt. of India, since November 2000 and State Medicinal Plants Board has been constituted in most of the States to coordinate the activities of cultivation and conservation of medicinal plants. So far more than 1.5 lakh acres of land has been brought under the *in-situ* conservation and *ex-situ* cultivation of medicinal plants. In the 11th Plan an ambitious Plan has been drawn up by the National Medicinal Plants Board for the provision of marketing and value-added services to the growers through State Medicinal Plant Boards and Herbal Mandis. A new promotional scheme for setting up herbal gardens in schools was also recently inaugurated.
10. The Department has been taking important steps for integrating AYUSH with the modern medicine. Mainstreaming of AYUSH is one of the core strategies envisaged under National Rural Health Mission with an objective to improve outreach and quality of health delivery in rural areas. This is meant to meet the unmet needs of health sector and to optimally utilize AYUSH infrastructure in health delivery. AYUSH systems being natural, holistic, comparatively safe, time-tested, accessible, affordable, culture-friendly and eco-friendly are more acceptable to the public and hence have been proposed to be mainstreamed with strategic interventions. In this regard the roadmap for mainstreaming of AYUSH was issued to the states seeking

placement of AYUSH services in primary health network with provisioning of AYUSH doctors (either by relocation or by contractual appointment) and medicines in PHCs and CHCs. AYUSH component is inbuilt in the training modules of Accredited Social Health Activists (ASHAs), for which orientation training in two rounds has been given to the master trainers from the States at National Institute of Health and Family Welfare, New Delhi. Officers from the Department of AYUSH were involved in the training as resource persons. AYUSH specific orientation about integration of health facilities, the Centrally Sponsored Scheme for promotion of AYUSH facilities in allopathic hospitals and the role of ASHAs in helping the community to access AYUSH services and provide simple AYUSH remedies was given to the State master trainers. AYUSH facilities in Sub-centres, PHCs, CHCs and District/Sub-divisional hospitals are proposed to be developed in accordance with the Indian Public Health Standards, for which necessary inputs from a Department of AYUSH have been forwarded. IPHS are being finalised in the Department of Health and FW for bringing uniformity *inter alia* in implementing mainstreaming of AYUSH strategy at the level of primary health care. One Ayurveda medicine—'Punarnavadi Mandoor' is included in the ASHA kit for the management of anemia and for pregnancy care. The approved implementation framework of NRHM provides for supporting need-based contractual appointment of AYUSH doctors/paramedics in proportion to the number of PHCs/CHCs of EAG states. During 2006-07 support from NRHM for contractual appointment of 1000 AYUSH doctors in such PHCs/CHCs of EAG states is intended, where relocation of AYUSH dispensaries is not possible.

11. Mainstreaming of AYUSH is being facilitated through a Centrally Sponsored Scheme of the Department of AYUSH by supporting States to set-up AYUSH facilities in allopathic hospitals. So far establishment of as many as 375 specialty clinics, 56 specialised therapy centres and 213 AYUSH wings in allopathic hospitals has been supported under this scheme. During the year 2005-06 proposals of 13469 dispensaries in different states were: approved with grants of Rs. 3372.60 lakhs for supply of essential drugs. With the approval from Empowered Programme Committee and Mission Steering Group of NRHM, it has been decided to establish AYUSH wings in Maternity and Children. Health Hospitals of Tamilnadu and Kerala and in the Guwahati Medical College Hospital. In order to ensure adequate implementation of mainstreaming of AYUSH strategy as envisaged under NRHM, the Department of AYUSH took up the matter in a meeting with State Health Secretaries and AYUSH Directors on 21 st July 2006. States were advised

to prepare action plans fo setting up AYUSH facilities in PHCs, CHCs and District hospitals; for training of ASHAs, ANMs and other health workers on AYUSH health concepts and remedies; and for utilisation of AYUSH practitioners in the National Health and Family Welfare Programmes.

12. The Department is also aware that bio-piracy of codified traditional knowledge of India has been quite prevalent at international level. Thus the second phase of Department's Traditional Knowledge Digital Library (TKDL) project has commenced with work on database for Unani, Yoga and Siddha along with more formulations from Ayurvedic texts. In its meeting held on 29th June 2006, the Cabinet accorded approval to make the Traditional Knowledge Digital Library (TKDL) database available to the International Patents Offices as per the desired aim of the project.

13. The Department has also been striving hard for promotion and propagation of Indian Systems of Medicine within the country and abroad. With a view to creating awareness among the public about the efficacy and efficiency of the AYUSH systems of medicine, their cost effectiveness and the availability of the herbs used for prevention and treatment of common ailments, messages are spread through various media channels and organisation of fairs and expos. Non-Governmental Organisations have also been associated to promote the strengths of AYUSH systems. The Department of AYUSH has been organizing Arogya exhibitions at New Delhi and other places and participating in Health Melas at district level with a view to creating awareness regarding the strengths of AYUSH systems. The sixth annual AROGYA was organized at New Delhi in October 2006. Regional Arogyas were organized at Chennai (February 2006) and Hyderabad (November 2005). The Department of AYUSH participated in the Guest of Honour Presentations, aimed at projecting the multi-faceted development of the country, at the Frankfurt Book Fair in October 2006. The display by the Department included presentations on Ayurveda and Yoga. As per the approved scheme, AYUSH industry was provided incentives for participation in national and international trade fairs/exhibitions to improve the visibility of AYUSH products.

14. The Department of AYUSH has been sending experts to participate in various international meetings and a number of delegations have visited the Department of AYUSH for exploring cooperation in the field of traditional system. As already mentioned, the first International Conclave on Traditional Medicine was organized on 16th-17th November 2006 in New Delhi and it has come up with important recommendations for Traditional Medicine at the global level.

15. Keeping in view the experience of implementation of various Central Sector and Centrally Sponsored Schemes, the Department of AYUSH has formulated an ambitious proposal for the 11th Five Year Plan in which following new initiatives have been proposed:
    1. Development of common facilities for AYUSH Industry Clusters for upgradation of small and medium size ASU&H manufacturing units.
    2. Substantial increase in financial assistance provided to ASU&H manufacturing units for training of its manpower and acquiring quality control and R&D equipment by way of 50% subsidy subject to a maximum of Rs. 50 lakh.
    3. Scheme for Development of Centres of Excellence in AYUSH education.
    4. Assistance to NGOs for revitalization of local health traditions/midwifery and birth attendant practices, etc. Assistance to AYUS Centres of Excellence in public and private sector engaged in AYUSH education/drug standardization and development/clinical trials, etc.
    5. Re-structuring and revamping of National Medicinal Plants Board and providing marketing/value-added services to medicinal plants farmers through State Medicinal Plants Boards/State Minor Forest Produce Corporations and Herbal Mandis.

    All the above initiatives are designed to build upon the achievements of the Department of AYUSH in the 9th and 10th Five Year Plans and to create all round capacities in AYUSH sector for bringing AYUSH systems center stage in National Health Care System as well as for globalization of AYUSH systems and capturing a fair share of global herbal market.
16. The Department of AYUSH is an equal opportunity employer and has a significant representation of women at all levels in the Department and its autonomous bodies. The Right to Information Act, 2005 has been implemented in the Department and requisite information on all manuals as required under Section 4(1)(b) of the Act has been displayed at the web site of the Department (http://www.indianmedicine.nic.in).

SECRETARY
Department of Ayurveda, Yoga and Naturopathy,
Unani, Siddha and Homeopathy (AYUSH)
Government of India, New Delhi

Appendix 5.2

Central Council of Indian Medicine

The Central Council of Indian Medicine is a Statutory Body constituted/established under the Indian Medicine Central Council Act, 1970 vide Government of India Gazettee Notification Extraordinary Part II Section 3 (ii) dated 10.8.1971. The main objectives of the Central Council are as under:

1. To prescribe Minimum Standards of Education in Indian Medicine viz. Ayurveda, Siddha and Unani Tibb.
2. To advise Central Government in matters relating to 'inclusion' (Recognition) and 'withdrawal' (De-recognition) of medical qualifications in Second Schedule to the Indian Medicine Central Council Act, 1970.
3. To maintain the Central Registrar of Indian Medicine and revise the Register from time to time.
4. To prescribe Standards of Professional Conduct, Etiquette and Code to Ethics to be observed by the practitioners.

Source: Ministry of Health and Family Welfare, GOI, Annual Report, 2006-07.

APPENDIX 5.3

CENTRAL COUNCIL OF HOMEOPATHY (CCH)

The Central Council of Homeopathy is a statutory body constituted by the Government of India under the provisions of Homeopathy Central Council Act, 1973. Its main objectives are: (a) the regulation of Homeopathy medical education, (b) the maintenance of a Central Register of Homoeopathic Practitioners in the country, and (c) prescribing standards of professional conduct, etiquette and a code of ethics for the practitioners of Homeopathy.

The Central Council is constituted of elected members from the State Boards/Councils of Homeopathy and from the University Faculties/ Departments of Homeopathy and of members nominated by the Central Government. The Council functions through various Committees like the Executive Committee, Finance Committee, PG committee, etc. The General Body of the Council is the supreme decision-making body.

The Homeopathy Central Council Act, 1973 was amended in 2002 and the power to grant permission for starting new colleges, introducing new or higher courses of study and increasing the number of seats in a College is now vested with the Central Government. There are 184 undergraduate Homeopathy colleges in the Country offering a five and half year Bachelor of Homoeopathic Medicine and Surgery (B.H.M.S). degree course. The PG course is of three years duration leading to the award of M.D. (Hom.). There are 30 colleges which offer Post-Graduate courses in the country. There are also two colleges that exclusively offer PG courses.

The Central Council of Homeopathy is supported by the Central Government through annual budget grants. During the year 2006-7 the CCH was provided with Rs. 70.00 lakhs under Non-Plan and Rs. 10.00 lakhs under Plan under Budget Estimates.

The HCC Act, 1973 has been amended in 2002 for making it mandatory for prior permission of the Central Government for establishing new colleges; starting new and higher courses and increasing admission capacity in colleges of Homeopathy systems of medicine. It also provides for ensuring conformity of standards in existing colleges within three years. Necessary resolutions for the purpose under Section 12-A of HCC (Amendment) Act, 2002 have been approved by competent authorities. These provisions aim to improve the education standards of Homeopathy in existing colleges as well as curb the unwanted growth of sub-standard colleges. HCC (Amendment) Act, 2005 has been introduced in the Parliament with a view to bring about transparency in the functioning of these councils as a part of the Department's priority to improve standards of graduate and post-graduate education in Ayurveda, Siddha, Unani and Homoeopahty.

Ministry of Health and Family Planning at State Level

HEALTH ADMINISTRATION AT THE STATE LEVEL

Health, according to the Constitution of India, is a State subject. The main responsibility for providing health services to all people lies with the State Health Department with the assistance of local health organisations wherever these exist, e.g., Corporations, Municipalities, Panchayati Raj, *ad hoc* statutory bodies like the Mines Board of Health, Employees' State Insurance Corporation and so on.

The Executive machinery of the government at the State level is headed by the Governor. Article 163 of the Constitution provides for a Council of Ministers with the Chief Minister as its head to aid and advise the Governor. The business of the government of the State (viz. law and order administration, the developmental functions like general administration, local government, public works, irrigation, health, education, cooperation, etc.) is allocated by the Governor amongst the Ministers in accordance with the provisions contained in Article 166(3) of the Constitution.

We shall now discuss the organisation of State Health Department in one State of the Indian Union, i.e. Punjab.

ORGANISATION OF STATE HEALTH DEPARTMENT

(a) Political Head

In the State of Punjab, a Minister of a Cabinet rank is the political head of the Health Department. He/she has to bear a heavy responsibility for formulating policies and monitoring the implementation of these policies and programmes.

The Health Minister has to perform both types of activities, viz., political as well as administrative. These can be broadly discussed as follows:

(i) As a member of the State Legislature, it is his duty to support and safeguard the total policies of the Government because of the collective responsibility of the cabinet.
(ii) As a member of the Ministry, he brings all the bills pertaining to his Department for the approval of the legislature.
(iii) As political head of the Health Department, he acts as an executive and administrator. He has to see that the policies approved by the legislature are faithfully implemented.
(iv) He is the custodian of the interests of the people in general and of his constituency in particular.
(v) As a member of the Government, he performs ceremonial duties.

As far as the administrative functions of the Minister are concerned, we find that for a number of reasons these activities to not receive the time and attention they deserve. Being busy with political activities, the Minister does not find enough time for administrative works. Lack of professional knowledge and lack of aptitude are the other contributory factors.

It was also pointed out by the Administrative Reforms Commission that there was a growing feeling among the public that most of the ministries lacked interest in efficient discharge of their administrative duties and did not possess the aptitude required for the purpose. The Administrative Reforms Commission in its report on State Administration recommended that, "the head of Council of Ministers (the Chief Minister) should, in selecting his colleagues, give special attention to considerations of political stature, personal integrity, intellectual ability and capacity for taking decisions and sustained application to work. Further, in assigning a portfolio, due regard should be paid to the aptitude and capacities of an incumbent.[1] The suggestion of A.R.C. must be accepted by the Chief Ministers to bring about innovations in political leadership.

(b) Administrative Head

In order to keep a record of the policies framed by the political heads and to watch over their implementation and execution, the State administration has to take the help of an office, which is known as the state secretariat. The word 'Secretariat' refers to the complex of departments, which vary from State to State.

Secretary Health and Family Welfare (SHFW)

SHFW is the overall in-charge of the department. By virtue of his posting, he is also Vice-Chairman of the Punjab Health Systems Corporation, Chairman of Punjab AIDS Control Society, Chairman SCOVA (RCH Society), TB Society and Leprosy Society. SH-*cum*-MD-PHSC is assisting the SHandFW in connection with the administrative issues concerning to the PCMS doctors, which include Recruitment, Posting, Transfers, Disciplinary Actions, Service Rules, etc. In addition to this, he has also been designed as Head of Department (HOD) of Government Mental Hospital, Amritsar. He is assisted by Superintendents of Health-I and II Branches of the Department.

Special Secretary Health (SSH)-cum-PD-PSACS

SSH is assisting SH&FW in connection with all other administrative issues concerning to the Department, i.e. Policy Issues, Coordination, Planning, Budget Estimates (Plan and Non-Plan), Issuance of Budget Sanctions, Opening of New Institutions and Upgradation, Food and Drug Issues, Disease Control, Immunization and Family Welfare Programmes, Administrative Issues of paramedics. All the issues of PHSC, Family Welfare, ESI, Homeopathic, Ayurveda Department, etc.

Under Secretary Health

The assists SSH in finalization of the issues allocated to him. USH is supported by Superintendent of Health.

Punjab Aids Control Society

In order to strengthen the National AIDS Control Programme Management, the State Government established in 1998 their own managerial organisation, i.e. Punjab State AIDS Control Society (formerly, State AIDS Cell), which constitute Technical Advisory Committee and Empowered Committee as per the guidelines of the National Aids Control Organisation (NACO). The Chairman of the society is SH&FW who is supported by Special Secretary Health-*cum*-Project Director AIDS. Assistant Project Director (APD) provides technical support to PD. ADP is supported different Assistant Directors who look after various AIDS-related programmes in the State.[2]

Administration at the top level in India is manned mostly by generalist services recruited through All India Competitive examinations. These so-called generalists are engaged in running all activities of the Machinery of Government at the Union and State levels. It is opined that their inherent intelligence coupled with their experience at all levels and in many sectors of Government make them fit for top level policy positions and experts in handling any assignment entrusted to them. In spite of the changed role of the Government as enshrined in the preamble and the Directive Principles of State Policy of the Indian Constitution, the administrative machinery of the Government has remained unchanged.

Generalists move frequently from one department to the other, which makes them jacks of all trades but master of none. In some cases, the transfers of Generalists are very frequent, resulting in lower quality of output from these departments. Even the Second Pay Commission, as early as 1959 had observed in its report:

> "Where the work of a department is mainly technical it is desirable, in our view, that the Secretary should be a person who, while possessing administrative ability and capable of taking a broad government wide view of matters, has a technical background in the particular field."

The controversy between the generalists and specialists is harmful to the smooth functioning of the Government. Both are essential to man the apparatus of the Government. The Fulton Committee has rightly said, "our aim is not to replace specialists by administrators or *vice-versa*. They should be complementary to one another."[3] The need is to remove this growing gap and utilize the potential in them for accelerating the tempo of development.

Parity of Status

Both generalists may function at places best suited to their caliber and requirements but should be given parity of status. Kuldip Nayar has supported this idea with examples from other countries. Dr. Rajendra Prasad, the first President of India, speaking on this issue observed as early as in 1956, "I see no reason why technical personnel and technical services should not be given the same emoluments and advantages as the treated at par with administrative personnel and services and should be country's administrative service. I am sure, sooner or later, it is bound to happen..."[4] Third Pay Commission in 1973 was constrained to make the following observation in their Report, which however was not backed by their final recommendation:

> "We have given a good deal of thought to the demand for parity with the Indian Administrative Service. The aptness and relevance of the basic premise which has been advanced in support of this demand has to be readily conceded...We have come to the conclusion that, consistent with the important role assigned to the Engineering Services, they should not suffer either from a sense of deprivation in emoluments or in the estimation of the value that Government puts to their services."

U.K. has already given up the old system and has adopted a new set-up, which gave specialists, parity with the generalists. In France, both the generalists and the specialists are given in-service training. Hence, after recruitment both stand on the same footing. The USA does not have a senior corps of qualified generalists. In the erstwhile Soviet Union the scientists and experts had a position superior to that of generalists. In Australia, the Specialist is given higher grade than generalists.[5]

The ARC Report has rightly concluded, "The Generalist has his place, and an important one at that, in the scheme of things, so has the specialist, the scientist and the technologist. In a growing democracy committed to rapid socio-economic development, the administration has to be good, no less than it has to be effective. This twin purpose needs the devoted services of the specialists no less than those of Generalists. Preference for the Generalist should give place to a preference for those who have acquired competence in the concerned field."[6]

The main duties and responsibilities of the health department are as under:

(i) Assisting the Minister in policy-making, in modifying policies from time to time and in the discharge of his legislative responsibilities;
(ii) Framing draft legislation and rules and regulations;
(iii) Coordination of policies and programmes, supervision and control over their execution and review of results;
(iv) Budgeting and control of expenditure;
(v) Maintaining contact with the Government of India and other State Governments; and
(vi) Overseeing the smooth and efficient running of administrative machinery and initiating measures designed to develop greater personnel and organisational competence.[7]

(c) Technical Head

Below the State Secretariat, there are Executive Departments. These departments are headed mostly by the specialists and are concerned with the supervision, coordination and control of the policy framed by the State Government. Based on our personal observation and discussion, it was revealed that notwithstanding the apparently clear demarcation of functions as between the secretariat and the Executive Department a lot of duplication and overlapping still persists between the Secretariat (Health Department) and the Executive Department. This results in too much interference in the day-to-day functioning of the Executive Department. As a matter of policy the Secretariat should restrict its activities only to policy-making.

Director of Health Services

There are Four Directorates for different services. These four Health Directorates provide technical knowledge to the Secretary and the Minister. They also coordinate, supervise and control the implementation of health programmes and projects. The success of failure of the health department depends upon the leadership of the Directors of various systems of medicine.

A part from allopathy, the Indian System of medicines, namely, Ayurveda, Homeopathy and Unani systems are also now beginning to receive proper attention. Their functioning is being regulated by the Director Ayurveda, Punjab. This Directorate constitutes a separate organisation and deals with all the three indigenous systems of medicines.

1. Directorate of Medical Education

Recently, there has been separate Directorates of Medical Education and Family Welfare. The area of medical education which was integrated with the Directorate of Health Services at the state, has once again shown a tendency of maintaining a separate identity as Directorate of Medical Education, who is answerable directly to the Health Secretary/ Commissioner of the state. Directorates of Medical Education and Research are found in the States of Jammu and Kashmir, Punjab, Haryana, Maharashtra, Karnataka and others.

2. Directorate of Employee State Insurance

The Directorate of ESI is headed by Director Health Services (DSI). The Department has been divided into 5 zones, i.e. Amritsar, Jalandhar, Ludhiana, Mohali and Rajpura. The first two zones are headed by Medical Superintendent of each ESI Hospital, Ludhiana Zone by separate Sr. Medical and other two are headed by incharge ESI Hospital, Ludhiana, Mohali and Rajpura. These MS/SMO/In-charge are supervising the activities of 68 ESI dispensaries.

3. Directorate of Ayurveda

The Directorate of Ayurveda is headed by Director Ayurveda (DAY) who is assisted by two officers of District Ayurvedic and Unani Officer (D.A.U.O.) rank. The district level establishment of the department is headed by a D.A.U.O. in each district except newly carved districts of Nawan Shahr, Moga and Muktsar. The DAY is also entrusted with the duties/ functions of Licensing Authority for the state of Punjab. Licensing Authority is assisted by Drug Inspectors the functions of which are being performed by D.A.U.O. in the State to control and regulate about 562 Drug Manufacturing Ayurvedic pharmacies in the public sector in the State.

Department of Homeopathy

The State Government established a separate Homeopathy Department in the year 1980 (May 1980). Earlier it was under the Ayurveda Department. The Government at that time declared an IAS officer Joint Secretary Health as Head of Homeopathy Department, Punjab and to assist him on Technical Side Assistant Director Homeopathy was appointed. Presently, the charge of the HoD of Homeopathy Department is with DAY. There are 14 In-charge district level dispensaries, which coordinate the working of the department at district level.[8]

4. Department of Health and Family Welfare

Department of Health and Family Welfare is providing preventive, promotive and curative health care services in the State through a good network of Public Sector Medical Institutions.

CHART 6.1

Organisation of Department of Health and Family Welfare

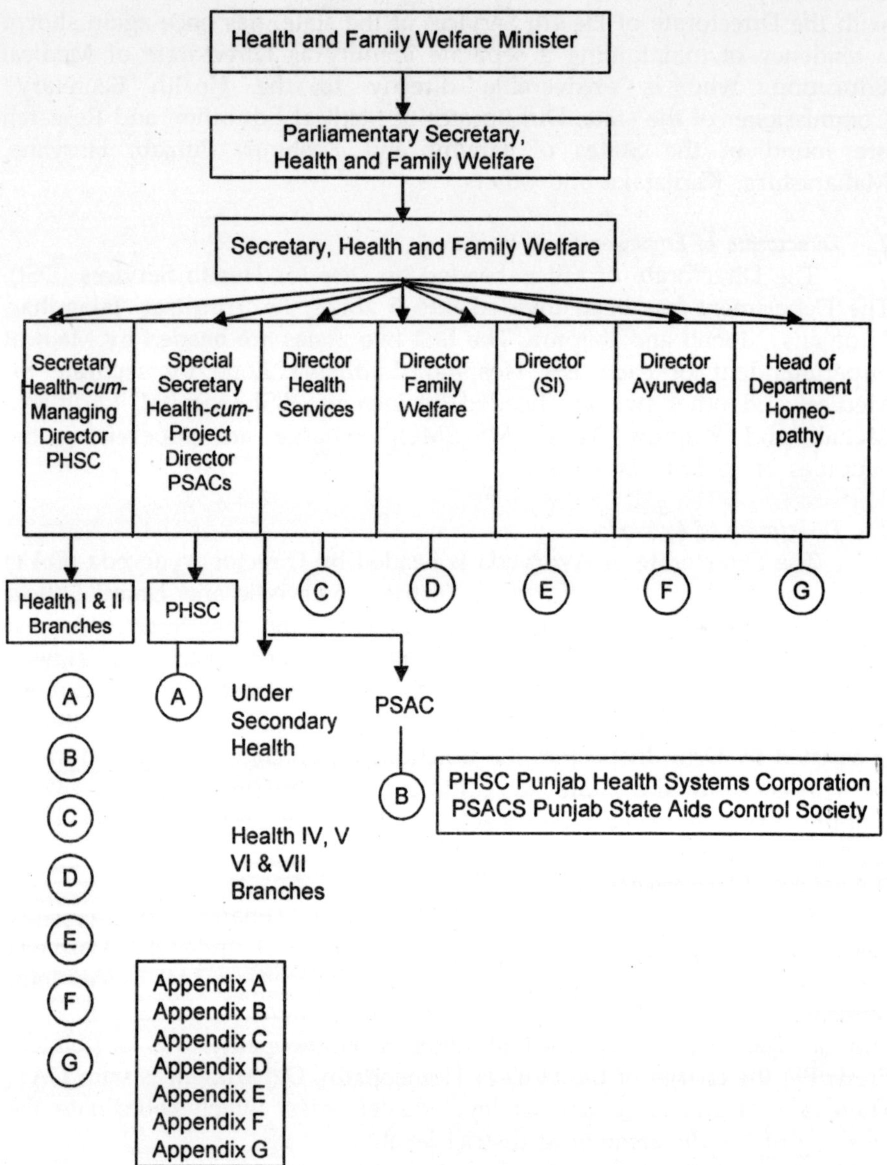

Primary Level Preventive and Curative Care

There are 2858 Sub-Centres (each for population of 5000 manned by one Male and one Female Health Worker). This is the first contact point with the masses. Manpower deployed there support in implementation of (i) Universal Immunization Programme (DPT, Polio, BCG, Measles and TT

Chart 6.2

Punjab Health System Corporation

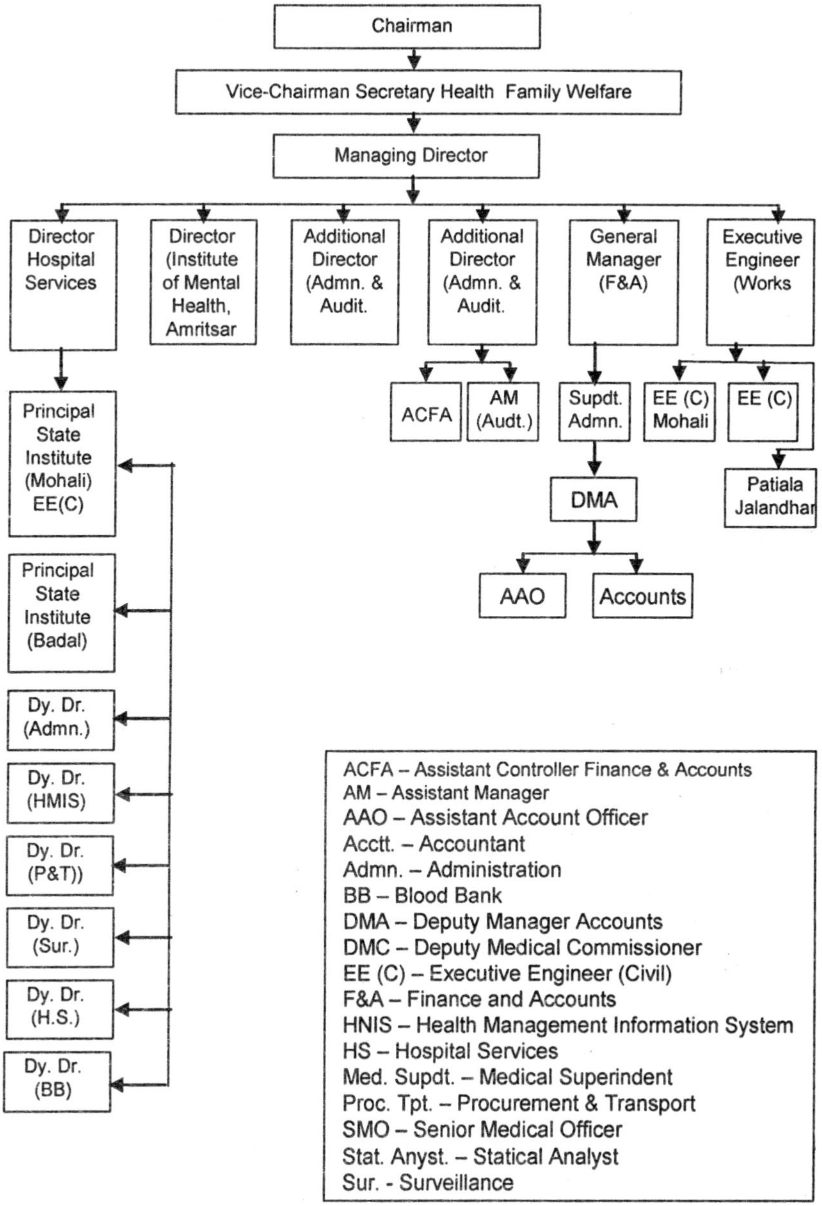

Chairman

Vice-Chairman Secretary Health Family Welfare

Managing Director

Director Hospital Services

Director (Institute of Mental Health, Amritsar

Additional Director (Admn. & Audit.

Additional Director (Admn. & Audit.

General Manager (F&A)

Executive Engineer (Works

Principal State Institute (Mohali) EE(C)

Principal State Institute (Badal)

Dy. Dr. (Admn.)

Dy. Dr. (HMIS)

Dy. Dr. (P&T))

Dy. Dr. (Sur.)

Dy. Dr. (H.S.)

Dy. Dr. (BB)

ACFA

AM (Audt.)

Supdt. Admn.

EE (C) Mohali

EE (C)

Patiala Jalandhar

DMA

AAO

Accounts

ACFA – Assistant Controller Finance & Accounts
AM – Assistant Manager
AAO – Assistant Account Officer
Acctt. – Accountant
Admn. – Administration
BB – Blood Bank
DMA – Deputy Manager Accounts
DMC – Deputy Medical Commissioner
EE (C) – Executive Engineer (Civil)
F&A – Finance and Accounts
HNIS – Health Management Information System
HS – Hospital Services
Med. Supdt. – Medical Superindent
Proc. Tpt. – Procurement & Transport
SMO – Senior Medical Officer
Stat. Anyst. – Statical Analyst
Sur. - Surveillance

for pregnant mothers). (ii) Maternal and Child Health Planning; (iii) Counselling/motivation. (iv) Management of diarrhea especially in infants. (v) Health Education: educating the community about the various available services. (vi) Control of Acute Respiratory Infection especially in infants. (vii) Identify the women requiring help for medical termination of

CHART 6.3

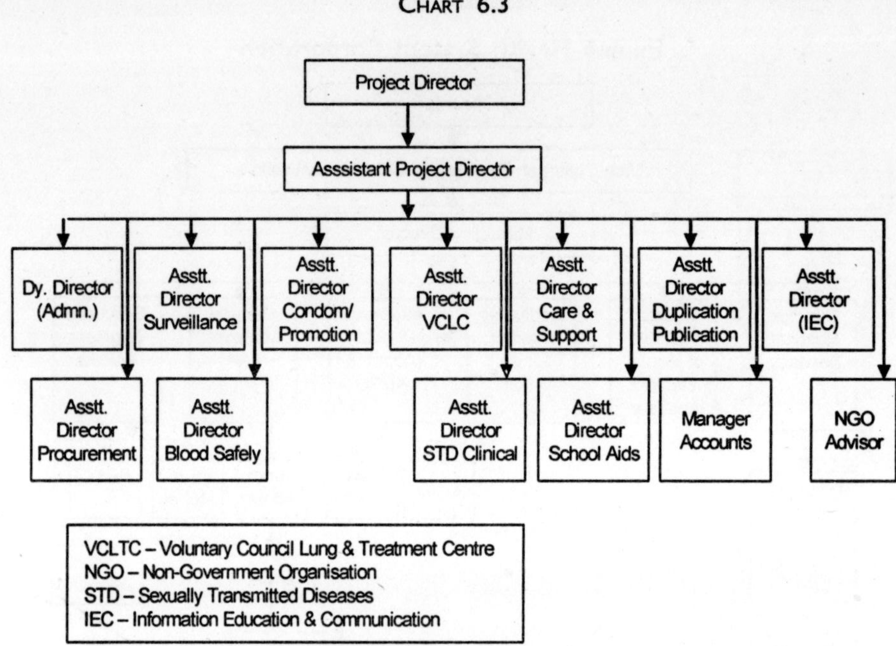

pregnancy and refer them to nearest approved institution. (viii) Health Survey.

There are 1200 Subsidiary Health Centres for the population of 10,000 having staff, i.e. one Medical Officer, one Pharmacist, one Sewadar, and one Sweeper. Through these institutions, all the above programmes along with curative health care (OPD) is being rendered.

There are 484 Primary Health Centres for every 30,000 population having staff of one Medical Officer, one Pharmacist, one Staff Nurse, one Lab Technician, one Sewadar, and one Sweeper. 4-bedded institutions providing curative and preventive health care.

There are 126 Community Health Centres for every 1,00,000 population having 4 specialists, two Pharmacists, one Block Extension Educator Officer, one Senior Malaria Inspector, Seven Staff Nurses, One Lady Health Visitor, and other Para-medics and supporting staff. 25/30 bedded CHC providing promotive, preventive and curative health care.

State Level Curative Care

Under secondary level health care services, all type of curative treatment for various diseases is provided. All types of surgeries and other interventions are being carried apart from by-pass and transplantations, which are being carried in the tertiary level institutions (Medical Colleges). In these institutions, all the preventive healthcare services and other disease control programme are being taken care of. Presently, there are 164 secondary level hospitals in the State as per following details:

CHART 6.4

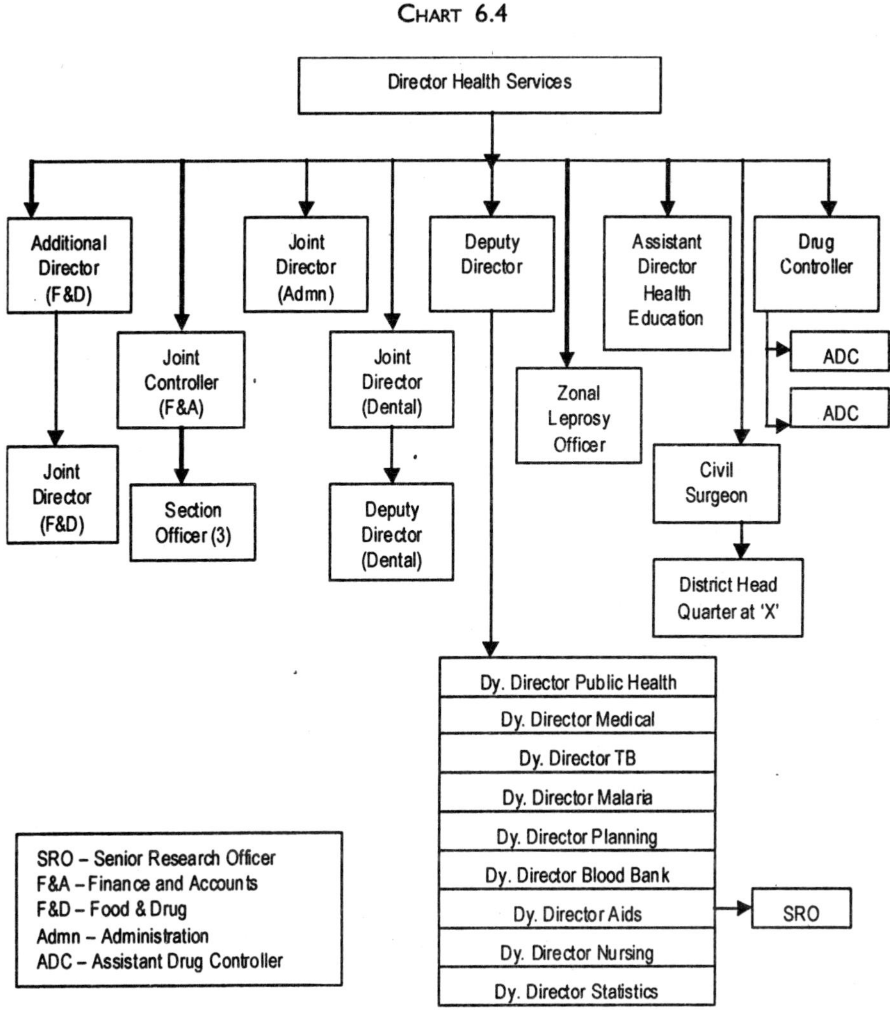

There are 16 District Hospital having bed range 50-400 beds. These hospitals are situated in all the districts except Patiala.

There are 2 Special Hospital, i.e. Special Gyane Hospital Mata Kaushyla Hospital at Patiala having 200-beds and Special Children Hospital at Bathinda having 100-beds.

There is one Special Mental Hospital at Amritsar having 400-beds, which has been reconstructed recently and is functioning under the name and style of "Institution of Mental Health", Amritsar.

39-Sub-Divisional Hospitals are there having bed range of 50-60 beds.

Out of 126 above mentioned CHCs, 107 CHCs are managed by the Punjab Health Systems Corporation, (98 CHCs have been recently revamped under World Bank project along with all District, Special and Sub-Divisional Hospitals). In these CHCs, apart from preventive healthcare services mentioned above, curative health services are being provided.

CHART 6.5

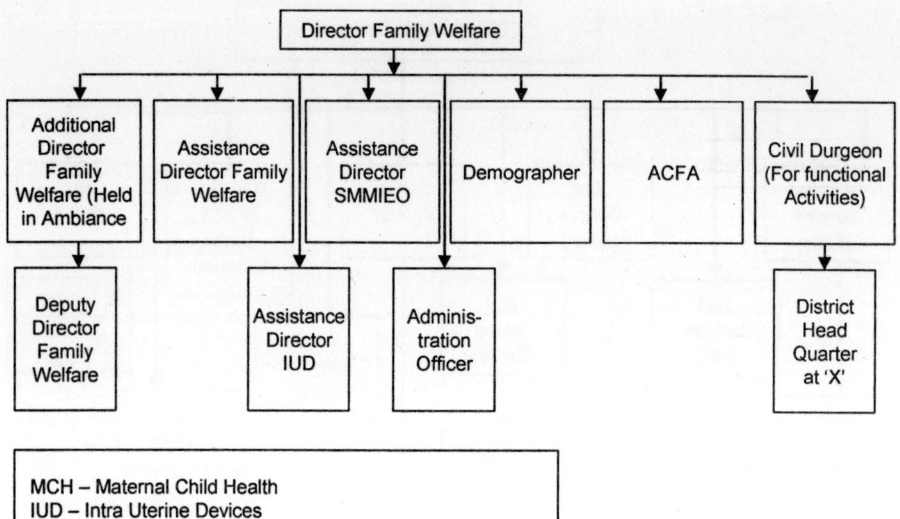

MCH – Maternal Child Health
IUD – Intra Uterine Devices
SMMIEO – State Mass Media Information & Education Officer
ACFA – Assistant Controller Finance & Accounts

Teaching and Training Institutions

There is one state level Regional State Institute of Health and Family Welfare Training Centre at Mohali. There are 17 district level Training Centres. In the State level institution, apart from the monitoring the district level training centers, in-service training relating to various disease control programmes, RCH, TB, MCH and other management trainings are being given. Statutory trainings are also being given in the S.I.H.F.W., Mohali to the students of private schools of MPHW (M).

There is one State Institute of Nursing and Paramedical Sciences, Badal for the women. 3 Multipurpose Health Worker (Male) Schools at Nabha, Khanna and Amritsar and 6 Multipurpose Health Worker (Female) Schools at Gurdaspur, Bathinda, Nangal, Moga, Hoshiarpur and Sangrur. In these institutions, mainly Diplomas are being awarded.

Drug and Food Laboratories

There are two Food Laboratories at Bathinda and Jalandhar, one Food and Drug Laboratory at Chandigarh and one Chemical Examination Laboratory at Patiala. In Drug and Food Laboratories drawn samples are being tested and in Chemical Examination Laboratory Patiala pathological medico-legal examination analysis are being done.

Indian System of Medicine (ISM)

The main function of this Department is to provide medical services through Ayurveda, Yoga and Unani system of medicine. This department extends these services through a network of 5 hospitals, 17 Swasth Kendras

CHART 6.6

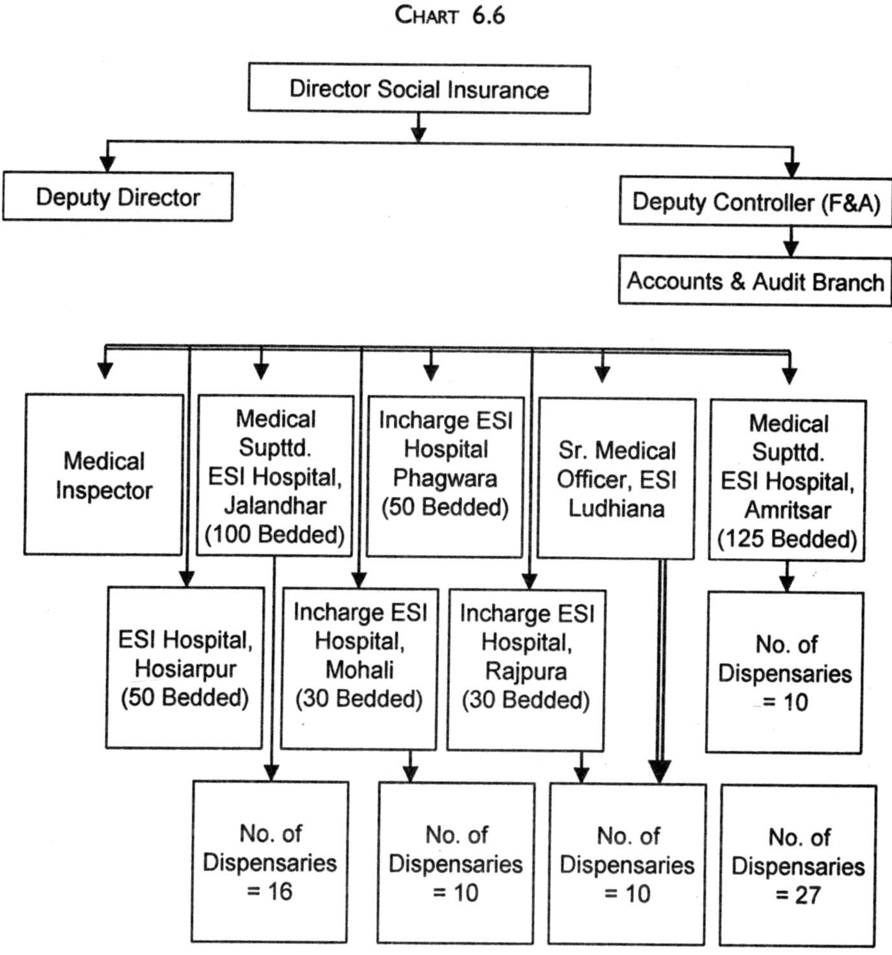

(One 100-Bedded ESI Hospital has been taken over by ESI Corp. w.e.f. 1.10.2002).
SI – Social Insurance (ESI).

and 472 Ayurvedic and 35 Unani dispensaries in the State. To encourage cultivation of the quality raw drugs, their conservation and optimum utilization by Drug Industries and also to encourage the farming community to adopt diversification of crops, the State Medical Plant Board constituted in the State under Health Department.

Homeopathic

Under this system, at present there are 107 Homeopathy Dispensaries functioning in the State, which provide curative care in the rural and urban areas.

Medical Services Under Employees State Insurance (SI)

Under the Government of India/Employees State Insurance Corporation sponsored programmes to provide medical facilities to

CHART 6.7

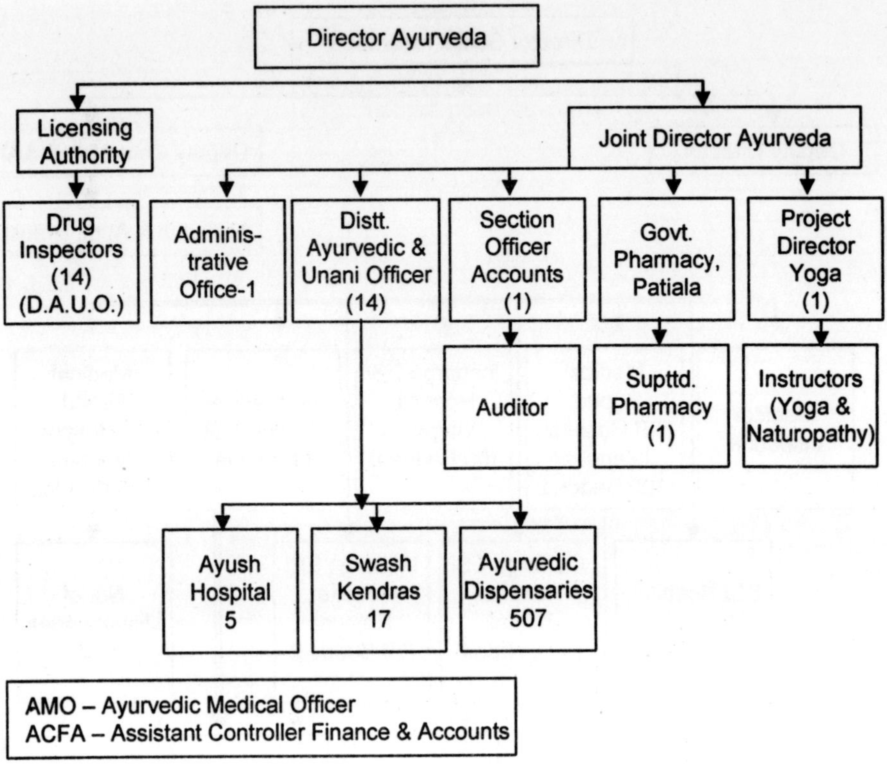

Director Ayurveda
Licensing Authority
Joint Director Ayurveda
Drug Inspectors (14) (D.A.U.O.)
Adminis-trative Office-1
Distt. Ayurvedic & Unani Officer (14)
Section Officer Accounts (1)
Govt. Pharmacy, Patiala
Project Director Yoga (1)
Auditor
Supttd. Pharmacy (1)
Instructors (Yoga & Naturopathy)
Ayush Hospital 5
Swash Kendras 17
Ayurvedic Dispensaries 507
AMO – Ayurvedic Medical Officer
ACFA – Assistant Controller Finance & Accounts

CHART 6.8

Head of Department Homeopathy
Assistant Director
In-Charge District Level Homeopathic Dispensaries
Assistant Controller (Finance & Accounts)
Homeopathic Medical Officer
Accounts Assistance
Supporting Staff
Senior Assistant & Supporting Staff

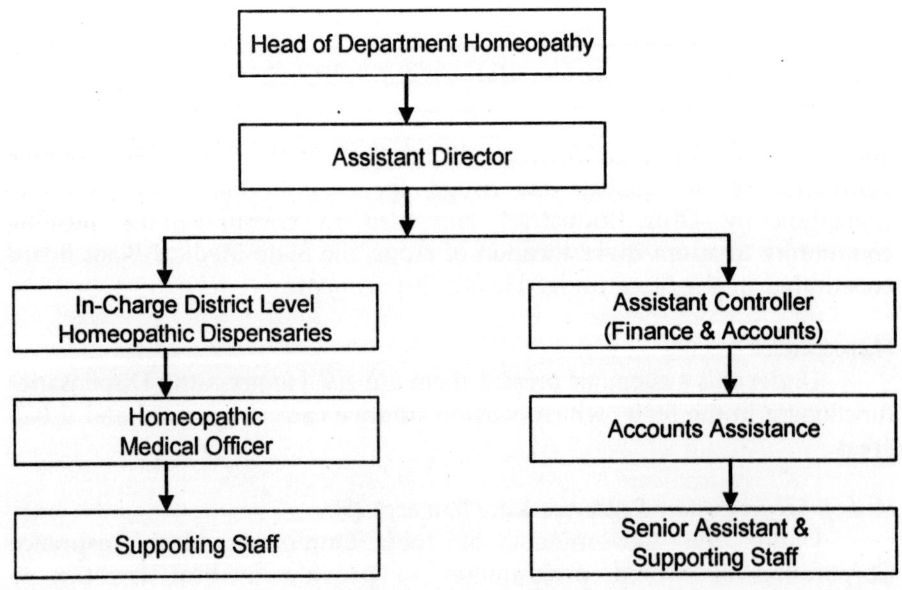

CHART 6.9

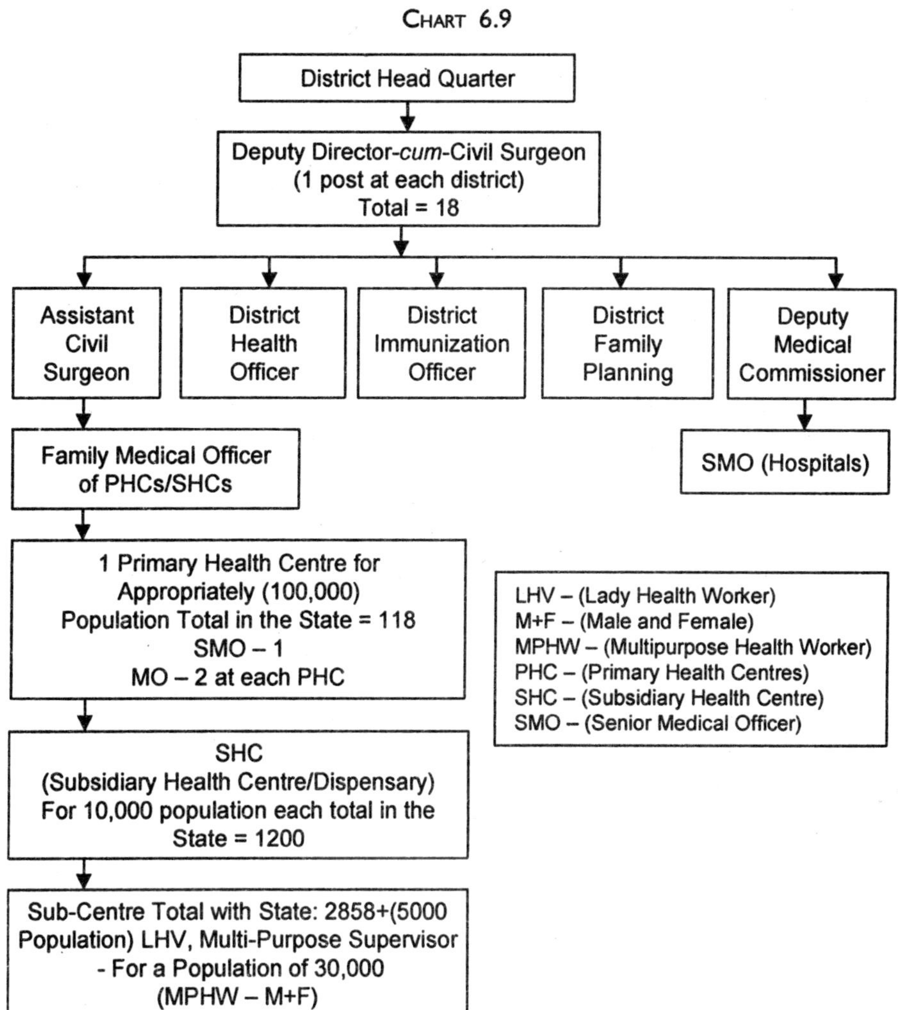

industrial and other workers (Insured Persons IP), there are six ESI hospitals, 68 ESI dispensaries, one TB center (Amritsar). In these institutions, preventive and curative healthcare services are being provided to workers covered under this scheme.[9]

The department is rendering the following services through its network of Medical and Health Institutions in the State. In brief the functions of Health and Family Department at State Level are:

1. Common Minimum need Programme;
2. Curative Services;
3. Reproductive Child Health Programme;
4. Prevention and control of communicable diseases, National Leprosy Control Programme, National Aids Control Programme,

National Tuberculosis Control Programme, National Guinea Worm Eradication Programme, National programme for control of blindness, etc.;

5. National Vector Borne Disease Control Programme including National Anti Malaria Programme, National Filaria Control Programme, Anti-JE Programme and Dengue Control Programme;
6. Laboratory services;
7. Implementation of Food Adulteration;
8. Environmental sanitation;
9. Vital Statistics;
10. Nutritional Services;
11. Health Education and School Health Services;
12. Training Programme;
13. Primary Health Care through CHC, PHC, SC, TBA; and
14. Reproductive and Child Health.[10]

CRITICAL APPRAISAL OF WORKING OF THE HEALTH AMINISTRATION AT THE STATE LEVEL

We have already examined the organisation and functions of the Karnataka State Health Department. From the quantitative analysis, it becomes quite clear that the department is doing well. On qualitative examination, it appears that the progress is superficial, unplanned and not directed to the needs of the clients. We give here some facts and suggestions, which can help in the improvement of the organisation and functions of the health administration at the State Level.

I. Imbalance between the Rural and Urban Areas

There has been an imbalance in the availability of medical facilities and health manpower in rural area. Rural people have become conscious of their rights. They demand and deserve good quality health services. Even the Government itself is critical of this situation. It was stated officially, "It is an unfortunate fact that thirty years of health services development resulted in concentration of 80 per cent of medical manpower and facilities in urban areas where just 24 per cent of the total population resides. Paradoxically enough, Punjab's rural areas where 76 per cent of the State's total population lives, were getting just 20 per cent institutional health services. Even 80 per cent of the total health budget was being spent on urban hospitals, etc. So the challenge of providing primary health care services to the ruralites was quite sizable in magnitude."[11]

What is being done to ensure health care to the rural people? The State governments are diverting more funds to develop infrastructure for providing health care to the rural people especially during the last five years. The basic question is how to ensure whether the rural people are being benefited or not. It is a common ill of Indian Administration that the people are not getting benefits because of the apathy of the personnel associated with the programmes. It is high time that we must ensure the fruitful working of our health schemes benefiting the villagers. Otherwise there is a likelihood of this imbalance increasing further. Health programmes could no more look mere political lollipops. These ought to be structured and designed in a fashion that meets the needs of the people. In the next century, we have to improve the health care for the rural people otherwise there can be violence.

2. Status and Role of the Director of Health Services

In the execution of health policy, programmes and activities, persons who have an exceedingly important role to play are the Directors of Health Services. Thus, a great deal depends on their competence, method of approach and managerial ability. If they have the right kind of leadership qualities, there is no reason why they should not succeed in the implementation of programmes under their control. If one has to identify factors affecting the role or performance of a Director of Health Services at the State level, one cannot possibly miss the most important factor related to his relative inferior position as compared to the prestigious position of the Secretary of Health Services. The Secretary/Deputy Secretary/Under-Secretary of Health Services as a rule is a senior member of the Indian Administrative Services. The Director is generally the senior most member belonging to the State Medical Service Cadre. The issues, which involve them in conflicts range from decision-making regarding health programmes to their actual implementation in the field. The Director often feels that by virtue of his professional knowledge and competence, his judgment is better than the judgment of his administrative counterpart. The domination of technocrats by the administrators in their day-to-day work has been debated in many national forums. The scientists feel that if they are given the freedom to decide, they can take much more interest and take rational decisions. The Administrative Reforms Commission (1666-70) pointed out: "An effort is needed to match jobs with the men possessing the needed qualifications, which means that the preference for the generalist, pure and simple should give place to a preference for those who have acquired competence in the concerned field."[12]

The Fulton Committee which was set-up in Great Britain in 1966 and which submitted its report in 1968 similarly said, "Many scientists, engineers and members of other specialist classes get neither the full responsibilities and corresponding authority, nor the opportunities they ought to have. Too often: they are organized in a separate hierarchy while the policy and financial aspects of the work are reserved for a parallel group of generalist administrators, and their access to higher management and policy-making is restricted. In the New Civil Service a wider and more important role must be opened up for specialists trained and equipped for it."[13]

Mr. P. Lal in his article, "Saying bye-bye to bureaucracy" in the Sunday *Tribune* rightly sensed the role of specialists in 21st century. To quote him: The bureaucratic system worked well when organisations were static, challenges small, expectations low, knowledge limited and information confined to local areas. Turnover of her individual's relations with people, institutions and ideas was also quite manageable. However, with the advent of the age of information technology some three decades back when computers came of age, knowledge burst upon the planet globally. What happens in one corner of the world now becomes known instantly in another. Internet has provided access to the common man, to information earlier available to specialists and professionals. High-speed decisions are required to be taken by men and organisations.

As the governance and management functions require more and more of inputs from specialists, systems analysts, computer programmers, engineering specialists, operation researchers—the importance of the latter increases and their advice and opinion cannot be brushed aside by the top management. Thus, they acquire a new decision-making function.

Says Professor William H. Read of the Graduate School of Business at McGill University, USA, "More and more of specialists do not fit neatly together into a chain-of-command system and can not wait for their expert advice to be approved at a higher level." They assume the role of decision-maker, they may well consult the ground level worker but would merely inform the top-executive who nods and accepts as the system benefits the organisation.

Thus, the specialists should be given parity with the Indian Administrative Service in the matter of conditions of service. Besides, they must be given top positions at the policy-making levels in Government. This would raise the morale of the technocrats and would improve the efficacy of the Government.

3. Absence of Comprehensive Health Legislation

In the States, legal provisions in regard to health lie scattered over a number of acts. At present, there is only one State, i.e. Tamil Nadu, which has a comprehensive public health Act satisfying reasonably the requirements of the modern health administration. The present corpus of health legislation is inadequate resulting in piecemeal decisions. Regulations are lacking in many vital subjects. In several respects the legislation is ineffective and outdated. There is need for comprehensive legislation embracing all aspects of health in a State. This would result in good health policies and plans.

4. Medical Education not Oriented to Rural Needs

A group on medical education and support manpower set-up in 1974 noted with concern that "Medical Education in India over the years has been essentially urban-oriented, relying heavily on curative method and sophisticated diagnostic aids, with little emphasis on preventive and promotional aspects of community health. Programmes of training in the field of nutrition, family welfare, planning, maternal and child health have tended to develop in isolation from medical education and thus do not subserve the total needs of the community. Although the number of doctors has speedily increased over the successive plan periods, the alienation of doctors from the rural environment has deprived the rural communities of total medical care." The same feeling was voiced in the Fifth Five-Year Plan. The Sixth Plan also went on to point out that, "the basic problem is to produce a doctor who will be able to provide good health care and medical service to the community and will be able to work effectively in rural areas." Thus, it is high time for the State governments to take policy decisions to reorient medical education with a view to progressively make the training of the medical students more community-based. It is suggested that the internship of medical college students may be arranged in villages. The students may be asked to execute a bond to serve in the villages atleast for a period of five years. The curriculum may be curtailed and may be oriented to the community needs.

5. Lack of Community Health and Health Administrative Research

Huge sums of money are poured out annually on clinical hospital-based research in most States of India. One would not underestimate the importance of this type of research because it adds to knowledge. However, one has to think in terms of defining the priorities of research. A country, where the bulk of people are living in the rural areas, should normally involve the greater number of doctors doing research in community health. India is one country, which cannot boast of even a single good epidemiological study of such communicable diseases as tuberculosis, from which a sizable number of people suffer every year. In fact, the area of community health research does not encourage clinicians to work in the rural areas. The problems of community health, no doubt, are vast and intriguing. Yet, the country cannot afford to ignore them. India lives primarily in the villages and it is the villagers who are the recipients of probably the poorest quality of medical care. The future of India also depends on the progress made in the villages, particularly in the area of health. One has to watch and see how different States plan administer their health programmes so that their rural beneficiaries are not outnumbered by their urban beneficiaries. Thus, the present trend of our spending on curative medicine research has to change in favour of community health research particularly in the rural areas. This is a challenge, which no State of India can afford to ignore.

Further, the health administration at the State level is poorly equipped. Most of the health administrators have got no training in the modern knowledge of management. There is no effort on the part of the personnel working in health departments to use modern methods to improve health care delivery. Moreover, the health departments, training institutions, medical colleges, nursing colleges do not seriously concern themselves with finding methods for optimum utilization of resources. Health services research should be multidisciplinary, involving not only medical professionals and experts but also system analysts, operational researchers, social scientists, health economists, public administrators, anthropologists, etc. The State health department may encourage research in consonance with priority problems of its health care delivery system. The health department may encourage researches, which affect programme delivery. Some areas are mentioned below:

(a) Health manpower—their training, development, utilization, availability, needs and demands, etc., including experimentation with the development of various categories of health manpower.
(b) Equipment, materials, etc., their availability, utilization, needs and demands.
(c) Organisational and management process in health and family welfare services, their linkages, etc., including referral systems.
(d) Performance and impact of health and family welfare services.
(e) Needs and demands of population for health and family welfare services.
(f) Perception, attitude, utilization factors (promoters and barriers) effecting utilization, etc., of population towards health and family welfare services.
(g) Problems and bottlenecks in the existing organisational systems and redesigning of existing systems to eliminate the same.
(h) Information systems for health and family welfare.
(i) Cost-benefit and cost-effectiveness analysis of health and family welfare services, programmes and projects.
(j) Cost-analysis of health and family welfare services programmes and projects.
(k) Development and testing of technology suited to the Indian health scene and needs.
(l) Studies focused on the inter-phase between community and health services organisations.
(m) Studies on health status and social and economic development.
(n) Materials Management in a hospital.
(o) Working of Intensive-care units.
(P) Cost of running hospital services.
(q) Staffing of emergency services.
(r) Utilization of operation theaters.
(s) Enlisting of community participation.
(t) Development of planning and management techniques.
(u) Identification of goals and priorities of the health services.

6. Absence of Well-Designed Management Information System

Many State governments have performed the ritual of-setting up statistical bureaus dealing with health. Huge health statistics have also been collected but these have been put to a bare minimum use in terms of utilizing this information for developing a realistic health care delivery system. Thus, the ever-widening gap between accumulation of health statistics and their utilization for improving health services has of late acquired new significance. While in the developed countries management information system is increasingly being given the importance it deserved, in the developing countries it has not yet become an integral part of the state health system. It would indeed be very profitable for all the States to organize data banks and critically examine the quality of their health services. Because of the many uses of health statistics in scientific analysis, planning, administration and evaluation, the health statistician must begin to think in terms of a fully coordinated health information system, in which all relevant data are collected, compiled stored, retrieved, analyzed and published.[14]

However, the Health Information System has to be planned properly. A Health Information System was defined by Conference on Health Information Systems held by WHO in Copenhagen from 18-22 June 1973, as:

> "A mechanism for the collection, processing, analysis and transmission of information required for organizing and operating health services and also for research and training."[15]

We must ensure the accuracy of data; otherwise the whole of our planning would go wrong. Goddard has rightly said, "One of the greatest possible contributors to wastage of our precious resources, whether at the local, national or international levels, is the failure of those at any level of administration, and at all stages in the management of the activity, to base all decisions on verifiable facts. There should be no tolerating errors in administrative action, which occur because someone failed to get all of those facts. In the evolution, execution and control of work plans, obtaining the factual evidence should always be the first step."[16] Mahdi Elmandjra in his article, "Informatics and telematics: the future" in *World Health,* Aug./ Sept. 1989 warns the use of borrowed systems. To quote him, "he says that knowledge—which has become the most strategic raw material in all the domains of human activity—is simply information produced by sound research and managed by people well-trained in the pursuit of clear objectives and goals. Informatics is of course not a panacea especially if it is used as a purchased gadget and implanted as a foreign body in an environment, which does not meet its minimum conditions. Yet it represents today the most efficient instrument which man has so far invented to help him to analyze and solve problems."

7. Inadequate Financial Resources

It is one thing to define health needs of a given population and another thing to adequately plan health services in accordance with their needs. No aspect of planning health services appears to be more important than the consideration of finance. The paucity of financial resources because of poor allocations has often proved to be a major obstacle in the execution of health programmes. With the meagre resources, one cannot expect much. At present, the health department of Punjab is being allocated only 3-4 per cent of the total resources for the promotion of health. The task of providing health care to improve the quality of life of the people is challenging. The State governments must allocate at least 10 per cent of their total budget for health. Besides, there is a need to make the best use of the resources already allocated.

However, financial resources mobilized through alternative mechanisms, such as cost recovery and user fees, are minimal at this stage, being less than 10% of the total recurrent health expenditure. It has therefore become increasingly difficult to meet the unprecedented rising costs of health care.[17]

8. Non-availability of Dedicated Doctors/Workers to Serve in the Villages

The doctors prefer to serve in the cities than in the villages. When they are forced to work in the villages, their mind is always in the cities. This results in lower efficiency of the Primary Health Centres. It is suggested that the Government while selecting the students for medical education must ensure that a large number of students should come from villages, i.e. rural areas. The missionary zeal may be cultivated among the doctors during their education so that they take up the rural assignments with dedication.

(i) Human Resource Development to Inject Creativity and Dynamism among Health Personnel

The provision of Health Care at lower levels is not a mechanical process, it is a human enterprise and its success will depend ultimately on the skill, the quality and motivation of the persons associated with it, e.g. Medical Officers. Workers of Health at the lower echelons of Health Administration are vital link between people and the health care system.

The quality of personnel appointed to take care of health care activities, levels of efficiency, motivation and enthusiasm have not been maintained at a high level and there is lack of devotion to duty on the part of the medical and para-medical personnel. Complaints by the citizens regarding inefficiency and lack of devotion to duty on the part of medical and para-medical personnel have become quite articulate, and many people are even losing confidence in the existing primary health care system thereby widening the credibility gap.

HRD is concerned with organizing, in systematic fashion, the goals, objectives, priorities and activities of manpower development in order to ensure that the right number of staff with the appropriate skills is provided at the right time to meet the requirement of the work to be done.

There should be only one-yard stick to judge the effectiveness of Manpower Development, namely, continuous improvement of the status and, the quality of health of the population with the least friction to those who supply the services and maximum satisfaction for those who receive it. We have to achieve all this with the minimum cost and maximum efficiency.

(ii) Developing Missionary: Spirit among the Health Personnel

The problems of public health are challenging as gauged from the statistics already enumerated. It is very difficult to solve these problems with bureaucratic and inhuman attitude. It requires hard work, sympathy, and tolerance on the part of the health personnel engaged in this arduous and challenging task. Most respondents felt that the personnel working are fulfilling only their legal duties, and that too reluctantly. We do not need highly specialized people in these areas. We, however, require dedicated people with missionary zeal to serve the people suffering from illness. Prof. J.S. Neki has rightly said in the context of health personnel which is true for all categories of personnel:

> "To help, to heal, to reconstruct, to comfort—and all along the line to act with compassion-all these bear testimony to the moral consciousness of the doctor. Whatever the new strains imposed upon medical ethics, this structure will survive and continue to guide doctors in their professional conduct...Legal and judicial obligations they have, of necessity, to fulfil. But these are not genuine ethics. Genuine ethics has to be ingrained into character and does not have to depend upon external controls.[18]

R.S. Pathak, Former Chief Justice of India rightly mentions: "The vitality of an ethical dimension in the discharge of public responsibilities is essential to a developing nation. In a developing nation, the release of nascent national energy is a great moment. It provides the power necessary for building of a nation."[19]

9. Under-utilization of Indigenous System of Medicine

Indian health problems are of such magnitude that if left only to the allopathic system of medicine, one cannot possibly hope to achieve much success. In the past, a policy of drift has been followed with regard to Ayurveda and other Indian systems of medicine. The supporters of Ayurveda and Homeopathy feel that this system did not get a chance to demonstrate its utility. It has been claimed by the practitioners of the indigenous system of medicine that the facilities provided to them have been too patchy and the services were inadequately supplied to prove the true worth of the system. The Punjab government has shown its keenness to promote the system but the tempo is very slow. The government should take a bold decision to encourage these systems, which can provide health care to a large number of people with little cost.

10. Unsatisfactory Management of Employees' State Insurance Scheme

Employees' State Insurance Scheme has not been functioning well. The shortage 'of doctors and medicines is the common ill of these institutions. There have been complaints from the beneficiaries about the malfunctioning of these hospitals. It was mentioned in the *Tribune* by C.M. Kumbhkarni with reference to E.S.I. Hospital, Jullundur:

> "The indoor patients take their meals like beggars on paper and towel. The hospital is provided with stainless steel utensils but these are kept under lock and key."

Besides, it is widely felt that there is lot of corruption among the doctors working in these hospitals. The State government must tighten the control over these hospitals and monitor the reactions and feelings of the patients to streamline the functioning of the ESI scheme.

11. Poor Nutritional Status of the People

Punjab is an economically well-off State but the majority of the people suffer from diseases arising from nutritional deficiencies and mal-nutrition.

The following recommendations were made by the South-East Regional Committee to solve the problems of nutritional deficiencies, which need the immediate attention of the State health department:

(1) Nutrition activities should be recognized as crucial components of health programmes, particularly of those directed at the mother and child.

(2) The nutrition activities of health programmes should be very clearly defined and their implementation at all levels and especially at the local level, should receive sufficient attention and allocation of resources.

(3) In the package of services, nutrition should receive the same priority as other components, so that it is not relegated to a position of secondary importance, as has been many times the case.

(4) The delivery system for nutrition activities catering to the needs of the under served population should be rationalized applying the principles of primary health care and using primary health workers within the context of national health administration.

(5) Nutrition education relevant to the local situation as a part of health education of the community and its inclusion in formal and non-formal education need to be improved.

(6) Service-oriented nutrition research to solve public health nutrition problems must receive priority.

(7) To fulfil the inter-sectoral and intra-sectoral responsibilities of health in nutrition, the role of the nutrition unit at the central level of the health services needs to be considerably

strengthened with its increased participation in health planning and programming.

12. Lack of Community Participation in Health

Community participation is perceived as a dynamic partnership process that is reinforced by information feedback. Health personnel are responsible for explaining and advising, and for providing clear information on health options. Community participation enables people to become agents of their own development, instead of being passive beneficiaries of development aid. The channeling of a community's human resources generated by the health volunteer movement is advantageous to both the health care providers and the recipients. Volunteers in community health activities not only bring health services to the community, but also act as agents for health development.

Social preparation of and capacity building in the community are prerequisites for mobilizing communities for health activities. This could be supported through information, education and communication (IEC) material in both electronic and print media, the formation of support groups, shared efforts of health volunteers through village exchange visits, and the development of joint plans of action and inter-sectoral activities at village level.[20]

Community health development through education is a critical issue that requires an investment of time and resources by the health care system.

In the new millennium, State Health Department must change its emphasis from merely examining files sitting in the offices and should instead ensure implementation of the programmes through personal visits, monitoring and regular guidance. We have to discard the old method of paper approach and focus on action approach in new millennium. Health Departments must be guided by the motto that "words written or spoken are of no use unless put to action."

The big task in new millennium is not only to enable change but to communicate it as widely as possible. Can the field functionaries visualize what the headquarters policy-makers dream of such congruence is sure to fillip progress.

In the new millennium, the State Government has to play a more dynamic role through Panchayati Raj System, urban local bodies, etc. in ushering in a new era of health development by exploiting local resources. This can be achieved through transparency, accountability and good governance. People's empowerment is the only answer to solve many national and bureaucratic ills from which the system suffers.

13. Excessive Centralization: Need for Decentralization

The State health system, within whose structure the services required to deliver care to the urban, suburban and rural family nucleus must be organized, is a mechanism of such administrative complexity that it cannot possibly be run on a centralized basis. Hence the need to decentralize the administrative process. This decentralization should include the extensive delegation of functions from the higher to the intermediate and local echelons, so as to produce effective decentralization in staff management, budgetary control, application of laws and regulations and if possible, financing as well.

The existing centralization results in delays, and consequential inefficiencies. The Secretary and Director are overburdened with files and a lot of routine administrative duties, which could easily be dealt with at much lower levels. As the Director is fully occupied in small matters relating to administration, he has little or no time for monitoring important programmes, making filed visits and providing quality leadership to this team. Though a large army of senior officers exists at the Directorate, they are not made accountable and responsible for their sphere of work. This also tends to rob them of some of their initiative, which they might have otherwise displayed. There has been no systematic effort to delegate powers to the Divisional Joint Directors. Similarly, Superintendents of sub-district hospitals have little authority even in the routine day-to-day management of the hospitals. For example, they have virtually no powers to attend to petty repairs to the building or attend to minor repairs of hospital equipment.

A senior health administrator suggested that the top personnel should concentrate on "A" category of functions, which account for 10 per cent of all total work; the rest 90 per cent should be decentralized to middle and lower levels.[21]

14. Planning and Management outdate: Need for Scientific Planning and Management

There are major weaknesses in the management of the health system in the State. At the Directorate level, there is a lack of clarity in the roles of various functionaries. There is also a lack of adequate administrative and financial accountability. At the lower levels, the hiatus is often sharper. While the medical officer is required to manage the hospital, all decisions on medical and financial aspects are taken by the Directorate. In specific areas, the delegation of powers such as the maintenance of infrastructure viz., building and equipment, both at the district and State Levels is poor, leading to deterioration of assets.

15. Building and equipment maintenance systems not effective: Need of Sound Set-up

The equipment management structure is very weak, with only one junior equipment officer for the entire state, who is expected to deal with both procurement and maintenance of equipment for all hospitals in the State including those in the teaching institutions. In-house capability for effecting even minor repairs of equipment is almost non-existent. Similarly, the capacity of the system to construct and maintain physical facilities, such as hospital buildings, residential quarters is limited on account of the fact that all building design, construction and maintenance works are managed by the PWD, who also deal with the buildings of other departments. As a result, there is no expertise to design, construct and maintain hospital buildings, activities which require a great deal of specialization.

16. Lack of Adequate Information Required for Health Planning, Implementation and Evaluation: Need of Developing Reliable MIS.

Information is the life-blood of an organisation. According to R.R. Duresch, "it is a system which provides management with the information, it requires to monitor progress, measure performance, detect trends, evaluate alternatives, make decisions and to take corrective action."[22]

There is an urgent need to integrate the MIS activity and expand its functions not only to monitor various activities but also to aid in preparation of medium and long-term plans.

It is also to be borne in mind that supplying unnecessary or unwanted information is also a sign of inefficiency of the system. To quote a UNICEF Report:

> "Information Services should be recast according to the priorities of the health system and should be aimed strictly at problem-solving."[23]

A Health Information System was defined by Conference on Health Information Systems held by WHO in Copenhagen from 18-22 June 1973, as "A mechanism for the collection, processing, analysis, and transmission of information required for organizing and operating health services and also for research and training."[24]

The existing MIS is restricted to providing monthly and annual reports on MCH and FW and other National Programmes. Some of the information essential for strategic planning is being compiled manually by the Planning and MIS wing. Up to date information on important aspects such as status of civil works, availability of equipment, personnel, analysis of expenditure, is not readily available.

Some of the aspects, which are important for planning health care services and monitoring performance are:

- Birth Rates according to Sex, Region and Family background.
- Death Rates according to Age, Sex, Region, Family background and cause.
- Morbidity Data according to Disease, Sex, Age and Region.
- Surveillance system for communicable diseases.
- Allocation of Personnel, Equipment, Facilities at different hospitals vis-à-vis norms.
- Existing plans and status for each unit.
- Expenditure tracking for each unit.
- Monitoring training of different categories of personnel.

- Equipment availability at each unit.
- Drugs and supplies tracking for each unit.
- Building maintenance of each unit.
- Quality Assessment programme monitoring.
- Monitoring of the Referral System.[25]

We can conclude by saying that Punjab Government can take bold and innovative decisions to accommodate management of change and thus provide decent Health Care to all the people in the State.

(i) Need for decentralized planning and policy-making involving the participation of the target communities and beneficiaries.
(ii) Establishment of sound administrative organisation, necessary competence and capability and devolution of authority and responsibility for the implementation and development of the programme in a team spirit and a well-designed information system to help in planning, implementation and evaluation.
(iii) Strengthening existing rural establishment and graded extension of national administrative structures to provide adequate and accessible referral, Supervisory, logistical and other supporting services to ensure the judicious use of health services.
(iv) Designing health technology to suit the environment and making the best use of existing technology of indigenous system of medicine.
(v) Improving research and development capacity to solve community health problems.[26]

Finally, there are a large number of other problems in the areas concerning Health Planning, Health Manpower Planning, Health Project Management, Hospital Management, Administration of Health Education and Environmental Sanitation Programmes, which would be discussed in the relevant chapters.

A COMPREHENSIVE STRATEGY FOR BETTER HEALTH

The 10th Plan aimed at providing essential primary health care, particularly to the underprivileged and underserved segments of our population. It also sought to devolve responsibilities and funds for health care to PRIs. However, progress towards these objectives has been slow and the 10th Plan targets on MMR and IMR have been missed. Accessibility remains a major issue especially in areas where habitations are scattered and women and children continue to die en route to hospitals. Rural health care in most states is marked by absenteeism or doctors/health providers, low levels of skills, shortage of medicines, inadequate supervision/ monitoring and callous attitudes. There are neither rewards for service providers nor punishments for defaulters. As a result, health outcomes in

India are adverse compared to bordering countries like Sri Lanka as well as countries of South East Asia like China and Vietnam.

India and Comparable Countries

	India	*Sri Lanka*	*China*	*Vietnam*
Infant mortality (per 1000 live births)				
	60 (2003)	13 (2003)	30 (2003)	19 (2003)
One year olds fully immunized for measles (%)				
	58.0 (2002-04)	99 (2003)	84 (2003)	93 (2000)
Population with sustainable access to improved sanitation (%)				
	30 (2002)	91 (2002)	44 (2002)	41 (2002)
Under-five mortality (per 1000 live births)				
	87 (2003)	15 (2003)	37 (2003)	23 (2003)
Births attended by skilled birth attendants (%)				
	47.6 (2002-04)	97 (1995-2003)	97 (1995-03)	85 (1995-03)
Maternal mortality (per 100,000 deliveries)				
	407 (adjusted 2000)	92 (adjusted 2000)	56 (adjusted 2000)	130 (adjusted 2000)

Achievement of health objectives involves much more than curative or even preventive medical care. We need a comprehensive approach, which encompasses individual health care, public health, sanitation, clean drinking water, access to food and knowledge about hygiene and feeding practice. This is a difficult area because of our socio-cultural complexities and also regional diversity. Policy interventions therefore have to be evidence-based and responsive to area specific differences. With concerted action including enabling pregnant women to have institutional deliveries and receive nutritional supplements; connecting PHCs and CHCs by all weather roads so that they can be reached quickly in emergencies; (accessibility to hospital should be measured in terms of travel time, not just distance from nearest PHC); providing home-based neo natal care including emergency life saving measures, etc. we can be on track to reach the

Millennium Development Goals for IMR, MMR and for combating diseases by the end of the 11th Plan.

To improve the primary health care system, the 11th Plan will first lay emphasis on integrated district health plans and second, on block specific health plans. These plans will ensure involvement of all health-related sectors and emphasize partnership with NGOs. The NRHM has already been launched to ensure quality health care in rural areas. The next step should be to extend this to make it a Sarva Swasthya Abhiyan that also covers the health needs of the urban poor, particularly the slum dwellers by investing in high caliber health professionals and appropriate technology.

Besides reducing the burden and the level of risk of existing, growing and emerging diseases, the 11th Plan will also take care of the special needs of people living with AIDS, in particular the women. The 11th Plan will recognize the feminine face of HIV and accord it the highest priority.

The 11th Plan will continue to advocate fertility regulation through voluntary and informed consent. The Plan will address the special healthcare needs of the elderly, especially those who are economically and socially vulnerable.[27]

Notes and References

1. GOI: Report of Administration of the State Level, Administrative Reforms Commission, New Delhi, 1969, p. 10.
2. Sarwan Singh, An Analysis of Secondary Health Care Administration in Punjab, A Thesis submitted for the degree of Doctor of Philosophy, Panjab University, Chandigarh, August 2005, pp. 48-49 and 52.
3. Fulton Committee Report, 1966-68.
4. R. Rostagi, IAS and Other Services, *The Time of India*, November 11, 1972.
5. Kuldeep Nayar, "Between the Lines: A Year of Drift and indecision", *The Statesman*, January 3, 1974.
6. ARC, Report on Personnel Administration, Government of India, p. 12.
7. GOI: Report of Administration of the State Level, Administrative Reforms Commission, New Delhi, 1969, p. 10.
8. Sarwan Singh, An Analysis of Secondary Health Care Administration in Punjab, A Thesis submitted for the degree of Doctor of Philosophy, Panjab University, Chandigarh, August 2005, pp. 51-52
9. Sarwan Singh, An Analysis of Secondary Health Care Administration in Punjab, A Thesis submitted for the degree of Doctor of Philosophy, Panjab University, Chandigarh, August 2005, pp. 62-64.
10. Government of Karnataka, Health and Family Welfare Department, Performance Budget (2007-08), p. 1.
11. Government of Punjab, Bold Planning and Solid Action: Health Services in Punjab, 1979.
12. Administrative Reforms Commission, Report on Personnel Administration, New Delhi, Manager of Publications, 1969, p. 10.
13. Report of the Committee of Civil Services (The Fulton Committee) Cmnd: 3638, London, H.M.S.C., 1968, p. 12.
14. Forest E. Linder, Director, International Programme of Laboratories for

Population Statistics, School of Public Health, University of North California at Chapel Hill, N.C., USA, "Recent Trends in Health Statistics" in *WHO Chronicle*, 30: 58-63 (1976).

15. M.R. Aderson, Honorary Director, Medical Information Unit, Wessex Regional Hospital Board, Winchester, U.K.: "Health Information System" in *WHO Chronicle*, 1974, 28, pp. 52-54.
16. H.A. Aderson, Principles of Administration Applied to Nursing Services, World Health Organisation, Geneva, 1958, p. 84.
17. SEA/RC20, pp. 39-40.
18. J.S. Neki, "Medical Ethics, A view point from the Developing World," *World Health*, July 1979, p. 15.
19. R.S. Pathak, Ethics in Public Life, Some Observations in IJPA, July to Sept. 1995, p. 265.
20. WHO: SEARO: Health Situation in the South-East Asia Region, New Delhi, 1994-97, p. 193.
21. Based upon Personnel Discussion.
22. Mortoff Meltzer, The Information Centre, Management Hidden Asset, American Management Association, New York, 1967, pp. 136-37.
23. UNICEF: Health and Basic Services: Keys to Development, New Delhi, 1984, p. 50.
24. M.R. Anderson, Health Information Systems, *WHO Chronicle*, 1974, 28, 52-54.
25. Rajneesh Goel, Thesis, An Analysis of Primary Health Care Administration in Karnataka, January 2000, pp. 106-11.
26. *Ibid.*, pp. 115-16.
27. Planning Commission, Government of India, 17th November 2006, An Approach to the 11th Five Year Plan, pp. 69-70.

District Health Care Administration

The District is the most peripheral fully organized unit of local government and administration. It is geographically compact and every part of it can normally be reached within a day. The District is often the natural meeting point for "bottom-up" planning and organisation and "top-down" planning support. It is a place where community needs and national priorities can be reconciled. We can develop good plans for a small area and ensure implementation.

District level health structure is a middle level Management Organisation and has been set-up to provide an organic link between state level health infrastructure as well as regional level infrastructure on the one side and district level and lower level health institutions on the other side. District health administration is the nerve centre of health infrastructure as upon its efficiency depends the efficiency of primary health care to a substantial extent.

SIGNIFICANCE OF DISTRICT HEALTH SYSTEM

The district health office is truly the nerve centre of the health care delivery system and an important aid to health care management. It acts as an intermediary between the State and the grass-root level health organisations. "The basic territorial unit of administration in India is the 'district' and 'district administration' is the total management of public affairs within this unit."[1]

Eighth General Programme of work covering the period (1990-95). Geneva, WHO (Health For All series No. 10) defines District Health System as:

A district health system based on primary health care is a more or less self-contained segment of the national health system. It comprises first and foremost "a well-defined population living within a clearly delineated administrative and geographical area. It includes all the relevant health care activities in the area, whether governmental or otherwise. It therefore consists of a large variety of interrelated elements that contribute to health in homes, schools, workplaces, communities, the health sector, and related social and economic sectors. It includes self-care and all health care personnel and facilities, whether governmental or non-governmental, up to and including the hospital at the first referral level, and the appropriate support services, such as laboratory, diagnostic, and logistic support. It will be most effective if coordinated by an appropriately trained health officer working to ensure as comprehensive a range as possible of promotive, preventive, curative, and rehabilitative health activities.[2]

The term district is used in a generic sense to denote a clearly defined administrative area, which commonly has a population of five to twenty lacs, where some form of local government or administration handles many of the responsibilities for central government sectors or departments, and where a general hospital for referral support exists. The actual organisation of district health systems depends on the specific situation in each country and each district, including the administrative structure and personalities involved. Nevertheless, the general principles for developing such systems are based on the Declaration of Alma-Ata and the global strategies for health for all. They incorporate the elements of equity, accessibility, emphasis on promotion and prevention, intersectoral action, community involvement, decentralization, integration of health programmes, and coordination of separate health activities.[3]

STRENGTHENING DISTRICT HEALTH SYSTEM BASED ON PRIMARY HEALTH CARE

Since its inception in 1978, the concept of the district health system has come to be accepted as a valid one and, in addition to the WHO headquarters programme on strengthening District Health System, the WHO Regional Office has taken up many activities to strengthen district health systems in the countries of their respective regions. A number of international, multilateral, and bilateral aid agencies have also supported the development and strengthening of district health systems, either through the WHO programme mentioned above or through direct bilateral support to countries.

In the recent past, states in India have recognized their health services structure in order to bring all health care programmes in a district under unified control.

39th World Health Assembly discussed "Evaluation of the Strategy for Health for All by the year 2000...", Seventh Report on the World Health Situation and considering the importance of strengthening the primary health care at the "District" level passed a resolution WHO 39.7, which urges member states to lay particular emphasis on district health system based on primary health care, defining targets for the integrated delivery of essential elements of primary health care.[4] Management at district level can be strengthened by the governments by providing:

(i) training programmes, particularly in services training, for senior district staff.
(ii) Model information systems, often the information required locally within a district is similar to that required elsewhere. Governments can provide examples of simple indicators and methods of recording, aggregating and analyzing data to provide useful information. These systems may be very simple, but may be considered an insurmountable and difficult problem to those inexperienced in setting them up.
(iii) Universal budgeting system to be applied at district level. Often systems are well established at the national level, but are extremely *ad-hoc* in each district. Simple guidelines on budgeting and cost control should be provided to each district.
(iv) Experts in evaluation of services: Until district staff have had some training and experience in evaluation, government may well have to provide experts on a short term *ad-hoc* basis to train local staff and demonstrate how evaluations may be carried out.
(v) Better coordination at national level of supplies, logistic and maintenance. Although governments can make recommendations on how these may be improved locally; so often the root of the problem lies in poor provision at the state level. For example, a district can hardly be expected to improve its supply of essential drugs, if the ordering and acquisition is deficient at the national level.[5]

District Health System is most convenient for health care delivery system. To quote WHO "The district, which is the peripheral organisational unit of national health systems, is particularly suitable as a channel for services to communities, and as a link with more central policies and support systems. It is at district level that the health needs of the population can best be matched with the resources to be allocated. The district health system initiative and approach were therefore designed to help countries implement their primary health care strategies more effectively, the district being the most appropriate level for coordinating "top-down" and "bottom up" planning, organizing community involvement in planning and implementation, supporting health care workers, and improving coordination between the government and private health sectors. In addition, many key development sectors are represented at this level, thereby facilitating intersectoral cooperation and management of services across a broad front."[6]

The head of the District Organisation is designed differently in different states of the India, e.g. Chief Medical Officer or District Health Officer, or District Health and Family Planning Officer. He has under him a lot of staff to supervise, co-ordinate and control the field activities as well as report to the headquarters. In some of the states of the Indian Union, District Health System has been entrusted to the control of Panchayati Raj System while in others; it is still under the total control of the State Government.

There has been a tendency in developing countries, including India, to allocate more and more powers to Union and State Governments, resulting in centralization and lack of initiative at local levels. In recent times, there has been a trend to decentralize health system to ensure fruitful results. Through decentralization, lower level units can meet local variations in ecological, geographical, economic, social and cultural conditions (e.g. 73rd and 74th Amendments of the Indian Constitution).[7]

A. DECENTRALISATION IN HEALTH CARE SYSTEM

Speedy and realistic decision-making is one of the essentials of efficient administration. In a big and complex organisation, the number of decisions to be taken from time to time is so large and the points at which the decisions are to be implemented are so many that it becomes necessary to distribute decision-making powers among a number of organs, rather than let these concentrate in one organ. This is expected to prevent the emergence of bottlenecks, which bedevil highly centralized power structures. Thus, one of the important problems of organisation is to reconcile the administrator's desire for centralized control for the sake of uniformity and certainty of decisions and action with the people's view that administration should be so organized as to deal with the needs of the different segments of the society in an effective manner. Decentralization has many other advantages.

(a) Decentralization Lightens the Works of the Upper Echelons in Administration

Most of the personnel at top level remain too busy and thus cannot devote time to everything they do. The result is mere signing.

(b) Decentralization Promotes Quick Disposal of Work

Decentralization can promote quick disposal of work as the decision-making authorities are in the field itself.

(c) Decentralization Generates Interest among Employees

Decentralization generates participation which increase the motivation of employees as they get the opportunity to express themselves and not simply act as ordered. In the words of J.C. Charles worth, "Decentralization has a more important justification than mere administrative efficiency. It bears directly upon the development of a sense of personal adequacy in the individual citizen; it has spiritual connotations."[8]

(d) Decentralization Develops Leadership

Through decentralization, opportunity is provided to people to put their ideas into practice. This gives a boost to experimentation and creativity, which are the essential qualities of leadership. According to Dimock and Dimock, "Decentralization permits to less standardization and hence allows more variation and experimentation, more freedom to innovate and choose, encourages more experience and a wider scope for initiative, both of which stimulate leadership."

(e) Decentralization Promotes Effective Supervision and Control

Control and supervision become easier at lower levels since operations are being done at lower levels. In a WHO document "Strengthening Ministries of Health for Primary Health Care", a question is raised about the extent of decentralization to provide primary health care. The answer goes in favour of decentralization to districts.[9]

How far down the line should decentralization go? Should it stop at large geographical areas, such as regions or states, or should matters be taken further down, to the provincial, district or municipal level? Answers are necessarily tentative. In part, they depend on the system's initial degree of centralization. If it is built downwards from a "top-heavy top", then decentralization to a small number of regions could be indicated. Human resource constraints may add force to such a strategy. There may, for example, be few health planners, appropriately trained district medical officers, PHC nursing supervisors, pharmacists, or administrators with a broader understanding of management. It is easier to assemble a few teams of capable officials than to find the expertise to staff large numbers of them. Some countries, which have decentralized to lower levels, have been seriously hampered by a lack of appropriate skills, especially in administration and management (Sudan). Yet there are also factors to be considered which point the other way.

Larger (and fewer) decentralized units will find it harder to ensure the required adaptability, flexibility and efficiency and to promote devolution of power and accountability towards the grassroots, where the services operate. There is growing evidence that an important cause of the limited efficiency of the health care system is often found at the "district" level, i.e. the level from which the basic PHC services are organized and managed, and where the primary backup services are situated. The weakness of district level organisation often leads to the breakdown of support and supervision, to shortage in essential supplies, and to lack of facilities for training (and retraining) grassroots health workers.

Conversely, strong and well-organized district health teams with access to relevant information sources appear to be an essential ingredient of the PHC approach. It may even be argued that district PHC teams are the key units of the entire organisational structure, and that their leaders are placed in the most critical positions of the health sector. Such teams can be responsible for all basic health care activities, for the promotion and sustaining of community involvement, and for the operational link-up between PHC and hospital activities. The district, therefore, needs resources and authority under its own control to be able to fulfil its tasks properly. Decentralization should go down all the way to the district, wherever possible.

A review of primary health care system by world health organisation has resulted in a resolution (WHA 39.7) in May 1986 in which it has urged countries to strengthen further the health system infrastructure based on primary health care, laying particular emphasis on district health systems based on primary health care, and defining targets for the integrated delivery of essential elements of primary health care until all districts and all elements are covered. It also called on WHO to intensify support for countries in this regard.

In order to facilitate a common understanding, the WHO Global Programme Committee in 1986 defined the district health system based on primary health care as "a self-contained segment of the national health system comprised of a well-defined population living within a clearly delineated administrative and geographical area, whether urban or rural. It includes all institutions and individuals providing health care in the district, whether governmental, social security, non-governmental, private, or traditional. A district health system therefore consists of a large variety of interrelated elements that contribute to health in homes, schools, work places and communities, through the health and other related sectors. It includes self-care and all health care workers and facilities, up to and including the hospital at the first referral level and the appropriate laboratory, other diagnostic, and logistic support services. Its component elements need to be well coordinated by an officer assigned to this function in order to draw together all these elements and institutions into a fully comprehensive range of promotive, preventive, curative and rehabilitative health activities."[10]

With regard to development, the objectives of the WHO Programme on Strengthening District Systems are to improve the quality of life and reduce mortality and morbidity by strengthening the effective implementation of primary health care in participating countries, with due consideration to equity, effectiveness, efficiency, and flexibility within the context of national, regional and global strategies for reaching the goal of Health for All.[11]

(f) Government Responsibility for District Health System

1. Government should strengthen support and encourage the decentralization process to give necessary autonomy and responsibility to district health systems and to ensure the development of an appropriate network of facilities, including at least one first referral hospital in each health district, together with the first contact services without which the hospital cannot function coherently and efficiently.

2. Governments should ensure that first referral hospitals have a high degree of technical and administrative competence and equipment to deal with clinical problems that cannot be handled at the health facility at first contact level. These hospitals should be equipped with reliable laboratory, imaging services, a pharmacy, and a blood bank. In this way further referrals up the chain can be reduced and rationalized.
3. Governments should ensure effective supervision, communication and control.
4. District Health System should provide leadership to motivate Personnel at the periphery level.
5. Governments should develop networks of urban primary health facilities so that the services of urban hospitals at first referral level may be used more rationally and efficiently.
6. Governments should review the allocation and use of hospital resources, and encourage the mobilization of additional sources of revenue for individual district health systems. Local financial resources should as much as possible, be retained and administered locally.
7. District Health System should ensure that the equipment remain functional.
8. Governments should ensure that, no capital investment is made unless the attendant recurrent expenditure can be assured.
9. District Health System should supply drugs of good quality and in time to field centres.
10. In order to reduce and rationalize referrals to hospital, governments should ensure that adequate diagnostic facilities are extended to health centres and other community-based units, together with appropriately trained personnel.
11. Governments should design training curricula for health workers involved in district health care to suit changing environment.
12. District health system should be transparent and responsive.

B. ORGANISATIONAL STRUCTURE OF DISTRICT HEALTH SYSTEM

District Health System is under the control of State Health Department. The head of the district health system, generally called Chief Medical Officer, is directly responsible to the state health department and is not accountable to elected Panchayati Raj Institutions. This system has many disadvantages as it is bureaucratic in style and functioning, it has no mechanism to involve the people, and the health system is not in tune with the needs of the people. Let us explain with an example of District Health System in Punjab.

The district is the most crucial level in the administration and implementation of medical health services. At the district level, there is a

District Medical and Health Officer (DMHO); Chief Medical Officer who is overall responsible for the administration of medical and health services in the entire district and for the implementation of all the national health and family welfare programmes. He is assisted by the Additional District Medical and Health Officers or Deputy District Medical and Health Officers along with other district officers for various national health programmes in the district. Their number varies from state to state.

Effective development strategies require a process of planning and implementation, which enables local people and officials to equally express their needs and to share in deciding what is to be done. Neither party has control. Their motivation is based on the desire to satisfy both personal (individual, family, community) needs as well as compatible joint project objectives. To the extent that communities and outside agents view the rewards they receive from performance as supportive of their personal objectives, they will be productive within the limits of their individual and group capacities and within the restraints placed upon them by their situation. One of the rural development manager's tasks is that of analyzing the situation to determine the most appropriate conditions and resources, which can lead to improving the situation and the equitable merger and attainment of personal and project needs.

This process of analysis, likewise, should be done not just by the manager but also on an equal basis with the people, incorporating popular knowledge as much as possible. This consultative process must go much deeper than the usual diplomatic and technical channels, for it must first and foremost involve people below the level of government officials; it must involve people in non-governmental organisations and in the communities. Thus, we come to the need for partnership, that is, for a means of enabling people to work together in a spirit of mutual trust and respect which encourages people to volunteer information and resources because they believe they are being taken seriously. Partnership is thus a means for improving the process of development by creating linkages, which will bring more people into the process, which will provide better information and participation, and which will more widely disperse responsibility for decisions.[12]

Let us now explain the District Health System with an example from Karnataka. Establishment of three-tier Panchayat Raj System is the first step towards decentralization of power. It provides for a Gram Panchayat, Taluka Panchayat and Zilla Panchayat. The Zilla Panchayat or District Panchayat has authority over the entire district except the urban areas under municipal or city or town councils.

There is provision for transfer of power and functions and devolution of funds to Panchayats. Practically all the development programmes are transferred to the District Panchayat and an officer of the rank of the collector is the Chief Executive Officer of the Zilla Panchayat.

It has an elected president and vice-President from among its elected members. Elected members alone have a right to vote. There are associate members too who are nominated and can only discuss and express their views in the meetings of Panchayat. The Chief Executive Officer of the rank of collector is posted to Panchayat who acts as an *ex-officio* Secretary of the Panchayat and has a pivotal role. This district panchayat functions through various committee structures and the Health Committee is one of the important committee to work for health development.

Thus, Zilla Parishad with Taluka and Gram Panchayats are ushering in democratic decentralization of administration. They are the active instruments at peoples' level. The panchayat system is taking strong roots and providing a solid base for building up and strengthening the decentralization of the planning process. The District Planning Board (DPB) provides a forum for all sectors and organisations engaged in development work, including panchayats, to pool their efforts and assist in evolving a well-coordinated and participatory approach to planning.

The Karnataka Panchayat Raj Act, 1993, which is now in force in the State, specifies the following functions to be performed by the Zilla Panchayat, in respect of Health and Family Welfare, at the district level:

(1) Management of hospitals and dispensaries excluding the District hospital and other hospitals under the direct management of government (above 50 beds);
(2) Implementation of maternity and child health programmes;
(3) Implementation of family welfare programmes; and
(4) Implementation of immunization and vaccination programmes.

The Taluka Panchayats deal with:

(1) Promotion of Health and Family Welfare programmes;
(2) Promotion of immunization and vaccination programmes at the Taluka level; and
(3) Health and sanitation at fairs and festivals.

At the village level, the Gram Panchayats deal with implementation of family welfare programmes, preventive measures against epidemics, regulation of sale of food articles, participation in immunization programmes, licensing of eating establishments and regulation of offensive and dangerous trades. Apart from operating the District Sector budget, the Zilla Panchayats also implement such State Sector Schemes as are entrusted to them by Government.

The State plan and centrally sponsored or assisted schemes and the normal schemes of the district are budgeted accordingly. Only innovative district specific schemes have to be funded under decentralized district planning for which either DPB provides 100 per cent discretionary funds or funds flow under incentive outlay where local community has to contribute on 50:50 or 25:75 basis of its proportion of the funds or from special outlays for backward areas. Otherwise, the district budget is

CHART 7.1

Organisation Structure of Panchayati Raj Institutions

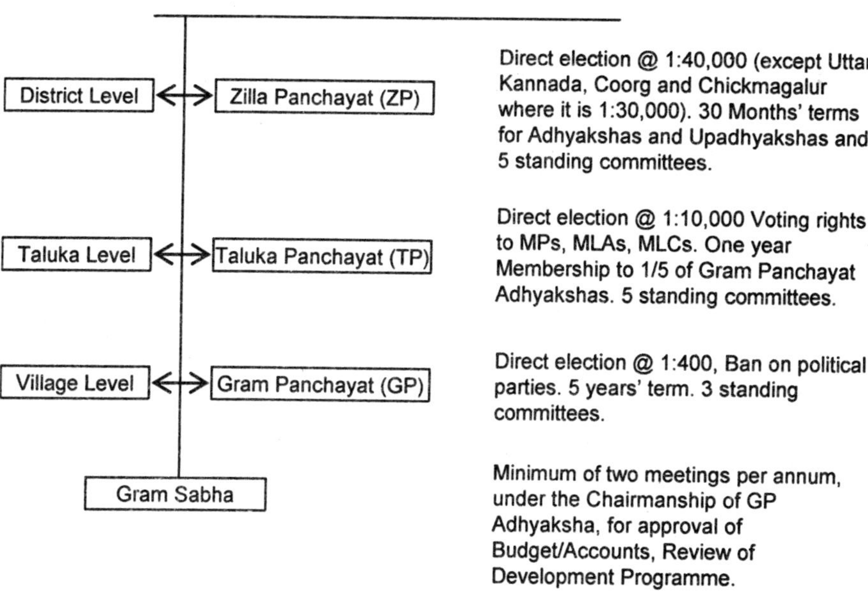

proportional to the number of institutions functioning in the district and the norms set for Central and State programmes being operated in the district under various approved budgetary heads of expenditure. Each programme officer at district level is drawing and disbursing officer and there is no integrated budget for the district. The delay in release of budget is generally the normal constraint affecting the utilization.[13]

ADMINISTRATIVE MACHINERY

Below this political set-up, there is administrative health machinery to implement the Plans made by ZP. This machinery helps PRI system in the formulation of Health Plans as well. The district administrative machinery under ZP consists of the Chief Executive Officer (CEO), an IAS officer, as head of the administrative organisation.

Besides CEO, the ZP secretariat comprises of 2 Deputy Secretaries in-charge of administration and development respectively, a Council Secretary for organizing ZP meetings, a Chief Planning Officer to assist in planning exercise and a Chief Accounts Officer to supervise the money transactions in the ZP (See Chart 7.3). There are field officers, i.e. Executive Officer, Block Development Officer and G.P. Secretary. Besides, there are departments headed by specialists. Let us explain with the examples of one of the Districts, i.e. Dakshina Kannada, where there are 17 departments (See Chart 7.3)

CHART 7.2

Committee System in Panchayati Raj Institutions

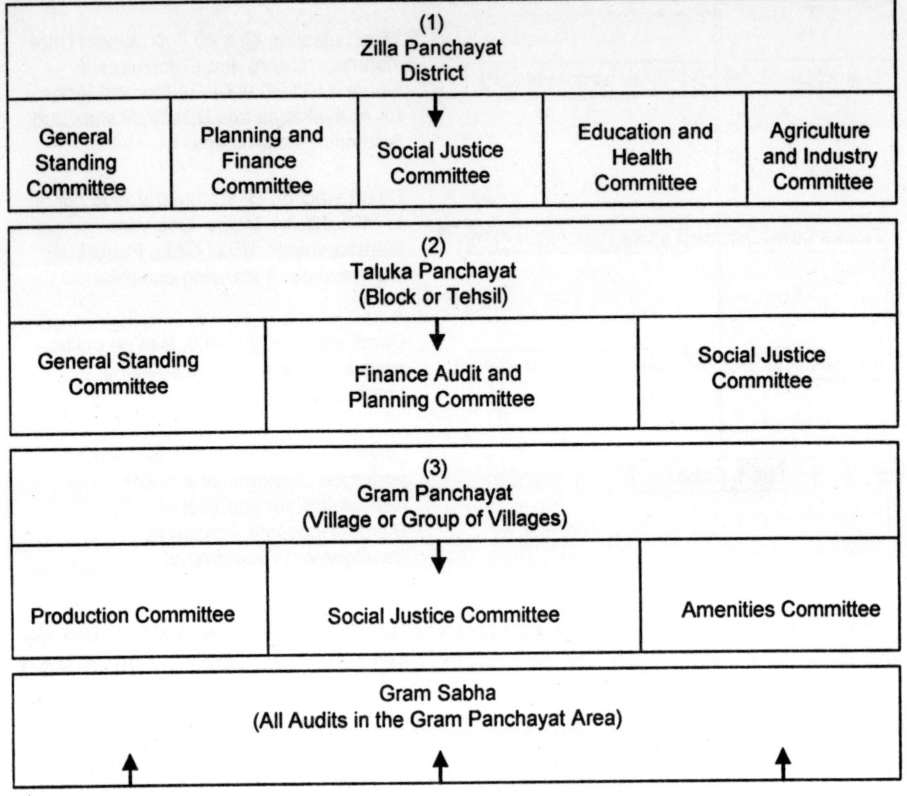

ROLE OF CHIEF EXECUTIVE OFFICER ZP

Chief Executive Officer (CEO) has to play an important role in ushering the benefits of democratic decentralization. However, CEO's tenure is not fixed and in practice is very short. Hence, it is very difficult to maintain continuity and interest in programmes. We can explain with the help of a case study of CEO in the district of Dakshina Kannada.

Since inception in 1987 to 01.04.98, there have been 9 incumbents to the post of CEO, with an average tenure of one and a half year. The CEO is expected to provide requisite linkage between the elected representatives and administration personnel within the ZP, between the District Administration and the State Government. The Chief Executive Officer attends every meeting of the ZP and has the right to attend the meeting of any committee thereof and to take part in the discussion, but does not have the right to move any resolution or to vote.

It is also very difficult to control and coordinate so many

CHART 7.3

The Administrative Structure of Panchayati Raj Institutions

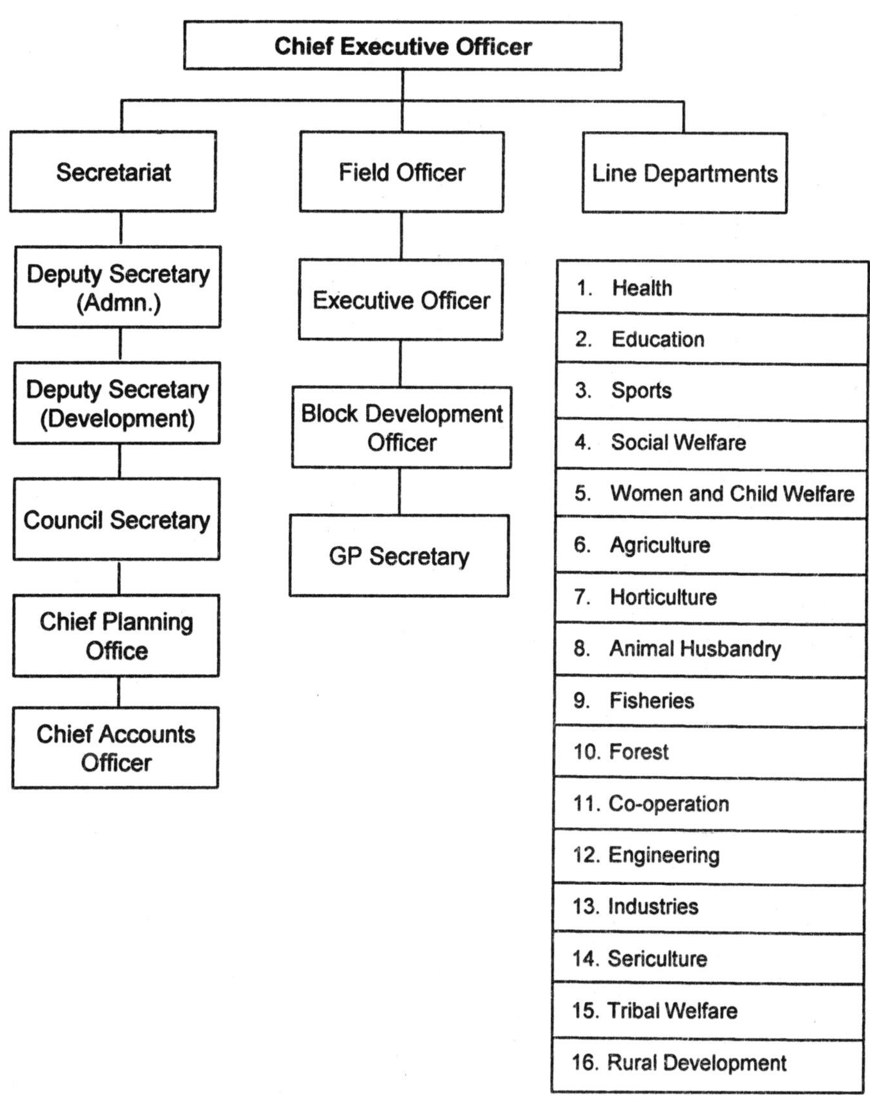

departments. Specialists, who head the District Departments, find it very difficult to meet the CEO as he is burdened with the affairs of many departments.

District Health Department

It may be interesting to note that the Health Department in the district is the second biggest department. For example, in Dakshina Kannada, out of total employees of 14184, 3130 belong to health, more than 20 per cent of the total. In Group A, out of 216 employees 137 belong to Health Department, more than 50 per cent. Thus, CEO has to devote a lot of time to the Health Department in the District.

A discussion with the Chief Planning Officer of District revealed the following constraints, which need be overcome to make decent health plans:

(a) Lack of adequate health information system for planning, implementation and monitoring;
(b) Natural resistance to change;
(c) The relatively low priority often accorded to health by political decision-makers and the public;
(d) The frequency of governmental, political and administrative changes, with concurrent changes in commitment to support to the health plan; and
(e) The imperfect state of the art of planning, i.e. the absence of trained health administrators and planners, and particularly the lack of precise tools to measure need, demand, cost and benefit.

Functions of District Health and Family Welfare Officer

The district officer with the overall responsibility for health is designated as the District Health and Family Welfare Officer (DHO).

In a district, the overall responsibility of implementation of health care delivery system lies with the DHO, who is assisted by a number of other district officers (Family Planning, Health, Malaria, T.B., U.J.P., etc. (See Chart 7.4). These district officers are declared as "Head of Office." The head of office is declared by the head of department under certain rules framed by the State Government/Central Government. The head of office has overall responsibility of carrying out all office functions. In this task, he is assisted by Administrative Officer/Office Superintendent/Office Assistant. The office work is allocated amongst the employees of the office by dividing them into different sections, i.e. Establishment, Accounts, Stores, Statistics, Transport, General, etc. The number of employees in a section depends upon the workload in that section and the number as well as the nature of sections may vary from office to office depending upon the type of work and the quantum of work.

In line with the government of India guidelines in the implementation of minimum needs programme, the State has revised its Health Policy and decided to establish a 3-Tier Health Infrastructure, viz. Sub-Centres, Primary Health Centres and Community Health Centres to provide health for all under the overall supervision and control of District Health System.

Role of DHO

DHO is given authority and is therefore responsible for the personnel, money and resources allocated to health. Authority in the managerial context of a DHO is usually identified with the legitimate base of power.

CHART 7.4

Organisational Structure of Health Department

- District Health and Family Welfare Officer
  - Dy. CMO/ Medical Officer (FW & MCH)
  - Assistant District Health and Family Welfare Officer (HQ)
  - Assistant District Health and Family Welfare Officer (Sub-Division Level/Dy. CMOS)
  - District Malaria Officer
  - Senior Malaria Officer
  - Senior Medical Superintendent
    - Medical Officers of Dt. General Hospital and other Govt. Hospitals
  - District Leprosy Officer
  - District Health Education Officer/DMEIO
  - Medical Officer (District Lab.)
  - Medical Officers of Primary Health Centres (Co-ordinators at PHC Level)
  - District Tuberculosis Officer (TB Centre)
  - District Nursing Supervisor
  - Gazetted Assistant
  - Assistant Statistical Officer
  - Lady Medical Officers/DMO of Primary Health Centres
  - Service Engineer (Mobile Workshop)

It may be defined as the legal right to command action by others and to enforce compliance. A DHO, however, might gain compliance in a number of ways through persuasion, sanctions, requests, coercion, cooperation or force...The responsibilities of a DHO are made clear by the State Health Administration through the statement of "Function, Duties, and Responsibilities of DHO." In the absence of such role description, it may lead to role ambiguity and ultimately to role conflict, where role boundaries have an overlap. The working relationship with other district health offices, district hospital and other programme officers has to be clarified and clearly understood. In fulfilling his responsibilities, the DHO often delegates authority and responsibility to other district health officials. By delegation, we mean conferring authority from DHO to another in order to accomplish particular activity/programme. Of course, such delegation has, in most districts, been very limited. When a DHO delegates authority and

CHART 7.5

Primary Health Care Infrastructure at District Level

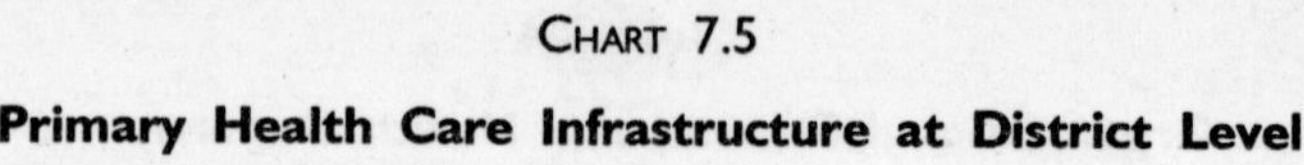

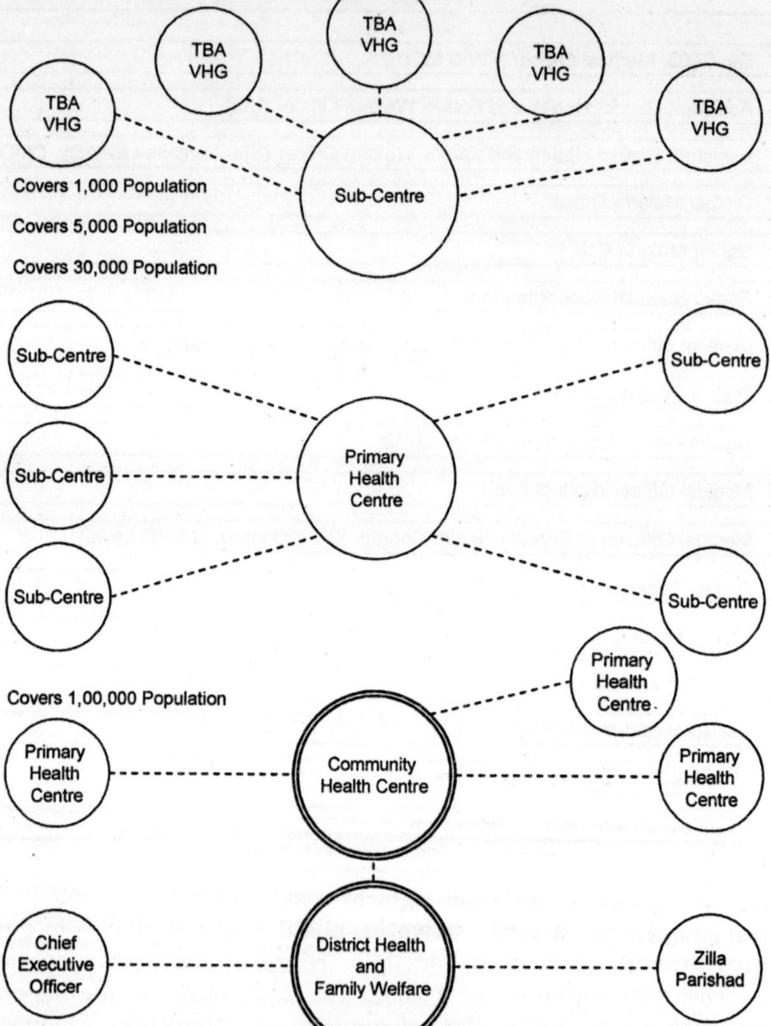

responsibility, it can never be abdicated. That means the DHO cannot throw the blame on others to whom he has delegated. Ultimately, it is the DHO who is accountable for everything in the district health services delivery.

For every recognized position in any organisation, there is an expectation widely shared by members of the organisation as to what would be the behaviour of persons who occupy that position. What a typical occupant of a given position such as DHO is expected to do, constitutes the role associated with that position. A role can be seen as encompassing, among other things, the duties or obligations of the position. DHO being the supreme authority of the district health care services structure is expected to translate into action, in his district, the broad health policies and programmes. In doing so, the DHO is expected to provide direction and guidance to the peripheral health care structure in the district.

The roles of DHO are several and they are interlinked; he is the district health-action planner: he is the director and supervisor of peripheral health structure in his district. He is the manager of entire district including lower levels of health care structure. In addition, the DHO might also have other roles in the district development administration and activities. DHO should create "prideful tradition of integrity, excellence and fellowship...Human beings breathe an ethos around them almost unconsciously and these traditions make for that ethos."

DHO should ensure "a planned system of co-operative effort in which each person has a recognized role to play and duties and tasks to perform."[14] "The key to the whole process is effective co-operation among the persons engaged in the operation."[15] According to Mooney, "Organisation is the form of every human association for the attainment of a common purpose."[16] Organisation is both structure and human relations.[17]

C. ADMINISTRATIVE FUNCTIONS OF DISTRICT HEALTH OFFICER

I. Health Planning

The most important activity of DHO is to plan for the district. District planning is crucial if primary health care is to be made successful. Planning is an intellectual exercise to adapt the health system to the district environment in order to achieve the goals of primary health care.

Planning of community health services means the careful analysis, intelligent interpretation and orderly development of these services, in accordance with modern knowledge, techniques and experience, to meet the health needs of a nation within its resources.[18] A health plan is a predetermined course of action that is firmly based on the nature and extent of health problems, from which are devised priority goals.[19] Health planning is an aid to political and administrative authorities to decide how health services can be modernized and improved to provide effective and decent health care to the community. Health planning is not an independent exercise. It is an integral part of the overall socio-economic development. National health planning has been defined as "the orderly process of defining community health problems, identifying unmet needs and surveying the resources to meet them, establishing priority goals that are realistic and feasible and projecting administrative action to accomplish the purpose of the proposed programme."[20] Planning is essentially a process of making choice between available alternatives at all levels of decision-making. Planning is the exercise of intelligence to deal with facts and solutions as they are and find a way to solve problems. Planning is, in essence, an organized, conscious and continual attempt to select the best available alternatives to achieve specific goals. As expressed by Ackoff (1970, p. 1):

Planning is one of the most complex and difficult intellectual activities in which man can engage. Not to do it well is not a sin, but to settle it for doing it less than well is.

According to Dr. Montoya

Health Planning is the phase of the total process which leads from the policy statements to the concrete identification of the populations whose needs and demands will be served; the indication of the types of activities that will be performed for those populations, with their general attributes, and the specification of the type of instruments that will be required to carry out the activities.[21]

2. Implementation

Plan implementation is an integral part of the planning process. It requires responsibility for translating the objectives of health plan into action. However, looking from the broader point of view, plan implementation requires cooperation, coordination and commitment at all levels of the implementing machinery in the field at the district, block or village level. It is at the implementation level that the difficulties creep in resulting in lower output. Implementation must be watched properly and timely action should be taken to improve administrative, technical, financial or personnel inadequacies.

3. Intersectoral Action

District Health Officer should promote intersectoral action to attain full impact of health services.

4. Leadership

The District Health Officer should provide leadership to the personnel working with him and at lower levels: Leadership is an indispensable phenomenon associated with the effective functioning of the district health services.

The attributes that are required in district health leadership may be briefly summarized as: technical competence, missionary zeal, the capacity to motivate others, the capacity to communicate with others, the ability to get along with people, cultural adaptability, the capacity to organize and manage, the capacity to inspire confidence in others, patience and dignity. Besides, a leader must believe in the ideals of the organisation, be willing to accept hardships and be prepared to work in a spirit of service. His ambition and enthusiasm should not be dampened by local conditions, which may not provide him with the necessary facilities.

5. Supervision

Planning, communication and supervision are the three main steps in the process of direction. Like every other aspect of organisation, supervision by district health team is also becoming very complicated and complex. The responsibilities of a supervisor have increased and a good supervisor is expected to have the qualities of head and heart. There is an old saying that "which is not inspected is not done." Hence inspection, overseeing and supervision arise in response to needs inherent in the functioning of an organisation.

The purpose of supervision and control is to ensure that the purposes of the organisation, i.e. provision of primary health care are being fulfilled. In most organisations, the supervision and control is still based on the old philosophy, i.e. to find faults and award punishments. The purpose of supervision is not only to inspect and inquire but also to encourage and inspire, and thus achieve teamwork.

6. Communication

District Health Officer should ensure effective communication among all the members of the staff at district and lower levels. This is essential to create sound understanding.

Effective communications is essential for ensuring effective administration. Staff must be adequately and currently informed about plans, methods, schedules, problems, events and progress. It is necessary that instructions, knowledge and information be passed on for practical application to all concerned, and that they be so clearly presented as to make misinterpretation or misunderstanding impossible. Proper and adequate communication is not just in one direction. It requires two-way passage. Administrators must be certain that they know and understand the problems of workers for whom they are responsible. Communications must flow from the bottom upwards, as well as from the top down.

7. Co-ordination

Co-ordination implies the prevention of both duplication and overlapping so as to avoid administrative wastes of efforts, manpower and resources and to pool resources and experiences in dealing with problems and in achieving common objectives. Coordination, which is a means to an end and not an end in itself, must be considered in relation to its practical purposes, which is to facilitate better performance and greater administrative efficiency in the system. To ensure efficient and economical functioning of an organisation, coordination is not only desirable but also even essential. For the same reason, inter-organisation coordination is advisable, especially when the activities of the various organisations concerned are of a complementary nature.

8. Control

The most important activity of District Health Officer is to control the activities of the district health office.

The objectives of control are as under:

(a) to ensure that the work has been accomplished according to stated objectives within budgetary and time limits;
(b) to enable the administration to identify the causes of work deficiencies; and
(c) to enable the management to suggest remedial action, i.e. to improve upon the system.

For control to be effective, it must be:

(a) Timely-Control needs to be exercised timely, otherwise there can be additions to problems.
(b) Simple-Control mechanism should be simple so that it can easily make amends.
(c) Flexible—It should be flexible as too rigid control may be self-defeating.
(d) Minimal-Control must be exercised rarely but must be thorough. Whenever it is done, all aspects need to be diagnosed.

9. Finances

The distribution of finances within the district needs to be ascertained and alternative ways found for using available finances equitably.

10. Delegation

Delegation has been defined as "investing subordinates with authority to perform the manager's job on the manager's behalf."

The starting-point in the delegation process is to examine the district health officer's own job description. Some of the jobs that have to be done can be assigned to a subordinate. Delegation can be encouraged by including a specific mention of the function in the job description of the district health officer, e.g. assignment of work to others.

11. Monitoring

Monitoring is the process of measuring, coordinating, collecting, processing and communicating information of assistance to management and decision-making. The sources of information used in monitoring health activities include monthly, quarterly and annual reports from health centres and hospitals, data on notifiable diseases and special surveys. Good information systems are required for effective monitoring. There is a practice to collect unnecessary information resulting in wastage of human and material resources. It must be emphasized that the problem is not a shortage of data, there is often too much—but the fact that little useful information can be gleaned from them.

D. FUNCTIONING OF DISTRICT HEALTH SYSTEM

(a) Headquarter-Field Relationship

The important function of District Health System is to control, Supervise and Coordinate the activities of various field agencies, viz. CHCs, PHCs, and Sub-Centres to ensure their smooth functioning and providing: (a) Preventive, (b) Promotive, (c) Curative, and (d) Rehabilitative health services. This is achieved by DHO and his staff through (a) Field reports, (b) Inspections, and (c) Meetings. District Health System has to submit reports upward to Divisional and State headquarters.

(b) Field Reports (See Chart 7.6)

These are prepared according to set guidelines to facilitate the comparability of reports on related matters and reduce as far as possible, the element of subjectivity. The reports are occasionally sugar coated. Information that will evoke a favourable reaction is played up and the lapses are glossed over without some standard guide forms, it is all too tempting for reporters to inject extraneous bits of information.[22]

A large number of reports and returns are procured from the field by District Health office. Let us mention here some of them:

1. Household and Family Register.
2. Village Register.
3. Target Couple Register.
4. Sterilization and IUD Register.
5. Oral Pill and Nirodh Distribution Register.
6. Sterilization and IUD Follow-up Register.
7. MCH Register.
8. Malaria Blood Slide Proforma.
9. Malaria Positive Case Register.
10. Stock and Distribution Register.
11. Birth and Death Register.
12. Sub-centre Clinic Register.
13. Health Worker Male Diary.
14. Health Worker Female Diary.
15. Health Worker Monthly Report Proforma.
16. Supervisor compiled report Proforma.
17. Monthly report on Health and Family Welfare Programme.

All the reports after compilation at the District level are sent to the Division level and from there to the State level.

CHART 7.6

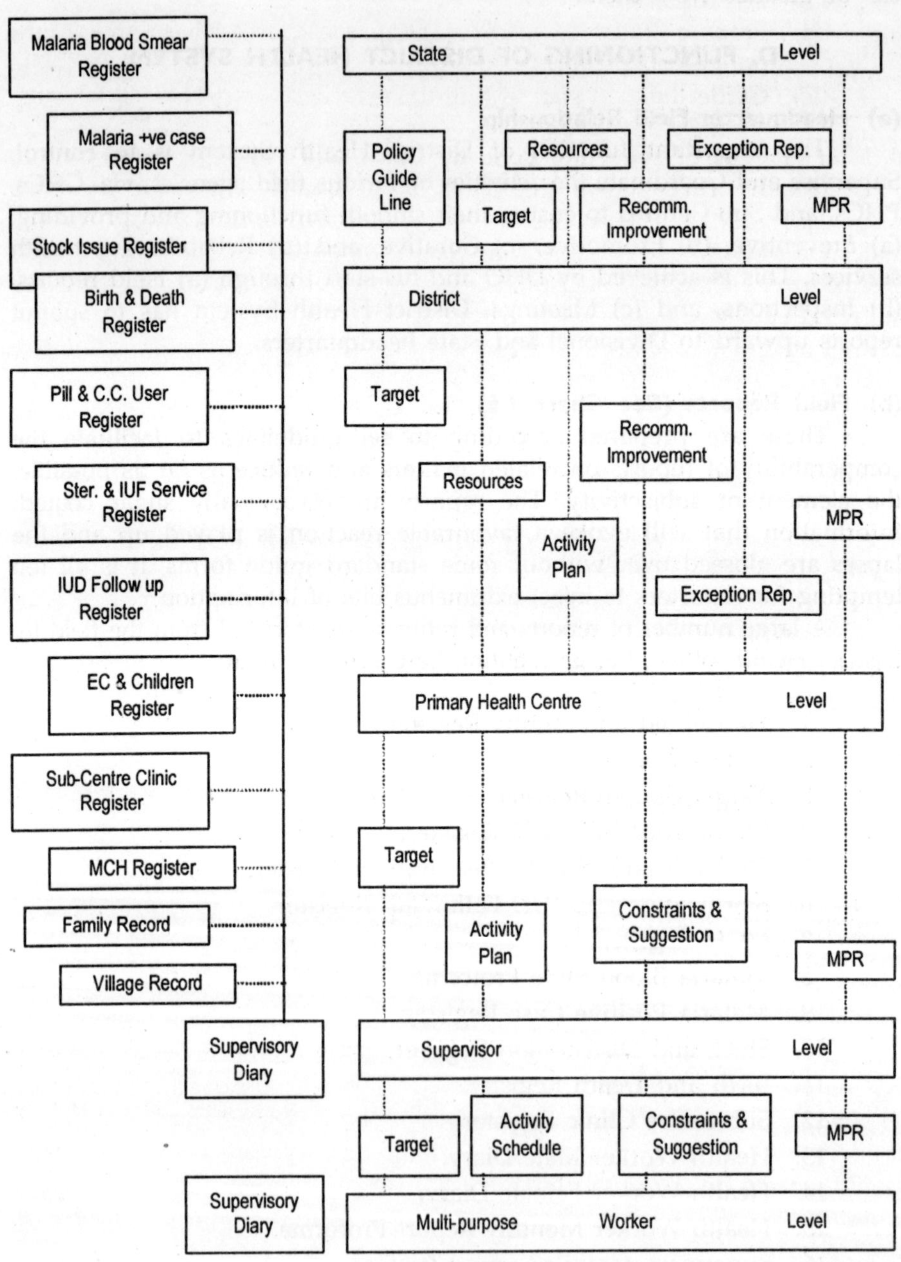

The purpose of report is to:[23]

(a) Measure the progress in the field.
(b) Locate problems in the field.

(c) Confirm that the arrangements for implementation of policies are adequate.
(d) Prepare statistical data for comparison, assessment and future policy-making and planning.
(e) Guide the field staff in future on the basis of past developments.

A brief analysis of reporting done by CHCs and PHCs to District Health office shows that it lacks in quality. Most of the staff responsible for this task has a very lukewarm attitude towards the collection of data, leaves aside their concern about its quality. In their own words, some of the field staff remarked during our field visits that 'data are collected to check the work and thus figures are mostly inflated.' At the district or the State level where it is used for the decision-making purpose, data are mostly found inconsistent and incomplete. The obvious answer submitted by the concerned staff is 'Proforma needed to be simplified' or 'less information should be collected'. As a matter of fact, whether the concerned staff is a worker, a supervisor or an official, the feeling is that the information collected has no relevance with their assigned jobs. Thus, attention paid to its quality has been minimal. The reports are usually prepared by a person with statistical background who is quite junior in status and has very little exposure of happenings in the field. It is also observed that whatever is prepared by him/her is forwarded blindly by the responsible officer to the next higher authorities. This has led to the gap between the real achievements and the reported figures. Further, since district authorities do not consider the utility and relevance of the records maintained and the reports received with the service delivery component, quality of the information has been rather poor.

Besides, the Health Staff feels that there is not much utility of such reporting. Our observation has been that most of the data does not get processed, analyzed or utilized at any level. Majority of the reports submitted to higher level after noting the achievements remain within the files and thus there has been very little utility of the information collected. In other words, no efforts are made to compare the resources utilized with that of the results obtained (cost effectiveness or cost-benefit). Further the data is so fragmented and objectives of data collection are so vague and limited that excepting matching of achievements with the set targets (Family Planning and Health Programmes), nothing more is done. Same holds true for follow-up data. For example, the follow-up cards are kept at the PHC level whereas field workers are supposed to do follow-up in the field. As a result, the follow-up cards are either not prepared or are incomplete or not updated.

One of the reasons for the indifferent attitude of the workers towards information system is that very little administrative monitoring at the field level is done by the district authorities. The only monitoring, which has been made, as a regular feature of the family welfare programme is whether targets have been met and respective feedback is given. Again, feedback is mostly to warn the staff, if achievements not commensurate with the targets or to congratulate those who have completed the targets. This is not adequate. To make the system effective and increase its use, adequate processing and appropriate analysis is needed.

Reporting and its analysis cost time and money. Therefore, only standardized, authenticated and useful reporting may be used to have genuine field control and field development. For this purpose, there is a need of designing and installing Management Information System to suit the needs of the organisation. This would hasten the exchange of information between headquarters and field. Besides, it would help in improving efficiency in operational functions, controlling organisational performance, and supporting intelligent planning by providing such information to the decision-makers, which is most relevant, accurate, complete, concise, timely, economical, reliable and efficient. In addition, the use of electronic gadgets can speed up the flow of information. In this context, district information centres set-up by the Government of India can serve as an effective link between headquarters and the field agencies.

(c) Supervision and Inspection of Field Organisations

The effectiveness of workers depends largely on the supervision they receive from district staff. In other words, quality of work is directly related to the degree of supervision. High degree of supervision improves the quality of work; poor supervision leads to poor work. So good supervision is very important for health workers, health guides and dais. Even well trained, highly motivated health workers eventually become discouraged and ineffective when supervision is lacking. Objectives of Supervision are:

To help subordinates to do their job skillfully/efficiently, develop subordinates capacity to the fullest extent, to guide/assist in meeting pre-determined work objectives (targets), to promote effectiveness of subordinates, to motivate subordinates and maintain high morale and promote teamwork.

In addition to formal reporting, observation and inspection are indispensible if field operations are to be kept under effective control and the mistakes made in one field are not to be repeated in another.

The inspection should not be conducted for isolated activities, as is the practice in most of the organisations, but should combine together all the issues needing attention at the field level. This combination of aims is necessary partly because travel costs have to be kept within the limited budgetary allocations and also to economize the use of staff time.[24]

However, in practice, inspections are not planned and no use is made of reports prepared, i.e. no action is taken upon them. The inspection is a formality and done hurriedly.

In spite of all these handicaps, the cumulative insight gained by the headquarters over field offices through observation and inspection helps in developing good relationships between headquarters and field agencies, as well as in effective evaluation.[25]

(d) Meetings between the District and Field Staff

One of the most common and useful techniques of improving workers' performance is staff meeting. It is held by supervisors at various levels of an organisation, who are responsible for getting the work done through a group of individuals placed under them. Staff meetings are productive if staff members participate freely, feel responsible, and contribute to the achievement of the organisation's goals. Staff conference may be held for different purposes. A staff conference may be called for: (a) for giving staff members certain information or to explain certain decisions taken at higher levels and to clarify certain points or doubts; (b) for solving problems arising out of day-to-day work situations for which the supervisor may have to draw upon the skills and talents of staff; (c) for giving instructions about a new skill which may need detailed explanation and demonstration. Thus, a staff conference, is not always a single purpose meeting, and the supervisor who calls and conducts it must be aware of the variety of objectives, each of which may require different patterns of leadership and participation. If staff meetings are planned and held regularly, they can certainly contribute to the development of teamwork.

The purposes of meeting are to discuss and solve a problem, communicate information, plan and organize, evaluate staff performance, evaluate the health services, coordinate the work of a health team, give training, motivate health workers and seek intersectoral meetings.

Every staff member should be well prepared for participation in a meeting. They should study the agenda and note carefully the topics to be covered. They should think about the items in terms of their own information and experience, and plan to share their ideas with others. They should feel free to make suggestions regarding the topics discussed during the meeting. Staff members should remain open-minded to listen to others reactions and accommodate the ideas of others. They should follow the discussions carefully and make notes of important decisions.

E. FACTS AND SUGGESTIONS

While district health systems have been developed and strengthened in varying degrees, a number of critical issues and problems remain. (i) the main emphasis has been on coverage, and quality of performance has been neglected; (ii) policy guidelines are inadequate to support planning and implementation at district level; (iii) decentralization is rare; (iv) the roles, responsibilities and procedures of district health staff are poorly defined and their leadership and management expertise is usually weak; (v) the integration of vertical programmes is still facing difficulties, and unipurpose workers, who have been trained as multipurpose workers, continue to give preference to their earlier programmes; (vi) there are deficiencies in collaboration within the health sector, and between the vertical programmes and the general health services; (vii) much of the information generated at district level is neither for the district health managers, nor required for decision-making, monitoring, and evaluation at district level, but only for transmission to the upper echelons, from which feedback is rarely provided; (viii) community involvement in health is weak and attempts to foster leadership capability in the community are inadequate; (ix) in district development committees, insufficient attention is paid to identifying health problems that require intersectoral action and individual sectoral priorities and different administrative structures often prevent the pooling and sharing of resources between sectors; (x) Finally, there are not enough financial or skilled human resources, at the district level, and those that are available are usually neither equitably distributed nor efficiently used.

Based on the discussions in the preceding paras, we seek to highlight various issues affecting district health system and also propose suitable suggestions to make this system effective.[26]

1. Democratic Decentralization not Effective in Practice

The experience with democratic decentralization has not been fruitful as expected. Our elected representatives are not the persons who want to serve their area without selfish motives. They, in connivance with district bureaucracy, want to exploit the system. In the new millennium, we have to ensure total transfer of power to people so that they can watch their interest and weed out bogus elected leaders and corrupt officials:

(a) Lack of able and mature leadership among office bearers at all levels of PRIs; need to strengthen their competence and capability through education and training.
(b) Mismatch of functions and resources; need for augmenting resources through local mobilization and participation.
(c) Inconsistencies in the Panchayat Raj Act, 1993; need for amendments to clarify issues to ensure a stable institutional framework of PRIs.
(d) Absence of continuous contact between the elected representatives and the people; need for people's association and organisations.
(e) Misconceptions about PRI's obligations for rural development; need for promoting self-reliance in the community.
(f) Lack of genuine will and faith in decentralization; need for transfer of full powers and authority to PRIs.
(g) Lack of cordial official-non-official relationship; need for creating harmonious conditions conducive to rural development.
(h) Undue interference by vested interests and pressure groups on PRI system; need for empowering the disadvantaged sections through education and awareness.

2. Poor Quality of Health Care

In the new millennium, quality is becoming an essential part of the health system in both developed and developing countries. Quality Assurance in Health Care is not a programme. Quality Assurance is a process, which is a continuous one. Quality of Medical Care is an index of Civilization. Health Care Quality is being demanded and expected and providers are judged by it. Quality is tangible and measurable. It is cost effective. Quality is as simple as doing one's job better continuously. There is a great pressure from patients and general public for quality health care, which is based on certain standards, accreditation, certification and bench marking. The quality of health care needs continuous improvements in services. Quality of health care should be effective, efficient, technically sound, safe and accessible. A WHO report of a meeting held in Indonesia recommended the following to improve quality health care.[27]

(1) Ensure that quality of health care is an integral part of health services delivery at all levels of health care covering public and private sectors;
(2) Organize advocacy/awareness workshops on quality assurance for policy-makers, administrators and the leadership of health care to get their commitment for quality assurance;
(3) Establish a coordinating mechanism for quality assurance activities at national level and constitute a multi-disciplinary task force of national experts to provide advice on technical aspects of quality assurance;
(4) Initiate quality assurance of health care in selected hospitals and in primary health care through the district health system approach, document the experiences and expand gradually to more health care facilities;
(5) Organize national strategic planning workshops with technical assistance from WHO;
(6) Formulate guidelines to set standards and select national key indicators on quality assurance to monitor compliance and measure performance;
(7) Invest on building local capacity in health care quality through the creation of a critical mass of expertise within the country;
(8) Mobilize potential resources from within the country including support from international agencies; and
(9) Ensure that orientation on quality assurance be integrated in both basic and in-service training programmes of all health care professionals.

3. Lack of Equity in Health Care

In the new millennium, we have to change our priorities to benefit the most deprived from the health services. We must plan and implement our health system to ensure quality health care to the poorest section of the society. Mahatma Gandhi has rightly suggested the providers of health care that "if modern medicine is to be humane, then compassion and wisdom on the part of clinicians are attributes that are needed perhaps as never before." First of all, an attitudinal change among health service staff has to be brought in so that they can make the patients feel important, wanted, cared and well looked after. This change in affective domain must start early as part of the teaching objectives for all medical and paramedical students. They should be made to realize that the hospitals of medical colleges need the patients for clinical teaching; thus the academia is dependent on patients and not *vice versa*.

Empowerment of patients will lead to medical uprising of the society by creating a class educated and aware, informed and health conscious, striving to improve their quality of life with justified use of their rights. They can curb exploitation in the name of medicine and ensure a decline in quackery.

The empowered can be easily motivated and channelised to enlist support for health programmes and achievement of health goals. Thus, health programmes will be a truly peoples' programme since indifference will cease to exist in health matters. Voluntary participation in health activities will increase.

We have to empower the poor people so that they can take their duo from health care system. As long as the services do not reach the needy people, there cannot be any perceptible change in the health status of the people. Services are not to be merely accessible but must reach those most in need.

Today, there is great alienation between the goals of District Health System and the personnel working in them resulting in inefficiency, tensions, conflicts, and low morale. Personnel system needs overhauling and reform to suit the health needs of the people in the next century. We may not get the result from the existing health personnel in the district without bringing about changes in them to usher an era of hard work, ethics, responsiveness and transparency.

4. Resistance of Bureaucracy to change itself to suit the needs of Democratic Decentralization

The greatest contribution of PRIs is breaking the hegemony of a few and empowering the masses. The concepts of transparency in administration and accountability to the people have a potential for being translated into reality through PRIs. The public mandate for a party-less development-oriented institution forces us to unlearn our present practices and beliefs.[28]

It is for the government to take certain tough decisions in overhauling the work culture and infusing ethics in administration. It is argued that appropriate action be initiated by policy-makers, administrators, political and social scientists to overcome the obstacles undermining the potential of these local institutions.

We know that it is easy to move the mountains than to change the minds of the people and without such changes, impact of Primary Health

Care would be temporary and ineffective. Shri R. Srinivasan, Secretary (Health), Government of India in his message to Regional Review meeting on Primary Health Care System Development for Southern Zone held at Bangalore on 22-23 February, 1990 said that "These tasks cannot be achieved by mere investment of further resources for buildings, residence, training centres, etc., but call for both professional and local accountability to the community. Unless the health care work force in a district remains accountable to the community and takes a large hand in health education and public information, Primary Health Care System can never do justice to its challenges. Within Government, even though the departmental organisation assigns specific responsibility at different levels, all policy level functionaries must keep the above considerations fully in mind."

For democracy to be successful at the national level, the grassroots organisations have to be strong. PRI system has to respond to the felt needs of the people. The citizens have to have faith in the efficacy of the administrative system so that the distance between people and the government is reduced.[29]

5. Primary Health Care Delivery Programme not Effective at District-level

(i) Implementation of national health programmes is weak. In particular, the routine operations should be managed well; campaigns should be properly organized and integrated well with other health activities.

(ii) Promotive health programmes such as health education, school health, nutritions, food adulteration and environmental sanitation are usually neglected. District officials should be able to plan, implement and monitor them well.

(iii) Epidemic control activities need to be streamlined.

(iv) District has to perform several functions to support functioning of PHCs which at present suffer because of resources and lack of support. These include:
- guidance/supervision to PHCs,
- exercise financial and administrative powers,
- maintenance of equipment,
- supplies,
- allocation of staff,
- appraise performance of PHCs systematically, scientifically and objectively,
- assess training needs of MOs, and
- create favourable community environment for health workers and PHCs to function..

6. Inadequate and Non-functional Infrastructure

Committed and reputed NGOs may be involved in the development of primary health care system by handing over certain proportion of infrastructure facilities, namely, Sub-centre or primary health centre along with building, funds and staff with relatively more management freedom to VOs/NGOs depending upon their capability of funds, staff, etc. after ascertaining their credibility.

Mechai Viraavaidya in his article, "Utapped Potential" in *World Health* rightly states, "The NGO sector has the potential to be a much greater force than it is at present...A working partnership between government agencies and NGOs can make tremendous progress in the next fifteen years."[30]

NGO-supported and organized health care services must be an integral part of the total health system of a country, including the referral system.[31]

7. Lack of Enlightened Community Participation and Involvement: Need of Empowering People

Although academics, voluntary organisations, government and funding agencies and UN agencies have promoted and supported the participation concept of development and much has been written and spoken about participation, authentic participation of the poor has hardly taken place in real life situation. Peoples' participation in development process has been elusive.[32] Same is true about participation of the people in health services.

To quote WHO: Community participation is a political process insofar as community members acquire a say in decision-making about health and health care issues that affect them, and a measure of control over the persons that are supposed to serve their needs. Community participation in this sense raises the most serious organisational problems, and even dilemmas, for ministries of welfare.[33] Community participation also has political implications when community members are involved in monitoring the services from which they are supposed to benefit.

They can demand that the necessary attention be paid to the needs of the people at the grassroots, and of those expected to serve them. The mechanisms of community involvement are also important to give the authorities responsibility at the district level, adequate information about the grassroots functioning of the health care system: without direct inputs from the communities, those authorities may only receive information from the very system they are supposed to control.[34]

Ministry of personnel has also realized the neglect of elected bodies from being given the real power to monitor. To quote: "The agenda for real empowerment of elected local bodies, has largely not gone beyond conforming legislation in most states-centralized system for planning and service delivery often through functional agencies still persist, and the local self-government bodies and the elected functionaries are not able to function with adequate control over local functions and resources.[35]

8. Lack of Inter-sectoral and Intrasectoral Coordination

The concept of primary health care encompasses the overall socio-economic development of communities concurrent to the improvement of the health status. Therefore, the health sector cannot function in isolation while implementing primary health care programmes. More important and relevant to the technical discussions is the acceptance by other sectors involved in the socio-economic development—agriculture, housing, public works and communications, education, mass media—that they cannot work in isolation to the exclusion of the health sector. The establishment of intersectoral coordination is therefore an important primary health care approach.

Aleyco El Bindari Hammad in his Article, "Intersectoral Cooperation in Primary Health Care" in *World Health* rightly mentions that the broader aim of increasing well-being and resistance to disease as a whole while promoting and maintaining good health will require the combined efforts of many sectors not immediately related to health.[36]

9. Non-involvement of Universities in Promoting, Health Care

Universities must act as bridges between the community and the Government. We have various universities and medical colleges who can help in the promotion of Primary Health Care. In May 1984, world health assembly chose the theme, "The Role of Universities in the Strategies for Health for all." To quote:

> Universities are seeking new relationships with health policy-makers, extending the concept of health care beyond that of the individual to that of whole communities, and adapting their under-graduate curriculum to ensure that education equips students to undertake those supervisory and managerial roles, which have not hitherto been seen as appropriate for health professionals."[37]

Now at last, the universities seem prepared to lend whole-hearted backing to three of the main imperatives of Health for All: political commitment to social equity, community participation and the use of appropriate and affordable technology.[38]

10. Stereotyped Health Management System

The challenge of Health for All calls for a permanent and systematic managerial process, ranging from planning and policymaking, in collaboration with other sectors, to implementation, monitoring and evaluation, for the development of an effective health system. The managerial process entails the formulation of a health policy with defined priorities, and the preparation of programmes and budgets to put the policy into effect. It also calls for the assessment of manpower requirements and the formulation of plans to train the requisite manpower, together with the integration of well formulated programmes into the general health system.

A dynamic civil society and a professionally trained and dedicated civil service (Insulated from political interference) are the twin pillars of a constructive relationship between State and Society.[39]

Mr. M.G. Devashayam, ex-IAS officer, in his Article 'Good Administration' in the *Daily Tribune* dated December 27, 1998 mentions the components of responsible administration. These are:

(i) Openness in the sense of having wide contact with the people administered;
(ii) A sense of justice, fair play and impartiality in dealing with men and matters;
(iii) Sensitivity and responsiveness to the urges, feelings and aspirations of the common people;
(iv) Securing the honor and dignity of the human being, however humble he or she might be;
(v) Humility and simplicity in the persons manning the administrative machinery and their easy accessibility;
(vi) Creating and sustaining an atmosphere conducive to development, growth and social change; and
(vii) honest and integrity in thought and action.

11. Lack of Reliable and Scientific Referral System

At present, the referral system does not function effectively. This is due to the following reasons: (i) Overloading of hospitals with self-referrals; (ii) lack of confidence in lower-level facilities because of perceived low quality of care; (iii) lack of organisational and management links between hospitals at various levels. An effective referral system has to be designed by focusing on three important areas: the structure of the referral system, management coordination and quality improvement.

The District Health System has the potential capacity and means to deliver decent health services to the people. However, the administrative system and the ethos and perceptions of the personnel working there do not possess confidence in achievement.

A visit to various health offices at District level reveal the poor functioning of these offices. People mentioned the following problems faced by them in dealing with the officials:

(i) Unhelpful attitude,
(ii) Inordinate delay in transacting business,
(iii) Corruption amongst the officials,
(iv) Shortage of medicine,
(v) Faulty procedure,
(vi) Intentional delays,
(vii) No arrangements for persons on leave, and
(viii) Improper behaviour

In the new millennium, we have to change the District Health System as envisaged in World Health Assembly Resolution WHA 39, in terms of its structure, approach, and methodology to meet the health needs of the people. We have to appoint persons who have vision, vitality, dedication, clarity and who can get the results and not simply move the papers.

In the new millennium, District Health System has to introduce new technology of Telematics, and ensure equity and quality in health care.

A Report of a WHO Inter-country Workshop on Telemedicine for Health Development in the 21st century Bangkok, Thailand, defines the meaning, use and gives recommendations to promote Telemedicine.[40]

Health Telematics is defined as a composite term for health related activities, services and systems carried out over a distance by means of information and communication technologies for the purpose of global health promotion, disease control and health care, as well as education, management and research for health.

The process of planning which includes the formulation of policy and strategies is followed by the choice of technology, which is implemented in three phases. The first phase of implementation includes the development and adoption of standards and laying down of specifications to meet the health telematics strategies. Standardization is required at different levels varying from Data Standards; Technical Standards; Work Standards, and Equipment Standards to Training Standards and Professional Standards. The second phase deals with the selection of computing hardware, peripherals, telecommunication infrastructure, operating and utility software, while the third phase concentrates on procurement, implementation, training and support.

Health Telematics raises certain ethical issues, such as the acceptability of transmitting personal information across cultural boundaries; young doctors getting professionally affected, and the confidentiality of the relationship between the patient and the treating doctor does not exist. Full cooperation of the medical and paramedical staff involved, as well as patients is essential. Even in the most advanced form, Health Telematics might not provide a blanket solution for each situation. There would be cases where human intervention is needed. It also raises concern on widening the gap between the poor and the privileged.

Based on the presentations by various resource persons, and the experiences shared between SEARO countries during the workshop, the participants appreciated the potential of Telemedicine. However, the group proposed to change the term "Telemedicine" to the broader term of "Health Telematics" in order to avoid a narrow interpretation of the scope of technology.

The participants made the following recommendations:

(1) Conduct advocacy and awareness of Health Telematics so as to gain the commitment of policy-makers, administrators and professional groups.

(2) Incorporate Health Telematics into the renewed HFA policies/strategies.
(3) Conduct situation analyses, and define priorities for initiating plans of action, through pilot projects on Health Telematics.
(4) Develop the national capacity, through training of human resources required to set-up and manage Health Telematics activities.
(5) Constitute national coordination committees for the development of Telematics as an integral component of social development, thus ensuring the participation of relevant sectors right from the beginning.
(6) Build Health Telematics on the available infrastructure, and choose appropriate technology based on country resources and the health needs of the people.
(7) Develop the monitoring and evaluation criteria as integral parts of the project.
(8) Develop partnerships with various stakeholders: the industry, academic institutions and research centres, and public and private sectors in support of Health Telematics.

District Health System need be strengthened to provide integrated and comprehensive health care to the people.

FACTS AND SUGGESTIONS

Let us mention here the facts identified by World Health Organisation in District Health System.

While district health system have been developed and strengthened in varying degrees, a number of critical issues and problems remain. (i) the main emphasis has been on coverage and quality of performance has been neglected; (ii) policy guidelines are inadequate to support planning and implementation at district level; (iii) decentralization is rare; (iv) the roles, responsibilities, and procedures of district health staff are poorly defined and their leadership and management expertise is usually weak; (v) the integration of vertical programmes is still facing difficulties and unipurpose workers, who have been trained as multipurpose workers, continue to give preference to their earlier programmes; (vi) there are deficiencies in collaboration within the health sector and between the vertical programmes and the general health services; (vii) much of the information generated at district level is neither for the district health managers, nor required for decision-making monitoring and evaluation at district level, but only for transmission to the upper echelons, from which feedback is rarely provided; (viii) community involvement in health is weak and attempts to foster leadership capability in the community are inadequate; (ix) in district development committees, insufficient attention is paid to identifying health problems that require intersectoral action, and individual sectoral priorities and different administrative structures often prevent the poking and sharing of resources between sectors; and (x) Finally there are not enough financial or skilled human resources, at the district level, and those that are available are usually neither equitably distributed nor efficiently used.[41]

Notes and References

1. S.S. Khera, District Administration in India, Asia, New Delhi, 1964, p. 21.
2. Eighth General Programme of Work Covering the Period, 1990-93, Geneva, WHO, 1987 (Health for All Series No. 10).
3. WHO: SEARO: Health Situation in the South-East Asia Region, 1994-97, New Delhi; 1999, p. 185.
4. WHO: World Health Assembly Resolution, 39.7.
5. Rajneesh Goel, Thesis, An Analysis of Primary Health Care Administration in Karnataka, January 2000, pp. 120-22.
6. WHO: District Health System, Geneva, 1995, p. 9.
7. James C. Charlesworth, Government Administration, Harpur, New York, 1951, p. 207.
8. *Ibid.*
9. WHO: Strengthening Ministries of Health For Primary Health Care, Geneva, 1984, pp. 31-32.
10. WHO: District Health Systems, Geneva, 1995, p. 8.
11. *Ibid.*, pp. 9-10.
12. Krasae Chanawonges, Rural Development Management, Mahidol University, Thailand, 1996, p. 13.
13. Based on Personal Discussion.
14. *Ibid.*
15. H. Simon, Public Administration, p. 5.
16. J.D. Mooney, Principles of Organisation, p. 1.
17. Dimok and Dimok, Public Administration, p. 104.
18. WHO: Technical Report Series, 215, 1961, p. 4.
19. WHO: Public Health Paper 46, p. 9.
20. WHO: Public Health Paper 44, p. 15.
21. Dr. Montoya, Programme Technology, in the Context of Health Planning, Mimeographed.
22. Walter R. Sharp, Field Administration in the United Nations System, The Carnegie Endowment, London, Stevens, 1961, p. 266.
23. S.L. Goel, Advanced Public Administration, New Delhi, Sterling, 1994, p. 290.
24. *Ibid.*
25. *Ibid.*, p. 291.
26. WHO: District Health Systems, Geneva, 1995, p. 28.
27. WHO: SEARO, Report of a WHO Inter-country Meeting, Sarabayo, Indonesia, 16-20, December 1996, New Delhi, p. 8.
28. Shailini Rajneesh, Democratic Decentralization in Karnataka, a Ph.D. thesis, unpublished, p. 293.
29. A.P. Barnabas, Good Governance at Local Level, in *IJPA*, July-September 1998, p. 453 (Special Number on Towards Good Governance).
30. Mechai Vira Vaidya, Untapped Potential, in *World Health*, March 1985, p. 4.
31. S.K. Vettivel, People's Participation in Social Development, Role of NGO's, New Delhi, Vetri Publishers, 1992, p. 5.

32. P.K. Bajpai, People's Participation in Development-A Critical Analysis, in *IJPA*, October-December, 1998, p. 817.
33. WHO: Strengthening Ministries of Health of Primary Health Care, Geneva, 1984. p. 39.
34. *Ibid.*, p. 42.
35. Documents, Action Plan for an Effective and Responsive Government Prepared by Department of Administrative Reforms and Public Grivances, Ministry of Personnel Public Grivances, New Delhi, Quoated in *IJPA*, Vol. XLIV, No. 3 (July-September, 1998), p. 637.
36. WHO: *World Health*, March, 1986, p. 5.
37. George C. Salmot, New Problems, New Strategies in *World Health*, January, 1980, p. 15.
38. WHO: *World Health*, April 1984, p. 3.
39. R.K. Sapru, Development Administration Crises and Continuities, in *IJPA*, October-December, 1998, p. 779.
40. SEARO, Report of WHO: Inter-country Workshop on Telemedicine For Health Development in the 21st Century, Bangkok, Thailand, 30 March-3 April, 1998, pp. 1-21
41. WHO: District Health Systems, Geneva, 1995, p. 28.

Role of Ministry of Women and Child Development

Government of India in Health Promotion of Women and Children

Growth of the economy has to be not only faster but also inclusive to achieve overall human development. The flow of benefits should be sufficiently widespread and equally distributed among all sections of society especially women and children. The dreams of the founding fathers of India—to have an India which is prosperous and equitable; an India which is caring and inclusive; an India which provides opportunities for every citizen to excel in her chosen area of work and live up to her fullest potential, are to be realized and the various development programmes are to aim in this direction.

The tenth plan continued with the approach of empowering women as agents of social change and development using the three-pronged strategy of social empowerment, economic empowerment and gender justice. One of the six basic principles of Governance laid down in the National Common Minimum Programme is "To empower women politically, educationally, economically and legally." The National Common Minimum Programme envisages universalisation of Integrated Child Development Scheme and Anganwadi Centres in each settlement.

Vision

The Ministry of Women and Child Development (MWCD), Government of India, is the nodal ministry for all matters pertaining to the welfare, development and empowerment of women and children in the country. A separate Ministry for Women and Child Development came into existence from 30th January 2006. The vision of Ministry of Women and Child Development is "Ensuring overall survival, development, protection and participation of women and children of the country." The Ministry has

CHART 8.1

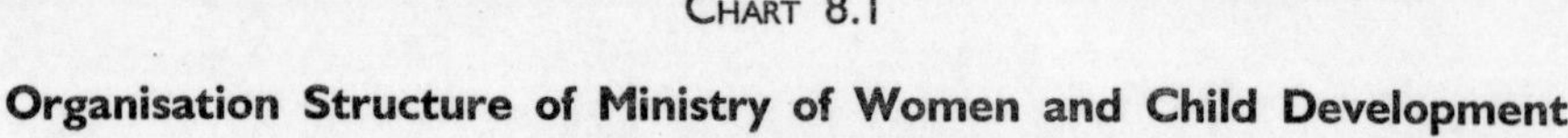

Organisation Structure of Ministry of Women and Child Development

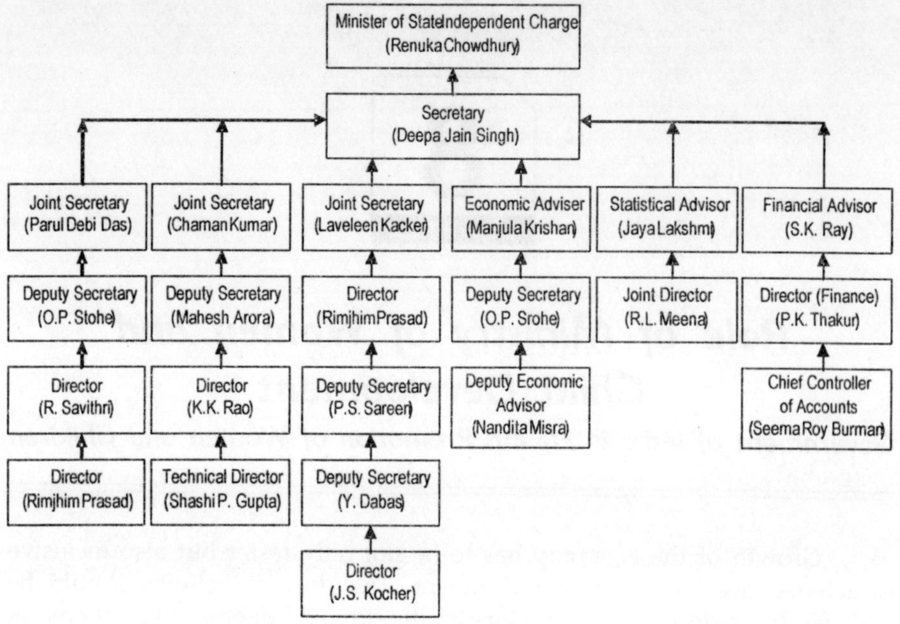

evolved policies, plans of action, legislations, programmes and schemes for advancement of women and children and has been implementing these with the support of State Governments, other Government agencies and voluntary sector for achieving its mandate.

Organisation

The Ministry of Women and Child Development is headed by Minister of State and the Secretary of the Ministry. Secretary is assisted by three Joint Secretaries, Economic adviser and a Statistical Adviser who head the five Bureaux of the Ministry namely; Child Development (also Food and Nutrition Board); Women Welfare and Development; Child Welfare and Protection; Prevention of Trafficking, Gild Child and Gender Budgeting; and Plan, Research, Monitoring and Statistics. Besides Joint Secretary, Financial Adviser of the Ministry looks after the financial matter of the Ministry.

The Ministry has 4 autonomous organisations, viz. National Institute of Public Cooperation and Child Development (NIPCCD), Rashtriya Mahila Kosh (RMK), Central Social Welfare Board (CSWB) and Central Adoption Resource Agency (CARA) working under its aegis. NIPCCD, RMK and CARA are societies registered under the Societies Registration Act, 1860. CSWB is a charitable company registered under section 25 of the Indian Companies Act, 1956. These organisations are fully funded by the Government of India and they assist the Department in its functions including implementation of some programmes/schemes. The National Commission for Women was constituted as a national apex statutory body in 1992 for protecting and safeguarding the rights of women.[1]

There are many agencies for Women Development and Empowerment, the most important being the Ministry of Women and Child.

The WCD department is the nodal Ministry of the government of India for the welfare and development of women and children of the country. The specific issues like health, education, employment, etc. of women and children are looked after by the sectoral Ministries/ Departments, but the Department of Women and Child Development has the overall responsibility to coordinate the activities of all other Ministries and organisations on this subject.

The list of subjects allocated to the Department of Women and Child Development include:

1. Welfare of the Family.
2. Women and Child Welfare and co-ordination of activities of other Ministries and Organisations in connection with this subject.
3. References from the United National Organisations relating to traffic in women and children.
4. Care of pre-school children including pre-primary education.
5. National Nutrition Policy, National Plan of Action for Nutrition and National Nutrition Mission.
6. Charitable and religious endowments pertaining to subjects allocated to this Department.
7. Promotion and development of voluntary effort on subjects allocated on this Department.
8. Implementation of—
   a. The Immoral Traffic (Prevention) Act, 1956 (as amended upto 1986);
   b. The Indecent Representation of Women (Prevention) Act, 1986 (60 of 1986);
   c. The Dowry Prohibition Act, 1961 (as amended upto 1986);
   d. The Commission of Sati (Prevention) Act, 1987 (3 of 1988), (excluding the administration of criminal justice in regard to offences under these acts.)
9. Implementation of the Infant Milk Substitutes, Feeding Bottles and Infant Food (Regulation of Production, Supply and Distribution) Act, 1992 (41 of 1992).
10. Coordination of activities and programmes of Cooperative for Assistance and Relief Everywhere (CARE).
11. Planning, Research, Evaluation, Monitoring, Project Formulations, Statistics and Training relating to the welfare and development of women and children, including development and gender sensitive data base.
12. United Nations Children's Fund (UNICEF).
13. Central Social Welfare Board (CSWB).

14. National Institute of Public Cooperation and Child Development (NIPCCD).
15. Food and Nutrition Board.
16. (i) Development and popularization of subsidiary and protective foods.
    (ii) Nutrition extension.
17. Women's Empowerment and Gender Equity.
18. National Commission for Women.
19. Rashtriya Mahila Kosh.
20. Juvenile Justice (Care and Protection of Children) Act, 2000 (56 of 2000).
21. Probation of Juvenile offenders.
22. Issues relating to adoption, Central Adoption Resource Agency and Child Help Line (Child line).
23. The Children Act, 1960 (60 of 1960).
24. The Juvenile Justice (Care and Protection of Children) Act, 2000 (56 of 2000).
25. The Child Marriage—Restraint Act, 1929 (19 of 1929).[2]

CRITICAL APPRAISAL

Policy-making and Planning

Policies may be thought of as the main system, which provides the framework for the accomplishment of intended objectives. Formulation of policies involves making explicit various assumptions regarding "the basic premises, needs and the priorities and allocating the finances accordingly. Besides, policies are intended to spell out the parameters in the context of which organisation's decisions are to be made. Policy gives a concrete shape to the political and social objectives, which the government lays down in the form of laws, rules, regulations, etc. Davis states: A policy is basically a statement either expressed or implied of those principles and rules that are set-up by executive leadership as guides and constraints for the organisation's thought and action. Its principal purpose is to enable executive leadership to relate properly the organisation's work to its objectives.

Ensuring Survival and Welfare of Girl Child, Prohibition of Child Marriage Bill

The rising incidence of female foeticide and infanticide, which has led to decline in the sex ratio from 976 in 927 in the year 2001 (for 0-6 years) is a reflection of society's perception of the values and respect accorded to a girl child. The problem of child marriage needs to be tackled in order to reduce maternal mortality and infant mortality.

Nation-wide awareness and sensitization campaigns have been organized to educate the masses that the girl child is an asset and not a burden. A number of awareness programmes and sensitization programmes have been organized by the Ministry during 2006-07 to sensitize and generate awareness among different sections of societies and stakeholders about ill effects of female foeticide and infanticide. The Ministry is closely working with M/o Health and Family Welfare in implementing and monitoring "Preconception and Prenatal Diagnostic Techniques Act, 1994."

The cabinet in its meeting held on 21.9.2006 approved the proposal on proposed Legislation on Child Marriage Prohibition Act, 1929. Thereafter the amendment to the prevention of Child Marriage Bill, 2004 was passed by the Rajya Sabha on 14.12.06 and the Prohibition of Child Marriage Bill, 2006 was passed by the Lok Sabha on 19.12.2006.

Legislations, Programmes for Child Protection

A Child Budget exercise carried out by the Ministry of Women and Child Development revealed the persistently low level of fund allocation for child protection. The total share of child protection in the Union Budget for 2005-06 was just 0.034% and the budget estimates for the current financial year 2006-07 has remained the same. Scarcely any allocations have been made for child protection since independence, a reflection of the low priority it has received in government's own planning and implementation, resulting in scant state interventions toward child protection.

Various legal measures, programmes and initiatives have been taken by the Ministry for child protection and these are as follows:

Commission for Protection of Child Rights Act, 2005

The Government notified the Commissions for Protection of Child Rights Act, 2005 in the Gazette of India on 20th January 2006 as Act No. 4 of 2006. The Act envisages setting up of a National Commission at the National level and the State Commission at the State level. The Commission would be working for proper enforcement of children's rights and effective implementation of laws and programmes relating to children. The National Commission is likely to be set-up shortly.

Offences Against Children (Prevention) Bill

Offences Against Children (Prevention) Bill provides for dealing with offences against children and punishments for offenders along with procedures to be followed. There are other provisions for reporting obligations and monitoring also. The draft cabinet note on Bill defining the various offences against children and corresponding punishments has been circulated among various ministries dealing with child sector.

Amendment to the Juvenile Justice (Care and Protection of Children) Act, 2000

This amendment was passed by both houses of the Parliament and it came into effect from 23.08.2006. An important amendment has been made in the Act with the sole objective to provide for the effective implementation of the Act through constitution of Child Protection Unit at State and District level.

An Integrated Child Protection Scheme

The Ministry of Women and Child Development has also initiated steps for formulate a comprehensive scheme. An integrated Child Protection Scheme which will seek to have a complete child protection framework in place across the country. The proposed scheme includes components for providing institutional as well as non-institutional support for the children in difficult circumstances in order to provide for their immediate care and protection as well as long-term rehabilitation. It also seeks to address the capacity building and training needs for all categories of functionaries concerned with children, be they police, judiciary, voluntary organisations and State Governments besides advocacy and awareness generation.

Schemes for Welfare of Working Children in Need of Care and Protection

A scheme for welfare of working children in need of care and protection which was started from January 2005 provides non formal education, vocational training to working children to facilitate their entry/re-entry into main stream education in cases where they have either not attended any learning system or where for some reason their education has been discontinued.

Integrated Scheme for Street Children

The objective of this programme is to prevent destitution of children and facilitate their withdrawal from life on the streets. The programme provides for basic facilities like shelter, nutrition, health care, education and recreation facilities to street children and seeks to protect them against abuse and exploitation.

Innovative Scheme for Women and Children

Under the scheme, assistance is given to voluntary organisation working in the filed of child and women welfare for innovative projects and activities, which are not covered in the existing schemes of the Ministry of Women and Child Development.

A number of programmes are being supported for rehabilitation of children of sex workers, destitute children and rehabilitation of families of Drug de-addicted people particularly in North-East, rehabilitation of widows providing counselling and support to traumatized women and children particularly those who have been victims of physical violence and sexual abuse.

Scheme for Prevention and Control of Juvenile Social Maladjustment

The scheme aims at:

(i) To extend help to State Governments to bear the cost of infrastructure and services development under the Juvenile Justice Act.
(ii) To ensure minimum quality standards in the juvenile justice services.

(iii) To provide adequate services for prevention of social maladjustment and rehabilitation of socially maladjusted Juveniles.

Under the scheme, the Ministry provides 50 per cent assistance to State Governments and UT Administrations for establishment and maintenance of various levels of institutions for juveniles in conflict with law and children in need of care and protection.

Adoption of Orphans

Taking care of children who have become orphan due to various reasons and rehabilitating them through adoption is one of the important functions undertaken by the Ministry. The Central Adoption Resource Agency (CARA) which is an autonomous body under the Ministry promotes domestic adoption and regulates inter country adoption. Sishu Grih Scheme (for assistance to homes) to promote in country adoption of children is implemented by CARA in which grant-in-aid is provided to Government organisations for increasing and promoting adoptions within the country.

Prevention of Trafficking in Women and Children

The growing incidence of trafficking for prostitution is a matter of growing concern, especially as it is estimated that as much as 40% of the prostitutes are children. To deal with this problem, the Ministry of Women and Child Development is implementing a pilot project for prevention and combating trafficking in source, destination and traditional areas. During 2006-07, the Ministry initiated action to deal with the emerging problems such as repatriation of cross-border victims, development of training modules and training and capacity building of various functionaries, streamlining inter-State rescue and repatriation measures, etc. The premier legislation, Immoral Traffic (Prevention) Act, 1956 (ITPA) is being amended in order to widen its scope, focus on the trafficker and prevent revictimization of the victims. The ITPA Amendment Bill has been examined by the Parliamentary Standing Committee and their recommendations are being processes.

The Ministry of External Affairs has been requested to set-up an internal Task force to ensure that the legislations, programme, etc. are in place for operationalizing the provisions of the SAARC Convention on Preventing and Combating Trafficking of Women and Children in Prostitution. Further, the need for helpline and emergency rescue facilities to be made available in embassies/high commissions for trafficked victims abroad has been emphasized.

National Plan of Action for Children, 2005 (NPAC)—Monitoring

Ministry of Women and Child Development has prepared a National Plan of Action for Children, 2005 after harmonizing the goals for children set in the UN General Assembly Special Session on Children held in 2002 and the monitorable targets set in the Tenth Five Year Plan, and goals for children in related Ministries/Departments. The Action Plan has been prepared in consultation with concerned Ministries and Departments, States/UT Governments, non-Governmental Organisations and experts. The National Plan of Action includes goals objectives, strategies and activities for improving nutritional status of children, reducing IMR and MMR, increasing enrolment ratio and reducing dropout rates, universalization of primary education, increasing coverage for immunization, etc. The Ministry is preparing quarterly monitoring reports for the National Plan of Action for Children, 2005 on the basis of eight parameters prescribed by the Prime Minister's Office and sends in regularly to PMO.

Socio-economic Empowerment of Women Micro Credit for Women

The Ministry of Women and Child Development has been implementing various programmes and schemes aimed at improving the socio economic empowerment of women, support services for enabling the women reach the take-off level for empowerment, schemes providing relief, protection and rehabilitation to women in difficult circumstances and policies, legislations and initiatives to enable gender justice.

Schemes for Socio-economic Empowerment of Women

The poor assetless women suffer from the high poverty incidence levels and in order to tackle this problem, initiatives such as mobilization of women into Self Help Groups (SHGs), provision of training in various livelihood skills, upgradation of skills to enable them take up income generation activities through self-employment or wage employment have been undertaken by the Ministry. Swayamsidha, STEP are some of the important programmes of the Ministry working in this direction. Under the scheme of Swayamsidha, women's SHGs have been formed and these SHGs are involved in various development activities. Under the programme STEP, updated skills and new knowledge are provided to poor and asset-less women in the traditional sectors such as Agriculture, Animal Husbandry, Dairying, Fisheries, Handlooms, Handicrafts, Khadi and Village Industries, Sericulture, Social Forestry and Wasteland Development for enhancing their productivity and income generation.

Micro Credit for Women

The Rashtriya Mahila Kosh (RMK) which is the micro credit agency of M/o Women and Child Development has in place a unique credit delivery model 'RMK-NGO-SHG-Beneficiaries' and has flexible credit norms, hassle loans, no collateral and reasonable rate of interest to help women start livelihood activities.

Support Services for Women

To facilitate the employment of women away from their homes/

towns, schemes providing support services for women such as Working Women Hostels with day-care centres and crèches/day care centres are implemented. Revamping of the scheme of working women hostels is in pipeline.

Provision of support facilities such as crèche for children of working and ailing mothers will enable the mothers to engage themselves in income generation activities. Crèche facilities for children have been increased under the aegis of Rajiv Gandhi National Crèche Scheme initiated in January 2006 by the Ministry. This scheme is implemented by Ministry through CSWB and the two voluntary organisations Adim Jati Sevak Sangh and Indian Council for Child Welfare.

Schemes Providing Relief, Protection and Rehabilitation of Women

Providing relief, protection and rehabilitation of women in distress is one of the focused areas and this is achieved through Swadhar Shelter Homes, Short Stay Homes and Women Helplines. The women in the Swadhar and Short Stay homes are provided shelter, food, clothing, emotional support and counselling in order to rehabilitate them socially and economically. While Swadhar Shelter homes scheme is run directly by the Ministry. The Scheme of short stay homes is implemented through CSWB. During 2006-07, Rs. 1750 lakhs is allocated and an amount of Rs. 1247.47 lakhs released to voluntary organisations as on 6.2.2007.

Schemes of Mahila Mandals, Awareness Generation, Condensed Course of Education, Family Counselling Centre implemented by Central Social Welfare Board.

Mahila Mandals provides services like Balwadis for children, craft activities, social education, maternity services for women, etc.

Awareness Generation Programme aims at generating awareness amongst women and community at large on rights, status and problems of women in particular and other social concerns. The main objective of awareness generation camps is to identify the needs of rural and poor women and to increase women's active participation in development and other allied programmes.

The scheme of Condensed Course of Education aims to provide educational opportunities to girls/women above the age of 15 years alongwith additional inputs of skill development/occasional training. The contents of the course are need based and modified according to local requirement.

The scheme of Family Counselling Centre provides counselling, referral and rehabilitative services to women and children who are victims of atrocities, family maladjustments, etc. The centers work in close collaboration with local administrator, police, courts, medical institutions, etc.

Some of the Family Counselling Centres are being run at Police Headquarters, Mahila Jails, Rape Crisis Intervention Centres, Pre-Marital Counselling Centre and Centre for Devdasis/Red Light Areas.

GENDER JUSTICE AND LEGAL SAFEGUARDS

Attending to Complaints relating to Atrocities on Women, Review of Central Acts concerning Women

Safeguard the interest of women covering all aspects of women's rights is a mandate of National Commission for women (NCW). NCW receives and attends to complaints received from women. NCW has also sponsored many workshops, awareness programmes, legal awareness programmes and Parivarik Mahila Lok Adalats concerning women related issues. Online registration of complaints has been started at www.ncw.nic.in with effect from 9th September 2005. The National Commission for women conceptualized a nation wide programme titled 'CHALO GAON KI ORE' in February 2006. The programme is a step towards empowerment of the rural woman throughout the country with knowledge of their rights under the law. The programme has been launched in the States of Punjab, Haryana, Madhya Pradesh, Bihar and Tripura.

There are about 44 Central Acts concerning or impacting women of which 41 acts have been reviewed by the National Commission for Women for their efficiency and removing gender discriminatory provisions.

Legislation on Domestic Violence, Bill on Prevention of Sexual Harassment of Women at Workplace

To fulfil the commitment made in the National Common Minimum Programme regarding enactment of legislation on domestic violence, the Ministry of Women and Child Development has enacted the "Protection of women from domestic violence Act, 2005" which is a comprehensive legislation to protect women from all forms of domestic violence. This act has been brought into force on 26.10.2006 and it provides immediate and emergent relief to women who face situation of violence in their homes. The protection of women from domestic violence rules, 2006 have also been notified as per the provisions contained in the act. The code of criminal procedure has been amended through CrPC Amendment Act, 2005 w.e.f. 23.6.2006 to provide that no women shall be arrested after sunset and before sunrise and where exceptional circumstances exist, the women police officer shall, by making a written report, obtain the prior permission of the judicial magistrate of the first class within whose local jurisdiction, the offence is committed or the arrest is to be made.

The Ministry is examining a Bill on prevention of sexual harassment of women at the workplace to give effect to the guidelines and norms laid down by the Supreme Court in the Vishaka judgment.

Rehabilitation of Victims of Rape

The Supreme Court, in a judgment dated 19.10.1994, had directed the Government to evolve a scheme to mitigate the sufferings of victims of rape and to constitute Criminal Injuries Compensation Board to pay them compensation. It is in this context that the new scheme 'Scheme for relief and rehabilitation of victims of rape' is being formulated. The scheme is proposed to be administered by the National Commission for Women and has broadly two components. The first component is the constitution of a Criminal Injuries Relief and Rehabilitation Board at every district to award compensation to the victims; the second component calls for district monitoring committees to provide shelter, protection, legal and medical aid and rehabilitation to the victims. The scheme has been included in the report of the working group on empowerment of women for the XIth Plan. The scheme is under examination of the Ministry in consultation with other line Ministries.

National Plan of Action for implementing the National Policy for the Empowerment of Women

The Government has adopted the National Policy for the Empowerment of Women on 20th March 2001. The main objective of this policy is to bring about the advancement, development and empowerment of women and to eliminate all forms of discrimination against women and to ensure their active participation in all spheres of public life and activities.

To ensure that the Policy prescriptions get implemented, the Department is in the process of drafting a Plan of Action (POA). Under the Policy's operational strategy, the Action Plan has to be drawn up with goals achievable by the year 2010. The POA will also identify commitment of resources and responsibilities for implementation and strengthen institutional mechanisms and structures for monitoring. The operational strategy also mentions the need to develop Gender Development Index as a method of gender auditing and stresses the importance of collecting gender-disaggregated data which will be useful for planning, implementation and monitoring.

Gender Disaggregated Database and Gender Budgeting

Gender disaggregated database and gender budgeting have been emphasized as the major monitoring tools to examine that the benefits of policies and programmes are reaching those for whom these are intended. Gender budgeting is perceived as a powerful tool not only for tracking allocation of resources for women but also covers implementation issues and outcomes. Ministry of Women and Child Development has been identified as the Nodal Ministry for Gender Budgeting and the Ministry is pursuing vigorously with the Central Ministries/Departments and State Governments to implement the techniques of gender budgeting.

The 2006-07 budget speech revealed and estimated allocation of Rs. 28,737 crores for benefit of women under 24 Demands for grants in 18 Ministries and Departments. In 2006-07, the task was to carry forward the exercise of universalizing Gender Budgeting exercises in the centre and the States. So far Gender Budget cells have been set-up in 50 Central Ministries/Departments and several States have also undertaken steps in this regard. Apart from quantification of allocation of resources for women, the other initiatives include mainstreaming gender concerns in policies and implementation process, collection and compilation of gender disaggregated data, gender development indices, review and analysis of programs, policies/interventions with a gender perspective. Several new initiatives such as review and effective implementation of all legislations and laws with a gender perspective to eliminate all forms of discrimination against women. Sensitizing gender concerns in various organs of administrative set-up, training and capacity building.

The Ministry has also initiated steps to compile and prepare Gender Development Index and Gender Empowerment Measure for India and States with UNDP assistance. The Ministry is also taking steps to set-up a full-fledged Statistical Division in the Ministry, which may, *inter-alia* create and maintain databases on women and children. The task of preparation of a gender database for SAARC member-countries is being undertaken by SAARC-UNIFEM. In India, the Ministry of Women and Child Development has been identified as the focal point for the database. The National Planning Commission, Centre for Women Development Studies, Delhi University, National Statistical Office, National Sample Survey Office and Representative for Tata Institute of Social Sciences, Mumbai. The first meeting of the National Committee was held on 23rd August 2006 to discuss the issues related with the preparation of database. The SAARC-UNIFEM review meeting on preparation of gender database was held on 29-30 August 2006 in Bhutan. The thematic areas identified for the database are:

- Violence against women (with focus on trafficking and domestic violence)
- Feminization of poverty and livelihood
- Health issues including HIV/AIDS
- Access to factors of production (productive resources)
- Decision-making
- Qualitative information

Currently, the indicators reflecting the above areas are being identified.

Promoting Gender Equality—GOI—UNDP Project

Ministry signed a Memorandum of Understanding with UNDP in July 2004 for implementation of a project titled "Promoting Gender Equality." The project has three components as given below:

- Action Research on Women Leaders—Increased understanding of the factors that enable/constrain women to assume leadership in various spheres.
- Action research on Vulnerable women—Increased information

base of the approaches and actions adopted by the diverse agencies to address the social security concerns of women belonging to the vulnerable groups.

- Impact of macroeconomic policies on women workers—National and State level dialogue and consensus on benchmarking and tracking gender-related impacts of key processes such as globalization, liberalization and WTO.

During the year 2005-06, an amount of Rs. 1,186 crores have been released under the project.

During the year 2006-07, the following proposals were approved:

- A study on ageing, Disability and Gender Trade.
- Documenting lessons and learning in organizing Home Based Workers.
- On Gender and Trade by National Productivity Council and IIT.
- Preparation of GDI/GEM.
- Preparation of a Women's Development Report.
- Engendering the process of XIth Plan.
- Second Time Use Survey.
- Printing a volume on gender and macro-economics.

Convention on Elimination of Discrimination against Women (CEDAW)

India signed the Convention on Elimination of Discrimination against Women (CEDAW) on 30th July 1980 and ratified it on 9th July 1993 with one reservation and two declaratory statements. The convention obligates the State parties to undertake appropriate legislative and other measures to eliminate discrimination against women and for guaranteeing them the exercise and enjoyment of human rights and fundamental freedom on the basis of equality with men. The first report was submitted (on 24th and 30th) in June 2000, when the Indian delegation led by the Secretary, Ministry of Women and Child Development made on oral presentation before the Committee. A combined 2nd and 3rd Periodic Report was submitted in June 2005. The UN Committee on CEDAW considered the Report on 18th January 2007.

As the implementation of the provisions of CEDAW requires a greater dialogue and convergence among the various ministries responsible for implementing different legal provisions, policies and programmes that work towards women's equality and elimination of discrimination against women, an Inter-Ministerial Committee has been constituted, under the chairpersonship of the Secretary, Ministry of Women and Child Development. India is the second country in the world to have such a Committee for implementation of CEDAW.

Beijing Platform for Action

The Fourth World Conference on Women, held in Beijing in 1995 was a landmark event that set the pace for women's empowerment when a Declaration and Platform for Action (BFPA) were adopted. India adopted both without any reservations and identified critical areas of concern. The Committee on Status of Women reviews progress made by member-countries in the critical areas. The 50th session of the committee was held in New York form 27th February to 10th March 2005. A delegation headed by Dr. Sayeda Hamid, Member Planning Commission attended the meeting. The 51st session of Committee on Status of Women has been scheduled from 26th February – 9th March 2007.

Grant-in-aid for Research, Publications and Monitoring

The Ministry of Women and Child Development is implementing the Scheme of grant-in-aid for research, publication and monitoring since 1986-87 with the objective to promote research studies for testing the feasibility and efficacy of existing programmes and services on emerging issues in the field of women and child development. Under the scheme, the Ministry also supports workshops/seminars which help in formulating research proposals and disseminating research findings or in social situational analysis, likely to be helpful in planning, programming and review of implementation.

Notification of Guidelines for Adoption

The Central Adoption Resource Agency has notified "Guidelines for Adoption from India-2006, Family Adoption Guidelines and definition of special needs."

Felicitation of Recipients of the National Child Bravery Awards, 2006

The Hon'ble Minister of State for Women and Child Development (Independent Charge) felicitated the recipients of the National Bravery Awards, 2006 in a function held on 23.1.2007 which was followed by a dinner hosted in honour of them. In all 21 awardees were present in the function (out of 24 awardees, 3 have been posthumously awarded) alongwith their parents and guardians. During the function, the representative of Sahara Airways announced that the airways will provide two free tickets to the awardee and an escort for any place in India.

National Nutrition Week

The National Nutrition Week was observed throughout the country from 1-7 September 2006. The theme selected for this year celebration was "Nutrition Literacy."

National Guidelines on Infant and Young Child Feeding

The second edition of the National Guidelines on infant and young child feeding was released on 17th May 2006 and these guidelines have been integrated into the reproductive and child health programme under the National Rural Health Mission and in the training curricula integrated Child Development Services personnel.

Observation of World Breastfeeding Week

The world breast feeding week (1-7 August 2006) was observed on the theme "Infant Milk Substitute Act: Making it Known to People."

Double Fortification of Salt

The double fortification of salt with iron and iodine was considered by the Central Committee for Food Standards and approved. The standard for the double fortified salt is under finalization.

Health Awareness Week for Parliamentarians

Health Awareness week was organized for parliamentarians at Parliament Annex during 7-11 August 2006. Food and Nutrition Board put up a nutrition exhibition in the Vatsalya Mela organized by Ministry of Women and Child Development in New Delhi during 14-19 November 2006.

Investigation into Child Abuse and Murder in Nithari Village, Noida

The Ministry of Women and Child Development constituted a Committee under the chairpersonship of Smt. Manjula Krishnan, Economic Adviser in the Ministry to investigate into the allegations of large scale sexual abuse, rape and murder of children in Nithari village of Noida on 3rd January, 2007. The committee also had Joint Secretary, Ministry of Home Affairs and director, Ministry of Women and Child Development, as members. The Committee Visited Noida twice and met officials of the District Administration, local police and Chief Medical Superintendent apart from the members of the affected families and local community. They also examined the various documents made available to them by the District Officials/Police. Based upon these documents as well as the information gathered from their meetings with all concerned, the Committee prepared a report which was submitted to the MOS(WCD) on 17th January 2007.

Visit of Committee of National Commission to Resettlement Colonies for Riot Victims in Gujarat

A committee for the National Commission for Women led by the Chairperson Dr. Girija Vyas visited on 6th May 2006, the resettlement colonies in Gujarat set-up for riot victims affected by the 2002 Communal riots to assess the conditions of living of the affected women. Expressing deep concern at the deplorable living conditions of women and emphasizing on the lack of basic amenities in the colonies, the NCW has asked the Government to take steps to improve the infrastructure to ensure better living conditions for the riot victims.

New Scheme of Resources Centres launched by RMK

The Governing Board of Rashtriya Mahila Kosh (RMK) under the chairmanship of Hon'ble MOS (Independent Charge), MWCD, in its meeting on 6 September 2006 has approved a new scheme called Resource Centre Scheme which will enable RMK to identify/designate various national level organisations like IIMs, NIDM, Universities, Research Centres, and reputed NGOs, etc. with requisite infrastructure as RMK Resource Centres to provide the facilities of capacity building, training for new skills, vocations and professions, skill upgradation, design improvement, enterprise development, livelihood management, etc. which are key component of micro-credit programme. These facilities will be provided in a regular and periodic manner to the grassroot beneficiaries (SHG members/leaders), and staff of implementing agencies including NGOs.

Stree Shakti Puraskar

As a measure of recognition of achievement of individual women in the field of social development, the Government of India has instituted five national awards, known as 'Stree Shakti Puraskar'. These awards will be in the name of the following eminent women personalities in the Indian history, who are famous for their personal courage and integrity:

- Devi Ahilya Bai Holkar
- Kanngi
- Mata Jijabai
- Rani Gaidenlou Zeliang
- Rani Lakshmi Bai

The award carries a cash prize of Rs. 1 lakh and a citation. Ministry of State (Independent Charge) for Women and Child Development gave the awards to the women who have been selected for the year 2002 and 2003 on 19th November 2006.

Ananya Festival

During the week 5-9 March, Ananya festival was celebrated with great fervor to mark the International Women's Day 8th March 2007. On 5th March a film festival was inaugurated for showing films portraying and glorifying the role of women. On 6th March 2007, a special flag on women's empowerment was hoisted; on 7th March 2007, the foundation stone was laid for working women's hostels for women from North-East; on 8th March 2007 a set four stamps was released in honour of women and on the concluding day 9th March 2007, women achievers were felicitated. "Survival to Success Celebrate Her Life" was the theme of the Ananya festival.

Working Groups on Women Empowerment and Integrating Nutrition with Health 11th Five Year Plan 2007-12.

Working Group on Empowerment of Women

The Planning Commission vide its order dated 17th April 2006 constituted a Working Group on "Empowerment of Women" for the 11th

Five Year Plan under the Chairpersonship of Secretary, Ministry of Women and Child Development with the basic objective to carry out a review, analysis and evaluation of the existing provisions/programmes for women and make recommendations for the Eleventh Five Year Plan.

The working group met on 12th June 2006 and it was decided to set-up four Sub-Groups:

- Engendering Policies and Strategies.
- Violence against Women.
- Schemes of Empowerment, Advocacy, Awareness Generation and Support Services for Women.
- Women's Component Plan and Gender Budgeting.

As a part of the plan process, five regional workshops to cover North, South, East, West and North-East and one at the National level were held with assistance from UNDP and UNIFEM to engenders the XIth Plan were held.

Based on the Sub-group Reports and the recommendations that emerged from the Workshops on Engendering the XIth Plan, a draft Working Group Report was prepared and was placed before the Group in its second meeting held on 10th November 2006. Based on the deliberations of the Working Group, the Report of the Working Group was finalized. The vision or philosophy of empowerment for the XIth Plan is Inclusive and integrated economic, social and political empowerment with gender justice.

Recommendations of the following topics were made in the working group report:

- Women and the Economy;
- Women and the Law;
- Socio-economic and Cultural Interventions for Vulnerable Groups;
- Social Empowerment;
- Political Empowerment;
- Institutional Mechanisms; and
- Schemes of the Ministry of Women and Child Development.

The working group on empowerment of women for formulating XIth Five Year Plan has recommended that feasibility of developing pilot projects to address specific requirements of vulnerable women such as women impacted by violence, women impacted by internal displacement, disasters and migration, domestic or bonded women labour, landless or marginal women in agriculture, women affected by HIV/AIDS or with disabilities, elderly and aged or suffering form life threatening diseases, slum dwellers, women prisoners, women belonging to ethnic and socially vulnerable communities, women of religious minorities, single women like widows, divorcees, women whose husbands are absent due to conflict, economic migration, widows of farmers who commit suicide due to failure of crops or heavy indebtedness. In the context of growing globalization and resultant liberalization of economy as well as increased privatization of services, women have to be mainstreamed into new and emerging areas of growth by providing them training and upgrading their skills. Globalization also paves way for setting up of more industrial parts, special economic zones and national highway, resulting in massive displacement; thus resettlement policy needs to be formulated and put in place to clearly reflect the needs of displaced women. The women in local self-governments need to be empowered so that they can play a more proactive role in decision-making.

Working Group on Child Development

The Planning Commission constituted the working group on development of children under the Chairpersonship of Secretary (WCD) on 17.4.2006.

The Working group on 'Development of Children' suggested constitution of the following 4 sub-groups on the following:

- Child Protection,
- Girl Child,
- ICDS and Nutrition, and
- Early Childhood Education.

The sub-group held meetings independently and finalized their reports. The sub group reports were considered by the working group and the report of the working group was finalized and copies furnished to Planning Commission for consideration in the steering committee of the Planning Commission.

Some of the important recommendations made by the working group are the following:

- Universalization of ICDS equality
- Provision of an additional Anganwadi Worker to impart pre-school education in Anganwadi Centre
- In cessation of a new centrally sponsored Integrated Child Protection Scheme (ICPS)
- Expansion of Crèche and Day Care Programme
- Review and reorganisation of adoption system in India
- Data Systems research
- A cradle baby scheme for girl child
- Expansion of Nutrition Programme for Adolescent Girls (NPAG) and its merger with Kishori Shakti Yojana (KSY)
- Pilot Scheme on conditional cash and non-cash transfer for girl child.

National Policy for Empowerment of Women

One of the landmark achievements of the year 2001 was the approval of the first ever-National Policy for the Empowerment of Women. The main objective of this Policy is to bring about the advancement, development and empowerment of women and, to eliminate all forms of discrimination against women and to ensure their active participation in all spheres of life and activities.

The policy prescribes affirmative action in areas such as Legal System, Decision-making Structure, Mainstreaming of Gender Perspective in Development Process, Economic Empowerment through increased access to resources like micro-credit, better resource allocation through Women's component Plan, Gender Budget exercises and development of Gender Development Indices and Social Empowerment of Women through, *inter-alia,* universalisation of education, adoption of holistic approach to women's health, etc. *The policy commits to making compulsory the registration of marriages and to eliminate child marriage by 2010.* The Policy takes into account the new developments initiated by the process of economic reforms and the impact of globalization and liberalization on women, particularly in the informal sector. The policy further prescribes that the provisions of various legislation including personal laws, which are discriminatory against women shall be reviewed and amended with the support and initiatives of concerned communities. *Review of women oriented legislations will be completed by 2003.*

The Policy envisages setting up of a Council at the National level to oversee the implementation of the Policy. The National Council will be headed by the Prime Minister. Similar Councils will also be set-up at the State levels to be headed by the concerned Chief Ministers. All Central and State Ministries/Departments would be required to draw up Action Plans with measurable goals to be achieved in a time frame of the next 10 years.

National Nutrition Policy

The National Nutrition Policy was adopted in 1993 under the aegis of Department of Women and Child Development. The Policy recognized the multifaceted problem of malnutrition and advocated a multi-sectoral approach for controlling the same. A series of actions were identified in various spheres like food production and distribution, health and family welfare, agriculture, horticulture and rural development. In pursuance of this Policy, the Food and Nutrition Board was transferred to this Department on 1 April, J993. A National Nutrition Mission has been launched in 180 selected nutritionally backward districts of the country to further carry forward the goals on National Nutrition Policy.

Women Component Plan

The Department of Women and Child Development, which was designated as the Nodal machinery for the development and empowerment of women, is playing crucial role in the formulation and monitoring of women's component. Plan, which was devised as an *operational strategy in the Ninth Plan to ensure that not less than* 30 *percent of funds/benefits earmarked for women in all the women-related sectors.*

The Department has advised all the concerned Ministries/ Departments for inclusion of an identifiable Women Component plan in their programmes, right from the planning process and implementation and monitoring of their programmes to ensure that the benefits reach the women. The Department has further requested all the Ministries/ Departments to set-up Advisory Committees for women in each sector to help in the preparation, monitoring and implementation of Women's Component Plan, set-up a women's cell and to include a Chapter on Women's Component Plan in their Annual Report.

On the instruction of Prime Minister's Office (PMO), the Department has also been monitoring 27 Beneficiaries Oriented Schemes for Women implemented by Central Government. It has been decided to extend the scope of the monitoring to include the entire gamut of the Women's Component Plan.

The review of the disabilities and constraints on women, which stem from socio-cultural institutions, indicates that the majority of women are still very far from enjoying the rights and opportunities guaranteed to them by the Constitution. Society has not yet succeeded in framing the required norms or institutions to enable women to fulfil the multiple roles that they are expected to play in India today. On the other hand, the increasing incidence of practices like dowry, indicate a further lowering of the status of women. They also indicate a process of regression from some of the norms developed during the Freedom Movement. We have been perturbed by the findings of the content analysis of periodicals in the regional languages that concern for women and their problems, which received an impetus during the Freedom. Movement has suffered a decline in the last two decades. The social laws that sought to mitigate the problems of women in their family-life have remained unknown to a large mass of women in this country, who are as ignorant of their legal rights today as they were before independence.

Changes in social attitudes and institutions cannot be brought about very rapidly. It is, however, necessary to accelerate this process of change by deliberate and planned efforts. Responsibility for this acceleration has to be shared by the State and the community, particularly that section of the community, which believes in the equality of women. We, therefore, urge that community organisations, particularly women's organisations, should mobilize public opinion and strengthen social efforts against oppressive institutions like polygamy, dowry, ostentatious expenditure on weddings and child marriage and mount a campaign for the dissemination of information about the legal rights of women to increase their awareness. This is a joint responsibility, which has to be shared by community organisations, legislators, who have helped to frame these laws and the Government, which is responsible for implementing them.[3]

Women of India have a background of history and tradition behind them, which is inspiring, but they have suffered much from various kinds of suppression and all these have to go so that they can play their full part in the life of the nation.[4]

2. Social and Economic Empowerment of Women

The Report 6f the Committee on the Status of Women in India: Towards equality (1974) rightly mentioned, "The status of any given section of population in a society is intimately 'connected with its economic position,' which (itself) depends on rights, roles and opportunities for participation in economic activities. The economic status of women is now accepted as an indicator of a society's stage of development. This does not, however, mean that all development results in improving women's economic status. Patterns of women's activity are greatly affected by social attitudes and institutions, which stem from the social ideology concerning basic components of status in any given period. These may differ according to the stage of economic development."[5] Discrimination against women is incompatible with human dignity and the welfare of the family and of society, prevents their participation on equal terms with men in the political, social, economic and cultural life of their countries and is an obstacle to the full development of the potentialities of women in the service of their countries and humanity.[6] "To maintain proper quantitative balance between various economic activities was one of the principal functions of the economic system, which, it was felt, should operate to give equal freedom of choice to men and women. The orientation of society as a whole regarding the desirability that women should play an equal part in the country's development was taken as very important precondition for the advancement not only of the women but of the country as well."[7]

Let us now discuss the recent developments of promote Socio-Economic Empowerment of Women:

Swayamsiddha

Swayamsiddha which is an integrated scheme for women's empowerment, was formally launched on 29th November, 2001, replacing the erstwhile Indira Mahila Yojana and subsuming the Mahila Samriddhi Yojana. Like the Indira Mahila Yojana the programme is based on the formation of women into Self-Help Groups (SHGs) but it aims at more comprehensive and holistic empowerment of women through awareness generation, economic empowerment and convergence of various schemes.

The long-term objective[8] of the programme is the all-round empowerment of women by ensuring their direct access to, and control over, resources through a sustained process of mobilization and convergence of all the on-going sectoral programmes. The immediate objectives of the programme are:

- Strengthening and institutionalizing the savings habit in rural women and their control over economic resources;
- Improving access of women to micro-credit;
- Involvement of women in local level planning; and
- Convergence of services of DWCD and other Departments.

Swa-Shakti Project

The Swa-Shakti Project, also known as Rural Women's Development and Empowerment Project, was sanctioned on 16 October, 1998 as a Centrally-sponsored Project for a period of 5 years.

The specific objectives of the project are:

- Establishment of 7400 to 12000 Self-reliant women's self-help groups (SHGs) having 15-20 members each;
- Developing linkage between SHGs and lending institutions to ensure women's continued access to credit facilities for income generation activities;
- Increased control of women over earning and spending, through their involvement in income generation activities, which will help in poverty alleviation;
- Enhancing women's access to resources for better quality of life, including those for drudgery reduction and time-saving devices; and
- Sensitizing and strengthening the Institutional capacity of support agencies to pro-actively address women's needs.[9]

Promotion of Health of Women

According to the World Health Organisation health is "a state of complete physical, mental and social well-being and not merely the absence of disease and infirmity."[10] Health is both an important factor as well as an indicator of social status, particularly for women, whose health is conditioned to a great extent by social attitudes. The health status of women, includes their mental and social condition to their by prevailing norms and attitudes of society in addition to their biological and physiological problems. Societies delineate women's roles partly according to their biological functions and partly from prevailing attitudes regarding their physical and mental capacity. These social attitudes also influence the provision and use of preventive and curative health care, including material care.[11] The health care facilities offered by a community in the form of medical particularly maternity services for women, is a significant index of the emphasis that community places on the health of its women. Some studies in both the developed and developing countries have shown a definite link between low status of women and deficiencies in the knowledge and utilization of preventive health services.[12]

Committee on Empowerment (2001-02) 4th Report, 12th Lok Sabha of Health and Family Welfare Programmes for Women states that: "There is a growing recognition that since women also suffer from other disabilities and morbidities, some of which are again very gender specific, there is need to examine the adequacy of our strategies in ensuring that they are appropriately covered. The scanty data available has shown that women in reproductive age groups of 18-45 years, constituting a bulk of the working population, suffer from TB, Malaria, UTI, STDs, Cancer, Leprosy, etc. Women working in cities are also subject to stressful conditions and are seen to suffer from mental health problem to stressful conditions and are seen to suffer from mental health problem as well as heart ailments, blood pressure and other stress induced diseases. Likewise, the National Commission for Women also brought out the special needs of women working in agriculture and informal sectors where they are exposed to chemicals and pesticides. Besides, the longevity of life has resulted in a higher burden of diseases among the older aged women. The women in this age group suffer medical disorders such as Alzheimer's and Arthritis, etc."[13]

Since the vast majority of women live in rural areas, where there are hardly any medical facilities available, women become victims of various diseases due to mal-nutrition, lack of clean and safe drinking water, unhygienic conditions, etc. The Government ought to integrate various programmes and take a holistic approach to immunization, nutrition, health care, drinking water, cleanliness, health infrastructure, trained personnel, etc. so as to improve the health of the rural women. As 33 per cent women are now in panchayats and other local bodies they can be utilized for improving the condition of omen all over the country.

The Demand and Supply of Health Facilities is Highly Skewed

There is urgent need to improve the conditions of the Government hospitals by making available doctors, para-medical staff, requisite medicines and necessary medical equipments. Not only is there need for more doctors and nurses but the norms for doctor-patient ratio and nurse-patient ratio needs to be reviewed and appropriate steps taken to provide medical staff as per those norms. It is known fact that the emergency wards of Government hospitals in major cities are managed by junior doctors while the senior doctors have to be called, if need arises. The Government should take appropriate steps to ensure the presence of senior doctors round the clock in each discipline in the emergency wards of major Hospitals.

The Committee would like the Government to pay immediate attention to the vital aspect of providing health services and take early action to open more Hospitals in rural and semi-urban areas, making it compulsory for all doctors to serve in rural areas for a specified period and ensuring that sufficient numbers of lady doctors are posted there. In order to improve the efficiency and effectiveness of the family planning programme, and to achieve better health for both the mother and the child, the committee insisted that 100% ante-natal registration should be made mandatory. This should form the basis of identifying high risk pregnancies and the eligible couples for permanent sterilization.

Training Empowerment and Education

A report on Status of Women in India by ICSSR rightly says: "The general purpose and objective of women's education cannot, of course, be different from the purpose and objective of men's education. . . At the Secondary and even at the university stage women's education should have a vocational or occupational bias."[14]

In a democratic society where all citizens have to discharge their civic and social obligation, differences which may lead to variation in the standard of intellectual development achieved by boys and girls cannot be envisaged.[15]

In the progressive society of tomorrow, life should be a joint venture for men and women. Men should share the responsibility of parenthood and home-making with women, and women in their turn should share the social and economic responsibilities of men.[16]

Women's and men's education should have many elements in common, but should not in general be identical in all respects, as is usually the case today. A woman should learn something of problems that are certain to come up in all marriages, and in the relations of parents and children, and how they may be met. Her education should make her familiar with problems of home management and skills in meeting them, so that she may take her place in a home with the same interest and the same sense of competence that a well trained man has in working at his calling.[17]

Support of Training and Employment Programme for Women (STEP)

This Programme launched in 1987, seeks to provide updated skills and new knowledge to poor and asset less women in the traditional occupations, such as, agriculture, animal husbandry, dairying fisheries, handlooms, handicrafts, khadi and village industries, sericulture, social forestry and wasteland development for enhancing their productivity and income generation. This would enhance and broaden their employment opportunities, including self-employment and development of entrepreneurial skills. Women beneficiaries are organized into viable and cohesive groups or cooperatives. A comprehensive package of services, such as, extension, inputs, market linkage with credit for transfer of assets.

According to the Department of Elementary Education and Literacy/ the National Policy on Education (NPE), 1986, recognizes that the education of girls is possibly the most critical pre-condition for the empowerment of women, The consequent Programme of Action which includes Education for Women's Equality, privileges the role of education as an instrument to bring about change in the status of women. *Departing from the First National Education Policy of* 1968 *which was committed to the provision of equal education opportunity, the NPE,* 1986, *brought the fundamental issue of women's equality to the centre Stage.* According to this policy,

"Education will be used as an agent of basic change in the status of women. In order to neutralize the accumulated distortions of the past, there will be a well-conceived edge in favour of women. This will be an act of faith and social engineering. The removal of women's illiteracy and obstacles inhibiting their access to, and retention in, elementary education will receive overriding priority, through provision of special support services setting time targets and effective monitoring."

Balika Samriddhi Yojana

The Scheme of Balika Samriddhi Yojana was launched on 2 October 1997 with the objective of raising the overall status of the girl-child and bringing about a positive change in family and community 'attitudes' towards her. The Scheme covers up to two girl children born on or after 15 August, 1997 in a family living below the poverty line as defined by the Government of India in any rural or urban area. During 1997-98 and 1998-99, the scheme was implemented as a Central Sector Plan Scheme under which the funds were released to district-level implementing agencies such as DRDAs and, DUDAs for giving a grant of Rs. 500 to the mother of the new born girl children.

The scheme was reviewed in 1999 and was recast as a Centrally Sponsored Scheme to extend 100% Central Assistance to States and UTs to provide benefits under the scheme through Integrated Child Development Services (ICDS) Scheme infrastructure. *As per the recast scheme, the post delivery grant of Rs. 500 will be deposited in an interest bearing account in a bank or post office in the name of girl-child. In addition,* the girl child will be entitled to receive scholarship for each class of study successfully completed by her, ranging from Rs. 300 for class 1st to Rs. 1000 for class X. The scholarship amounts will also be deposited in the above account. The accumulated value of the deposits in the account will be payable to the girl child on her attaining the age of 18 years and having remained unmarried till then.

Hostel for Working Women

Under the scheme of construction/expansion of Hostel Building for Working Women with a Day Care Centre, financial assistance is given to voluntary organisations, local bodies and cooperative institutions engaged in the field of women's/social welfare/women's education, Public Sector Undertakings, Women Development Corporations, Educational Institutions and State Governments for the construction of hostels for working women in order to enable women seek employment and participate in technical training. The objective of the Scheme is to provide cheaper and safe hostel accommodation to working women living out of their homes. The target beneficiaries are single working women, widows, divorcee, separated and working women whose husbands are out of town. Women getting training for employment and girl students studying in post-school professional courses are also eligible to stay in hostel.

Swadhar

This is a new scheme launched by the Department during the 2002 year in the central sector for the benefit pf women in difficult circumstances, like destitute widows deserted by their families in religious places like Vrindavan, Kashi, etc., women prisoners released from jail and without family support; women survivors of natural disaster who have been rendered homeless and are trafficked, women/girls rescued or runaway victims of sexual crimes who are disowned by family or who do !tot want to go back to respective family for various reasons; women victims of terrorist violence who are without any family support and without any economic means for survival; mentally disordered women who are without any support of family or relatives, etc.

The package of assistance that will be available under the scheme shall include provision for shelter, food, clothing, health care and counselling for such women; measures for social and economic skill upgradation and personality development through behavioural training, etc. help line or other facilities to such women in distress; and such other services will be required for the support and rehabilitation to such women in distress.

Women Rights and the Law: Education for Prevention of Atrocities on Women

The Department of Women and Child Development is reviewing the following five Acts with which it is administratively concerned with a view to make the provisions more stringent and to remove the lacunae:

(a) The Indecent Representation of Women (Prohibition) Act, 1986.
(b) The Immoral Traffic (Prevention) Act, 1956.
(c) The Dowry Prohibition Act, 1961.
(d) The Commission of Sati (Prevention) Act, 1987:
(e) The National Commission of Women Act, 1990.

Implementation of Supreme Court Order Regarding Sexual Harassment of Women at Workplaces and other Institutions

The Hon'ble Supreme Court in its order dated 13 August, 1997 had passed an order laying down the norms and guidelines to be followed by the employers for tackling the incidents of sexual harassment of women at workplace and other institutions. The guidelines issued by the Supreme Court included setting up a complaints redresser forum in all workplaces and amendment of the disciplinary/conduct rules governing employees by incorporating the norms and guidelines. The Department has circulated the Supreme Court's order to all Ministries/Departments of the Government of India, Women Development Corporations and National Commission for Women for compliance. A complaint redressal forum regarding sexual harassment of women at workplace has been constituted in the Department in compliance of the directions of the Supreme Court.

National Resource Centre for Women (NRCW)

This Department has proposed to set-up National Resource Centre for Women. The objectives of the centre will be to:

(i) Orient and sensitize elected representatives, policy planners, administrators, members of the judiciary, police, bankers, etc. towards gender issues;

(ii) Facilitate leadership training for grass-root level workers, newly elected panchayat leaders, members of NGOs, etc.;

(iii) Create an. information base and disseminate information in the fields of women's development and also facilitate generation of data on contemporary issues of women in development;

(iv) Facilitate and coordinate the monitoring and evaluation of existing Government programmes relating to women development;

(v) Undertake and coordinate policy and programme-related research on women's development;

(vi) Provide networking facilities to institutions and individuals actively engaged in the field of women's development;

(vii) Strengthen institutional capacity of Department of Women and Child Development in relation to planning and implementation processes which are gender sensitive and participatory;

(viii) Assimilate gender perspective; in policies, planning, implementation and monitoring in selected sectors;

(ix) Undertake advocacy and provide policy support on women's issues; and

(x) Take up all or any other activity for the holistic development for women.

The proposal has been approved by the Standing Finance Committee of the Department, but in view of the restrictions imposed by the Government on the creation of new organisation the possibility of anchoring the proposed Resource Centre with an existing institution is being explored.

Crime against Women

Crime against women, reproduced from Crime Against Women, Bureau of Police Research and Development, New Delhi, rightly suggests,[18] "There is a necessity to review the system of manning the investigating machinery and the prosecution branch in the state civil police to make it more responsive to women victims of' atrocities. It is necessary that the state police should revise the strength of their investigating officers and have a mix of women investigating cadre should be developed by filling up existing vacancies with women officers of suitable basic qualifications as well as by marginal addition to augment areas of extreme deficiency. Although it is not possible to have a parallel force of women investigating officers, as this would not only be inconvenient in management but would lead to a division of duties in the work of police investigation. Women police officers should be posted as investigating officers in all police stations in urban areas where the urban population is' above 1 lakh. The states may devise, systems as suitable to them, keeping in view the local needs and facilities to post women police officers of lower rank in police stations in rural or semi-urban areas. Special training in social welfare works should be imparted to the women police officers as part of their basic training.

We reiterate that women victims of atrocities should not be put in the police station premises at night, pending their questioning and the rules already existing in the police manuals or orders of the State IGP should be strictly enforced. The State IGE should make a review of his existing orders to ensure that they have a practical applicability.

The insistence of police officers, where such a practice exists, asking women victims of atrocities to appear before police stations or to report in writing at the police stations, should be dispensed with. Police officers under the Acts are empowered to record an FIR if they themselves receive information of crime and this practice should be further applied in the cases of atrocities against women. Written reports sent to the police station by courier or mail from women victims of atrocities in particular should be accepted as FIR and not kept for enquiries under Section 154 Cr.P.C. A large number of complaints received, on atrocities on women are 'filed' after enquiry in police records and, therefore, will escape future surveys and research activity.

The State/UTs should develop their departments of Serology in their Forensic Science Laboratories to meet the challenge of quick results and easy accessibility of this facility for women victims of atrocities particularly in rape cases. Wherever possible an outpost of the Forensic Laboratory dealing with examination in serological and chemical divisions should be considered.

Crime against women, e.g. rape, kidnapping/abduction, abetment to suicide, Dowry Acts, procurement of minor girls, unnatural offences involving women, importation of girls, buying or selling of minors for the purposes of prostitution, if not already being treated as "Special Report Cases" should be termed as such for direct cognizance and attention of the senior supervisory police officers.

A time limit of 90 days should be fixed for completion of the police investigation, with a maximum period of further 30 days for the scrutiny and filing of the case by the prosecution agency in the criminal courts.

Mass media can contribute to a great extent in releasing the social tensions which otherwise promote some types of crimes against women. We, therefore, recommend the following:

(a) The Indian film industry may be advised to eschew the exhibition of violence against women. Rape or molestation of women can be at best only suggestive. Where it becomes essential to use the rape scene in the development of the story which is centred on women, the audio-visual presentation should be kept to a minimum. These yardsticks should apply equally to the Indian as well as foreign films exhibited in India.

(b) Films idealizing the protection of women's honour, and their rights of equality and their special rights in the preservation of social culture should be encouraged.

(c) Pictorial displays in advertising, must exhibit good taste and display material directly linked to the scenes and frames passed by the Board of the Censors in the main film. The use of sensual poses of women in college with fire-arms and liquor in the composition of film posters and other mass media should be discouraged as much as possible and where good counts does not prevail, local municipal laws should be enacted to impose heavy fines and forthright confiscation of the pictorial displays.

The artist involved in commercial contributes should have vicarious liability for such offences.

Critical Appraisal

The special attention given to the needs, and problems of women, to enable them to enjoy and exercise their Constitutional equality of status along with other specific provisions relating to the hitherto suppressed sections of our society, have led many scholars to describe the Indian Constitution as a "social" document embodying the objectives of a 'social revolution'. There is no doubt that the constitution contemplates attainment of an entirely new social order by making deliberate departures in norms and institutions of democratic governance from the inherited social, political and economic systems. In doing so the Constitution assigns primacy to law as an instrument of directed social change. It thus demands of the legislature, the executive and the judiciary continuous vigilance and responsiveness to the relationship between law and social transformations in contemporary India.

We have seen that there is nothing wrong in policies and programmes of women Empowerment but implementation is slack and needs innovation. Robert McNamara, Former President of World Bank has rightly observed, "It is action that matters. . . .But knowing does not guarantee a change of feeling; and a change of feeling does not guarantee a change of behaviour. So we come to the final, paradoxical reversal; to start by acting. . . .Not everything can or should be foreseen. It is often best to start, to do something, and to learn from doing."

To fulfil the aspirations of the people as mentioned in the Preamble and later stressed through Directive Principles of State Policy and Fundamental Rights and other constitutional provisions, an elaborative machinery of Government, consisting of a complex of organisations, exists at Union; State and Regional and local levels and is in operation. Similarly, the existing structure, which has became redundant, needs to be eliminated. However, in India and other developing countries, the process of removing the redundant structures is very slow, resulting in wastage of resources in maintaining them. Besides, there are many duplicate structures with overlapping functions which also lead to a great wastage of resources and efforts.

Procedures are laid out to define the steps according to which administration puts policies into action. "It is procedure", as Waldo says, "that governs the routine internal and external relationship between one individual and another; between one organisational unit and another; between one process and another; between one skill or technique and another; between the organisation and the public; and between all combinations and permutations of these." These procedures, in Indian administration, instead of being an asset, have created innumerable problems, leading to red tapism. Procedures have taken precedence over performance. Many reforms in financial, personnel and general procedures have been introduced. Based upon ARC recommendation, Desk Officer System, Functional File Index system, Proper Space Layout, etc. were introduced in the machinery of Government. In spite of awareness of some acting, administrative procedures are acting as hurdles in the process of development and modernization. A consistent and persistent attention is required to keep the procedures in tune with the administration aimed at positive action.

Ever since the creation of the Department of Women and Child Development, it has been doing a great service to promote the development *of* women and children. However, we may bring some facts and suggestions which can improve the functioning of the Department.

Generalist Staff: Need of Technical Experts

The ministry has a staff which belongs to general category. Most of them are on deputation, merely carrying out traditional administrative activities. There is a need to appoint technical advisors in the different areas of women development and empowerment from the disciplines of psychology, public Administration, law, sociology, Women Studies, etc. to inject expertise and dynamism.

Duplication between the Department of Women and Child Welfare and National Council for Women

There is a lot of duplication and overlap between the two agencies working in the Government of India. There is a need of clear cut divisions in functions so that there can be optimization of resources.

More Theoretical Approach: Need of Practical Approach

The Ministry of women and child development mostly lays down policy which is more theoretical than practical. There is a need of detailing the policy in units so that those who are engaged in implementation are clear about means and ends. This would lessen the repeated references to the Department from field offices, causing delays in programme implementation.

Routine Activities: Need of Innovation

The department of women and child development is not like any other department. It is dealing with living persons who have emotions, ideas and preferences. Therefore, to deal with these women, we have to draw innovative programmes based on field survey, study and research. The department should design these programmes based upon the felt needs of women.

Lack of Co-ordination: Need of Providing Leadership

The department of women and child development should coordinate all the work done in the domain of women development and disseminate this after vetting by all the concerned organisations. The Department should implement merely essential activities.

Less Emphasis on Empowering Rural Women: Need of Providing Assistance to Women in General and Panchayati Raj Institutions in Particular

It has been now more than a decade since the 73rd Amendment Act, 1992. Nothing substantial has been achieved inspite of 33 percent reservation for women. The Department of Women and Child Development must concentrate on equipping women in rural areas with leadership qualities and awareness of their rights as non-official members of PRIs. Once this process takes a definite shape, then surely, rural India would awaken to fulfil the ideals of Mahatma Gandhi.

No Attempt to Change the Attitudes and Mind-set of Women towards themselves and Mind-set of Men towards Women: Need of Cultivating Self-Confidence and Faith in Women

General Recommendations

National perspective plan of action for women, 1988-2000 AD, Report of the core group set-up by the Department of Child and Women Development, Ministry of HRD, Government of India, recommends the following which should be followed by Ministry of Women and Child Welfare, Government of India. Certain important issues, however, impinge on all spheres of women's lives and work. With a view to enhancing women's status and capacities to participate in the process of nation-building, the following general recommendations are made:

1. The overall approach of this National perspective Plan is to perceive women in a holistic manner. While the programmes for

women will continue to be implemented by different ministries as part of their department plans, it is essential to have a strong inter-ministerial coordination and monitoring body along with its own supportive facilities service by the Department of Women and Child Development.

2. All ministries must reflect the concern for the all round development of women. *The concerned ministries must all have a women's cell* which currently only exists in the Ministries of Labour, Small Scale Industry, Science and Technology and Rural Development.
3. An essential pre-requisite for the implementation of these new policy directives would be a *women's unit in the Planning Commission, to redefine categories of data collection for women, modify existing terminology and identify gaps in data collection relating to women* and to give direction to plans and programmes for women's development. It is also essential to analyze the impact of the different macro-policies on women while planning new endeavours.
4. Financial and fiscal resources should be apportioned and preferential allocations for women's employment in mainstream programmes and projects should be made. This would imply the rationalization of resource allocation within mainstream programmes so as to benefit women, rather than only seeking separate allocations for women. *Critical emphasis must be placed on rate of investment in women preferred industries and occupations.*
5. At the state level, the Departments/Directorate of Women's Development should be initiated. Currently, there is no separate department for women in many States. Social welfare, handicapped, Scheduled Castes and Tribes are subjects that are bracketed together with the development of women at the State level. This new department could also be the State level implementation body for the programmes/policies of the Ministry of Women and Child Development of the Government of India.
6. In terms of programme implementation, the two major implementing bodies envisaged, are the Social Welfare Boards and the Women's Development Corporations. *There can be a rationalization of service provision between these two bodies.* The State Social Welfare Advisory Boards could eventually concentrate on implementing welfare/supportive programmes for women (homes for women in distress, working women's hostels, counselling centres fat legal aid and para-legal training, condensed courses, etc.); Women's Development Corporations would be responsible for the implementation of economic programmes through non-governmental and governmental agencies/departments wherever necessary, concentrating on

technical inputs like credit, marketing, design development, etc. and reaching out to women at the district and village level.

7. Women should be entitled to a package of services at the block level created by the convergence of schemes such as Development of Women and Children in Rural Areas (QWCRA), Integrated Child Development Schemes (ICDS), Adult Education, Health Care, etc. at the grass-roots administrative level. Every district should have a coordinator to assist in the integration of these programmes aimed at the development of women. The coordinator should also be responsible for motivating local planning of programme and assist in their implementation and provide feed-back for effective planning and evaluation. Since decentralization of planning, monitoring and implementation of development programmes for women is suggested as also devolution of finance at district level, appointment of District coordinators for women's programmes would facilitate this process and control over finance would empower them. The National Commission on Self Employed Women and Women in the Informal Sector has also recommended the appointment of District coordination officers to be responsible for planning, monitoring, coordination and evaluation of the programmes affecting women. Rationalization of functionaries at the block and village level to ensure coordination of programmes affecting women at the grass-roots level also needs to be undertaken.

8. There are today sufficient number of programmes in the government of India as well as innovative programmes in any States and sectors. *What is needed is not merely larger resource allocation but technical inputs for greater, effectiveness* of *these programmes, to* guarantee better resource utilization. Emphasis has to be placed on more effective planning, monitoring and evaluation of existing programmes through a result-oriented mechanism operating at different levels.

9. Recognizing that a critical input for women's development would be training and wider dissemination of information backed by research data and documentation, *it is proposed to set-up a National Resource Centre for Women.* This resource centre would translate national developmental needs of women into a systematic grid of programmes and schemes for training at different levels in skills/knowledge/attitudes. The Centre would identify and if necessary, strengthen existing governmental and non-governmental agencies including women's universities/ women's centres and colleges through which the training; research/dissemination could be carried out. The national commission on self-employed women and those in informal sector has also recommended the need for a national institution to cater to women's training as well as formulate guidelines and

help the other constituent units at the state level, divisional level and district level to carry out training programmes.

10. Reorientation and sensitization of the administrative machinery at all levels in the government of India, the States, as well as specialized technical agencies (both Government and Voluntary) to the issues of women in development is essential. Three levels of orientation are necessary, i.e. at the policy and planning level, at the district or intermediary level, and at the block and, village level. The training of functionaries and their orientation to women's issues must also be in the right perspective, i.e. *women should be perceived as producers and participants, not clients for welfare.* The dynamic role of women's contribution to the national economy as partners and equal citizens must be reiterated and translated into programmes and projects. The National Resource Centre would be responsible for revamping the existing content/methodology and monitoring of training at all levels.
11. *A special division should be created in the Ministry of Women and Child Development for the enforcement of law for women.* The officer-in-charge may be designated Commissioner for Women's Rights and must liaise with various Special Cells for women created by the police, the CBI as well as with the Departments of Public Grievances at Centre and State levels as also the Women's Cell in the Home Ministry. This division will be concerned with the enforcement of law to ensure women's rights, to facilitate action-oriented research in fields such as discrimination against women, protection at work, etc.
12. *This Plan recommends that the Census in future must take into account women's unpaid work in the household and outside as well as the value added in performing her many survival tasks for the family.* A greater conceptual clarity has to emerge on 'work' and 'non-work' as well as a distinction between works that produces economic value and other activities that are consumption-oriented. Data relating to women, especially in the unorganized sector should be reflected in the data of the National Sample Survey and the Central Statistical Organisation.
13. It has been observed through various studies, that education of citizens not builds-up knowledge and information but also helps the citizen understand the complexities of the political process. It is therefore, recommended that the programme of free universal education upto the age of 14 should be vigorously implemented. Further, *serious attention needs to be paid to the content of education.* The courses of studies and the text books should inculcate values of gender equality, self-respect, courage, independence, etc., which would help develop the personalities of women.

14. *The Planning Commissions and all ministries and government departments must have a Women's Cell.* All government delegations to international meetings must include at least one or more women members. Wherever a Committee or Commission is set-up by Government for any purpose, 30 per cent *of* its representation must be of women. The .Union and all State-level Public Service Commissions must have women representatives. The Planning Commission and State Planning Boards must have adequate representation of women.
15. All women members of panchayats and other executive bodies must be trained and empowered to exercise their authority. Both men and women members must be sensitized to women's issues. A committee should be formed to look into the training needs of women panchayat members and to help in designing modules. Separate allocations may be made for this purpose. Particular attention must be paid to the development of interpersonal communication skills amongst the trainees/ community leaders.
16. Media should play a productive role in enhancing women's participation. It should give wider coverage to various activities and measures taken by women, and should highlight the problems of women. In order to project women's issues and achievements, perhaps mainstream media may not be adequate and, therefore, it is necessary to develop an alternate media system that could portray women's struggles and experiences, help generate values which encourage gender equality and justice, and build-up a positive image of women participating in public life.

"Lord why have you not given women the right to conquer her destiny?
Why does she have to wait head bowed,
By the roadside, waiting with tired patience,
Hoping for a miracle in the morrow?"

—*Rabindranath Tagore*

Notes and References

1. Ministry of Women and Child Development, GOI, Annual Report, 2006-07, pp. 3-4.
2. Ministry of Women and Child Development, Government of India, Annual Report, 2006-07, p. 177.
3. Ministry of Women and Child Development, GOI, Annual Report, 2006-07, pp. 4-15.
4. GOI, Department of Social Welfare, Ministry of Education and Social Welfare, Towards Equality, Report of the Committee on the Status of Women in India, New Delhi, December 1974, p. 101.

5. "The present division of labour between the sexes in member-countries of the U.N. is also the result of special factors, such as basic difference in social culture, customs and type of Economy," Report of the Inter-regional meeting of Experts on the Integration of Women in Development....UN Doc. St.SOA.
6. Declaration on the Elimination of Discrimination Against Women, United Nations, 1967.
7. *Ibid.*, p. 5.
8. Annual Report of the Department of Women and Child Development, Ministry of HRD, GOI, 2001-02, pp. 65-66.
9. *Ibid.*, pp. 67-68.
10. Preamble to Constitution of World Health Organisation.
11. Among some tribal communities, medical services are welcome except during maternity.
12. Koos, E.S., "The Health of Region-wise", Columbia University Press, New York, 1954.
13. Committee on Empowerment of Women (2001-02), No. 4, Health and Family Welfare Programmes for Women, Ministry of Health and Family Welfare and Department of Indian System of Medicine and Homeopathy, Lok Sabha Secretariat, New Delhi, pp. 13, 21, 46.
14. First Five Year Plan, Government of India, 1951, Chapter XXXIII.
15. Report of the Secondary Education Commission, Government of India, 1953, Chapter IV.
16. Report of the Committee on Differentiation of Curricula for Boys and Girls, Government of India, 1954, Chapter IV.
17. Report of the University Education Commission, 1949, Government of India, Chapter 12.
18. Crime Against Women, Document 3, Reproduced from Crime Against Women, Police Research and Development, New Delhi, Quoted in *IJPA*, July-September 2002, pp. 485-88.

National Commission for Women at Union and State Level

GENESIS OF NATIONAL COMMISSION FOR WOMEN ACT, 1990

The UN Commission on the Status of Women in its 25th Report had recommended establishment of National Commissions or similar bodies with a mandate to review, evaluate and recommend measures and priorities, to ensure equality between men and women, and the full integration of women in all sectors of national life. Surveying the scenario, the Government of India set-up a high powered Committee on the Status of Women in India. The Committee in 1974 recommended the constitution of a Commission at the Centre and in the States with the functions of collection of information, evaluation of existing policies, programmes and laws that have a bearing on the status of women, and recommendations for new laws, policies or progammes, as well as redressal of grievances. The National Commission on Self-Employed Women and Women in the Informal Sector, in its report submitted in 1988, recommended the setting up of an Equal Opportunities Commission under Central law. In order to meet the enormous challenge of fighting atrocities against women and effectively raising their status, it was felt that a nodal agency should be set-up. This agency would be responsible for enforcement of the constitutional guarantees on the equal status of women, for review as and when necessary of existing legislation for monitoring its effect on women, for ensuring training and legal literacy and awareness amongst women, for providing a forum for women for redressal of their grievances and complaints. Successive Committees/Plans including the National Perspective Plan for Women (1988-2000) recommended the constitution of such an apex body for women.

Women's voluntary organisations and women activists had also made persistent demands for a National Women's Commission. During

1990, the Central Government held consultations with NGOs, social workers and experts, regarding the structure, functions, powers, etc. of the Commission proposed to be set-up. Women's organisations and gender experts rejected the suggestion to set-up a commission under an executive order of the Government and instead agreed on an autonomous, statutory commission armed with adequate powers.

Keeping in mind the various suggestions, the Ministry of Human Resource Development prepared the National Commission for Women Bill and consulted Central Ministries and State Governments. In May 1990, the Bill was introduced in the Lok Sabha. In July 1990 a national level conference was organized by the Ministry of Human Resource Development seeking suggestions from the women MPs, Women's organisations and experts regarding the Bill. Subsequently, the Government itself introduced new provisions in the Bill to vest the Commission with powers of a civil court for the purpose of investigation.

The National Commission for Women Bill was passed by the Lok Sabha and the Rajya Sabha on 9th and 23rd August 1990 respectively. The Bill received the assent of the President on the 30th August, 1990. In pursuance of the National Commission for Women Act, 1990 the National Commission for Women was constituted on 31st January 1992 as an autonomous statutory body. The State Government were also requested to set-up similar State Commission for Women in their respective States. The Department of Women and Child Development is the nodal Department for the National Commission for Women.

The State Commission for Women have been set-up in the 18 states under their own executive or statutory orders, viz., Andhra Pradesh, Assam, Delhi, Goa, Haryana, Himachal Pradesh, Karnataka, Kerala, Madhya Pradesh, Mizoram, Maharashtra, Orissa, Punjab, Rajasthan, Tamil Nadu, Tripura, West Bengal and Jammu and Kashmir.

ORGANISATIONAL STRUCTURE

The National Commission for women consists of a full time chairperson, five members and a member secretary. They are all appointed by the Government of India, Department of Women and Child Development for a period of three years from the date of assumption of office.

The Standing Committee on Empowerment of Women interacted with the former Chairpersons and Members of the National Commission for Women and 22nd February 2001 and the following suggestion s have emerged there from—

(i) There should not be any *ad-hocism* in the appointment of the Chairperson and Members.

(ii) There should not be any post of Member-Secretary. There should be only a Secretary for the administrative set-up for the Commission and Secretary should facilitate the functioning of the Commission in administrative matters only.

CHART 9.1

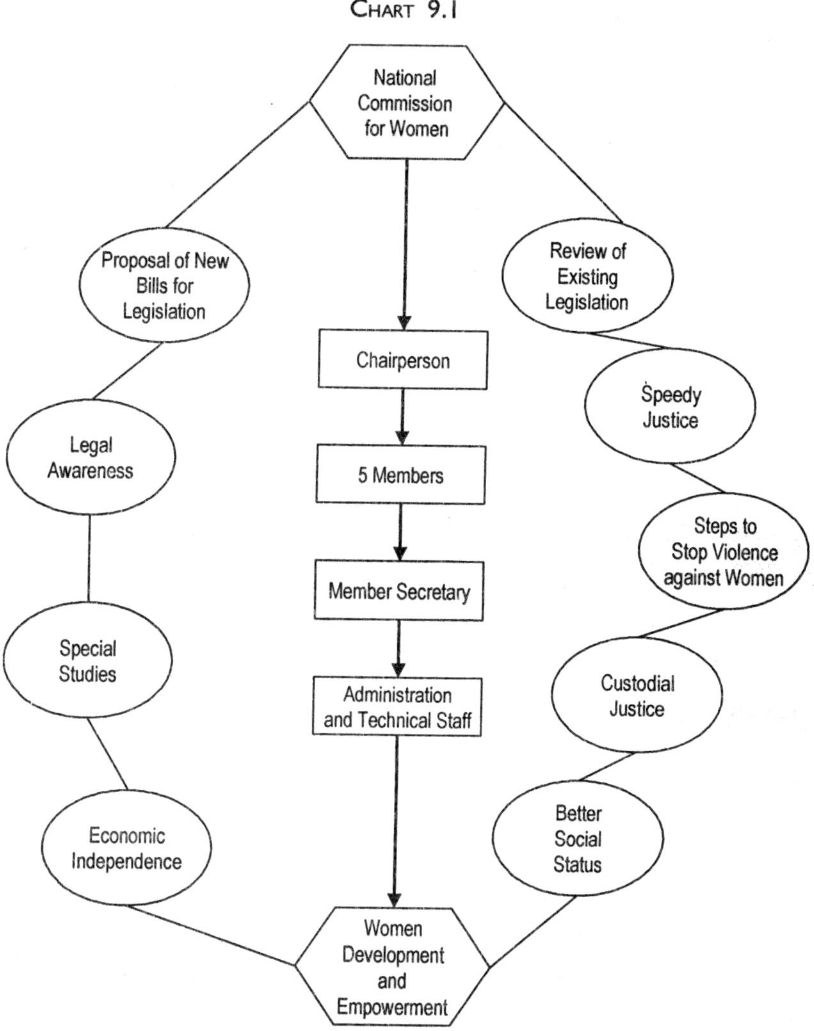

(iii) The Commission should have the powers to appoint experts.

(iv) The Commission must be consulted by the various Departments whenever they frame policies pertaining to women and the girl child.

(v) Commission ought to be totally accessible to the public.

(vi) National and State Commissions should identify the areas of work and there should not be any overlapping of their activities.

The various points/suggestions put forth by the NGOs in its meeting were as under:

(i) NCW should be strengthened to work as a high-powered autonomous and statutory body to protect the constitutional rights of women.

(ii) National Commission for Women must be given autonomous status along the line of National Human Rights Commission and the status of the Chairperson and Members of the Commission should be suitably enhanced.

(iii) There ought to be strong network of State Commissions that should work in coordination with National Commission for Women.

(iv) There should be time limit within which the new appointments are made at all levels in the Commission.

(v) The Chairperson should have the powers to authenticate the decisions taken by the Commission.

(vi) More publicity needs to be given to the work and powers of National Commission for Women.

(vii) Autonomous functioning of the Commission, its role as a watchdog body as well as mandatory consultations by Government on policy matters has been under severe pressure by Government at various times.

(viii) The necessary staff and infrastructural facilities essential to ensure proper functioning of the Commission need to be provided.

(ix) Delay on the part of the Government in taking action on the specific recommendations made by the commission should be taken seriously.

During interaction by the Committee with State Commissions, the following points emerged:

(i) Status of Chairperson and Members of the Commission to be defined to invoke response.

(ii) Lack of adequate powers and statutory status to the Commissions need attention.

(iii) Need to fill up the vacancies for Members in some State Commissions.

(iv) Powers to appoint its own staff rather than getting staff on deputation basis from the Government.

(v) Shortage of adequate and competent staff support.

(vi) Allocation of insufficient funds to the commission.

(vii) Most of the commissions do not have their own building.

(viii) Non-availability of computers, fax and other facilities to some of the commissions.

(ix) Non-availability of adequate infrastructure, conveyance and other facilities.

(x) Delay in acceptance of recommendations made by the State Commissions by the Government.

(xi) In order to ensure continuity of its functions, amendment to the Act needed to ensure that 1/3rd of Members retire every year.

The State Governments were also required to take proper action to set-up State Commissions in their respective States. So far, as per the information made available to the Committee only 18 States have constituted the State Commission for Women in their respective States. In some States the Women Commissions have been set-up recently. The Committee observed that despite the National Commission for Women Act, 1990 having been in existence for more than a decade, the setting up of such Commissions in some States is yet to become a reality (Arunachal Pradesh, Bihar, Gujarat, Manipur, Meghalaya, Nagaland, Sikkim, Uttar Pradesh and in three newly created States, i.e. Chhattisgarh, Uttrananchal and Jharkhand). There are other States like Karnataka where the Commission is not reconstituted for over a year and a half, leaving it to be seen by an official of the State Government. The absence of an autonomous statutory Commission armed with adequate powers have deprived millions of women in those States the right to effectively fight for redressal of their grievances and to facilitate implementation of the Gender policies. The Committee would urged upon the Department of Women and Child Development to impress upon those State Governments to constitute the State Commissions for Women in their States without any further loss of time.

It has also come to the notice of the Committee that whereas the National Commission for Women is constituted as per the National Commission for Women Act, 1990, some States' Commissions are just appointees of the Government and there is no uniformity in appointment of such Commissions in States. The Committee, therefore, urged upon the Department of Women and Child Development to take up the matter with the State Government to ensure that the State Commissions in all the States are appointed by a statutory order.

(I) Internal Re-organisation (Chart 9.2)

To optimize the resources of the Commission, the whole organisation was reviewed in relation to its expected functions and different cells were created as separate nodes of authority and responsibility to focus on the important areas of the Commission's activities. While doing this both the statutory mandate as well as working requirements and the experience in the past decade were given due consideration. The work of the Commission has now been organized among the following cells/sections:

(a) Legal Cell;
(b) Complaints and Investigation Cell;
(c) Research and Studies Cell.
(d) Monitoring Cell;
(e) Public Relations Cell;
(f) Administrative Section;
(g) Cash Section; and
(h) Accounts Section.

CHART 9.2

Organisation Chart—National Commission for Women

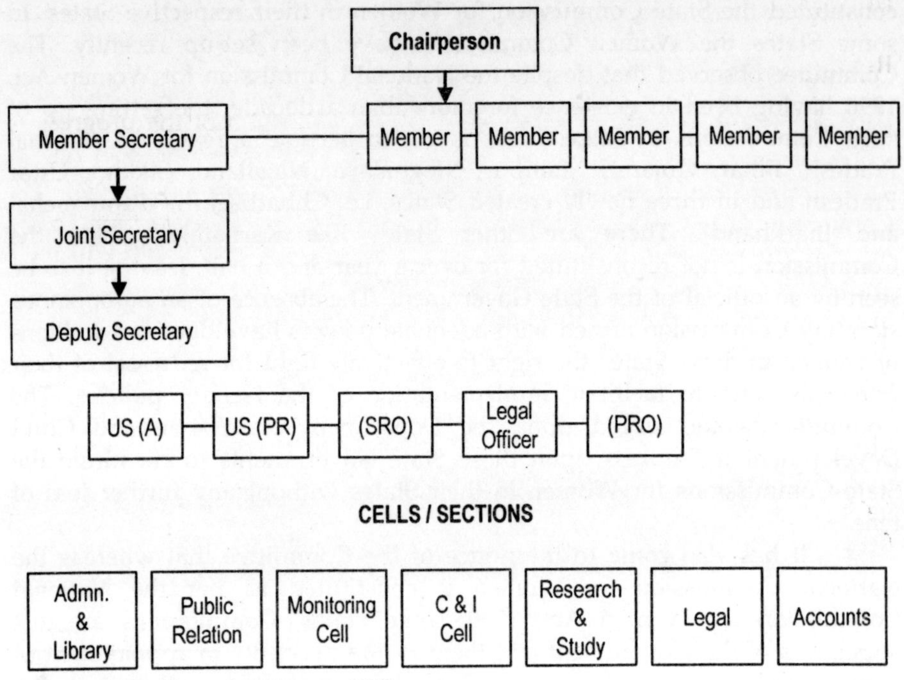

Source: NCW, Year of Endevour, 2002.

Legal Cell

Since one of the primary functions of the Commission is to review the working of various laws and policies which have a bearing on the status of women, the Cell deals with the review and examination of legislation concerning women. The Cell also coordinates the working of the Parivarik Mahila Lok Adalats through which the Commission provides speedy justice. It also looks after the country-wide legal awareness programme for women to impart practical knowledge about the basic legal rights and remedies provided under various laws to prepare them to face the challenges of real life situations.

Complaints and Investigation Cell

One of the most important functions of the Commission, by which ordinary women across the country relate to the Commission, is the handling of complaints from women who are in distress or are otherwise the victims of social and economic wrongs or a gender biased system. Though the Commission received complaints by the tons, there had been a virtual clogging up of the channels of hearing and redress because of organisational deficiencies. The refocusing of the cell involved bringing the Members of the Commission into a more direct role vis-à-vis these complaints. Now it has been ensured that each and every complaint, never mind, their number, would be handled by one or the other Member personally and would not be filed away or summarily closed at the administrative level.

Research and Studies Cell

The Commission has a salient role in promotional and educational research into the problems of women, in the evaluation of the progress of various developmental schemes and in the advice to be rendered on the planning process of socio-economic development concerning women. The Commission has carried out various studies and brought out reports and monographs on several important issues. While the Commission will push ahead with its future agenda on numerous other issues, the Cell will help in underpinning this effort through the development of gender profiles for different States and augment its research efforts by collaborating with State Commissions across the country.

Monitoring Cell

Various plans and initiatives, however well conceived, can end up in naught for want of effective systems of follow-up. The Monitoring Cell has been specifically created to keep a watch on every initiative from its conception through initiation, implementation and evaluation. The visits of the Members to the States, the deliberations of various committees and working groups, the reports of various investigations, the recommendations sent to the Government all need to be monitored constantly so that what was considered an emergency yesterday does not fade into a non-entity today because of the onrush of new problems. Equally, the Cell would monitor internal processes of the Commission and keep track of how its current activities correspond to the mandate under Sec. 10 of the Act and the planned agenda for the year.

Public Relations Cell

The effectiveness of the Commission and its image have long suffered for want of a proper public relations mechanism. Both the people and their representatives, including MPs and MLAs; had often voiced their frustration that the Commission did not respond adequately and promptly to queries, suggestions or information sought or brought by them. The appointment of a Public Relations Officer and the creation of a Cell in this area will no doubt help to disseminate requisite information to the media as well to the general public and also spread awareness of the activities and programmes of the Commission at all levels.

Other Cells

The administration, cash and accounts sections carry out their usual duties but they have been revitalized through a clear delineation of lines of authority and command.

(II) Functional Review

Though the functions of the Commission are statutorily laid down (Section 10), there had been, over the years, digressions leacl.ing to occasional forays into executive areas which properly belonged to the administrative departments and some shift away from legitimate duties like hearing of complaints and grievances. A decision was taken therefore to refocus the lenses and, as already mentioned, Members of the commission took up this challenging task of attending to individual complaints with great earnestness. Members have also taken responsibility for handling specific functional area of work in keeping with their interests and expertise. In addition, States have been allocated to Members on a geographical basis in order to facilitate intensive concentration of work in specific areas.

(III) Procedural Revamping

Sec. 9(2) of the NCW Act, 1992, stipulates that the Commission shall regulate its own procedure and the procedure of the Committees thereof. After ten years of working, however, the Commission lacked a duly authenticated set of procedures covering various aspects of its working. This resulted in endless confusion concerning the authority and responsibility of various functionaries who invoked different sets of rules and regulations and accompanying powers under various statutes of the Government. Since working procedures are as vital as formal structures for the functioning of any organisation the Commission formulated and adopted the National Commission for Women (Procedure) Regulations, 2002.

Term of Office and Conditions of Service of Chairperson and Members

(1) The Chairperson and every member hold office for such period, not exceeding three years, as may be specified by the Central Government in this behalf.

(2) The Chairperson or a Member (other than the Member Secretary who is a member of a civil service of the Union or of an all-India service or holds a civil post under the Union) may, by writing and addressed to the Central Government, resign from the office of Chairperson or, as the Case may be, of the Member at any time.

(3) The Central Government can remove a person from the office of Chairperson or a Member referred to in sub-section (2) if that person—

   (a) becomes an undischarged insolvent;

   (b) get convicted and sentenced to imprisonment for an offence which in the opinion of the Central Government involves moral turpitude;

   (c) becomes of unsound mind and stands so declared by a competent court;

(d) refuses to act or becomes incapable of acting;

(e) is, without obtaining leave of absence from the Commission, absent from three consecutive meetings of the Commission; or

(f) in the opinion of the Central Government has so abused the position of Chairperson or Member as to render that person's continuance in office detrimental to the public interest:

Provided that no person shall be removed under this clause until that person has been given a reasonable opportunity of being heard in the matter.

(4) A vacancy caused under sub-section (2) or otherwise is filled by fresh nomination.

(5) The salaries and allowances payable to, and the other terms and conditions of service of, the Chairperson and Members shall be such as may be prescribed.

Officers and other Employees of the Commission

(1) The Central Government shall provide the Commission with such officers and employees as may be necessary for the efficient performance of the functions of the Commission under this Act.

(2) The salaries and allowances payable to, and the other terms and conditions of service of the officers and other employees appointed for the purpose of the Commission shall be such as may be prescribed.

Salaries and Allowances to be paid out of Grants

The salaries and allowances payable to the Chairperson and Members and the administrative expenses, including salaries, allowances and pensions payable to the officers and other employees referred to in section 5, shall be paid out of the grants referred to in sub-section (1) of section 11. Grants released by the Department of Women and Child Development has released. 2 crores in 1995-96 which increased to three and a half crores in 2000-01.

Vacancies, etc., not Invalidate Proceedings of the Commission

No act or proceeding of the Commission shall be questioned or shall be invalid, on the ground merely of the existence of any vacancy or defect in the constitution of the Commission.

Committees of the Commission

(1) The Commission may appoint such committees as may be necessary for dealing with such special issues as may be taken up by the Commission from time to time.

(2) The Commission shall have the power to co-opt as members of any committee appointed under sub-section (1) such number of persons, who are not Members of the Commission, as it may think fit and the persons so co-opted shall have the right to attend the meetings of the committee and take part in its proceedings but shall not have the right to vote.

(3) The persons so co-opted shall be entitled to receive such allowances for attending the meetings of the committee as may be prescribed.

Procedure to be Regulated by the Commission

(1) The Commission or a Committee thereof shall meet as and when necessary and shall meet at such time and plate as the Chairperson may think fit.

(2) The Commission shall regulate its own procedure and the procedure of the Committees thereof.

(3) All orders and decisions of the Commission shall be authenticated by the Member-Secretary or any other officer of the Commission duly authorized by the Member-Secretary in this behalf.

Functions of the Commission

The Commission shall perform all or any of the following functions, namely:

(a) investigate and examine all matters relating to the legal safeguards provided for women under the Constitution and other laws;

(b) present to the Central Government, annually and at such other times as the Commission may deem fit, reports upon the working of those safeguards;

(c) make in such reports and recommendations for the effective implementation of those safeguards for improving the conditions of women by the Union or any State;

(d) review, from time to time, the existing provisions of the Constitution and other laws affecting women and recommend amendments thereto so as to suggest remedial legislative measures to meet any lacunae, inadequacies or shortcomings in such legislations;

(e) take up the cases of violation of the provisions of the Constitution and of other laws relating to women with the appropriate authorities;

(f) look into complaints and take suo moto notice of matters relating to:

i. deprivation of women's rights;

ii. non-implementation of laws enacted to provide protection to women and also to achieve the objective of equality and development; and

iii. non-compliance of policy decisions, guidelines or instructions aimed at mitigating hardships and ensuring welfare and providing relief to women, and take up the issues arising out of such matters with appropriate authorities;

(g) call for special studies or investigation into specific problems or situations arising out of discrimination and atrocities against women and identify the constraints so as to recommend strategies for their removal;

(h) undertake promotional and educational research so as to suggest ways of ensuring due representation of women in all spheres and identify factors responsible for impeding their advancement, such as, lack of access to housing and basic services, inadequate support services and technologies for reducing drudgery and occupational health hazards and for increasing their productivity;

(i) participate and advise on the planning process of socio-economic development of women;

(j) evaluate the progress of the development of women under the Union and any State;

(k) inspect or cause to be inspected a jail, remand home, women's institution or other place of custody where women are kept as prisoners or otherwise, and take with the concerned authorities for remedial action, if found necessary;

(l) fund litigation involving issues affecting a large body of women;

(m) make periodical reports to the Government on any matter pertaining to women and in particular various difficulties under which women toil; and

(n) any other matter which may be referred to it by Central Government.

PROBLEMS AND SUGGESTIONS

The author conducted a discussion with present and past members of NCW and present and past Chairpersons, Members of Parliament and State Legislatures, eminent women in metropolitan cities and elected members of Panchayats about their views pertaining to the functioning of National Council For Women. More than 80 percent of the women were of the view that the creation of National Council for Women is a progressive step and is essential to promote the cause of women in all areas especially in 12 areas as specified by Beijing Conference. However, in practice, the NCW could not make desired impact inspite of its existence for a decade. They mentioned that nomination to commission is mostly based on influence and not merit. Most of the members are merely decorative. There is a need of overhauling its administrative structure both political and administrative. In addition, NCW is doing duplicate work as activities undertaken by NCW are also undertaken by many other agencies. The NCW has failed to provide the role of leadership as a Nodal agency. Hence, there is a need of strengthening of National Council for Women. We give here some of the problems and suggestions to improve the capability and capacity of NCW.

I. Shortage of Staff

The Commission is short of staff inspite of the fact that there is a provision in the Act that the central government shall provide the Commission with such officers and employees as may be necessary for the efficient performance of the functions of the Commission [section 5(1)], no such personnel were provided to NCW except for administrative and house keeping jobs. The Commission had made some *ad-hoc* arrangement by availing of the services of retired government officials which was asked to be discontinued in 1998. Government must look into this matter seriously otherwise this would affect the functioning of NCW.

Based upon the SID Study, the Department of Expenditure has since approved creation of five additional posts in National Commission for Women. Besides creation of the 5 posts mentioned above, National Commission for Women has been allowed to engage 4 full-time Counsellors at a consolidated monthly fee of Rs. 4000 as and when their services are required by it. It may, however, be added that the Commission had recruited a number of (nearly 104) persons over and above the sanctioned strength of 37. When NCW tried to dispense with their services, they filed a writ petition in the Delhi High Court and 24 of such persons unauthorisedly recruited by NCW have obtained a stay order against their retrenchment. The Commission has therefore to retain them in service. They are in the grade of LDC Steno and Peon. Until and unless, NCW is well equipped in terms of human beings, money and material, no impact can be made. It is also necessary for NCW to concentrate on very important activities till these are consolidated and then take other activities when the NCW has developed capacity and capability.

2. Finances not Released in Time

The process of actual release of funds is not timely and being in a piecemeal fashion, does hamper the commission efforts to work in a planned and structured manner.

3. Nomination of Affluent Urban Women

Most of the members appointed on NCW including chairperson belong to affluent sections of the society and are based in urban areas. The problems before NCW are mostly from rural areas, which defy solution with such composition of NCW. We must encourage the women with initial background and based in villages to be nominated on NCW. Only such women, who have seen, experienced and lived among rural women facing problems whether these may be in the areas of dowry, or violence or divorce or maltreatment or education. The Government of India should nominate at least half of the women who belong to rural areas, backward areas and are also living there otherwise NCW would look only ornamental.

4. Involving of Women in Commission's Activities Living in Cities who are already busy with their other Activities

The NCW generally deals with cases from urban life as they: have knowledge and access to NCW as well. However, the need is to solve the problems of rural women who because of their poverty and illiteracy go on tolerating the injustices and privations and never approach NCW, most of the women who came in my contact even did not know about NCW. It is high time that through Panchayati Raj Institutions NCW approaches the women in villages and creates awareness among them. This is the challenge of 21st century.

5. Lack of Effective Implementation

NCW has been effective in mobilizing MLAs, MPs to enact new laws and. amend old one's to protect women from injustice. However, those who are engaged in their implementation whether in administration or judiciary fail to do justice. The existence of law would not make women happy. What is needed is to monitor the cases dealt under those laws and also assess the impact these had made on the conditions of women. It requires constant monitoring as well as action in a bold manner. The government functionaries responsible for implementation need to be adequately trained and re-oriented for desired results.

6. Lack of Awareness Generation Programmes among Women belonging to Villages/Disadvantages Sections of Society

Most of the women are not aware of the role of NCW and its programmes. NCW with the help of Women teachers in schools, women Panchayat members and other enlightened women in Mahila Mandals, etc. should make a programme to educate the women of the rural areas in a simple language or the language of the areas. Pamphlets may be kept in village school library. NCW may keep in mind that it is easier to destroy the mountains than to change the minds of the people. Hence, it is a very difficult and challenging task which require tremendous efforts before women can be able to get their lawful rights.

7. Studies got Conducted by NCW are not in Priority Areas

NCW promotes research to get insights into women's problems. However, these studies are not in priority areas, which result in the wastage *of* resources. NCW may provide small amounts to scholars (M. Phil., Ph.D) and get the study conducted. In addition, the University Grants

Commission has set-up women study -centres in most of the Universities in India. NCW can entrust this work to them rather than spend its own money, which can be used for other productive purposes.

Thus, NCW may become a Nodal agency for coordinating researches done by different agencies.

8. Lack of Effective Linkages with State Women Commission

NCW should provide leadership to state women commission, central social welfare board, NGO's as to, how they should operate which can benefit women allover the country. NCW should be a think tank to guide other agencies. NCW should do more of a qualitative work rather than merely carry out its statutory activities. NCW should be innovative and action-oriented. NCW has to struggle for the rights of women till these are achieved.

9. Lack of Adequate Status

The National Commission for Women was constituted for the safeguard of almost half of the population of the country. It has neither been given the same status as intended by the Parliament nor a status equivalent to the other national level Commissions. The Commission, therefore, recommends that the Chairperson of NCW be given the status of the Union Cabinet Minister and the Members that of Ministers of State.

Role of Central Social Welfare Board

> Economic growth means not only creation of wealth but also creating people's capacity to create wealth and that resides in their health, education, knowledge, skills, etc. It is very difficult to separate the two. Social Welfare has to be the society's organized expression of concern for the total well-being of its members. It is not some temporary relief measures but consists of long-term rehabilitation.
>
> —*Durgabai Deshmukh*

Before India embarked upon planned development, social work was, by and large, in the hands of voluntary organisations. Lack of trained personnel paucity of financial resources, lack of leadership hampered their useful work. Planned development aimed at evolution of a national plan for social welfare with co-ordination of government and voluntary effort; and organisation of a programme of financial and technical assistance to voluntary organisations. It was, therefore, considered necessary to provide specialized agency, which, could help the voluntary organisations with financial and technical assistance to dovetail their efforts in the planning and implementation of social welfare programmes.

The State, however, has to undertake the responsibility of providing aid to the voluntary organisations *for the maintenance,* expansion and development of welfare services. Consequently, in 1953 the Central Social Welfare Board was created with an allocation of forty million rupees for grants-in-aid to voluntary organisations, by a resolution of the then Ministry of Education.

Central Social Welfare Board (CSWB) was conceived as an institution to be instrumental in bringing the neglected, weak, handicapped and backward sections of society into the national mainstream. *Established on 13th August, 1953, the Board initiated several programmes for delivering welfare services to the most backward, marginalized and deserving sections of the society.*

As a follow-up, the State Social Welfare advisory Boards were set-up with the task of implementing and monitoring of different programmes *or* the CSWB.

Over the years, the Board has not only widened the scope of its programmes but has also moved its policy approach from welfare to development to empowerment. Today, it is the pioneering national level organisation in the field of development and empowerment of women in the country.[1]

CHART 10.1

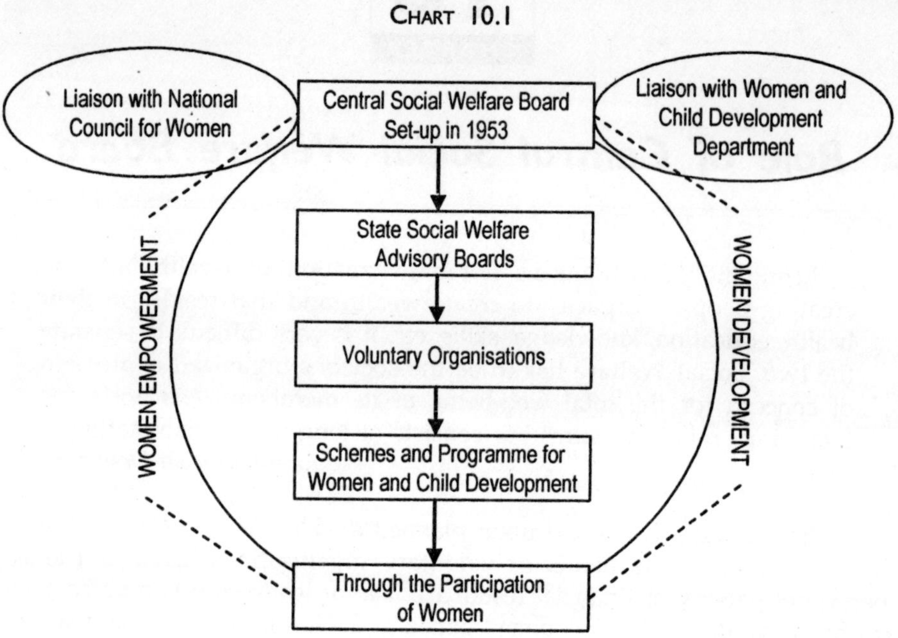

It was declared by Jawaharlal Nehru, (the then Prime Minister of India) that "this attempt that we are making to encourage social welfare activities is in a sense rather unique. It is not some 'Central Authority' that is doing it by itself, not does the burden of this fall on the local social welfare organisations. It is certainly a combination of the two where the Central Social Welfare Board comes as a helper and advises and at the same time the local welfare organisations, which are best suited for it, undertake the work. In this case, we can utilize the energy, enthusiasm and initiative of vast number of persons all over the country."[1]

The CSWB was also envisaged as an interface between the Government and the voluntary sector for social development in the country. It *has made a signal contribution in encouraging, assisting and promoting the growth of nearly twenty-five thousand voluntary organisations for reaching the neglected women and children of the country.*

FUNCTIONS

The Board in 1953 was assigned the functions as: generally to assist in the improvement and development of social welfare activities and in particular: (i) to cause a survey to be made of the needs and requirements of Social Welfare Organisations; (ii) to evaluate the programmes/projects of the aided agencies; (iii) to co-ordinate assistance extended to social welfare activities by various Central Ministries/Departments/State Governments; (iv) to promote the setting up of, Social Welfare Organisations on a voluntary basis in places where such organisations do not exist; and (v) to render financial aid, when necessary, to deserving organisations or institutions on terms to be prescribed by the Board.

This list of functions for the Board appear to reflect: (a) the spirit of continued partnership between statutory and voluntary welfare services to act as complementary and supplementary to each other; (b) change over from un-organized charity to systematic welfare work on systematic lines to be supported by State assistance wherever considered necessary or desirable; (c) need of proper co-ordination of all welfare services, voluntary and statutory and the dovetailing thereof into the general pattern of the overall development of the country as unfolded in the Five Year Plans; (d) change in the role of voluntary welfare organisations from the concept of charity or patronage 'to, that of social responsibility based on social justice; (e) need for rationalizing the system of rendering financial assistance to voluntary organisations; (f) the setting up of welfare institutions on voluntary basis for the uncovered areas; and (g) conducting of regular surveys regarding the needs and requirements of the social welfare organisations.

ADDITIONAL FUNCTIONS

In July 1960, on the recommendation of the Study Team on Social Welfare and Backward Classes, the following additional areas of responsibilities were assigned to the Board: (i) to organize field counselling service as an effective supplement to the working of the grants-in-aid programmes to assess the programmes and projects of aided agencies; (ii) to promote the setting up of voluntary organisations in uncovered areas; (iii) to initiate the organisation of pioneering welfare service; and (iv) to stimulate effective co-ordination among voluntary welfare agencies, especially at the national level and among agencies covered by the grants-in-aid programme.

The broad reasons for the addition of the above mentioned functions are the indicators of (a) ensuring proper utilization of funds by the voluntary organisations provided under the grants-in-aid programme, through an effective internal assessment or supervisory machinery (Field Counselling Service) (This internal assessment is different from evaluation which is normally entrusted to an external independent body); (b) non-existence of a large number of suitable voluntary organisations which could fulfil terms and conditions of grant, such as those of registration, auditing and accounting, raising of matching contribution, etc. for rural, remote, backward and hilly areas, i.e. for the uncovered areas;. (c) to encourage and motivate the voluntary organisations which did not take up earlier all types of social welfare services, through initiating such services as pilot services so as to cover different categories of social welfare services meant for vulnerable sections of society; (d) non-existence of required co-ordination and co-operation among the voluntary, organisations functioning at all levels, amongst themselves and with the governmental agencies, between the concerned government departments at Central and State level, between voluntary agencies at the Central, State, District and local levels; (e) demand of voluntary organisations for providing them with technical knowledge for the implementation of the social welfare programmes at their door steps; and (f) emerging needs and requirements to establish specialized social welfare services.

In 1969, the following function were also added to the functions of the Board: (i) to give technical and financial aid to Panchayati Raj Institutions in accordance with the schemes or principles approved by Government of India; (ii) to promote social welfare activities intended for the general welfare of the public such as welfare of the family, women, children and the handicapped and assistance in cases of unemployment, under-employment, old-age, sickness disablement and other cases of under served wants (i.e., categories which have not been covered); (iii) to organize or promote training in social work as and when required and also to organize and work out pilot projects whenever necessary; and (iv) to organize through its machinery, emergency relief in cases of national, natural calamity or otherwise whenever deemed fit.

The main reasons for the addition of these functions assigned to the Board include: (a) involving Panchayati Raj Institutions in the total perspective of social welfare services; (b) introducing social security measures through devices like social insurance and social assistance in conformity with achieving the goals of a welfare state; (c) coping with the increased necessity of trained personnel for manning the social welfare programmes and staff development; (d) changes effected in socio-economic environmental conditions of the country; (e) organizing relief measures on permanent Basis; (f) entrusting a positive land challenging role to the Central Board while keeping in view the changing needs and requirements of an individual, group and community in the field of social welfare; (g) attempting to make the Board the only agency responsible for promoting voluntary efforts in the field of social welfare at national, state, district and local level, (h) making the Board responsible for advising government on problems and provision of measures relating to social welfare; and engaging the Board itself in executive functions; (i) promoting, research (applied) in the field of social welfare and standards of norms meant for the voluntary organisations; (j) realizing that mass approach should give place to group approach and further to individual approach. (For example, there is a tendency now to set-up residential institutions for children on cottage basis with housemother, so as to give individual attention to a child in a family-like atmosphere rather than a composite home for them); (k) realizing the need to appoint paid workers to do field jobs in place of voluntary workers who usually are busy at the supervisory and managerial level; (l) realizing the need of training in social welfare administration to voluntary social workers; and (m) utilizing energies and newer channels of voluntary effort for national development programmes.

A review of these changes in functions over a period of time (i.e. from 1953 to 1987) reveals that the functions assigned to the Board demand many responsibilities and liabilities on the part of the Central Social Welfare Board and these gigantic functions assigned overlap with the functions of other governmental agencies, *inter alia* has to act as an agent of social change. An examination of these functions has also raised four basic issues viz., (i) the role of the Board in terms of making speedy and rational policy decisions; (ii) the role of the Board in the implementation of the social welfare programmes and problems of coordination and control; (iii) the relationship between the Board and the Panchayati Raj Institutions in the implementation of Social Welfare Programmes *vis-à-vis* giving grants to Panchayati Raj Institutions; and (iv) the relationship of the Board with other government departments discharging similar type of functions *vis-à-vis* arousing public opinion against social. evils.

Annual Report of the Central Social Welfare Board (2000-01) rightly mentions that under the leadership of the founding Chairperson, Dr. Durgabai Deshmukh, eminent social workers and national leaders gave patronage to the Board. Dr. Durgabai Deshmukh was instrumental in metamorphosing the Board into a medium, which initiated, the programmes and carried out careful monitoring of the implementing agencies. As a result of her vision and the continued efforts of her successors, there is today a widespread network of voluntary organisations that are carrying welfare services to the remotest corners of the country. Such a, network could not ordinarily have been envisaged in newly independent India. Owing to relentless efforts by the Board this network of voluntary agencies has been established and developed all over the country.

Today, the Central Social Welfare Board is major national; level organisation dedicated to the welfare, development and empowerment of women children and marginalized in society, through education and training, collective mobilization and awareness creation, income generation facilities and by the provision of support services.

ORGANISATIONAL STRUCTURE

In Central Social Welfare Board at the top, there is a General Body. Next, in hierarchy is the Executive Committee for decision-making. Next, in hierarchy is the Chairman who administers the day-to-day affairs of the Board.

The administrative structure has been broken into staff and line agencies, as the running of the administration of such a complex organisation cannot be a single man's show. Immediately after Chairman, there is an Executive Director, assisted by Five Divisional heads, namely, Joint Director, Planning, Monitoring and Co-ordination, Joint Director, Industrial Programme Administration, Joint Director, Welfare Programme Administration, Internal Financial Advisor-cum-Chief Pay and Accounts Officer, Finance and Accounts Division, Joint Director, Administrative Division, etc.

The first three constitute staff offices and remaining two line officers. The former acts as a filter and funnel to the Chairman by contributing special knowledge and ability to solve problems within specific area of operation. It also serves the line agency in matter of planning, co-ordination, fact-finding and research in achieving its objectives. The line agencies deal with substantive fields and are responsible for implementation.[2]

The success or failure of an organisation among other things, (team of competent and permanent employees) depend upon the quality of participation, interest and responsiveness of its management. These members adopt the mechanism of institutional bodies to formulate policies because they cannot manage the affairs individually and in isolation from one another. These bodies are:

- Participation in the policy-making by all the members through the Institution of General Body;
- Participation in the policy-making by the elected/nominated members of the General Body; and
- Allocation of special duties and responsibilities to different members of the General Body through Committees.

General Body

The functioning of the CSWB is sought to be ensured through the General Body in a democratic manner. All matters of policy planning substantive programme management and investment of funds in the organisation have to be carried out with the approval of General Body. The day-to-day management of the affairs of the organisation is, however, entrusted to the nominated executive committee subject to overall policy directives of the former.[3]

CSWB vests the power of administration of the Central Social Welfare Board in the General Body (except that it must conform to the Acts and the Rules). The General Body has various powers and functions such as consideration of the accounts, balance sheet, annual report and the reports of the executive committee and also of the Auditors. The composition of the General Body has direct relevance to the efficient and successful operations of the organisation. As provided in Article 4, (amended from time to time) the General Body of the Board consists of a Chairman nominated by the Government and members from the following:[4]

General body

- All Chairpersons of State Social Welfare Advisory Boards (33).
- Representatives from the Parliament: Lok Sabha 2 and Rajya Sabha 1.
- 2 Professionals from General Body.
- 3 eminent persons with extensive experience in social work.
- Representatives from Ministers/Departments/Government of India, Department of Women and Child Development, Department of Rural Development, Department of Education, Planning Commission, Ministry of Labour, Ministry of Social Justice and Empowerment, Department of Family Welfare.
- Executive Director, CSWB.

Executive Committee

- Chairpersons of State Social Welfare Advisory Boards: 5 by rotation.
- Representative from Ministers/Department of the Government of India, Department of Women and Child Development, Department of Family Welfare, Department of Rural Development and Poverty Alleviation, Department of Education and Ministry of Social Justice and Empowerment.
- Two Professionals.
- Executive Director, CSWB.

The composition of the body itself suggests that there is an effort to infuse in the decision-making, and planning those people who are connected with the implementation of programme so that it brings realism by feeling the experience gained in the process.

Committee Systems

The Committees are part of an effective system of checks and balances within an organisation. A committee can be defined as a body of persons entrusted with accomplishing specific functions of a group in a corporate capacity. In the words of Brech, a committee is "a meeting which has a formal constitution and formal proceedings and which will meet on a regular or periodic basis."[5] The committees are known by different names, e.g., Executive Committee, Administrative Committee, Standing Committee and the like.

In Central Social Welfare Board, there is a statutory committee viz., Executive Committee. Besides, the Board has been "authorized by its Article and Memorandum of Association to appoint other committees as it may deem fit. These committees have a variety of functions to perform—Advisory, informational and decision-making, etc. In Central Social Welfare Board, the Executive Committee consists of twelve members comprising of the Chairman. 4 government representatives, representing: the Ministry of Social Welfare; Ministry of Finance, Department of Rural Development and the Ministry of Health and Family. Welfare, six other members to be appointed by Government in consultation with the Chairman of the Board and the Executive Director."[6]

With regard to the functions and powers of the Executive Committee, these are as follows:

- to administer the general affairs of the Board,
- to determine what activities shall be undertaken and to manage the carrying out of such activities;
- to collaborate with activities with other organisations working in the field,
- to control the finance of the Board,
- to control the staff of the Board,
- to borrow money,
- to invest the funds of the Board,
- to appoint special committee consisting of experts in various fields with specific objectives provided that no one shall be a member in more than two such committees at a time,
- to delegate to any officer of the Board such administrative and financial powers as it may deem fit,
- to arrange for the audit of the annual accounts of the Board, and
- to do all such other lawful acts as would be conductive to the interests and objects of the Board.

The social and economic growth of our society is closely linked with our ability to create appropriate organisations that can serve the purpose for which they are created. Social welfare programmes are an integral part of planned development in India. The country increasingly depends on organisations for implementing these programmes.[7] It is essential for every such organisation to have an in-built capacity to adapt itself to changing circumstances. The Central Social Welfare Board is one of the major organisations in the field of social welfare.

The structure of the Central Social Welfare Board has been evolved over the years as dictated by diversification and expansion of its functions. The evolution has been from a comparatively small and less complex structure to a large and complex one. It is thus a result of gradual evolution. At the turn of the millennium, the Board is metamorphosing into a more proactive and flexible instrument for taking development to the needy and marginalized. *The primary focus of the Board has been the development of women and children.* This function assumes tremendous importance in the changing scenario that has thrown up new challenges and opportunities to the social sector. As the development idiom in the country has moved from welfare to development to empowerment, so too, the focus of the CSWB has widened in scope. The specific programmes of the Central Social Welfare Board haves undergone several mutations in order to become need and situation specific and sensitive to the changing social environment.

State Board Administration

33 State Social Welfare Boards are functioning in each State Capital and Union Territory with the objective of implementing various schemes for the welfare and development of poor women, girls and children through registered voluntary organisations. The State Board is headed by a non-official Chairperson who is a renowned social worker of the State. State Board members are nominated on the Board by Central Board and State Government in the ratio of 50:50. These members normally represent each district of the State.

The expenditure on the State Board Establishment Budget is met on 50:50 basis (i.e. 50% by the State Government and 50% by CSWB). An amount of Rs. 555.00 lakh has been released to State Boards during 2005-06 as Central Social Welfare Board's share and Rs. 371.49 lakh for 2006-07.[8]

Chief Executive

It is important to know how an organisation is influenced by the head of the organisation before we discuss his/her role. *One important factor for successful functioning of an organisation is the capability and integrity of its executives.*[9] Administrative capability is an important means of converting inputs into outputs, such as goods and services. It involves the ability to mobilize, allocate and co-ordinate actions that are essential to carry out developmental activities effectively. The chief executive especially has the responsibility of enabling the organisation to achieve its objectives in an efficient and effective manner. In CSWB, the Chairman is the chief executive at the administrative hierarchy. The chairman, being closely associated with many national and international committees, consultative committees, etc., brings a rich experience to the furtherance of the Board's programme and proper understanding of social welfare situations and conditions.

Functional Distribution

The Executive Director-functions directly under the chief executive. The executive director is responsible for authoritative advice on all-aspects of Working of the Board and is expected to participate in and contribute to management decisions. His/Her work is characterized by a substantial weight and range of complexities in view of the problems presented by various outside environmental factors and internal organisational elements. His/Her job combines and cuts across the lines of work included in two or more specialized fields and thus can be described as a network of various responsibilities. He/She has to perform many managerial and advisory functions, which arise from relatively intangible nature of activities and are performed in an informal manner. Under the executive director, there are five divisional heads directly responsible to him/her.

These divisional heads are assisted by supporting staff. The major duties and responsibilities assigned to the five divisions are mentioned following:

A. Industrial Programme Division

The division deals with socio-economic programme of the Board. The division deals mainly with, matters such as: (i) examination of applications of organisations or institutions with reference to their eligibility for grants, (ii) release of grants to the voluntary organisations/state boards; (iii) finalization and acceptance of the audited statements of accounts, (iv) examination of the inspection reports received from welfare officers and assistant project officers, (v) preparation of annual budget estimates and formulation of proposals for Annual Plan and Five Year Plan, (vi) attending to all matters concerning questions in Parliament, and (vii) maintaining liaison with Ministry of Social Welfare, Ministry of Industries, Khadi Commission and the concerned State Governments. The division is headed by a Joint Director assisted by 4 Deputy Directors and supporting staff with specific areas of functions.

B. Welfare Programme Division

The division deals with the following programmes; divided into three sections:

General Grant Unit; Section-I

This section is concerned with execution of, programmes in regard to giving grants to voluntary organisations. It concerns itself with Plan Period Grants, One Year Grants, Mahila Mandals, Welfare Extension Projects (Original Pattern), Welfare Extension Projects (Community Development), Welfare Extension Projects (Border Area), Welfare Extension, Projects (Urban) and Grants to Working Women Hostels.

The section performs functions such as: (i), planning and implementation of the above mentioned programmes according to financial allocations made for each programme, (ii) examination and consideration of applications and proposals received from voluntary welfare organisations or institutions as recommended by the state social welfare advisory boards, (iii) finalization of the cases for sanction of grants, (iv) conveying the sanctions to respective voluntary organisations or institutions, (v) ensuring proper utilization of funds released for decentralized programmes by verification of authenticated lists of sanctions received from the State Boards, (vi) correspondence with the state social welfare advisory boards and the instructions relating to decentralized programmes of the Central Board, (vii) obtaining and examining the audited statement of accounts and utilization certificates from the guarantee institutions or voluntary organisations and state boards, (viii) compilation of statistical information/ statements as are required by the executive director for the executive committee and general body meetings of the central board, (ix) preparation of the budget for these programmes for the ensuing year, (x) maintaining liaison with the outside concerned organisations, and (xi) examination of inspection reports received from the field inspection machinery for taking necessary action.

Child Welfare Unit: Section-II

This section is concerned with the nutrition programme crèches for working mothers, holiday camps, integrated pre-school project, demonstration projects and family and child welfare projects. Of these, the nutrition programme and crèches for children of working mothers are the programmes of the Ministry of Social Welfare implemented through the central social welfare board. The family and child welfare projects have since been handed, over to the state governments.

Major functions of the section include planning and implementation of the above-mentioned programmes according to financial allocations made for each programme, examination of the applications/proposals received from voluntary organisations state boards and finalization of the cases for sanction of grants, examining the audited statements of accounts and utilization certificates from the guarantee institutions and state boards, compilation of statistical information/statements as required by the executive director for the executive committee and general body meetings of the board, preparation of the budget for these programmes for the ensuing year, maintaining of liaison with the concerned organisations outside and examination of inspection reports received from the field inspection machinery for action.

Condensed Course Unit: Section-III

This section is concerned with condensed Course of education of two years' duration, one year courses for failed candidates and vocational training courses.

With regard to these programmes, this section deals with the scrutiny of applications of voluntary organisations recommended by the state boards and processing these reports furnished by the grant receiving institutions, examination of Inspection reports of welfare officers, examination of the statement of accounts and utilization certificates furnished by the state boards and preparation of annual budget estimates pertaining to these programmes. This division is headed by a Joint Director as aided by three Deputy Directors and supporting staff with specific areas of functions.

C. Administration Division

The division has the responsibility of overall planning, organizing, directing and accomplishment of the personnel matters.

(i) Personnel Function

Recruitment and selection, placement transfers, promotion, conduct rules and discipline, performance appraisal, motivation and incentive.

(ii) Service Functions

Record management, communication, property management, transportation, space control, procurement and supply, typing and stenographic pool, printing, tabulation and machine operations.

(iii) Advisory Functions

(a) to identify long and short range personnel needs of the Board,
(b) to help the executive director in planning procedural changes, and
(c) to suggest measures for full utilization of manpower resources available in the Board.

In addition, the division deals with matters such as reconstitution of state boards and their budget and annual reports and is responsible for the filed level staff in so far as administrative and establishment matter (such as recruitment, appointment, etc.) are concerned. The maintenance of data regarding vehicles, their repairs and disposal and the legal affairs pertaining to the Board are also looked after by this division.

The division is also responsible for administrative functions pertaining to the publication of two magazines 'Social Welfare' and 'Samaj Kalyan' as well as other publications of the Board. (There is also an Editorial Advisory Committee consisting of certain experts to provide general and overall guidance relating to publication matters). The work pertaining to public relations such as acquainting the outside persons or agencies with the various programmes of the Board as well as promotion in sales of these publications is one of the important functions of this division.

The division is headed by a Joint Director who is assisted by the following staff:

(i) Deputy Director responsible for work pertaining to head-quarters;
(ii) Deputy Director responsible for all matters pertaining to State Boards including a vehicle cell and a legal cell;
(iii) Editor (Social Welfare) responsible for publication for the monthly magazine in English;
(iv) Editor (Samaj Kalyan) responsible for publication of the monthly magazine in Hindi;
(v) Public Relations Officer for attending to all work pertaining to public relations and publicity; and
(vi) Other supporting staff.

D. Finance and Accounts Division

The work of this division involves accountability for the Board's funds and assets. The division is also responsible for proper economic management of all financial resources under the jurisdiction of the Central Social Welfare Board. The division performs, administers and supervises accounting as well as budgeting work and various financial transactions of the Board. It is responsible for designing, establishing and maintaining an integrated financial management system so that timely data is in use at the various levels of administration of the Board.

It is the concern of this division to synthesize and inter-relate the financial data for the purpose of obtaining a perspective of total financial situation and in interpreting the composite financial position, which is of use in programme planning. For integrated and effective financial control, the division supplies financial information produced by accounting system in respect of unfavourable trends It is the responsibility of the division to assist the officials in other divisions in analyzing the cost of various programmes.

The division is headed by an Internal Financial Adviser-*cum*-Chief Accounts Officer supported by a Pay and Accounts Officer and two Accounts Officers and supporting staff.

E. Planning, Monitoring and Co-ordination Division

The division is charged with the responsibilities as planning, research evaluation, monitoring, counselling and co-ordination. Major duties and responsibilities of this division are:

1. To assist in the overall planning .of social welfare programmes in consonance with the objectives of the Board and the Governmental policies;
2. To examine the statistical data required in the formulation of major policies and programmes of the Board and supplying relevant information for establishing priorities in the implementation of various programmes;
3. To conduct research in various fields of social welfare and/or to undertake feasible surveys on specified subjects related to the initiation of new programmes as suggested by other divisions of the Board;
4. To evaluate the efficiency of the completed as well as on-going social welfare programmes/projects of the Board in terms of their impact on the beneficiaries;
5. To maintain systematic relevant data about all the aided voluntary organisations under the various programmes of the Board (Data Bank);
6. To evolve new methods for improving the reporting system in the Board and its dealing with outside agencies;
7. To examine the functioning and performance of voluntary organisations dealing with the Board and submitting reports to the executive director;
8. To assess the local community needs of the weaker sections of

the community in different regions of the country and to assist in translating them into operational policies and programmes;

9. To provide an effective counselling and guidance service to voluntary organisations; and
10. To assist in overall co-ordination of welfare activities of different agencies, departments and ministries to establish effective internal co-ordination within the organisation.

The Planning, Monitoring and Co-ordination division consists of: (1) Information and Monitoring Section; (2) Statistical and Evaluation Section; (3) Field Counselling and Inspection Section; and (4) Coordination Section. These sections are under the charge of: (a) a Senior Management Analyst (Information and Monitoring), (b) a Senior Research Officer (Statistical and Evaluation), (c) a Deputy Director (Field Counselling), and (d) another Deputy Director (Co-ordination) respectively with supporting staff at each level. A Joint Director has the overall charge of the division.

Major Activities

The schemes evolved over the years by the Central Social Welfare either run directly or entrusted to the care of voluntary organisations, have been revised or scope enlarged, from time to time, based upon the field experiences, meetings, conferences, seminars, etc. and socio-economic changes and requirements. Now, let us examine in brief the achievements made under different programmes/projects of the Board.

PROGRAMMES OF THE BOARD

The Board is running a number of programmes for the development of women and children. All these programmes are fully funded by the Department.

Awareness Generation, Education and Training Programme for Rural and Poor Women

The scheme of Awareness Generation Programme provides a platform for the rural and poor women to come together, exchange their experience, ideas and in the process, develop an understanding of reality and also the way to tackle their problems and fulfil their needs. The programme also enables women to organize themselves and strengthen their participation in decision-making in the family and in the society and to deal with social issues including atrocities on women and children.

The programme was introduced by the Central Social Welfare Board in the year 1986-87. Under the programme voluntary organisations are provided a grant of Rs. 10,000 for organizing awareness generation camps for 8 days plus follow-up for two days. In 2006-07, 260 camps have been sanctioned and an amount of Rs. 163 lakhs has been released upto 15.12.2006.

Condensed Courses of Education for Women

The Scheme of Condensed Courses of Education for Women was initiated by the Central Social Welfare Board during the year 1958 with the objective of providing education to those women who for various social and economic reasons dropped out of school and could not pursue their studies. The scheme was designed particularly to benefit women like young widows, women deserted by their husbands and those belonging to economically backward classes.

Under this Scheme, grant is given to Voluntary Organisations to conduct two types of courses, one of two years duration for preparing women candidates for Primary/Middle/Matric Examination and the other of one year duration for Matric failed candidates. Girls and women of 15 years plus age groups are entitled to avail the benefit of the scheme.

During the year 2005-06, 700 courses have been sanctioned for 17500 women.

Vocational Training for Women

The Central Social Welfare Board had started the scheme of Vocational Training Programme during the year 1975 to train women in the trades which are marketable and also to upgrade their skills in order to meet the demands of changing work, environment. Main objective of training interventions is to enable and empower women to access remunerative employment, opportunities, which will instill self confidence and enhance their self-esteem.

From the year 1997-98, funds for Vocational Training are being provided under NORAD assisted scheme on Training and Employment of Women. The main emphasis of the programme is training and skill upgradation of women for their employment and self-employment on a sustainable basis. In view of a similar programme implemented by the Department through the Women Development Corporations of the States, CSWB concentrates mainly on the seven North-Eastern States and Sikkim from where adequate numbers of proposals are not received through the State Governments. The network of State Social Welfare Advisory Boards and the voluntary organisations provide very useful support for running this programme.

Socio-Economic Programme

The Socio-Economic Programme of the Central Social Welfare Board endeavours to provide employment opportunities on full or part-time basis to destitute women, widows, deserted and the physically handicapped, to supplement their meager family income. Besides, women entrepreneurs are encouraged to exhibit and sell their products through Exhibition-*cum*-Melas organized by State Boards at District level The Central Social Welfare Board, has two different types of schemes of assistance under this Programme:

Agro-based Units

The Board assists voluntary organisations for setting up agro-based units like dairy, poultry, piggery, goatery, etc. for poor and needy women, However, for the past few years proposals for Agro-based Units are not being considered since another Programme of the Department of Women and Child Development namely, Support for Training and Employment of Women (STEP) is taking care of these sectors.

Production Units

Voluntary organisations are encouraged to set-up Production Units, which can provide employment on full or part-time basis to women. Project proposals are examined by District Industrial Centres, KVICS, etc. who look into viability of the projects. A grant is provided by the Board to facilitate setting up a Production Unit by the grantee institution. The grant is finalized on a case-to-case basis subject to a limit of Rs. 3 lakh.

Rajiv Gandhi National Crèche Programme for the Children of workshop or Ailing Mothers.

The programme has been in operation since 1975. The scheme provides for day-care service to children in the age group of 0-6 years. The facilities are provided to the children of working women belonging to economically backward sections of casual, agricultural and construction labour in remote, rural and urban slum areas. Children of sick women also get the benefit of this programme.

The schematic pattern of the scheme has been revised from 1st January, 2006 and now Rs. 42,384 is provided for a year for one Creche Unit. The amount of non-recurring grant has also been enhanced from Rs. 4,000 to Rs. 10,000 for setting up new Crèche units and Rs. 5,000 for continuation per unit after every five years for equipment. During the year 2005-06 an amount of Rs. 2,849.65 lakhs was released for running 12,600 Crèche units throughout the country. The number of crèches sanctioned during 2004-05 were 9709 which were increased to 12600 crèches during the year 2005-06 which indicates 29.77% increase in number of units over the previous year. The amount released for these nits during 2004-05 was Rs. 1605.02 lakhs which was increased to Rs. 2849.65 lakhs during 2005-06.

During the year 2006-07 (Up to 31st October, 2006) 11475 units have been sanctioned and an amount of Rs. 1995.30 has been released to the voluntary organisations and State Boards.

The National Creche Fund (NCF) Scheme has been merged with the Rajiv Gandhi National Creche scheme for the children of working mothers.[11]

Working Women's Hostel

Under this scheme the Board provides, a maintenance grant to voluntary organisations for providing safe accommodation to working women whose salary does not exceed, Rs. 16,000 p.m. so that they are not exposed to undesirable and anti-social elements. The following types of maintenance expenses are covered under the scheme:

(i) Salary of Matron and Chowkidar,
(ii) Recreation facilities,
(iii) Difference of Rent of the building, and
(iv) Maintenance of Hostel building.

A minimum grant of Rs. 40,000 and maximum grant of Rs. 50,000 is sanctioned to an institution in a year keeping in view the class or category of the city.

Family Counselling Centres

The objective of the Family Counselling Centres is to provide preventive and rehabilitative services to women and children who are victims of atrocities and family maladjustments. The scheme is being implemented since 1984 through voluntary agencies. It was evaluated through NIPCCD during the year, 1990-91 and a revised scheme is in force since 1992-93. Under the revised scheme, a maximum of Rs. 1 lakh per center per annum is given for continuation of existing FCCs while Rs. 1.15 lakh is given for new FCCs. The salaries of two counsellors who are either Post-Graduate in Social Work or Psychology and Rs. 15000 for recurring items are borne fully by the Board while the institution is required to contribute 20% towards other recurring expenditure.

Short Stay Home Programme

The scheme Short Stay Home was launched by the Government of India in 1969 to provide temporary shelter to women and girls.

- who are being forced into prostitution;
- who as a result of family tension or discord are made to leave their homes without any means of subsistence and have no social protection from exploitation and are facing litigation on account of marital disputes;
- who have been sexual assaulted and are facing the problem of re-adjustment in the family or society;
- who are victims of mental mal-adjustment, emotional disturbances and social ostracism; or
- who escape from their homes due to family problems, mental or physical torture and need shelter, psychiatric, treatment and counselling for their rehabilitation and re-adjustment in family and society.

Temporary shelter to these women and girls from six months to three years with casework, counselling services, medical care and psychiatric treatment, skill development training, education, vocational and rehabilitative services are provided in the Short Stay Home.[12]

This scheme was earlier being implemented directly by the Department of Women and Child Development through the Non-Governmental Organisations. *While the power to sanction new Homes still vests with the Department, the responsibility of supervision and monitoring of the existing Homes and release of funds to the NGOs running the Homes have been delegated to the Central Social Welfare Board since April 1999.* The financial norms and guidelines of the scheme of Short Stay Home have also been revised in June 1999 to make it more relevant and effective.

OTHER PROGRAMMES OF THE BOARD

Border Area Projects

These Projects were taken up by the Central Board _in all the 14 Border States of the country after the Chinese Aggression in 1962 with the aim of achieving emotional and cultural integration of the Border population with the rest of the country. These Projects are of multipurpose nature and provide services for women and children in the field of maternity care, general medical aid, social education, craft training and balwadies. These services are rendered through multipurpose welfare centres, which cater to a compact area of 25 contiguous villages with a population of nearly 25,000 per centre. These are being phased out exception three states, Jammu and Kashmir, Tripura, and A & N Islands.

The Welfare Extension Projects

These were started in the Community Development Blocks in 1958 to organize welfare services in the rural and remote areas for the benefit of women and children. The programme includes running of balwadies, adult literacy and social education, elementary medical aid, maternity services, art-craft, cultural and recreational activities. Each Project covers 10 villages with population of 66,000 through 6 to 8 centres attached to a project. There are at present 41 Projects with 315 centres in 5 States.

Balwadi Demonstration Projects

Under this programme Balwadies are organized under the supervision of the State Boards. Each balwadi consists of a Balsevika and a helper. There are at present 11 Projects with 248 centres functioning in 11 States.

Mahila Mandal Programme

The Mahila Mandal Programme was started by the Board to provide social services to women and children in rural areas where such welfare services did not exist at all. The services like Balwadies for Children, Craft Activities, Social Education and Maternity Services for Women, etc. are provided under this programme. The expenditure under the scheme is being borne by the Central Social Welfare Board to the extent of 75% of the approved budget and remaining 25% is being shared either by the

Voluntary Organisation or by the State Government as matching contribution. At present there are 146 units running in 17 states covering 48752 beneficiaries.

Durgabai Deshmukh Award

Dr. Durgabai Deshmukh Award for Women's Development is awarded to Welfare Association which has done excellent work.

Publicity and Publications

The Board regularly brings out its magazine Social, Welfare on themes like Empowerment of Women, Empowerment through Education, Changing Family Trends, the Elderly and the Family, Child and Society, etc. The Hindi magazine 'Samaj Kalyan' brought out issues on Educational Policy, Nutrition and Child Health, Legal Rights of Women, Empowerment of Women and Development of Society, Participation of Women in Politics arid Administration, Violence against Women, and Social Security.

Field Counselling and Inspections

The Field Counselling and Inspection Division (FCI) monitors the performance of the field officers posted in various State Boards *vis-à-vis* their duties and functions in providing counselling and guidance to the institutions implementing the Board's programmes and promoting voluntarism in the districts allotted to them. Conferences, workshops, seminars, etc. are organized periodically on women-related and social issues through voluntary organisation, or directly' through State Boards and Central Social Welfare Board. Training programmes are regularly held for the EOs to update them on inspection skills, orientation on monitoring of different programmes and management of welfare services relieved by voluntary organisations.

The field officers in the ranks of Welfare Officer, Asst. Project Officers and Project Officers are attached with various State Social Welfare Advisory Boards. Presently against the sanctioned strength of 137 field officers only 125 field officers are in position to achieve the above objectives. These field officers also have the responsibility of furnishing performance reports of the institutions aided by the Board as well as pre-funding appraisal reports of institutions applying for grants for the first time.

As part of Herd work training, several students form Schools of Social Work from different parts of the country visit Central Social Welfare Board to get first hand-information about the Board's programmes and their implementation. Some of these are:

(i) Madras Christian College, Chennai;
(ii) Sri Narayan Guru College, Coimbatore;
(iii) Shri Rama Krishna Mission Vidyalaya, College of Arts and Sciences, Coimbatore;
(iv) Bharatiya Vidyapeeth Social Science Centre, Pune;

(v) 47 participants of a training programme organized by NCERT on "Women Education and Development"; and

(vi) One student from Kashi Vidyapeeth, Varanasi was placed in CSWB for 8 weeks block filed work training.

Research, Evaluation and Statistics

There is a Research, Evaluation and Statistics wing in the CSWB that is responsible for functions related to monitoring and evaluation of various programmes and the maintenance of a data bank on various indicators.

(i) A study on "Women Cashew Workers in Kollam of Kerala" was conducted with the help of Southern Institute of Social Science Research, Thiruvanthapuram. The study has been completed and the Central Social Welfae Board has received the report.

(ii) A study entitled "Women and Children in Tea Gardens with particular reference to Sonitpur District in Assam" has been initiated and assigned to an organisation "Mahila Sarathi", Guwahati.

(iii) Monitoring of Scheduled caste component of Plan (SCP) and Tribal Sub-Plan-I (TSp) continued during the year for the Annual Plan of the DWCD.

(iv) Monitoring of Monthly Expenditure Report! Quarterly Progress Report of the State Boards is in progress.

(v) Data Bank of NGOs at the instance of Planning Commission was completed.

(vi) Salary Software package developed with the help of NIC was modified and installed.

Innovative Schemes

Although, the Central Social Welfare Board has many structure programmes and schemes for the development of women and children, there are several problems relating to women and children, which are not fully covered within the existing schemes of the Board; therefore, Innovative Programme was launched by the Central Board. Several projects under the programme are being run for the welfare of children of prostitutes, rag pickers and children of leprosy patients, etc. who need special attention. Apart from above, campaigns have been launched for creating awareness against drug de-addition, alcoholism, etc. Counselling for the school girls prone to depression due to apprehension about their future career prospects and consequently attempt to suicide, needed special attention under Innovative Scheme.

Under this scheme, an institution is expected to prepare a project giving details of the area, the requirement of the proposed project, areas of intervention, methodology, tools budget, etc. There is no schematic budget for such projects; and the project proposal is prepared by voluntary organisations keeping in view the social necessities. No specific application forms are issued for this programme. However, voluntary organisations are advised to contact the State Social Welfare Board and submit their detailed project proposal through the State Board along with budget and details of activities to be organized. In the absence of a structured Proforma, the State Boards have to prepare the project proposal along with comprehensive justification, which requires the inclusion of basic data.[13]

Women's Help Line

Help Line is a project of Government of India, Ministry of Women and Child Development and Central Social Welfare Board in collaboration with voluntary organisations working for the welfare of women and girls in distress. The scheme is operational from 2002-03 and onwards. Help Line is a 24 hours phone emergency outreach programme for women and girls in distress or in moral danger needing immediate protection and shelter. It responds to the need of such women and girls and links them to long-term services as per their requirement and availability of services.

The Objectives of the Programme are as under:

- To provide quality services to women and girls in need of special care and protection and to ensure that proper care is provided till they are rehabilitated.
- To provide Crisis Intervention Services.
- To provide referral services like Short Stay Home, Free Legal Aid, Police, Assistance, Counselling, Hospitalization, etc.
- To arrange suitable rehabilitation service to the target group.
- To provide counselling.
- Awareness, opinion building and documentation.
- Documentation of the type of case being registered, to understand the trends in society.[14]

CONCLUSION AND SUGGESTIONS

Prior to the attainment of independence, social welfare services were, isolated, sporadic, ad-hoc and for the most part were un-coordinated as they were structured to meet purely local needs. The social welfare activities were dominated by the early reform movements and the struggle for independence by socio-political thinkers. The Central Social Welfare Board came into existence in 1953 as a realization of its need for establishing a specialized agency, which would guide assist and co-ordinate voluntary organisations and to encourage their multi-dimensional growth as well. *The Constitution provided the legal framework to it, while the Planning Commission gave the policy frame and programme outline.* The creation of the CSWB represents an experiment in the newer ways of public administration. It is, neither wholly government nor wholly voluntary organisation, but it is a combination of the two. The government through the CSWB, gives financial assistance and technical guidance to the voluntary welfare organisations who are the best suited to undertake such programmes. The novelty of the Board's administration consists in the basis of its constitution and in the participation of non-officials in the planning and administration of the social welfare programmes.

The Board is not a statutory body. Till 1969, the Board did not enjoy any legal status. After good deal of considerations, it was filially registered as a charitable company under Companies Act, 1956 on 1st April 1969. With this status of the Board, its functions are being considered as a debatable subject. It appears that the question of giving an appropriate status as well as assigning functions to the CSWB is still engaging the, top attention of the concerned agencies. The structural changes over the years and, assignment of gigantic functions from promoting voluntary efforts to social security measures has showed appropriation of the organisations multiple role within and outside the organisation. A close look at the objectives of the CSWB would indicate their complexity and diversity in character. Hence, there is a great need for resolving the issue by giving an appropriate status as well as functions to the CSWB as early as possible.

For perspective planning, the CSWB is functioning within the framework of policies provided to it by the Ministry of Women and Child, Welfare in the Government of India. The policies for the CSWB and its macro-programmes are formulated in the Ministry of Women and Child Development.

The status of the State Social Welfare Boards (counterparts or branches of the CSWB) still remains unresolved. In the final analysis the status of the Board will depend on the recognition given to it by the Government and on the degree of freedom and flexibility permitted to it in its day-to-day operation. It will also depend on the Board keeping itself free from environmental factors. An expert Committee known as Ranade Committee has however emphasized that the Government should seek the advice and guidance of the Board in all matters concerning voluntary organisations and give due weight to its views. The Government should lay down the broad policies and leave this execution to the Board. The very purpose of setting up the Board will be defeated if the same constraints as operate in the case of a Government Department, were to apply to the Board.

The Seventh Plan has rightly observed, when it states that the Central Social Welfare Board continued to function as the focal and apex agency in the voluntary sector. It made notable progress in its on going programmes and initiated new activities during the Plan period. *From the traditional role of a funding agency, the Board has assumed the role of a catalyst of social change.* The Central Social Welfare Board and its counterparts in the States would be required to shoulder more responsibility in promoting, strengthening and stimulating voluntary effort in different sub-sectors of social welfare and specially in the areas of children's and women welfare.[15] As regards the Board's infrastructure at district and block levels, it still remains a matter of opinion, as whether or not, the CSWB should have its own infrastructure at district and block levels. Expertise and assistance however should be made available to the voluntary organisations through the State Social Welfare Advisory Boards as and when required.

The Board practices an open system approach and. thus as an organisation, it is less rigid and is agreeable to accommodate new ideas. It provides an example of "open management" both in information and accessibility, thereby, establishing its credibility and readiness to respond to views expressed in its programme of social action.

Notes and References

1. Prime Minister's Letter No. 32-PMH/54, dated the April 23, 1954 addressed to Chief Minister of all States.
2. Willoughboury uses the term "primary or functional for line and Institutional or house-keeping for staff-agency." Similarly, Pfeiffer and Presthus, classifies the agencies as general, technical and auxiliary.
3. Herbert, A. Simon, Administrative Behaviour: A Study of decision-making Processes in Administrative Organisations; New York, Macmillan Company, 1954, Introduction.
4. Article 4: Memorandum and Articles of Association of the Central Social Welfare Board.
5. F.L. Brech, Organisation, London, Longmen, 1969, p. 412.
6. Article 10: Article and Memorandum of Association of Central Social Welfare Board.
7. S.N. Dubey, "Administrative of Social Welfare Programmes in India, Bombay," Somaiya Publications, 1973, p. 1.
8. Ministry of Women and Child Development, GOI, Annual Report, 2006-07, p. 144.
9. Avasthi and Maheswari, "Public Administration", *op. cit.*, pp. 60-62.
10. V. Gabrial, "Administrative Capability as a Neglected Dimension, in the Implementation of Development Programmes and Projects", Seventieth General Assembly and Conference of ECROPA, on Implementation of the Problems of Achieving Results, 24-31 Oct., 1973, Vol. III, pp. 3-14.
11. Ministry of Women and Child Development, GOI, Annual Report, 2006-07, pp. 144-45.
12. *Ibid.*, p. 149.
13. *Ibid.*, p. 150.
14. *Ibid.*, pp. 150-51.
15. Planning Commission, Seventh Five Year Plan (1985-90); Government of India, New Delhi, 1985, pp. 306-08.

Integrated Child Development Services (ICDS)

. The desire for our children well-being has always been the most universally cherished aspiration of mankind. Only as we move closer to realizing the rights of all children's will countries move closer to their goals of development and peace. There is no task more important than to building a world in which all of our children can grow up to realize their full potential in health, peace and dignity.

—*Kofi Annan*
Former Secretary General of UNO

A nation's children are its supremely important asset and the nation's future lies in their proper development. An investment in children is indeed an investment in the Nation's Future. A healthy and educated child of today is the active and intelligent child of tomorrow.

Bestow blessing on those Little, innocent lives Bloomed on earth, Who have brought the message of joy from heavenly garden.

—*Rabindra Nath Tagore*

Children are our future and our most precious resources. The quality of tomorrow's world and perhaps even its survival will be determined by the well-being, safety and the physical and intellectual development of children today. To predict the future of a nation, it has been remarked, one need not consult the stars; it can more easily and plainly be read in the faces of its children. Children are the mirror of a nation. Abraham Lincoln nicely explained the role of the child when he said,

"A child is a person who is going to carry on what you have started.

CHART 11.1

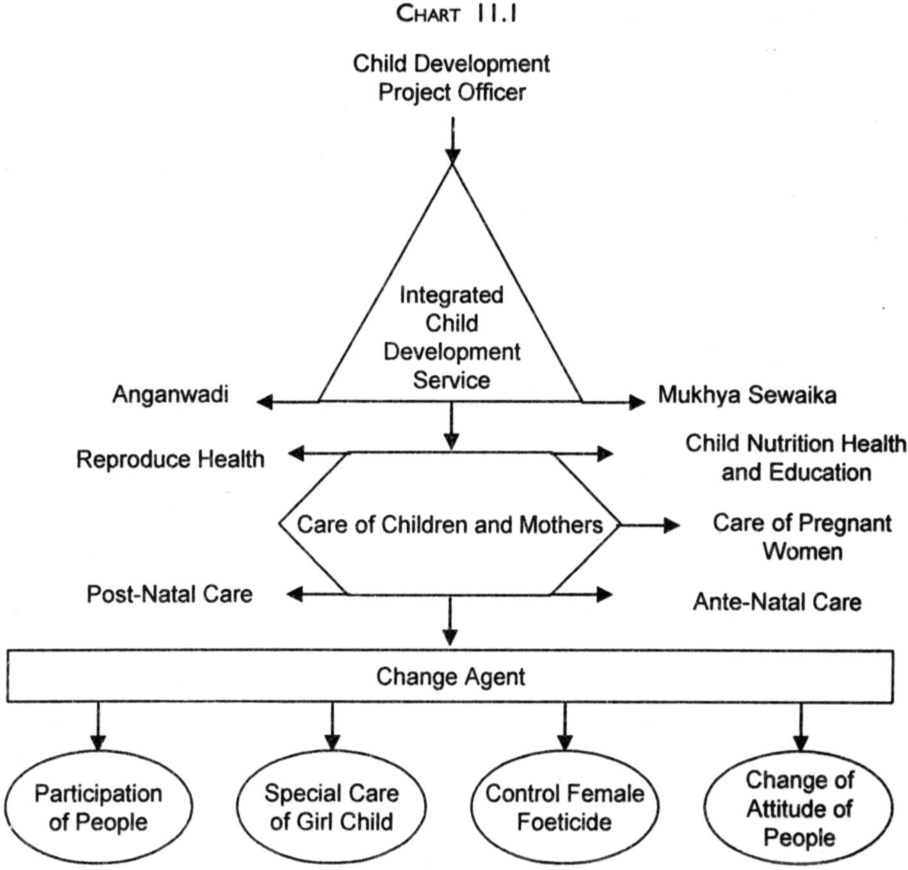

> He is going to sit where you are sitting, and when you are gone attend to those things which you think are important. You may adopt all the policies you please, but how they are carried out depends on him. He will assume control of your cities, states, and nations. He is going to move in and take over your Churches, Schools, Universities and Corporations. All your books are going to be judged, praised or condemned by him. The fate of humanity is in his hands."

The UN General Assembly in the Resolution comprising the Second Development Decade has stated:

> "Today youth, everywhere is in ferment. The 1970's must mark a step forward in securing the well-being and happiness not only of the present generation but also of the generations to come."[1]

One of the specific objectives of the Second Development Decade was that "the well-being of children shall be fostered."[2] Dr. P.C. Chunder, former Minister of Education and Social Welfare, Government of India in his

Foreword to the National Plan of Action for International Year of the Child, 1979 has rightly said that,

> "A Nation's children are its supremely important asset and the nation's future lies in their proper development. An investment in children is indeed an investment in the Nation's future. A healthy and educated child of today is the active and intelligent citizen of tomorrow."[3]

To quote C. Subramaniam, the former Finance Minister in the Government of India:

> "Giving high priority to children's welfare means singling out a target group which is intermingled with the rest of the population right down to the level of individual families. Therefore, it requires building up an organisation and an administrative set-up that goes all the way from international agencies to each village and town of less-developed countries."[4]

To quote Mahatma Gandhi:

> "If we are to reach peace in this world and if we are to carry on a real war against war, we shall have to begin with children; and if they will grow up in their natural innocence we won't have to struggle, we won't have to pass fruitless ideal resolutions, but we shall go from love to love and peace to peace."

Effective national policies and plans regarding children can make decisive contribution to all other long-term development activities and particularly to the success of the programmes aimed at raising the quality of life of lower income groups and at building national capacities and self-reliance.

There is no cause which merits a higher priority than the protection and development of children, on whom survival, stability and advancement of all nations—and indeed of human civilization depends. Plan of action of the World Summit for children, 20 Sept. 1990

As per the 2001 Census, India has around 347.54 million children (0.14 years) constituting 33.8% of the total population. These future human resources of the country deserve concerted support for their survival, development and protection. The Ministry of Women and Child Development's policies, programmes and schemes are aimed at a holistic full-fleged development of children in terms of tackling declining sex ratio, infant mortality, health and nutrition issues, early childhood education, protection of their rights, prevention of abuse of children, provision of care and protection and so on.[5]

EVOLUTION AND GROWTH OF ICDS

Genesis

On the basis of eight inter-ministerial study teams set-up by the Planning Commission, a scheme of Integrated Child Development Services was evolved. It is a centrally sponsored scheme Thirty-three experimental projects were started in different parts of the country on 2 October 1975. During 1978-79, 67 new ICDS projects were started

It was gradually expanded to 6277 projects as on 14.12.07 of which 5724 projects with 7.81 lakhs AWCs have become operational as on 30.9.2006. State-wise number of sanctioned and operational projects/AWCs are given in Table 11.1.

Beneficiaries

As on 30.9.06 services under the scheme are being provided to about 645.65 lakh beneficiaries, comprising of about 543.43 lakh children (0-6 years) and about 111.22 lakh pregnant and lactating mothers through a network of 9.46 lakh Anganwadi centres. State-wise details of beneficiaries are given at Table 11.2

Integrated Child Development Services (ICDS) programme continue to be the world's most unique early childhood development programe, which is being satisfactorily operated since three decades of its existence. The rich experience of ICDS has brought about a welcome transition from welfare orientation to a new challenging perspective of social change. The programme provides package of services, comprising supplementary nutrition, immunization, health check-up, referral services to children below six years of age and expectant and nursing mothers. Non-formal pre-school education is imparted to children of the age group 3-6 years and health and nutrition education to women in the age group 15-45 years. High priority is accorded to the needs of the most vulnerable younger children under three years of age in the programme through capacity building of caregivers to provide stimulation and quality early childhood care.

Holistic Development

The Ministry's emphasis has been on integrated and holistic development of children, as far as the two basic elements of human resource development, i.e. health and education, are concerned.

Article 45 of the Constitution has been recently amended to state that "The state shall endeavour to provide early childhood care and education for all children until they complete the age of 6 years."

In this light, in addition to emphasis on supplementary nutrition and convergence with health services, special focus is also being given to the pre-school education component of the ICDS schemes, so that the children are fully prepared for entering Class I at the age of 6 years under the Sarva Shiksha Abhiyyan and District Primary Education Progarmme. For this, the states have been requested to ensure necessary convergence between ICDS

TABLE 11.1

Statement indicating State-wise Number of ICDS Projects and Anganwadi Centres (AWCs) Sanctioned and Operationalized in the Country

S. No.	States/UTs	ICDS Projects		No. of Anganwadis	
		Total sanctioned as on 14.2.2007	*Operational as on 30.9.2006*	*Total sanctioned (as on 14.2.07)*	*Operational as on 30.9.2006*
1.	Andhra Pradesh	385	366	73609	858581
2.	Arunachal Pradesh	85	58	4277	2359
3.	Assam	223	196	37082	25447
4.	Bihar	538	394	80528	57767
5.	Chhattisgarh	163	153	34937	20401
6.	Goa	11	11	1112	1012
7.	Gujarat	260	227	44198	27512
8.	Haryana	037	124	17192	16967
9.	Himachal Pradesh	76	72	18248	7354
10.	Jammu and Kashmir	140	129	25358	10398
11.	Jharkhand	204	204	32097	21459
12.	Karnataka	185	185	54260	44609
13.	Kerala	163	136	28651	25382
14.	Madhya Pradesh	367	336	69238	49806
15.	Maharashtra	451	397	85457	68184
16.	Manipur	38	34	7639	4501
17.	Meghalaya	41	38	3388	3243
18.	Mizoram	23	23	1683	1592
19.	Nagaland	56	54	3194	2770
20.	Orissa	326	326	41697	34997
21.	Punjab	148	142	20169	14730
22.	Rajasthan	278	262	48372	38414
23.	Sikkim	11	9	988	757
24.	Tamil Nadu	434	464	47265	42677
25.	Tripura	54	51	7351	6069
26.	Uttar Prasdesh	897	834	157327	116740
27.	Uttaranchal	99	99	9664	7579
28.	West Bengal	416	357	92152	55064
29.	A & N Islands	5	5	672	621
30.	Chandigarh	3	3	370	329
31.	Delhi	50	29	6106	4011
32.	Dadra and N. Haveli	2	1	219	138
33.	Daman and Diu	2	2	107	97
34.	Lakshadweep	1	1	87	74
35.	Pondicherry	5	5	688	670
	ALL INDIA	6277	5724	1048762	781208

Source: Annual Report, 2006-07, Ministry of Women, p. 188.

TABLE 11.2

Statewise Number of Beneficiaries (Children 6 month–6 years and Pregnant and Lactating Mothers (P & LM)

(As on 30.9.2006)

Sl. No.	*States/UTs*	*Beneficiaries for Supplementary Nutrition*				
		Children (6 months–3 years)	*Children (3-6 Years)*	*Total Children (6 months–6 years)*	*Pregnant & Lactating Mothers (P&LM)*	*Total Beneficiaries (Children 6 month–6 years plus P&LM)*
1	*2*	*3*	*4*	*5*	*6*	*7*
1.	Andhra Pradesh	973791	1486253	2460044	644312	3104356
2.	Arunachal Pradesh	50008	38971	88979	13632	102611
3.	Assam	683842	576171	1260013	148176	1408189
4.	Bihar	2406720	2329167	4735887	836835	5572722
5.	Chhattisgarh	752290	506999	1259289	326650	1585939
6.	Goa	22180	16546	38728	9971	48699
7.	Gujarat	712947	822509	1535456	267434	1802890
8.	Haryana	563388	493419	1056807	264498	1321305
9.	HImachal Pradesh	196477	134450	330927	75628	4065555
10.	Jamm and Kashmir	163277	120520	273790	69856	343648
11.	Jharkhand	792645	669831	1562476	423472	1998948
12.	Karnataka	1349734	1250606	2600340	595216	3195556
13.	Kerala	349453	423911	773364	151652	925016
14.	Madhya Pradesh	1806039	1553961	3360000	760927	4120927
15.	Maharashtra	2379823	2680677	5060500	835782	5896282
16.	Manipur	94493	84412	178905	23704	217609
17.	Meghalaya	125674	152113	277787	53412	331199
18.	Mizoram	64574	45870	110444	26811	137255
19.	Nagaland	159864	105256	265120	50864	315984
20.	Orissa	1835287	1827287	3662574	675719	4338293
21.	Punjab	389634	455169	844803	250796	1095601
22.	Rajasthan	1388683	1134472	2523155	619447	3162602
23.	Sikkim	17194	3656	20850	5326	26176
24.	Tamil Nadu	649505	1113246	1762751	498218	2260969
25.	Tripura	96087	101428	197515	29921	227436
26.	Uttar Prasdesh	7063843	6707789	13771632	2829258	16600890
27.	Uttaranchal	151206	104253	255469	58645	314104
28.	West Bengal	1820722	1761866	3582588	447247	4029835
29.	A & N Islands	13671	9707	22378	5287	28656
30.	Chandigarh	19948	13796	33744	8108	41852
31.	Delhi	245439	142294	387733	73301	461034
32.	Dadra and N. Haveli	6120	5815	11935	2020	13555
33.	Daman and Diu	3492	3602	7094	1792	8886
34.	Lakshadweep	1998	2015	4013	965	4978
35.	Pondicherry	22088	3142	25230	9242	34472
	ALL INDIA	27362131	269811079	54343310	11122128	65465438

Source: *Ibid.*, p. 189.

CHART 11.2

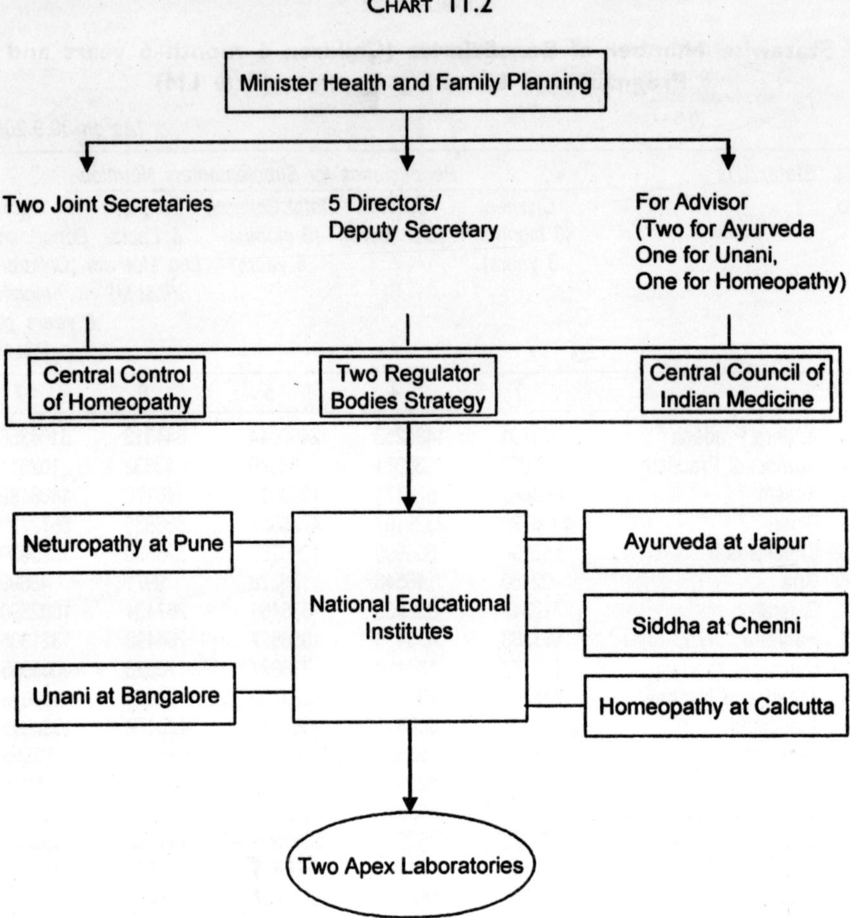

scheme and sarva Shikhsa Abhiyan and District Primary Education prgramme. There has been emphasis on convergence of services under various schemes/programmes viz. health, education, safe drinking water so as to achieve the desired impact. States have been requested to activate/set-up coordination Committee at State, district/block and village level to ensure proper delivery of services at Anganwadi level by concerned line functionaries of various departments.[6]

Objectives of the Scheme

(i) to improve the nutritional and health status of children in the age group, 0-6 years;

(ii) to lay the foundations for proper psychological, physical and social development of the child;

(iii) to reduce mortality, morbidity, mal-nutrition and school drop-out;

CHART 11.3

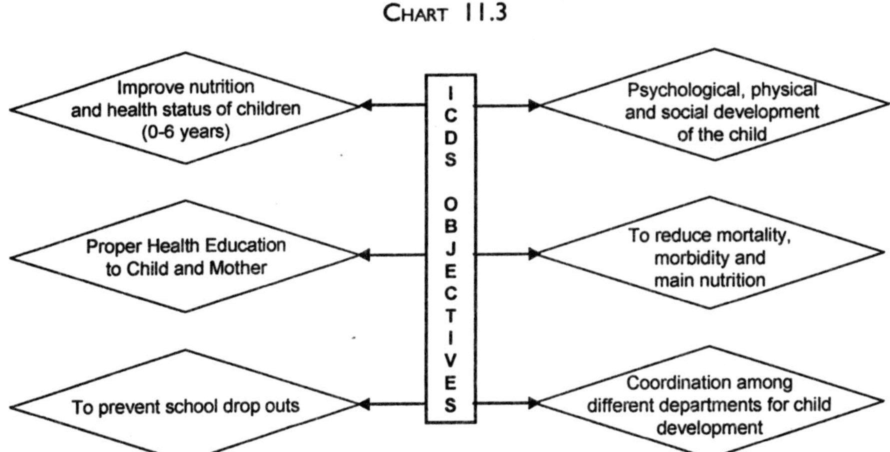

(iv) to achieve an effective coordination of policy and implementation amongst the various departments working for the promotion for child development; and

(v) to enhance the capability of the mother and nutritional needs of the child through proper nutrition and health education.[7]

To achieve the above objectives, the ICDS aims at providing the following package of services.[8]

Beneficiary Group	*Service*
Pregnant Women	Health Check-up Immunisation against tetanus Supplementary Nutrition and health education
Nursing mothers	Health check-up Supplementary nutrition Nutrition and health education
Other women 15-44 years	Nutrition and health education
Children below 3 years	Supplementary nutrition Immunization Health check-up Referral Services
Children in the age group 3-6 years	Supplementary nutrition immunization Health Check-up Referral services Non-formal pre-school education

These services can be utilised in many interventions under Family Welfare Programme. The LHV/ANMs should train the Anganwadi Workers in the areas given above. This training can be conducted at the Sub-centre on a monthly basis in consultation with the supervisor/senior officers of the Department of the Women and Child Development. The areas in which Anganwadi Workers can be oriented are:

Care of Pregnant Women

- Importance of early Registration.
- Why regular ante-natal check up is necessary.
- Motivate pregnant women to register early and seek ante-natal care.
- Use of DDKs.
- Nutritional advice during pregnancy.
- Common symptoms and signs (danger signs) when pregnant women should seek immediate medical help.

Care of Children

- Help mothers in care of normal newborn (exclusive breast feeding no pre-lacteal feeds, colostrum feeding, keeping baby warm, prevention of infections.
- Immunization.
- When?
- Where?
- Expected mild side effects and their treatment.
- Reporting of cases of AFP, NNT, measles and other VPDs to ANM.

Management of Dirrhoeal Diseases

- A WW can be depot holder for ORS.
- How to make ORS?
- How much ORS to be given?
- Danger signs for seeking medical help.
- Continue feeding during episode.
- Extra feeding during episode.

Management of ARI

- Child with cough who has rapid breathing or/and difficulties in breathing may have pneumonia. Immediate referral is necessary.
- Home remedies for cold/mild cough.
- Danger signs.
- Continue to feed child.
- Keep child warm.

Nutrition

- Concept of complementary (weaning) food.
- When to start?

- What (according to local tradition)?
- How much?
- Balanced diet.
- Promote consumption of iron and vitamin A rich foods.
- Gender sensitivity regarding eating with the family, adequate amounts as also extra food during pregnancy.

Reproductive Health

- Motivate newly wed women to delay pregnancy till they are 20 years of age.
- Motivate mothers who have delivered for birth spacing.
- Depot holder for OP/condoms wherever feasible.
- Counsel women with RTI/STD to seek immediate medical help.

Selection of Project Areas

The scheme envisages that:

(1) The administrative unit for an ICDS Project is the community development block in the rural areas and the tribal development block in the tribal areas and group of slums in urban areas.

(2) In the selection of projects in rural areas priority consideration is given to the following factors:
   (i) areas predominantly inhabited by tribes. Particularly backward tribes;
   (ii) backward areas;
   (iii) drought-prone areas;
   (iv) areas inhabited predominantly by Scheduled Castes;
   (v) nutritionally-deficient areas; and
   (vi) areas poor in development of social services.

(3) In the selection ward(s) in urban areas for urban projects priority consideration is given to the following factors:
   (i) location of slums; and
   (ii) areas predominantly inhabited by Scheduled Castes.

(4) The number of the villages in the rural project may be 100 while in a tribal project it may be only about 50, taking into account the difficult terrain in which tribal projects are located.

Population Norms

Existing Norms

The Scheme envisages that the administrative unit for the location of ICDs project will be the CD blocks in rural areas, tribal blocks in tribal areas and ward(s) or slums in urban areas. An Anganwadi Centre is sanctioned on an average for 1,000 population in rural/urban projects and 700 populations in tribal project, with suitable adjustments, wherever necessary, in the light of local conditions.

Sparsely populated hilly/desert areas

In hilly or desert areas, which may be sparsely populated, villages may be very small or divided into small hamlets. In such cases, an Anganwadi may be set-up in a village or a hamlet having a population of 300 or more.

Mini-AWCs

Mini Aganwadi Centre can be set-up to cover the remote and low populated hamlets/villages in tribal blocks, having population between 150-300.

Revised Norms

An inter-ministerial task force was set-up in 2004 to review the existing population norms for sanction of an ICDS Project/AWC and suggest revised norms. The Task Force Submitted its reports/ recommendations in May 2005. The revised population norms recommended by the Task Force are as follows:

Project

CD Block in a state should be the unit for sanction of an ICDS project, in Rural/Tribal areas, irrespective of number of villages/population in it.

Anganwadi Centre

(For rural projects)

Population

500 – 1500 — 1 AWC
150 – 500 — 1 mini AWC

(For Tribal Projects)

Population

300 – 1500 — 1 AWC
150 – 300 — 1 mini AWC

(For habitation with less than 150 population, specific proposal should be submitted by the State Governments for consideration and appropriate decision by the Govt. of India)

For Urban Project

Population

500–1000 — 1 AWC

To consider further expansion of the ICDS scheme, states/UTs were requested to carry out micro-level planning and furnish their requirement of additional AWCs/Mini-AWCs, if there are still some villages/habitations, which are not covered by the Scheme. Based on the requirements of States/UTs, further expansion of the Scheme can be done.

Supplementary Nutrition Norms

Nutritional Norms

On an average the effort should be to provide daily nutritional supplements as indicated below:

Supplementary Nutrition Norms

Beneficiaries	*Calories (cal)*	*Protein (g)*
Children below 3 years*	300	8-10
Children 3-6 years	300	8-10
Severely malnourished children (on medical advice after health check-up)	(double of above)	
Pregnant and Lactating (P & L) Mothers (Adolescent girls, (under KSY) should be provided supplementary nutrition at the same scale as admissible to P & L mothers)	500	20-25

* Provisions regarding promotion of breast-feeding in the Infant Milk Substitute Act are also relevant.
Source: *Ibid.*, p. 49.

Financial Norms

Under the schematic pattern, the states are responsible for providing supplementary nutrition. The nature and type of food provided as supplementary nutrition vary from state to state. In view of the Supreme Court's order and price escalation over the years, financial norms for supplementary nutrition under the ICDS Scheme, fixed in 1991, have been revised in October 2004 which are as follows:

Revised Financial Norms

The states have to necessarily assess the current unit cost of meeting the nutritional norms and budget accordingly and to ensure that supplementary nutrition is provided as per the prescribed nutrition norms of the Scheme to all ICDS beneficiaries.

In view of the fact that some states do not provide adequate funds in their budget for supplementary nutrition, the Planning Commission has been requested to address this aspects during formulation and monitoring of states Annual Plan and also consider earmarking of funds for supplementary nutrition in States Plans.[9]

	Old Rates	Revised rates
(i) Children (6 month to 72 months)	95 paise per children/per day	Rs. 2.00 per child/per day
(ii) Severely malnourished children (6 months, 72 months)	135 paise per child/per day	Rs. 2.70 per child/per day
(iii) Pregnant Women and Nursing mothers as per Kishori Shakti Yojana (KSY/Adolescent Girls)	115 paise per beneficiary/ per day	Rs. 2.30 per beneficiary/ per day

Source: Ibid., p. 49.

UNICEF

UNICEF extends technical and material support to strengthen the ICDS scheme. Material support of UNICEF during 2006 was to supply the weighing scales, growth monitoring charts and photocopies to new projects.

ICDS TRAINING PROGRAMME

Training is imparted to the Anganwadi Workers, Supervisors, Child Development Project Officers (CDPO) through the National (Institute of Public Cooperation and Child Development (and through its Regional Centres at Lucknow; Guwahati and Bangalore. 18 Middle-Level Training Centres (MLTCs) and 300 Anganwadi Workers' Training Centres (AWTCs). In addition, the Central Technical Committee-integrated Mother and Child Development (CTC-IMCD) also gives training to medical and para-medical staff.[10] In addition, Department of Women Studies and Development in Universities and State Institutes of Public Administration are also giving training to them.

Structure and Personnel

Child Development Officer (CDPO) is the in-charge officer of the project. Each village has an Anganwadi worker. She is assisted by a helper in organising supplementary nutrition feeding programme. Mukhya Sevika supervises the work of Anganwadi workers. (1 Mukhya Sevika Supervising about 20). The ICDS budget provides for one doctor, two lady health visitors/PHN and eight ANMs in the Primary Health Centre. In the case of tribal and urban areas instead of eight ANMs. four ANMs are provided. Even though funds are provided by the Central Government, this additional staff of PHC is borne on the State Cadre. Asha Das in her article, "Child Development and Empowering Women in India" in *IJPA*, July-Sept. 1997 rightly observes that the impact of the programme is evident from the remarkable improvements made in child survival and development indicators viz., decrease in prevalence in malnutrition among pre-school children, improved immunization coverage in ICDS areas, decrease in Infant Mortality Rate (IMR) in ICDS areas. improvement in school enrolment and reduction in school dropout rate in ICDS areas.

Anganwadi Karyakartri Bima Yojana

In line with the aim of the Government to provide risk coverage for workers in the unorganized sector, a benefit has been extended to Anganwadi Workers and Helpers through an insurance scheme under the Life Insurance Corporation's Social Security Group Scheme. The Scheme is optional for the target group.

Based upon the success of the programme, many new successful experiments have been taken up through innovative models like Ramakrishna Mission Project in Narendrapur, West Bengal. The Poriyawadi-Thabus Experiment in Madhya Pradesh, Alleppy Model in Kerala, the Spastics Society of Tamil Nadu, all these models and I.C.D.S. Schemes indicated the potential of the Scheme which can meet the needs of the children.

CRITICAL APPRISAL

The scheme has made a great progress. However, there are a number of problems which need examination and action. We give here some facts and suggestions based on this study which can be considered for the efficient functioning of this scheme.

I. To suggest methods of improvement in Professional and Administrative Competence

The success of the scheme depends on the faith of the people in the professional competence of the personnel administering services to them. Most of the beneficiaries are disillusioned with the performance of Anganwadi workers. These base line workers have not been sufficiently trained and are poorly equipped in terms of social. psychological and environmental understanding of the people of the area. It is suggested that intensive training may be given to these workers turn by turn (10 per cent at a time) to equip them to deal with this challenging and revolutionary task. Besides, their continuation in service may be subject to the good work done and the will of the beneficiaries.

The Mukhya Sevikas and CDPO possess no grounding in public administration and rural dynamics. They should be taught the art of supervision, motivation and coordination. It was mentioned by one of the Sarpanches of the Kathura block that CDPO and other staff are no different from the already bureaucratic set-up existing at the block level. The Government is withering away the resources through such functionaries. Such functionaries should be directly responsible to Panchayat Samiti.

It was mentioned by the NIPCCD report that selection of supervisors should be done carefully. It was stated that "While recruiting them, steps should be taken to ensure that they have the prescribed level of education, work experience and ability to perform the task allotted to them."

2. To Suggest methods of Administrative Support

The success of the programme depends upon the proper facilities provided to the staff. Most of the Anganwadi workers lack proper accommodation for the office. The helpers provided to the Anganwadi workers carry a meagre allowance. The absence of proper facilities makes a mockery of the scheme. One of the intellectual elite of the area remarked: "The Government is always interested to design a new set-up for every new scheme rather than utilising the existing framework which can be cheaper and effective. Why does the Government not make the functioning of Block Development Officers efficient and run this scheme through the already existing machinery. Besides, Indian Council of Child Welfare with its branches in the States is already well established. This programme can be run with the help of that agency." It is very difficult to provide facilities to different kinds of workers of different schemes in a village/city. If this is done, all our resources would be diverted to constructive activities. What is required is to provide a set-up for all the basic services in a block and administer all the programmes through this complex. People in the villages are bewildered when they find different workers under different schemes without any coordination. It is high time to streamline the functioning of various agencies operating in a village. Such independent costly programmes for all the blocks in the country are beyond the resources of our country. What is required is to economise expenditure and serve the community and the target groups through the already existing channels. It can be merged with the recently restructured infrastructure for women and child health under the head RCH (Reproductive and Child Health).

3. To Design Vertical and Horizontal Coordination

The scheme envisages the coordination among the ICDS staff, PHC staff, BDO staff, Panchayats, Panchayat Samiti and the field offices of Development departments. In actual practice, there is a lot of friction among the different agencies. For instance, it was mentioned that they never make use of the transport and other facilities in a coordinated way. Every officer is an empire unto himself. The focus of coordination should be the provision of efficient services to the beneficiaries rather than self-glory. All this would be possible only if all the programmes in a block are fitted into the already existing administrative structures rather than setting up loose structures.

4. To Suggest Ways of Promoting and Encouraging People's Participation

The ultimate objective of the ICDS programme is to convert these programmes into people's programmes with Government's assistance where necessary. Most of the people interviewed from the area of the project were of the view that this is a Government Programme and the people are getting a charity. No steps are taken to ensure people's cooperation. People interviewed indicated that they were not clear about the objectives of this programme. Simply by stating, it is not going to be people's programme to make them aware of this basic assumption. Setting up of local committees can be an effective step in this direction. It was suggested by the NIPCCD (National Institute of Public Cooperation and Child Development) that the project staff should try to work out not only with the structured leadership or established power groups but should also identify, strengthen and work with new, latent or potential leadership which can be of considerable help in implementing the project programmes. ...Primary School Teachers, village Dais Gram Sevaks and Sevikas, Patwaris, Women Panchas, traditional caste leaders, members of village Panchayats, block Samiti Mahila Mandals, Youth Clubs, Cooperative Societies, tanners' clubs, leaders of political parties should be educated and mobilised to assist the delivery of various services of ICDS projects.[11]

There was very little involvement of those who were not getting the benefits from this scheme. It was also found in a study conducted by J.P. Gupta, V.K. Manchanda, R.K. Juyal and C.B. Joshi that "The perception, utilisation, satisfaction and participation of the non-beneficiaries was low as they were not given complete knowledge about the scheme, its services and benefits through regular contacts by the workers and other states. There has been a tendency among the Anganwadi workers to visit beneficiaries more often than non- beneficiaries. Increased contacts with non-beneficiaries would be much more fruitful to achieve the desired results.[12]

5. Suggest Methods of Continuous Monitoring and Evaluation

Evaluation is being done by the monitoring cell in the Ministry of Education and Social Welfare. Government of India but such evaluation is not realistic as it is based upon the official reports submitted by the CDPO and his staff. There is need to appoint disinterested outside evaluators to measure the impact of the scheme. The Governments can get such evaluations done by the university teaching departments. The university teachers would be happy to undertake such work provided all the facilities are provided including access to all files and papers connected with the project at a particular place. This would also make the researches relevant and applied. These areas can be assigned to Doctoral students for pursuing their research.

6. How to Improve Storage System

It was observed that in most of these villages, there were no proper arrangements for storing of food items. There is a need of creating proper storing places and provision of boxes for storing supplementary nutrition food supply stuffs.

7. Need of Enhance Budgetary Grant

It was mentioned by a few officers that provision of Rs. 18,000 under

ICDS budgetary allocation for medicines and vaccination was not enough and also that most of the drugs/medicines were diverted towards other health schemes in the area.

8. Method of Proper Control and Supervision

It was observed that there were large variations in the number of children actually present at the Anganwadis and those shown in the attendance register. However, the supplies were being drawn on the basis of attendance in the register whereas the actual number was much less. Thus, nutrition supplements are not being used properly.

So, the resources were being either wasted or misutilized. It was, therefore. necessary to exercise proper and surprise checks, to plug this lacunae. The plan evaluation organisation of the Planning Commission in its report mentioned some of the deficiencies in the implementation of the programme: inadequate identification of target groups, lack of coordination between field level health staff and the project staff, bottlenecks in the supply of equipments, over-emphasis on educational aspects and lack of community involvement, particularly of women. These problems and suggestions may be taken into consideration while setting up the future projects and implementing them successfully.

Within the ICDS programme, a beginning was made to provide the much needed services to the hitherto-neglected school dropout adolescent girls. This is envisaged to imbibe in them a responsible future motherhood and impart necessary skills including functional literacy to act as social animators at later stage. The package of interventions for adolescent girls includes hands-on training and experience in anganwadis in the areas of health, nutrition, pre-school education and child care, including nutrition and health care. For effective delivery of services envisaged under ICDS, the training of ICDS functionaries at all levels is being concurrently undertaken. NIPCCD is the apex organisation for training of ICDS functionaries.[13]

9. Shift Emphasis to Child Development and Protection

Developing on the gains made in the Eighth Plan period, the Ninth Plan is entailing a shift in emphasis from promoting only child survival and growth to child development and protection. While the Eighth Plan viewed children as the nation's future human resource, the perspective in the Ninth Plan is to view child development not only as a desireable societal investment for the nation's future, but as the right of every child to achieve full development potential.

10. Moving Ahead: Changing the Policy Paradigm

The analysis shows that there has to be a change in the policy paradigm informing the planning of interventions for the Indian Child. In which case, what should the directions be?

Broadly the research recommends a move towards:

- An outcome-focused and child centered approach to planning for children.
- A multi-sectoral approach.
- A demand-driven, community-based, business plan approach.
- Contextualized, decentralized planning.
- Improved targeting and monitoring.
- Improved service delivery.
- Making the private sector more accountable and forging new partnerships.
- Better use of information, education and communication to mobilize the community and raise awareness.
- Greater investment in the very young child.
- Targeting Public financing for poor child.

11. From an Input Focus towards an Outcome Focused and Child Centered Approach to Planning for Children

Thus, the integrated conceptual framework calls for planning that Addresses the continuous and cumulative nature of child development, and recognizes the need to intervene in every stage of child development—since what precedes influences the quality of what follows:

- Recognizes the priority needs of each sub-stage of child development; and
- Emphaizes the synergistic; interdependent and complementary nature of health, nutrition, education and psychological development that operates within the dynamics of the child's proximal and distal environment.

The GOI and World Bank jointly organized a National Consultation cum workshop on "Child Under nutrition and ICDS in India: A Call for Reform and Action" in May 2006 to discuss the findings of a report that the bank had prepared in 2005 on child under nutrition in India and the ICDS program, and the preliminary findings of the endline evaluation under the project. The Consultation was inaugurated by Smt. Renuka Chowdhary, Hon'ble Minister For Women and Child Development.[14]

Key issues with recommendations, emerged from the National Consultation, are as follows:

- Preventing malnutrition as early as possible, in the life cycle.
- Improving family care and health-related behaviour targeting.
- Poorest and most marginalized households.
- Most vulnerable under 3 children.
- Worst off communities/blocks/districts/states.
- Local relevance and flexibility.

Key Recommendations

- Focus ICDS service delivery for under 3s on prevention of undernutrition.
- Ensure accountability in terms of nutrition outcomes.
- Develop two distinct cadres of functionally trained workers (for 0-3 and 3-6).
- Enhance convergence with health department for care of underweight babies, etc.
- Encourage community involvement to reach most vulnerable children/groups.
- Offer a basket of services to address micronutrient malnutrition including supplementation, fortification, dictary diversification and nutrition education.
- Promote optimal home-based care, breastfeeding and complementary feeding practices through nutrition education and counselling of mothers and families.
- Build a special thrust on states/blocks with poor indicators.
- Encourage customized local planning and management.
- Introduce decentralization in procurement, data management, human resources appointment, reporting and monitoring.
- Enhance role of community committees in planning and monitoring.

Working group on Child Development[15]

The Planning Commission constituted the working group on development of children under the Chairpersonship of Secretary (WCD) on 17.4.2006.

The working group on 'Development of Children' suggested constitution of the following 4 sub-groups on the following:

- Child Protection
- Girl Child
- ICDS and Nutrition
- Early Childhood education

The sub-group held meetings independently and finalized their reports. The sub group reports were considered by the working group and the report of the working group was finalized and copies furnished to Planning Commission for consideration in the steering committee of the Planning Commission.

Some of the important recommendations made by the working group are the following:

- Universalization of ICDS equality
- Provision of an additional anganwadi worker to impart pre-school education in Anganwadi centre.

- Incessation of a new centrally sponsored Integrated Child Protection Scheme (ICPS).
- Expansion of Creche and Day Care Programme.
- Review and reorganisation of adoption system in India.
- Data Systems research.
- A Cradle baby scheme for girl child.
- Expansion of Nutrition Programme for Adolescent Girls (NPAG) and its merger with Kishori Shakti Yojana (KSY).
- Pilot scheme on conditional cash and non-cash transfer for girl child.

NIPCCD in its study, "Three Decades of ICDS—An Appraisal", came out with excellent recommendations to improve ICDS. We mention here few general recommendations—

(i) Past experience as well as observations by the research teams has shown that mothers and children have responded enormously to supplementary nutrition programme wherever SHGs were involved in preparing cooked food in Anganwadis and serving the same to children and pregnant and lactating mothers. Since the ICDS programme is intended to be a people-based one, it should, in its stride, involve the Self-Help Groups (SHGs) which are potentially the most effective and active grass-root level action groups. It is high time that their contributions must be sought not only to enrich the supplementary nutrition component but also to consider the shifting of responsibility of running the AWCs to SHGs in those states where the SHG movement has shown positive contribution to the ICDS programme especially in the delivery of supplementary nutrition.

(ii) ICDS programme needs a complete face-lift order to bring in the element of participatory management in it. Project level functionaries need to be encouraged to reflect on the prevailing situation, analyse them, think about possible alternatives, plan for suitable appropriate action and more importantly grasp the necessity and urgency for change. All this could be carried out on the solid premise of collective thinking, decision-making and delegating responsibilities towards cultivating trust and strengthening the shared commitment for effective utilization of services of ICDS. As inbuilt mechanism of openness and freedom for exchange of ideas and views among ICDS functionaries on various issues concerning implementation of the programme on regular basis needs to be evolved. This needs to be done at all levels.

(iii) In order to make health services more effective, strategies need to be evolved to bridge the gap between knowledge and practice, and training and implementation. In this regard, two pronged training strategy is required—one for women and another for ICDS functionary concerned with health services. Training of women will lead to an increase in outreach and ultimate prevalence of widespread health practices necessary for a good living and generate demand for health services. Training of staff will result in developing concrete plans for subsequent action and follow-up of that action. All training and capacity building measures need to be focused on achieving health targets and improving coverage rates. In this context, adequate emphasis needs to be given on certain priority areas which include strategies for increasing coverage, observance of health day for pregnant women and mothers of children under 2, emphasis on individual counselling and expanding the number the type of community health workers.

(iv) The concept of community monitoring could be experimented with a different perspective by technically ensuring developmental goals of ICDS programme. A community level monitoring team comprising local people from all sections of life could be developed. The team members should be trained by service functionaries and professional experts to monitor ICDS programmes based on certain process indicators and outcome indicators. This will ensure tracking of locally relevant indicators *vis-à-vis* developmental goals set for children, adolescents girls and women at community level. These indicators could be based on household's accessibility to safe drinking water, means of waste disposal. Full immunization of children, children under 3 receiving regular doses of vitamin A, presence of a depot-holder for ORS, condoms and contraceptive pills within the community, all pregnant women and/or lactating mothers receiving supplementary nutrition, ante-natal care, iron and folic acid tables and TT doses regularly and without fail, every child above six months of age receiving compulsory feeding, every child above six months of age receiving compulsory feeding, every child above five years enrolled and attending formal schools, existence of a functional mothers or women's group, incidence of birth or death among children and pregnant women in a given period, accessibility to transport facility to go to health centre whenever a pregnant mother developing complications and so on.

(v) Moulding the mind of people, especially with such issues as discrimination against girl child is a major challenge to the ICDS programme. Female foeticide and infanticide are to be contained and the general population is to be educated adequately on these issues. Protecting girls child is a sensitive issue and persuastion is the only recourse. The institution of

Anganwadi can play an important role in creating awareness in the villages about the dwindling sex ratio and its likely impact on future of the country. It is therefore imperative that project functionaries including the AWWs and the helpers are involved in creating such an awareness through campaigns and other means.[16]

Notes and References

1. UN General Assembly, Second Development Decade, Report of the Second Committee (Part I) A/8/24.
2. Second Development Decade Resolution 2626 (XXV), para 18.
3. Govt. of India: Ministry of Education and Social Welfare, Department of Social Welfare, National Plan of Action for International Year of Child (1979), New Delhi, September 1978.
4. C. Subramaniam, A World Charter for Children, *The Hindu,* 28 September, 1978.
5. Annual Report, 2006-07, Ministry of Women and Child Development, GOI, New Delhi, p. 47.
6. Annual Report, 2006-07, Ministry of Women and Child Development, GOI, New Delhi, pp. 50-51.
7. Govt of India: Department of Social Welfare, Integrated Child Development Services Scheme, New Delhi, pp. 2-3.
8. NIPCCD: A Consolidated Report of ICDS Workshop on Coordination held at Imphal, New Delhi, Patna, Bombay and Hyderabad, November 1976, pp. 25.26.
9. Annual Report, 2006-07, Ministry of Women and Child Development, GOI, New Delhi, pp. 48-50.
10. J.P. Gupta, *et. al.,* "Integrated Child Development Services Schemes: A Study of Its Health Components in a Delhi Anganwadi", in *The Indian Journal of Public Administration,* Vol. XXV, No. 3, p. 748.
11. *Ibid.*
12. *Ibid.*
13. Deptt. of Family Welfare, Reproductive and Child Health (World Bank Component), Project Proposal and Implementation Plan, New Delhi, March 1997, pp. 135-37.
14. The World Bank, Reaching out to the Child, Human Development Sector, South Asia Region, Sept. 2004, pp. 103-04.
15. Annual Report, 2006-07, Ministry of Women and Child Development, GOI, New Delhi, pp. 15-16.
16. National Institute of Public Cooperation and Child Development, New Delhi, 2006.

Appendix I

NATIONAL HEALTH POLICY, 1983

National Health Policy, Government of India, Ministry of Health and Family Welfare, New Delhi, 1983

Introduction

1. The Constitution of India envisages the establishment of a new social order based on equality, freedom, justice and the dignity of the individual. It aims at the elimination of poverty, ignorance and ill-health and directs the State to regard the raising of the level of nutrition and the standard of living of its people and the improvement of public health as among its primary duties, securing the health and strength of workers, men and women, specially ensuring that children are given opportunities and facilities to develop in a healthy manner.

1.1 Since the inception of the planning process in the country, the successive Five Year Plans have been providing the framework within which the States may develop their health services infrastructure, facilities for medical education, research, etc. Similar guidance has sought to be provided through the discussions and conclusions arrived at in the Joint Conferences of the Central Councils of Health and Family Welfare and the National Development Council. Besides, Central legislation has been enacted to regulate standards of medical education, prevention of food adulteration, maintenance of standards in the manufacture and sale of certified drugs, etc.

1.2 While the broad approaches contained in the successive Plan documents and discussion in the forums referred to in para 1.1 may have generally served the needs of the situation in the past, it is felt that an integrated, comprehensive approach towards the future development of medical education, research and health services requires to be established to serve the actual health needs and priorities of the country. It is in this context that the need has been felt to evolve a National Health Policy.

Our heritage

2. India has a rich, centuries-old heritage of medical and health sciences. The philosophy of Ayurveda and the surgical skills enunciated by Charaka and Shusharuta bear testimony to our ancient tradition in the scientific health care of our people. The approach of our ancient medical

systems was of a holistic nature, which took into account all aspects of human health and disease. Over the centuries, with the intrusion of foreign influences and mingling of cultures, various systems of medicine evolved and have continued to be practised widely. However, the allopathic system of medicine has, in a relatively short period of time, made a major impact on the entire approach to health care and pattern of development of the health services infrastructure in the country.

Program achieved

3. During the last three decades and more, since the attainment of Independence, considerable progress has been achieved in the promotion of the health status of our people. Smallpox has been eliminated; plague is no longer a problem; mortality from cholera and related diseases has decreased and malaria brought under control to a considerable extent. The mortality rate per thousand of population has been reduced from 27.4 to 14.8 and the life expectancy at birth has increased from 32.7 to over 52. A fairly extensive network of dispensaries, hospitals and institutions providing specialised curative care has developed and a large stock of medical and health personnel, of various levels, has become available. Significant indigenous capacity has been established for the production of drugs and pharmaceuticals, vaccines, sera, hospital equipments, etc.

The existing picture

4. In spite of such impressive progress, the demographic and health picture of the country still constitutes a cause for serious and urgent concern. The high rate of population growth continues to have an adverse effect on the health of our people and the quality of their lives. The mortality rates for women and children are still distressingly high; almost one third of the total deaths occur among children below the age of 5 years; infant mortality is around 129 per thousand live births. Efforts at raising the nutritional levels of our people have still to bear fruit and the extent and severity of malnutrition continues to be exceptionally high. Communicable and non-communicable diseases have still to be brought under effective control and eradicated. Blindness, Leprosy and T.B. continue to have a high incidence. Only 31% of the rural population has access to potable water supply and 0.5% enjoys basic sanitation.

4.1. High incidence of diarrhoeal diseases and other preventive and infectious diseases, specially amongst infants and children, lack of safe drinking water and poor environmental sanitation, poverty and ignorance are among the major contributory causes of the high incidence of disease and mortality.

4.2. The existing situation has been largely engendered by the almost wholesale adoption of health manpower development policies and the establishment of curative centres based on the Western models, which are inappropriate and irrelevant to the real needs of our people and the socio-economic conditions obtaining in the country. The hospital-based disease, and cure-oriented approach towards the establishment of medical services has provided benefits to the upper crusts, of society, specially those residing in the urban areas. The proliferation of this approach has been at the cost of providing comprehensive primary health care services to the entire population, whether residing in the urban or the rural areas. Furthermore, the continued high emphasis on the curative approach has led to the neglect of the preventive, promotive, public health and rehabilitative aspects of health care. The existing approach, instead of improving awareness and building up self-reliance, has tended to enhance dependency and weaken the community's capacity to cope with its problems. The prevailing policies in regard to the education and training of medical and health personnel, at various levels, has resulted in the development of a cultural gap between the people and the personnel providing care. The various health programmes have, by and large, failed to involve individuals and families in establishing a self-reliant community. Also, over the years, the planning process has become largely oblivious of the fact that the ultimate goal of achieving a satisfactory health status for all our people cannot be secured without involving the community in the identification of their health needs and priorities as well as in the implementation and management of the various health and related programmes.

Need for evolving a health policy—the revised 20-Point Programme

5. India is committed to attaining the goal of "Health for All by the Year 2000 A.D." through the universal provision of comprehensive primary health care services. The attainment of this goal requires a thorough overhaul of the existing approaches to the education and training of medical and health personnel and the reorganisation of the health services infrastructure. Furthermore, considering the large variety of inputs into health, it is necessary to secure the complete integration of all plans for health and human development with the overall national socio-economic development process, specially in the more closely health-related sectors, e.g. drugs and pharmaceuticals, agriculture and food production, rural development, education and social welfare, housing, water supply and sanitation, prevention of food adulteration, maintenance of prescribed standards in the manufacture and sale of drugs and the conservation of the environment. In sum, the contours of the National Health Policy have to be evolved within a fully integrated planning framework which seeks to provide universal, comprehensive primary health care services, relevant to the actual needs and priorities of the community at a cost which the people can afford, ensuring that the planning and implementation of the various health programmes is through the organised involvement and participation of the community, adequately utilising the services being rendered by private voluntary organisations active in the Health sector.

5.1. It is also necessary to ensure that the pattern of development of the health services infrastructure in the future fully takes into account the revised 20-Point Programme. The said Programme attributes very high priority to the promotion of family planning as a people's programme, on a voluntary basis; substantial augmentation and provision of primary health care facilities on a universal basis; control of Leprosy, T.B. and Blindness; acceleration of welfare programmes for women and children; nutrition programmes for pregnant women, nursing mothers and children, especially in the tribal, hill and backward areas. The Programme also places high emphasis on the supply of drinking water to all problem villages, improvements in the housing and environments of the weaker sections of society; increased production of essential food items; integrated rural developments; spread of universal elementary education; expansion of the public distribution system, etc.

Population stabilisation

6. Irrespective of the changes, no matter how fundamental, that may be brought about in the over-all approach to health care and the restructuring of the health services, not much headway is likely to be achieved in improving the health status of the people unless success is achieved in securing the small family norm, through voluntary efforts, and moving towards the goal of population stabilisation. In view of the vital importance of securing the balanced growth of the population, it is necessary to enunciate, separately, a National Population Policy.

Medical and Health Education

7. It is also necessary to appreciate that the effective delivery of health care services would depend very largely on the nature of education, training and appropriate orientation towards community health of all categories of medical and health personnel and their capacity to function as an integrated team, each of its members performing given tasks within a coordinated action programme. It is, therefore, of crucial importance that the entire basis and approach towards medical and health education, at all levels, is reviewed in terms of national needs and priorities and the curricular and training programmes restructured to produce personnel of various grades of skill and competence, who are professionally equipped and socially motivated to effectively deal with day-to-day problems, within the existing constraints.

Towards this end, it is necessary to formulate, separately, a National Medical and Health Education Policy which (i) sets out the changes required to be brought about in the curricular contents and training programme of medical and health personnel, at various levels of functioning; (ii) takes into account the need for establishing the extremely essential inter-relations between functionaries of various grades; (iii) provides guidelines for the production of health personnel on the basis of realistically assessed manpower requirements; (iv) seeks to resolve the existing sharp regional imbalances in their availability; and (v) ensures that personnel at all levels are socially motivated towards the rendering of community health services.

Need for providing primary health care with special emphasis on the preventive, promotive and rehabilitative aspects

8. Presently, despite the constraint of resources, there is disproportionate emphasis on the establishment of curative centres—dispensaries, hospitals, institutions for specialist treatment—the large majority of which are located in the urban areas of the country. The vast majority of those seeking medical relief have to travel long distance to the nearest curative centre, seeking relief for ailments which could have been readily and effectively handled at the community level. Also, for want of a well established referral system, those seeking curative care have the tendency to visit various specialist centres, thus further contributing to congestions, duplication of efforts and consequential waste of resources. To put an end to the existing all-round unsatisfactory situation, it is urgently necessary to restructure the health services within the following broad approach:

(1) To provide, within a phased, time-bound programme a well dispersed network of comprehensive primary health care services, integrally linked with the extension and health education approach which takes into account the fact that a large majority of health functions can be effectively handled and resolved by the people themselves, with the organised support of volunteers, auxilliaries, paramedics and adequately trained multi-purpose workers of various grades of skill and competence of both sexes. There are a large number of private, voluntary organisations active in the health field all over the country. Their services and support would require to be utilised and intermeshed with the governmental efforts, in an integrated manner.

(2) To be effective, the establishment of the primary health care approach would involve large scale transter of knowledge, simple skill and technologies to Health Volunteers, selected by the communities and enjoying their confidence. The functioning of the front line workers, selected by the community would require to be related to definitive action plans for the translation of medical and health knowledge into practical action, involving the use of simple and inexpensive interventions which can be readily implemented by persons who have undergone short periods of training. The quality of training of these health guides/workers would be of crucial importance to the success of this approach.

The success of the decentralised primary health care system would depend vitally on the organised building up of individual self-reliance and effective community participation; on the provision of organised, back-up support of the secondary and tertiary levels of the health care services, providing adequate logistical and technical assistance.

(4) The decentralisation of services would require the establishment of a well worked out referral system to provide adequate expertise at the various levels of the organisational set-up nearest to the community, depending upon the actual needs and problems of the area, and thus ensure against the continuation of the existing rush towards the curative centres in the urban areas. The effective establishment of the referral system would also ensure the optimal utilisation of expertise at the higher levels of the heirarchical structure. This approach would not only lead to the progressive improvement of comprehensive health care services at the primary level but also provide for timely attention being available to those in need of urgent specialist care, whether they live in the rural or the urban areas.

(5) To ensure that the approach to health care does not merely constitute a collection of disparate health interventions but consists of an integrated package of services seeking to tackle the entire range of poor health conditions, on a broad front, it is necessary to establish a nation-wide chain of sanitary-*cum*-epidemiological stations. The location and functioning of these stations may be between the primary and secondary levels of the heirarchical structure, depending upon the local situations and other relevant considerations. Each such station would require to have suitably trained staff equipped to identify, plan and provide preventive, promotive and mental health care services. It would be beneficial, depending upon the local situations, to establish such stations at the Primary Health Centres. The district health organisation should have, as an integral part of its set-up, a well organised epidemiological unit to coordinate and superintend the functioning of the field stations. These stations would participate in the integrated action plans to eradicate and control diseases, besides tackling specific local environmental health problems.

In the urban agglomerations, the municipal and local authorities should be equipped to perform similar functions, being supported with adequate resources and expertise, to effectively deal with the local preventable public health problems. The aforesaid approach should be implemented and extended through community participation and contributions, in whatever form possible, to achieve meaningful results within a time-bound programme.

(6) The location of curative centres should be related to the populations they serve, keeping in view the densities of population, distances, topography, transport connections. These centres should function within the recommended referral system, the gamut of the general specialities required to deal with the local disease patterns being provided as near to the

community as possible, at the secondary level of the hierarchical organisation. The concept of domiciliary care and the field-camps approach should be utilised to the fullest extent, to reduce the pressures on these centres, specially in efforts relating to the control and eradication of Blindness, Tuberculosis, Leprosy, etc. To maximise the utilisation of available resources, new and additional curative centres should be established only in exceptional cases, the basic attempt being towards the upgradation of existing facilities, at selected locations, the guiding principle being to provide specialist services as near to the beneficiaries as may be possible, within a well-planned network. Expenditure should be reduced through the fullest possible use of cheap locally available building materials, resort to appropriate architectural designs and engineering concepts and by economical investment in the purchase of machineries and equipments, ensuring against avoidable duplication of such acquisitions. It is also necessary to devise effective mechanisms for the repair, maintenance and proper upkeep of all bio-medical equipments to secure their maximum utilisation.

(7) With a view to reducing governmental expenditure and fully utilising untapped resources, planned programmes may be devised, related to the local requirements and potentials, to encourage the establishment of practice by private medical professional, increased investment by non- governmental agencies in establishing curative centres and by offering organised logistical, financial and technical support to voluntary agencies active in the health field.

(8) While the major focus of attention in restructuring the existing governmental health organisations would relate to establishing comprehensive primary health care and public health services, within an integrated referral system, planned attention would also require to be devoted to the establishment of centres equipped to provide speciality and superspeciality services, through a well dispersed network of centres, to ensure that the present and future requirements of specialist treatment are adequately available within the country. To reduce governmental expenditures involved in the establishment of such centres, planned efforts should be made to encourage private investments in such fields so that the majority of such centres, within the governmental set-up, can provide adequate care and treatment to those entitled to free care, the affluent sectors being looked after by the paying clinics. Care would also require to be taken to ensure the appropriate dispersal of such centres, to remove the existing regional imbalances and to provide services within the reach of all, whether residing in the rural or the urban areas.

(9) Special, well-coordinated programmes should be launched to provide mental health care as well as medical care and the physical and social rehabilitation of those who are mentally retarded, deaf, dumb, blind, physically disabled, infirm and the aged. Also, suitably organised of various disabilities.

(10) In the establishment of the re-organised services, the first priority should be accorded to provide services to those residing in the tribal, hill and backward areas as well as to endemic disease affected populations and the vulnerable sections of the society.

(11) In the re-organised health services scheme, efforts should be made to ensure adequate mobility of personnel, at all level of functioning.

(12) In the various approaches, set out in (1) to (11) above, organised efforts would require to be made to fully utilise and assist in the enlargement of the services being provided by private voluntary organisations active in the health field. In this context, planning encouragement and support would also require to be afforded to fresh voluntary efforts, specially those which seek to serve the needs of the rural areas and the urban slums.

Re-orientation of the existing health personnel

9. A dynamic process of changes and innovation is required to be brought about in the entire approach to health manpower development, ensuring the emergence of fully integrated bands of workers functioning within the "Health Team" approach.

Private practice by governmental functionaries

10. It is desirable for the States to take steps to phase out of system of private practice by medical personnel in government service, providing at the same tome for payment of appropriate compensatory no-practising allowance. The States would require to carefully review the existing situation, with special reference to the availability and dispersal of private practitioners, and take timely decisions in regard to this vital issue.

Practitioners of indigenous and other systems of medicine and their role in health care

11. The country has a large stock of health manpower comprising of private practitioners in various systems, for example, Ayurveda, Uncanny, Sidha, Homeopathy, Yoga, Naturopathy, etc. This resource has not so for been adequately utilized. The practitioners of these various systems enjoy high local acceptance and respect and consequently exert considerable influence on health beliefs and practise. It is, therefore, necessary to initiate organised measures to enable each of these various systems of medicine and health care to develop in accordance wit its genius. Simultaneously, planned efforts should be made to dovetail the functioning of the

practitioners of these various systems and integrate their service, at the appropriate levels, within specified areas of responsibility and functioning, in the over-all health care delivery system, specially in regard to the preventive, primitive and public health objectives. Well considered steps would also require to be launched to move towards a meaningful phased integration of the indigenous and the modern systems.

Appendix II

NATIONAL POPULATION POLICY, 2000

ACTION PLAN OPERATIONAL STRATEGY

(i) and (ii) Converge Service Delivery at Village Levels

1. Utilise village self-help groups to organise and provide basic services for reproductive and child health care, combined with the ongoing Integrated Child Development Scheme (ICDS). Village self-help groups are in existence through centrally sponsored schemes of: (a) Department of Women and Child Development, Ministry of HRD, (b) Ministry of Rural Development, and (c) Ministry of Environment and Forests. Organise neighbourhood acceptor groups, and provide them with a revolving fund that may be accessed for income generation activities. The groups may establish rules of eligibility, interest rates, and accountability for which capital may be advanced, usually to be repaid in instalments within two years. The repayments may be used to fund another acceptor group in a nearby community, who would exert pressure to ensure timely repayments. Two trained birth attendants and the aanganwadi worker (AWW) should be members of this group.

2. Implement at village levels a one-stop integrated and coordinated service delivery package for basic health care, family planning and maternal and child health-related services, provided by the community and for the community. Train and motivate the village self-help acceptor groups to become the primary contact at household levels. Once every fortnight, these acceptor groups will meet, and provide at one place 6 different services for: (i) registration of births, deaths, marriage and pregnancy; (ii) weighing of children under 5 years, and recording the weight on a standard growth chart; (iii) counselling and advocacy for contraception, plus free supply of contraceptives; (iv) preventive care, with availability of basic medicines for common ailments; antipyretics for fevers, antibiotic ointments for infections, ORT/ORSI for childhood diarrhoeas, together with standardised indigenous medication and homeopathic cures; (v) nutrition supplements; and (vi) advocacy and encouragement for the continued enrolment of children in school up to age 14. One health staff, appointed by the panchayat, will be suitably trained to provide guidance. Clustering services for women and children at one place and time at village levels will promote positive interactions in health benefits and reduce service delivery costs.

3. Wherever these village self-help groups have not developed for any reason, community midwives, practitioners of ISMH, retired school teachers and ex-defence personnel may be organised into neighbourhood groups to perform similar functions.

4. At village levels, the aanganwadi centre may become the pivot of basic health care activities, contraceptive counselling and supply, nutrition education and supplementation, as well as pre-school activities. The aanganwadi centres can also function as depots for ORS/basic medicines and contraceptives.

5. A maternity hut should be established in each village to be used as the village delivery room, with storage space for supplies and medicines. It should be adequately equipped with kits for midwifery, ante-natal care, and delivery; basic medication for obstetric emergency aid; contraceptives, drugs and medicines for common ailments; and indigenous medicines/ supplies for maternal and new-born care. The panchayat may appoint a competent and mature mid-wife, to look after this village maternity hut. She may be assisted by volunteers.

6. Trained birth attendants as well as the vast pool of traditional dais should be made familiar with emergency and referral procedures. This will greatly assist the Auxiliary Nurse Midwife (ANM) at the sub-centres to monitor and respond to maternal morbidity/emergencies at village levels.

7. Each village may maintain a list of community mid-wives, village health guides, panchayat sewa sahayaks, trained birth attendants, practitioners of indigenous systems of medicine, primary school teachers and other relevant persons, as well as the nearest institutional health care facilities that may be accessed for integrated service delivery. These persons may also be helpful in involving civil society in monitoring availability, quality and accessibility of reproductive and child health services; in disseminating education and communication on the benefits of smaller and healthier families, with emphasis on education of the girl child; and female participation in the work force.

8. Provide a wider basket of choices in contraception, through innovative social marketing schemes to reach household levels.

Comment: Meaningful decentralisation will result only if the convergence of the national family welfare programme with the ICDS programme is strengthened. The focus of the ICDS programme on nutrition improvement at village levels and on pre-school activities must be widened to include maternal and child health care services. Convergence of several related activities at service delivery levels with, in particular, the ICDS programme, is critical for extending outreach and increasing access to services. Intersectoral coordination with appropriate training and sensitisation among field functionaries will facilitate dissemination of integrated reproductive and child health services to village and household levels. People will willingly cooperate in the registration of births, deaths, marriages and pregnancies if they perceive some benefit. At the village level, this community meeting every fortnight, may become their most convenient access to basic health care, both for maternal and child health, as well as for common ailments. Households may participate to receive integrated service delivery, alongwith information about ongoing micro-credit and thrift schemes. Government and non-government functionaries will be expected to function in harmony to ensure integrated service delivery. The panchayat will promote this coordination and exercise effective supervision.

(iii) Empowering Women for Improved Health and Nutrition

1. Create an enabling environment for women and children to benefit from products and services disseminated under the reproductive and child health programme. Cluster services for women and children at the same place and time. This promotes positive interactions in health benefits and reduces service delivery costs.

2. As a measure to empower women, open more child care centres in rural areas and in urban slums, where a woman worker may leave her children in responsible hands. This will encourage female participation in paid employment, reduce school dropout rates, particularly for the girl child, and promote school enrolment as well. The aanganwadis provide a partial solution.

3. To empower women, pursue programmes of social afforestation to facilitate access to fuel wood and fodder. Similarly, pursue drinking water schemes for increasing access to portable water. This will reduce long absences from home, and the need for large number of children to perform such tasks.

4. In any reward scheme intended for household levels, priority may be given to energy saving devices such as solar cookers, or provision of sanitation facilities, or extension of telephone lines. This will empower households, in particular women.

5. Improve district, sub-district and panchayat-level health management with coordination and collaboration between district health officer, sub-district health officer and the panchayat for planning and implementation activities. There is need to:

- Strengthen the referral network between the district health office, district hospital and the community health centres, the primary health centres and the sub-centres in management of obstetric and neo-natal complications.
- Strengthen community health centres to provide comprehensive emergency obstetric and neo-natal care. These may function as clinical training centres as well. Strengthen primary health centres to provide essential obstetric and neo-natal care. Strengthen sub-centres to provide a comprehensive range of services, with delivery rooms, counselling for contraception, supplies of free contraceptives, ORS and basic medicines, together with facilities for immunisation.

- Establish rigorous problem identification mechanisms through maternal and peri-natal audit, from village level upwards.

6. Ensure adequate transportation at village level, sub-centre levels, zila parishads, primary health centres and at community health centres. Identifying women at risk is meaningful only if women with complications can reach emergency care in time.

7. Improve the accessibility and quality of maternal and child health services through:

- Deployment of community mid-wives and additional health providers at village levels; cluster services for women and children at the same place and time, from village level upwards, e.g. ante-natal and post-partum care, monitoring infant growth, availability of contraceptives and medicine kits; and routinised immunisations at sub-centre levels.
- Strengthen the capacity of primary health centres to provide basic emergency obstetric and neo-natal health care.
- Involve professional agencies in developing and disseminating training modules for standard procedures in the management of obstetric and neo-natal cases. The aim should be to routinise these procedures at all appropriate levels.
- Improve supervision by developing guidance and supervision checklists.

8. Monitor performance of maternal and child health services at each level by using the maternal and child health local area monitoring system, which includes monitoring the incidence and coverage of ante-natal visits, deliveries assisted by trained health care personnel and post-natal visits, among other indicators. The ANM at the sub-centre should be responsible and accountable for registering every pregnancy and child birth in her jurisdiction, and for providing universal ante-natal and post-natal services.

9. Improve technical skills of maternal and child health care providers by:

- Strengthening skills of health personnel and health providers through classroom and on-the-job training in the management of obstetric and neo-natal emergencies. This should include training of birth attendants and midwives at district-level hospitals in life-saving skills, such as management of asphyxia and hypothermia.
- Training on integrated management of childhood illnesses for infants (1 week-2 months).

10. Support community activities such as dissemination of IEC material, including leaflets and posters, and promotion of folk jatras, songs

and dances to promote healthy mother and healthy baby messages, along with good management practices to ensure safe motherhood, including early recognition of danger signs.

11. Programme development comprising:

- Partnership in family health and nutrition. The aanganwadi worker will identify women and children in the villages who suffer from malnutrition and/or micro-nutritional deficiencies, including iron, vitamin A, and iodine deficiency; provide nutritional supplements and monitor nutritional status.
- Convergence, strengthening and universalisation of the nutritional programmes of the Department of Family Welfare and the ICDS run by the Department of Women and Child Development, ensuring training and timely supply of food supplements and medicines.
- Include STD/RTI and HIV/AIDS prevention, screening and management, in maternal and child health services.
- Provide quality care in family planning, including information, increased contraceptive choices for both spacing and terminal methods, increase access to good quality and affordable contraceptive supplies and services at diverse delivery points, counselling about the safety, efficacy and possible side effects of each method, and appropriate follow-up. Develop a health package for adolescents.

13. Expand the availability of safe abortion care. Abortion is legal, but there are barriers limiting women's access to safe abortion services. Some operational strategies are:

- Community-level education campaigns should target women, household decision-makers and adolescents about the availability of safe abortion services and the dangers of unsafe abortion.
- Make safe and legal abortion services more attractive to women and household decision-makers by: (i) increasing geographic spread; (ii) enhancing affordability; (iii) ensuring confidentiality; and (iv) providing compassionate abortion care, including post-abortion counselling.
- Adopt updated and simple technologies that are safe and easy, e.g. manual vacuum extraction not necessarily dependant upon anaesthesia, or non-surgical techniques which are non-invasive.
- Promote collaborative arrangements with private sector health professionals, NGOs and the public sector, to increase the availability and coverage of safe abortion services, including training of mid-level providers.

- Eliminate the current cumbersome procedures for registration of abortion clinics. Simplify and facilitate the establishment of additional training centres for safe abortions in the public, private, and NGO sectors. Train these health care providers in provision of clinical services for safe abortions.
- Formulate and notify standards for abortion services. Strengthen enforcement mechanisms at district and sub- district levels to ensure that these norms are followed.
- Follow norms-based registration of service provision centres, and thereby switch the onus of meticulous observance of standards onto the provider.
- Provide competent post-abortion care, including management of complications and identification of other health needs of post-abortion patients, and linking with appropriate services. As part of post-abortion care, physicians may be trained to provide family planning counselling and services such as sterilisation and reversible modern methods such as IUDs, as well as oral contraceptives and condones;
  - — Modify syllabus and curricula for medical graduates, as well as for continuing education and in-house learning, to provide for practical training in the newer procedures.
  - — Ensure services for termination of pregnancy at primary health centers and at community health centres.

14. Develop maternity hospitals at sub-district levels and at community health centres to function as FRUs for complicated and life-threatening deliveries.

15. Formulate and enforce standards for clinical services in the public, private, and NGO sectors.

16. Focus on distribution of non-clinical methods of contraception (condoms and oral contraceptive pills) through free supply, social marketing as well as commercial sales.

17. Create a national network consisting of public, private and NGO centres, identified by a common logo, for delivering reproductive and child health services free to any client. The provider will be compensated for the service provided, on the basis of a coupon, duly counter-signed by the beneficiary, and paid for by a system to be devised. The compensation will be identical to providers across all sectors. The end-user will choose the provider of the service. A group of management experts will devise checks and balances to prevent misuse.

(iv) Child Health and Survival

1. Support community activities, from village level upwards to monitor early and adequate ante-natal, natal and post-natal care. Focus attention on neo-natal health care and nutrition.

2. Set-up a National Technical Committee on neo-natal care, to align programme and project interventions with newly emerging technologies in neo-natal and peri-natal care.

3. Pursue compulsory registration of births in coordination with the ICDS Programme.

4. After the birth of a child, provide counselling and advocacy about contraception, to encourage adoption of a reversible or a terminal method. This will also contribute to the health and well-being of both mother and child.

5. Improve capacities at health centres in basic midwifery services, essential neo-natal care, including the management of sick neo-nates outside the hospital.

6. Sensitise and train health personnel in the integrated management of childhood illnesses. Standard case management of diarrhoea and acute respiratory infections must be provided at sub-centres and primary health centres, with appropriate training, and adequate equipment. Besides, training in this sector may be imparted to health care providers at village levels, especially in indigenous srstems.

7. Strengthen critical interventions aimed at bringing about reductions in maternal malnutrition, morbidity and mortality, by ensuring availability of supplies and equipment at village levels, and at sub-centres.

8. Pursue rigorously the pulse polio campaign to eradicate polio.

9. Ensure 100 per cent routine immunisation for all vaccine preventable diseases, in particular tetanus and measles.

10. As a child survival initiative, explore promotional and motivational measures for couples below the poverty line who marry after the legal age of marriage, to have the first child after the mother reaches the age of 21, and adopt a terminal method of contraception after the birth of the second child.

11. Children form a vulnerable group and certain sub-groups merit focused attention and intervention, such as street children and child labourers. Encourage voluntary groups as well as NGOs to formulate and implement special schemes for these groups of children.

12. Explore the feasibility of a national health insurance covering hospitalisation costs for children below 5 years, whose parents have adopted the small norm, and opted for a terminal method of contraception after the birth of the second child.

13. Expand the ICDS to include children between 6-9 years of age, specifically to promote and ensure 100 per cent school enrolment, particularly for girls. Promote primary education with the help of aanganwadi workers, and encourage retention in .school till age 14. Education promotes awareness, late marriages, small family size and higher child survival rates.

14. Provide vocational training for girls. This will enhance perception of the immediate utility of educating girls, and gradually raise the average age of marriage. It will also increase enrolment and retention of girls at

primary school, and likely also at secondary school levels. Involve NGOs, the voluntary sector and the private sector, as necessary, to target employment opportunities.

(v) Meeting the Unmet Needs for Family Welfare Services

1. Strengthen, energise and make publicly accountable the cutting edge of health infrastructure at the village, sub-centre and primary health centre levels.

2. Address on priority the different unmet needs detailed in Appendix IV, in particular, an increase in rural infrastructure, deployment of sanctioned and appropriately trained health personnel, and provisioning of essential equipment and drugs.

3. Formulate and implement innovative social marketing schemes to provide subsidised products and services in areas where the existing coverage of the public, private and NGO sectors is insufficient in order to increase outreach and coverage.

4. Improve facilities for referral transportation at panchayat, zilla parishad and primary health centre levels. At sub-centres, provide ANMs with soft loans for purchase of mopeds, to enhance their mobility. This will increase coverage of ante-natal and post-natal check-ups, which, in turn, and will bring about reductions in maternal and infant mortality.

5. Encourage local entrepreneurs at village and block levels to start ambulance services through special schemes, with appropriate vehicles to facilitate transportation of persons requiring emergency as well as essential medical attention.

6. Provide special loan schemes and make site allotments at village levels to facilitate the starting of chemist shops for basic medicines and provision for medical first aid.

(vi) Under-Served Population Groups

(a) Urban Slums

1. Finalise a comprehensive urban health care strategy.

2. Facilitate service delivery centres in urban slums to provide comprehensive basic health, reproductive and child health services by NGOs and private sector organisations, including Corporate houses.

3. Promote networks of retired government doctors and para- medical and non-medical personnel who may function as health care providers for clinical and non-clinical services on remunerative terms.

4. Strengthen social marketing programmes for non-clinical family planning products and services in urban slums.

5. Initiate specially targeted information, education and communication campaigns for urban slums on family planning, immunization, ante-natal, natal and post-natal check-ups and other reproductive health care services. Integrate aggressive health education programmes with health and medical care programmes, with emphasis on

environmental health, personal hygiene and healthy habits, nutrition education and population: education.

6. Promote inter-sectoral coordination between departments/ municipal bodies dealing with water and sanitation, industry and pollution, housing, transport, education and nutrition, and women and child development, to deal with unplanned and uncoordinated settlements.

7. Streamline the referral systems and linkages between the primary, secondary and tertiary levels of health care in the urban areas.

8. Link the provision of continued facilities to urban slum-dwellers with their observance of the small family norm.

(b) Tribal Communities, Hill Area Populations and Displaced and Migrant Populations

1. Many tribal communities are dwindling in numbers, and may not need fertility regulation. Instead, they may need information and counselling in respect of infertility.

2. The NGO sector may be encouraged to formulate and implement a system of preventive and curative health care that responds to seasonal variations in the availability of work. income and food for tribal and hill area communities and migrant and displaced populations. To begin with, mobile clinics may provide some degree of regular coverage and outreach.

3. Many tribal communities are dependent upon indigenous systems of medicine which necessitates a regular supply of local flora, fauna and minerals, or of standardised medication derived from these. Husbandry of such local resources and of preparation and distribution of standardised formulations should be encouraged.

4. Health care providers in the public, private and NGO sectors should be sensitised to adopt a "burden of disease" approach to meet the special needs of tribal and hill area communities.

(c) Adolescents

I. Ensure for adolescents access to information, counselling and services, including reproductive health services, that are affordable and accessible. Strengthen primary health centres and sub-centres, to provide counselling, both to adolescents and also to newly weds (who may also be adolescents). Emphasise proper spacing of children.

2. Provide for adolescents the package of nutritional services available under the ICDS programme.

Comment: Improvement in health status of adolescent girls has an inter-generational impact. It reduces the risk of low birth weight and minimizes neo-natal mortality. Malnutrition is a problem that seriously impairs the health of adolescent and adult women and has its roots in early childhood. The causal linkages between anemia and low birth weight, prematurity, pre-natal mortality, and maternal mortality has been extensively studied and established.

3. Enforce the Child Marriage Restraint Act, 1976, to reduce the incidence of teenage pregnancies. Preventing the marriage. of girls below the legally permissible age of 18 should become a national concern.

Comment: It will promote higher retention of girls at schools, and is also likely to encourage their participation in the paid work force.

4. Provide integrated intervention in pockets with unrnet needs in the urban slums, remote rural areas, border districts and among tribal populations.

(d) Increased Participation of Men in Planned Parenthood

1. Focus attention on men in the information and education campaigns to promote the small family norm, and to raise awareness by emphasising the significant benefits of fewer children, better spacing, better heath and nutrition, and better education.

2. Currently, over 97 per cent of the sterilisations are tubectomies. Repopularise vasectomies, in particular the no-scalpel vasectomy, as a safe, simple, painless procedure, more convenient and acceptable to men.

3. In the continuing education and training at all levels, there is need to ensure that the no-scalpel vasectomy, and all such emerging techniques and skills are included in the syllabi, together with abundant practical training. Medical graduates, and all those participating in "in-service" continuing education and training, will be equipped to handle this intervention.

(vii) Diverse Health Care Providers

1. At district and sub-district levels, maintain block-wise data base of private medical practitioners whose credentials may be certified by the Indian Medical Association (IMA). Explore the possibility of accrediting these private practitioners for a year at a time, and assign to each a satellite population, not exceeding 5,000 (depending upon distances and spread), for whom they may provide reproductive and child health services. The private practitioners would be compensated for the services rendered through designated agencies. Renewal of contracts after one year may be guided by client satisfaction. This will serve as an incentive to expand the coverage and outreach of high quality health care. Appropriate checks and balances will safeguard misuse.

2. Revive the earlier system of the licensed medical practitioners who, after appropriate certification from the IMA, may participate in the provision of clinical services.

3. Involve the non-medical fraternity in counselling and advocacy so as to demystify the national family welfare effort, such as retired defence personnel, retired school teachers and other persons who are active and willing to get involved.

4. Modify the under/post-graduate medical, nursing, and paramedical professional course syllabi and curricula, in consultation with the Medical Council of India, the Councils of ISMH, and the Indian Nursing Council, in order to reflect the concepts and implementation strategies of the reproductive and child health programme and the national population policy. This will also be applied to all in-service training and educational curricula.

5. Ensure the efficient functioning of the First Referral Units, i.e. 30 bed hospitals at block levels which provide emergency obstetric and child health care, to bring about reductions in Maternal Mortality Ratio (MMR) and Infant Mortality Rate (IMR). In many states, these FRUs are not operational on account of an acute shortage of specialists, i.e. gynaecologist obstetrician, anaesthetist and pediatrician. Augment the availability of specialists in these three disciplines, by increasing seats in medical institutions, and simultaneously enable and facilitate the acquisition of in-service post-graduate qualifications through the National Board of Medical Examination and open universities like IGNOU in larger numbers. As an incentive, seats will be reserved for those in- service medical graduates who are willing to abide by a bond to serve for 5 years at First Referral Units after completion of the course. States would need to sanction posts of Specialists at the FRUs. Further, these specialists should be provided with clear promotion channels.

(viii) *(a) Collaboration with and Commitments from the Non-Government Sector*

1. There remain innumerable hurdles that inhibit genuine long-term collaboration between the government and non-government sectors. A forum of representatives from government, the non-government organisations and the private sector may identify these hurdles and prepare guidelines that will facilitate and promote collaborative arrangements.

2. Collaboration with and commitments from NGOs to augment advocacy, counselling and clinical services, while accessing village levels. This will require increased clinic outlets as well as mobile clinics.

3. Collaboration between the voluntary sector and the NGOs will facilitate dissemination of efficient service delivery to village levels. The guidelines could articulate the role and responsibility of each sector.

4. Encourage the voluntary sector to motivate village-level self-help groups to participate in community activities.

5. Specific collaboration with the non-government sector in the social marketing of contraceptives to reach village levels will be encouraged.

(viii) *(b) Collaboration with the Commitments from Industry*

1. The corporate sector and industry could, for instance, take on the challenge of strengthening the management information systems in the seven most deficient states, at primary health centre and sub-centre levels. Introduce electronic data entry machines to lighten the tedious work load of ANMs and the multi-purpose workers at sub-centres and the doctors at the primary health centres, while enabling wider coverage and outreach.

2. Collaborate with non-government sectors in running professionally sound advertisement and marketing campaigns for products and services, targeting all segments of the population, from village level upwards, in other words, strengthen advocacy and IEC, including social marketing of contraceptives.

3. Provide markets to sustain the income-generating activities from village levels upwards. In turn, this will ensure consistent motivation among the community for pursuing health and education-related commonality activities.

4. Help promote transportation to remote and inaccessible areas up to village levels. This will greatly assist the coverage and outreach of social marketing of products and services.

5. The social responsibility of the corporate sector in industry must, at the very minimum, extend to providing preventive reproductive and child health care for its own employees 100 workers are engaged.

6. Create a national network consisting of voluntary, public, private and non-government health centres, identified by a common logo, for delivering reproductive and child health services, free to any client. The provider will be compensated for the service provided, on the basis of a coupon system duly counter-signed by the beneficiary and paid for by a system that will be fully articulated. The compensation will be identical to providers, across all sectors. The end user exercises choices in the source of service delivery. A committee of management experts will be set-up to devise ways of ensuring that this system is not abused.

7. Form a consortium of the voluntary sector, the non-government sector and the private corporate sector to aid government in the provision and outreach of basic reproductive and child health care and basic education.

8. In the area of basic education, set-up privately run/managed primary schools for children up to age 14-15. Alternately, if the schools are set-up/managed by the panchayat, the private corporate sector could provide the mid-day meals, the text-books and/or the uniforms.

(ix) Mainstreaming Indian Systems of Medicine and Homeopathy

I. Provide appropriate training and orientation in respect of the RCH programme for the institutionally qualified ISMH medical practitioners (already educated in midwifery, obstetrics and gynaecology over 5-1/2 years), and utilise their services to fill in gaps in manpower at appropriate levels in the health infrastructure, and at sub-centres and primary health centres, as necessary.

2. Utilise the ISMH institutions, dispensaries and hospitals for health and population-related programmes.

3. Disseminate the tried and tested concepts and practices of the indigenous systems of medicine, together with ISMH medication at village maternity huts and at household levels for ante-natal and post-natal care, besides nurture of the newborn.

4. Utilise the services of ISMH 'barefoot doctors' after appropriate training and orientation towards providing advocacy and counselling for disseminating supplies and equipment, and as depot-holders at village levels.

(x) Contraceptive Technology and Research on RCH

1. Government will encourage, support and advance the pursuit of medical and social science research on reproductive and child health, in consultation with ICMR and the network of academic and research institutions.

2. The international Institute of Population Sciences and the Population Research Centres will continue to review programme and monitoring indicators to ensure their continued relevance to strategic goals.

3. Government will restructure the Population Research Centres, if necessary.

4. Standards for clinical and non-clinical interventions will be issued and regularly reviewed.

5. A constant review and evaluation of the community needs assessment approach will be pursued to align programme delivery with good management practices and with newly emerging technologies.

6. A committee of international and Indian experts, voluntary and non-government organisations and government may be set-up to regularly review and recommend specific incorporation of the advances in contraceptive technology and, in particular, the newly emerging techniques, into programme development.

(xi) Providing for the Older Population

1. Sensitize, train and equip rural and urban health centres and hospitals towards providing geriatric health care.

2. Encourage NGOs and voluntary organisations to formulate and strengthen a series of formal and informal avenues that make the elderly economically self-reliant.

3. Tax benefits could be explored as an encouragement for children to look after their aged parents.

(xii) Information Education and Communication

1. Converge IEC efforts across the social sectors. The two sectors of Family Welfare and Education have coordinated a mutually supportive IEC strategy. The Zila Saksharta Samitis design and deliver joint IEC campaigns in the local idiom, promoting the cause of literacy as well as family welfare. Optimal use of folk media has served to successfully mobilize local populations. The state of Tamil Nadu made exemplary use of the IEC strategy by spreading the message through every possible media, including public transport, on mile stones on national highways as well as through advertisement and hoardings on roadsides, along city/rural roads, on billboards, and through processions, films, school dramas, public meetings, local theatre and folk songs.

2. Involve departments of rural development, social welfare, transport, cooperatives, education with special reference to schools, to improve clarity and focus of the IEC effort, and to extend coverage and outreach. Health and population education must be inculcated from the school levels.

3. Fund the nagarpalikas, panchayats, NGOs and community organisations for interactive and participatory IEC activities.

4. Demonstration of support by elected leaders, opinion-makers, and religious leaders with close involvement in the reproductive and child health programme greatly influences the behaviour and response patterns of individuals and communities. This serves to enthuse communities to be attentive towards the quality and coverage of maternal and child health services, including referral care. Public leaders and film stars could spread widely the messages of the small family norm, female literacy, delayed marriages for women, fewer babies, healthier babies, child immunization and so on. The involvement and enthusiastic participation of elected leaders will ensure dedicated involvement of administrators at district and sub-district levels. Demonstration of strong support to the small family norm, as well as personal example, by political, community, business, professional, and religious leaders, media and film stars, sports personalities and opinion-makers, will enhance its acceptance throughout society.

5. Utilise radio and television as the most powerful media for disseminating relevant socio-demographic messages. Government could explore the feasibility of appropriate regulations, and even legislation, if necessary, to mandate the broadcast of social messages during prime time.

6. Utilise dairy cooperatives, the public distribution systems, other established networks like the LIC at district and sub-district levels for IEC and for distribution of contraceptives and basic medicines to target infant/ childhood diarrhoeas, anaemia and malnutrition among adolescent girls and pregnant mothers. This will widen outreach and coverage.

7. Sensitise the field level functionaries across diverse sectors (education, rural development, forest and environment, women and child development, drinking water mission, cooperatives) to the strategies, goals and objectives of the population stabilisation programmes.

8. Involve civil society for disseminating information, counselling and spreading education about the small family norm, the need for fewer but healthier babies, higher female literacy and later marriages for women. Civil society could also be of assistance in monitoring the availability of contraceptives, vaccines and drugs in rural areas and in urban slums.

Appendix III

NATIONAL HEALTH POLICY, 2002

1. INTRODUCTORY

1.1 A National Health Policy was last formulated in 1983, and since then there have been marked changes in the determinant factors relating to the health sector. Some of the policy initiatives outlined in the NHP-1983 have yielded results, while, in several other areas, the outcome has not been as expected.

1.2 The NHP-1983 gave a general exposition of the policies which required recommendation in the circumstances then prevailing in the health sector. The noteworthy initiatives under that policy were:

(i) A phased, time-bound programme for setting up a well-dispersed network of comprehensive primary health care services, linked with extension and health education, designed in the context of the ground reality that elementary health problems can be resolved by the people themselves;

(ii) Intermediation through 'Health volunteers' having appropriate knowledge, simple skills and requisite technologies;

(iii) Establishment of a well-worked out referral system to ensure that patient load at the higher levels of the hierarchy is not needlessly burdened by those who can be treated at the decentralized level; and

(iv) An integrated net-work of evenly spread speciality and super-speciality services; encouragement of such facilities through private investments for patients who can pay, so that the draw on the Government's facilities is limited to those entitled to free use.

1.3 Government initiatives in the pubic health sector have recorded some noteworthy successes over time. Smallpox and Guinea Worm Disease have been eradicated from the country; Polio is on the verge of being eradicated; Leprosy, Kala Azar, and Filariasis can be expected to be eliminated in the foreseeable future. There has been a substantial drop in the Total Fertility Rate and Infant Mortality Rate. The success of the initiatives taken in the public health field are reflected in the progressive improvement of many demographic/epidemiological/infrastructural indicators over time (Box-I).

Box I

Achievements through the Years: 1951-2000

Indicator	*1951*	*1981*	*2000*
Demographic Changes			
Life Expectancy	36.7	54	64.6(RGI)
Crude Birth Rate	40.8	33.9(SRS)	26.1(99 SRS)
Crude Death Rate	25	12.5(SRS)	8.7(99 SRS)
IMR	146	110	70 (99 SRS)
Epidemiological Shifts			
Malaria (cases in million)	75	2.7	2.2
Leprosy cases per 10,000 population	38.1	57.3	3.74
Small Pox (no of cases)	>44,887	Eradicated	
Guineaworm (no. of cases)		>39,792	Eradicated
Polio		29709	265
Infrastructure			
SC/PHC/CHC	725	57,363	1,63,181 (99-RHS)
Dispensaries and Hospitals (all)	9209	23,555	43,322 (95-96-CBHI)
Beds (Pvt. and Public)	117,198	569,495	8,70,161 (95-96-CBHI)
Doctors (Allopathy)	61,800	2,68,700	5,03,900 (98-99-MCI)
Nursing Personnel	18,054	1,43,887	7,37,000 (99-INC)

1.4 While noting that the public health initiatives over the years have contributed significantly to the improvement of these health indicators, it is to be acknowledged that public health indicators/disease-burden statistics are the outcome of several complementary initiatives under the wider umbrella of the developmental sector, covering Rural Development, Agriculture, Food Production, Sanitation, Drinking Water Supply, Education, etc. Despite the impressive public health gains as revealed in the statistics in Box-I, there is no gainsaying the fact that the morbidity and mortality levels in the country are still unacceptably high. These unsatisfactory health indices are, in turn, an indication of the limited success of the public health system in meeting the preventive and curative requirements of the general population.

1.5 Out of the communicable diseases which have persisted over time, the incidence of Malaria staged a resurgence in the 1980s before stabilising at a fairly high prevalence level during the 1990s. Over the years, an increasing level of insecticide-resistance has developed in the malarial vectors in many parts of the country, while the incidence of the more deadly P-Falciparum Malaria has risen to about 50 percent in the country as a whole. In respect of TB, the public health scenario has not shown any significant decline in the pool of infection amongst the community, and there has been a distressing trend in the increase of drug resistance to the type of infection prevailing in the country. A new and extremely virulent communicable disease—HIV/AIDS—has emerged on the health scene since the declaration of the NHP-1983. As there is no existing therapeutic cure or vaccine for this infection, the disease constitutes a serious threat, not merely to public health but to economic development in the country. The common water-borne infections—Gastroenteritis, Cholera, and some forms of Hepatitis—continue to contribute to a high level of morbidity in the population, even though the mortality rate may have been somewhat moderated.

1.6 The period after the announcement of NHP-83 has also seen an increase in mortality through 'life-style' diseases—diabetes, cancer and cardiovascular diseases. The increase in life expectancy has increased the requirement for geriatric care. Similarly, the increasing burden of trauma cases is also a significant public health problem.

1.7 Another area of grave concern in the public health domain is the persistent incidence of macro and micro-nutrient deficiencies, especially among women and children. In the vulnerable sub-category of women and the girl child, this has the multiplier effect through the birth of low birth weight babies and serious ramifications of the consequential mental and physical retarded growth.

1.8 NHP-1983, in a spirit of optimistic empathy for the health needs of the people, particularly the poor and under-privileged, had hoped to provide 'Health for All by the year 2000 AD', through the universal provision of comprehensive primary health care services. In retrospect, it is observed that the financial resources and public health administrative capacity which it was possible to marshal, was far short of that necessary to achieve such an ambitious and holistic goal. Against this backdrop, it is felt that it would be appropriate to pitch NHP-2002 at a level consistent with our realistic expectations about financial resources, and about the likely increase in Public Health Administrative capacity. The recommendations of NHP-2002 will, therefore, attempt to maximize the broad-based availability of health services to the citizenry of the country on the basis of realistic considerations of capacity. The changed circumstances relating to the health sector of the country since 1983 have generated a situation in which it is now necessary to review the field, and to formulate a new policy framework as the National Health Policy-2002. NHP-2002 will attempt to set out a new policy framework for the accelerated achievement of Public health goals in the socio-economic circumstances currently prevailing in the country.

2. CURRENT SCENARIO

2.1 Financial Resources

2.1.1 The public health investment in the country over the years has been comparatively low, and as a percentage of GDP has declined from 1.3 percent in 1990 to 0.9 percent in 1999. The aggregate expenditure in the Health sector is 5.2 percent of the GDP. Out of this, about 17 percent of the aggregate expenditure is public health spending, the balance being out-of-pocket expenditure. The central budgetary allocation for health over this period, as a percentage of the total Central Budget, has been stagnant at 1.3 percent, while that in the States has declined from 7.0 percent to 5.5 percent. The current annual per capita public health expenditure in the country is no more than Rs. 200. Given these statistics, it is no surprise that the reach and quality of public health services has been below the desirable standard. Under the constitutional structure, public health is the responsibility of the States. In this framework, it has been the expectation that the principal contribution for the funding of public health services will be from the resources of the States, with some supplementary input from Central resources. In this backdrop, the contribution of Central resources to the overall public health funding has been limited to about 15 percent. The fiscal resources of the State Governments are known to be very inelastic. This is reflected in the declining percentage of State resources allocated to the health sector out of the State Budget. If the decentralized public health services in the country are to improve significantly, there is a need for the injection of substantial resources into the health sector from the Central Government Budget. This approach is a necessity—despite the formal Constitutional provision in regard to public health,—if the State public health services, which are a major component of the initiatives in the social sector, are not to become entirely moribund. The NHP-2002 has been formulated taking into consideration these ground realities in regard to the availability of resources.

2.2 Equity

2.2.1 In the period when centralized planning was accepted as a key instrument of development in the country, the attainment of an equitable regional distribution was considered one of its major objectives. Despite this conscious focus in the development process, the statistics given in Box-II clearly indicate that the attainment of health indices has been very uneven across the rural-urban divide.

Also, the statistics bring out the wide differences between the attainments of health goals in the better-performing States as compared to the low-performing States. It is clear that national averages of health indices hide wide disparities in public health facilities and health standards in

Box II

Differentials in Health Status Among States

Sector	*Population BPL (%)*	*IMR/ Per 1000 Live Births (1999-SRS)*	*<5 Mortality per 1000 (NFHS II)*	*Weight For Age-% of Children Under 3 years (<-2SD)*	*MMR/ Lakh (Annual Report 2000)*	*Leprosy cases per 10000 population*	*Malaria +ve Cases in year 2000 (in thousands)*
India	26.1	70	94.9	47	408	3.7	2200
Rural	27.09	75	103.7	49.6	-	-	-
Urban	23.62	44	63.1	38.4	-	-	-
Better Performing States							
Kerala	12.72	14	18.8	27	87	0.9	5.1
Maharashtra	25.02	48	58.1	50	135	3.1	138
TN	21.12	52	63.3	37	79	4.1	56
Low Performing States							
Orissa	47.15	97	104.4	54	498	7.05	483
Bihar	42.60	63	105.1	54	707	11.83	132
Rajasthan	15.28	81	114.9	51	607	0.8	53
UP	31.15	84	122.5	52	707	4.3	99
MP	37.43	90	137.6	55	498	3.83	528

different parts of the country. Given a situation in which national averages in respect of most indices are themselves at unacceptably low levels, the wide inter-State disparity implies that, for vulnerable sections of society in several States, access to public health services is nominal and health standards are grossly inadequate. Despite a thrust in the NHP-1983 for making good the unmet needs of public health services by establishing more public health institutions at a decentralized level, a large gap in facilities still persists. Applying current norms to the population projected for the year 2000, it is estimated that the shortfall in the number of SCs/ PHCs/CHCs is of the order of 16 percent. However, this shortage is as high as 58 percent when disaggregated for CHCs only. The NHP-2002 will need to address itself to making good these deficiencies so as to narrow the gap between the various States, as also the gap across the rural-urban divide.

2.2.2 Access to, and benefits from, the public health system have been very uneven between the better-endowed and the more vulnerable sections of society. This is particularly true for women, children and the socially disadvantaged sections of society. The statistics given in Box-III highlight the handicap suffered in the health sector on account of socio-economic inequity.

2.2.3 It is a principal objective of NHP-2002 to evolve a policy structure which reduces these inequities and allows the disadvantaged sections of society a fairer access to public health services.

Box III

Differentials in Health Status Among Socio-Economic Groups

Indicator	*Infant Mortality/ 1000*	*Under 5 Mortality/ 1000*	*% Children Underweight*
India	70	94.9	47
Social Inequity	—	—	—
Scheduled Castes	83	119.3	53.5
Scheduled Tribes	84.2	126.6	55.9
Other Disadvantaged	76	103.1	47.3
Others	61.8	82.6	41.1

2.3 Delivery of National Public Health

Programmes

2.3.1 It is self-evident that in a country as large as India, which has a wide variety of socio-economic settings, national health programmes have to be designed with enough flexibility to permit the State public health administrations to craft their own programme package according to their needs. Also, the implementation of the national health programme can only be carried out through the State Governments' decentralized public health machinery. Since, for various reasons, the responsibility of the Central Government in funding additional public health services will continue over a period of time, the role of the Central Government in designing broad-based public health initiatives will inevitably continue. Moreover, it has been observed that the technical and managerial expertise for designing large-span public health programmes exists with the Central Government in a considerable degree; this expertise can be gainfully utilized in designing national health programmes for implementation in varying socio-economic settings in the States. With this background, the NHP-2002 attempts to define the role of the Central Government and the State Governments in the public health sector of the country.

2.3.2.1 Over the last decade or so, the Government has relied upon a 'vertical' implementational structure for the major disease control programmes. Through this, the system has been able to make a substantial dent in reducing the burden of specific diseases. However, such an organisational structure, which requires independent manpower for each disease programme, is extremely expensive and difficult to sustain. Over a long time-range, 'vertical' structures may only be affordable for those diseases which offer a reasonable possibility of elimination or eradication in a foreseeable time-span.

2.3.2.2 It is a widespread perception that, over the last decade and a half, the rural health staff has become a vertical structure exclusively for the implementation of family welfare activities. As a result, for those public health programmes where there is no separate vertical structure, there is no identifiable service delivery system at all. The Policy will address this distortion in the public health system.

2.4 The State of Public Health Infra-Structure

2.4.1 The delineation of NHP-2002 would be required to be based on an objective assessment of the quality and efficiency of the existing public health machinery in the field. It would detract from the quality of the exercise if, while framing a new policy, it were not acknowledged that the existing public health infrastructure is far from satisfactory. For the outdoor medical facilities in existence, funding is generally insufficient; the presence of medical and para-medical personnel is often much less than that required by prescribed norms; the availability of consumables is frequently negligible; the equipment in many public hospitals is often obsolescent and unusable; and, the buildings are in a dilapidated state. In the indoor treatment facilities, again, the equipment is often obsolescent; the availability of essential drugs is minimal; the capacity of the facilities is grossly inadequate, which leads to over-crowding, and consequentially to a steep deterioration in the quality of the services. As a result of such inadequate public health facilities, it has been estimated that less than 20 percent of the population, which seek OPD services, and less than 45 percent of that which seek indoor treatment, avail of such services in public hospitals. This is despite the fact that most of these patients do not have the means to make out-of-pocket payments for private health services except at the cost of other essential expenditure for items such as basic nutrition.

2.5 Extending Public Health Services

2.5.1 While there is a general shortage of medical personnel in the country, this shortfall is disproportionately impacted on the less-developed and rural areas. No incentive system attempted so far, has induced private medical personnel to go to such areas; and, even in the public health sector, the effort to deploy medical personnel in such under-served areas, has usually been a losing battle. In such a situation, the possibility needs to be examined of entrusting some limited public health functions to nurses, paramedics and other personnel from the extended health sector after imparting adequate training to them.

2.5.2 India has a vast reservoir of practitioners in the Indian Systems of Medicine and Homeopathy, who have undergone formal training in their own disciplines. The possibility of using such practitioners in the implementation of State/Central Government public health programmes, in order to increase the reach of basic health care in the country, is addressed in the NHP-2002.

2.6 Role of Local Self-Government Institutions

2.6.1 Some States have adopted a policy of devolving programmes and funds in the health sector through different levels of the Panchayati Raj Institutions. Generally, the experience has been an encouraging one. The adoption of such an organisational structure has enabled need-based allocation of resources and closer supervision through the elected representatives. The Policy examines the need for a wider adoption of this mode of delivery of health services, in rural as well as urban areas, in other parts of the country.

2.7 Norms for Health Care Personnel

2.7.1 It is observed that the deployment of doctors and nurses, in both public and private institutions, is ad-hoc and significantly short of the requirement for minimal standards of patient care. This policy will make a specific recommendation in regard to this deficiency.

2.8 Education of Health Care Professionals

2.8.1 Medical and Dental Colleges are not evenly spread across various parts of the country. Apart from the uneven geographical distribution of medical institutions, the quality of education is highly uneven and in several instances even sub-standard. It is a common perception that the syllabus is excessively theoretical, making it difficult for the fresh graduate to effectively meet even the primary health care needs of the population. There is a general reluctance on the part of graduate doctors to serve in areas distant from their native place. NHP-2002 will suggest policy initiatives to rectify the resultant disparities.

2.8.2.1 Certain medical disciplines, such as molecular biology and gene-manipulation, have become relevant in the period after the formulation of the previous National Health Policy. The components of medical research in recent years have changed radically. In the foreseeable future such research will rely increasingly on the new disciplines. It is observed that the current under-graduate medical syllabus does not cover such emerging subjects. The Policy will make appropriate recommendations in respect of such deficiencies.

2.8.2.2 Also, certain speciality disciplines—Anesthesiology, Radiology and Forensic Medicine—are currently very scarce, resulting in critical deficiencies in the package of available public health services. This Policy will recommend some measures to alleviate such critical shortages.

2.9 Need For Specialists in 'Public Health' and 'Family Medicine'

2.9.1 In any developing country with inadequate availability of health services, the requirement of expertise in the areas of 'public health' and 'family medicine' is markedly more than the expertise required for other clinical specialities. In India, the situation is that public health expertise is non-existent in the private health sector, and far short of requirement in the public health sector. Also, the current curriculum in the graduate/post-graduate courses is outdated and unrelated to contemporary community needs. In respect of 'family medicine', it needs to be noted that the more talented medical graduates generally seek specialization in clinical disciplines, while the remaining go into general practice. While the availability of post-graduate educational facilities is 50 percent of the total number of qualifying graduates each year, and can be considered adequate, the distribution of the disciplines in the post-graduate training facilities is overwhelmingly in favour of clinical specializations. NHP-2002 examines the possible means for ensuring adequate availability of personnel with specialization in the 'public health' and 'family medicine' disciplines, to discharge the public health responsibilities in the country.

2.10 Nursing Personnel

2.10.1 The ratio of nursing personnel in the country *vis-à-vis* doctors/ beds is very low according to professionally accepted norms. There is also an acute shortage of nurses trained in super-speciality disciplines for deployment in tertiary care facilities. NHP-2002 addresses these problems.

2.11 Use of Generic Drugs and Vaccines

2.11.1 India enjoys a relatively low-cost health care system because of the widespread availability of indigenously manufactured generic drugs and vaccines. There is an apprehension that globalization will lead to an increase in the costs of drugs, thereby leading to rising trends in overall health costs. This Policy recommends measures to ensure the future Health Security of the country.

2.12 Urban Health

2.12.1.1 In most urban areas, public health services are very meagre. To the extent that such services exist, there is no uniform organisational structure. The urban population in the country is presently as high as 30 percent and is likely to go up to around 33 percent by 2010. The bulk of the increase is likely to take place through migration, resulting in slums without any infrastructure support. Even the meagre public health services which are available do not percolate to such unplanned habitations, forcing people to avail of private health care through out-of-pocket expenditure.

2.12.1.2 The rising vehicle density in large urban agglomerations has also led to an increased number of serious accidents requiring treatment in well-equipped trauma centres. NHP-2002 will address itself to the need for providing this unserved urban population a minimum standard of broad-based health care facilities.

2.13 Mental Health

2.13.1 Mental health disorders are actually much more prevalent than is apparent on the surface. While such disorders do not contribute significantly to mortality, they have a serious bearing on the quality of life of the affected persons and their families. Sometimes, based on religious faith, mental disorders are treated as spiritual affliction. This has led to the establishment of unlicensed mental institutions as an adjunct to religious institutions where reliance is placed on faith cure. Serious conditions of mental disorder require hospitalization and treatment under trained supervision. Mental health institutions are woefully deficient in physical infrastructure and trained manpower. NHP-2002 will address itself to these deficiencies in the public health sector.

2.14 Information, Education and Communication

2.14.1 A substantial component of primary health care consists of initiatives for disseminating to the citizenry, public health-related information. IEC initiatives are adopted not only for disseminating curative guidelines (for the TB, Malaria, Leprosy, Cataract Blindness Programmes), but also as part of the effort to bring about a behavioural change to prevent HIV/AIDS and other life-style diseases. Public health programmes, particularly, need high visibility at the decentralized level in order to have an impact. This task is difficult as 35 percent of our country's population is illiterate. The present IEC strategy is too fragmented, relies too heavily on the mass media and does not address the needs of this segment of the population. It is often felt that the effectiveness of IEC programmes is difficult to judge; and consequently it is often asserted that accountability, in regard to the productive use of such funds, is doubtful. The Policy, while projecting an IEC strategy, will fully address the inherent problems encountered in any IEC programme designed for improving awareness and bringing about a behavioural change in the general population.

2.14.2 It is widely accepted that school and college students are the most impressionable targets for imparting information relating to the basic principles of preventive health care. The policy will attempt to target this group to improve the general level of awareness in regard to 'health-promoting' behaviour.

2.15 Health Research

2.15.1 Over the years, health research activity in the country has been very limited. In the Government sector, such research has been confined to the research institutions under the Indian Council of Medical Research, and other institutions funded by the States/Central Government. Research in the private sector has assumed some significance only in the last decade. In our country, where the aggregate annual health expenditure is of the order of Rs. 80,000 crores, the expenditure in 1998-99 on research, both public and private sectors, was only of the order of Rs. 1150 crores. It would be reasonable to infer that with such low research expenditure, it is virtually impossible to make any dramatic break-through within the country, by way of new molecules and vaccines; also, without a minimal back-up of applied and operational research, it would be difficult to assess whether the health expenditure in the country is being incurred through optimal applications and appropriate public health strategies. Medical Research in the country needs to be focused on therapeutic drugs/vaccines for tropical diseases, which are normally neglected by international pharmaceutical companies on account of their limited profitability potential. The thrust will need to be in the newly-emerging frontier areas of research based on genetics, genome-based drug and vaccine development, molecular biology, etc. NHP-2002 will address these inadequacies and spell out a minimal quantum of expenditure for the coming decade, looking to the national needs and the capacity of the research institutions to absorb the funds.

2.16 Role of the Private Sector

2.16.1 Considering the economic restructuring under way in the country, and over the globe, in the last decade, the changing role of the private sector in providing health care will also have to be addressed in this Policy. Currently, the contribution of private health care is principally through independent practitioners. Also, the private sector contributes significantly to secondary-level care and some tertiary care. It is a widespread perception that private health services are very uneven in quality, sometimes even sub-standard. Private health services are also perceived to be financially exploitative, and the observance of professional ethics is noted only as an exception. With the increasing role of private health care, the implementation of statutory regulation, and the monitoring of minimum standards of diagnostic centres/medical institutions becomes imperative. The Policy will address the issues regarding the establishment of a comprehensive information system, and based on that the establishment of a regulatory mechanism to ensure the maintaining of adequate standards by diagnostic centres/medical institutions, as well as the proper conduct of clinical practice and delivery of medical services.

2.16.2 Currently, non-Governmental service providers are treating a large number of patients at the primary level for major diseases. However, the treatment regimens followed are diverse and not scientifically optimal, leading to an increase in the incidence of drug resistance. This policy will address itself to recommending arrangements which will eliminate the risks arising from inappropriate treatment.

2.16.3 The increasing spread of information technology raises the possibility of its adoption in the health sector. NHP-2002 will examine this possibility.

2.17 The Role of Civil Society

2.17.1 Historically, it has been the practice to implement major national disease control programmes through the public health machinery of the State/Central Governments. It has become increasingly apparent that certain components of such programmes cannot be efficiently implemented merely through government functionaries. A considerable change in the mode of implementation has come about in the last two decades, with the increasing involvement of NGOs and other institutions of civil society. It is to be recognized that widespread debate on various public health issues has, in fact, been initiated and sustained by NGOs and other members of the civil society. Also, an increasing contribution is being made by such institutions in the delivery of different components of public health services. Certain disease control programmes require close inter-action with the beneficiaries for regular administration of drugs; periodic carrying out of pathological tests; dissemination of information regarding disease control and other general health information. NHP-2002 will address such issues and suggest policy instruments for the implementation of public health programmes through individuals and institutions of civil society.

2.18 National Disease Surveillance Network

2.18.1 The technical network available in the country for disease surveillance is extremely rudimentary and to the extent that the system exists, it extends only up to the district level. Disease statistics are not flowing through an integrated network from the decentralized public health facilities to the State/Central Government health administration. Such an arrangement only provides belated information, which, at best, serves a limited statistical purpose. The absence of an efficient disease surveillance network is a major handicap in providing a prompt and cost-effective health care system. The efficient disease surveillance network set-up for Polio and HIV/AIDS has demonstrated the enormous value of such a public health instrument. Real-time information on focal outbreaks of common communicable diseases—Malaria, GE, Cholera and JE—and the seasonal trends of diseases, would enable timely intervention, resulting in the containment of the thrust of epidemics. In order to be able to use an integrated disease surveillance network for operational purposes, real-time information is necessary at all levels of the health administration. The Policy would address itself to this major systemic shortcoming in the administration.

2.19 Health Statistics

2.19.1 The absence of a systematic and scientific health statistics data-base is a major deficiency in the current scenario. The health statistics collected are not the product of a rigorous methodology. Statistics available from different parts of the country, in respect of major diseases, are often not obtained in a manner which make aggregation possible or meaningful.

2.19.2.1 Further, the absence of proper and systematic documentation of the various financial resources used in the health sector is another lacuna in the existing health information scenario. This makes it difficult to understand trends and levels of health spending by private and public providers of health care in the country, and, consequently, to address related policy issues and to formulate future investment policies.

2.19.2.2 NHP-2002 will address itself to the programme for putting in place a modern and scientific health statistics database as well as a system of national health accounts.

2.20 Women's Health

2.20.1 Social, cultural and economic factors continue to inhibit women from gaining adequate access even to the existing public health facilities. This handicap does not merely affect women as individuals; it also has an adverse impact on the health, general well-being and development of the entire family, particularly children. This policy recognises the catalytic role of empowered women in improving the overall health standards of the community.

2.21 Medical Ethics

2.21.1 Professional medical ethics in the health sector is an area which has not received much attention. Professional practices are perceived to be grossly commercial and the medical profession has lost its elevated position as a provider of basic services to fellow human beings. In the past, medical research has been conducted within the ethical guidelines notified by the Indian Council of Medical Research. The first document containing these guidelines was released in 1960, and was comprehensively revised in 2001. With the rapid developments in the approach to medical research, a periodic revision will no doubt be more frequently required in future. Also, the new frontier areas of research—involving gene manipulation, organ/ human cloning and stem cell research—impinge on visceral issues relating to the sanctity of human life and the moral dilemma of human intervention in the designing of life forms. Besides this, in the emerging areas of research, there is the uncharted risk of creating new life forms, which may irreversibly damage the environment as it exists today. NHP-2002 recognises that this moral and religious dilemma, which was not relevant even two years ago, now pervades mainstream health sector issues.

2.22 Enforcement of Quality Standards for Food and Drugs

2.22.1 There is an increasing expectation and need of the citizenry for efficient enforcement of reasonable quality standards for food and drugs. Recognizing this, the Policy will make an appropriate policy recommendation on this issue.

2.23 Regulation of Standards in Para Medical Disciplines

2.23.1 It has been observed that a large number of training institutions have mushroomed, particularly in the private sector, for para medical personnel with various skills—Lab Technicians, Radio Diagnosis Technicians, Physiotherapists, etc. Currently, there is no regulation/ monitoring, either of the curriculae of these institutions, or of the performance of the practitioners in these disciplines. This Policy will make recommendations to ensure the standardization of such training and the monitoring of actual performance.

2.24 Environmental and Occupational Health

2.24.1 The ambient environmental conditions are a significant determinant of the health risks to which a community is exposed. Unsafe drinking water, unhygienic sanitation and air pollution significantly contribute to the burden of disease, particularly in urban settings. The initiatives in respect of these environmental factors are conventionally undertaken by the participants, whether private or public, in the other development sectors. In this backdrop, the Policy initiatives, and the efficient implementation of the linked programmes in the health sector, would succeed only to the extent that they are complemented by appropriate policies and programmes in the other environment-related sectors.

2.24.2 Work conditions in several sectors of employment in the country are sub-standard. As a result, workers engaged in such employment become particularly vulnerable to occupation-linked ailments. The long-term risk of chronic morbidity is particularly marked in the case of child labour. NHP-2002 will address the risk faced by this particularly vulnerable section of society.

2.25 Providing Medical Facilities to Users from Overseas

2.25.1 The secondary and tertiary facilities available in the country are of good quality and cost-effective compared to international medical facilities. This is true not only of facilities in the allopathic disciplines, but also of those belonging to the alternative systems of medicine, particularly Ayurveda. The Policy will assess the possibilities of encouraging the development of paid treatment-packages for patients from overseas.

2.26 The Impact of Globalization on the Health Sector

2.26.1 There are some apprehensions about the possible adverse impact of economic globalisation on the health sector. Pharmaceutical drugs and other health services have always been available in the country at extremely inexpensive prices. India has established a reputation around the globe for the innovative development of original process patents for the manufacture of a wide-range of drugs and vaccines within the ambit of the existing patent laws. With the adoption of Trade Related Intellectual Property Rights (TRIPS), and the subsequent alignment of domestic patent laws consistent with the commitments under TRIPS, there will be a significant shift in the scope of the parameters regulating the manufacture of new drugs/vaccines. Global experience has shown that the introduction of a TRIPS-consistent patent regime for drugs in a developing country results in an across-the-board increase in the cost of drugs and medical services. NHP-2002 will address itself to the future imperatives of health security in the country, in the post-TRIPS era.

2.27 Inter-Sectoral Contribution to Health

2.27.1 It is well recognized that the overall well-being of the citizenry depends on the synergistic functioning of the various sectors in the socio-economy. The health status of the citizenry would, inter alia, be dependent on adequate nutrition, safe drinking water, basic sanitation, a clean environment and primary education, especially for the girl child. The policies and the mode of functioning in these independent areas would necessarily overlap each other to contribute to the health status of the community. From the policy perspective, it is therefore imperative that the independent policies of each of these inter-connected sectors, be in tandem, and that the interface between the policies of the two connected sectors, be smooth.

2.27.2 Sectoral policy documents are meant to serve as a guide to action for institutions and individual participants operating in that sector. Consistent with this role, NHP-2002 limits itself to making recommendations for the participants operating within the health sector. The policy aspects relating to inter-connected sectors, which, while crucial, fall outside the domain of the health sector, will not be covered by specific recommendations in this Policy document. Needless to say, the future attainment of the various goals set out in this policy assumes a reasonable complementary performance in these inter-connected sectors.

2.28 Population Growth and Health Standards

2.28.1 Efforts made over the years for improving health standards have been partially neutralized by the rapid growth of the population. It is well recognized that population stabilization measures and general health initiatives, when effectively synchronized, synergistically maximize the socio-economic well-being of the people. Government has separately announced the 'National Population Policy-2000'. The principal common features covered under the National Population Policy-2000 and NHP-2002, relate to the prevention and control of communicable diseases; giving priority to the containment of HIV/AIDS infection; the universal immunization of children against all major preventable diseases; addressing the unmet needs for basic and reproductive health services, and supplementation of infrastructure. The synchronized implementation of these two Policies—National Population Policy-2000 and National Health Policy-2002—will be the very cornerstone of any national structural plan to improve the health standards in the country.

2.29 Alternative Systems of Medicine

2.29.1 Under the overarching umbrella of the national health frame work, the alternative systems of medicine—Ayurveda, Unani, Siddha and Homeopathy—have a substantial role. Because of inherent advantages, such as diversity, modest cost, low level of technological input and the growing popularity of natural plant-based products, these systems are attractive, particularly in the underserved, remote and tribal areas. The alternative systems will draw upon the substantial untapped potential of India as one of the eight important global centers for plant diversity in medicinal and aromatic plants. The Policy focuses on building up credibility for the alternative systems, by encouraging evidence-based research to determine their efficacy, safety and dosage, and also encourages certification and quality-marking of products to enable a wider popular acceptance of these systems of medicine. The Policy also envisages the consolidation of documentary knowledge contained in these systems to protect it against attack from foreign commercial entities by way of malafide action under patent laws in other countries. The main components of NHP-2002 apply equally to the alternative systems of medicines. However, the Policy features specific to the alternative systems of medicine will be presented as a separate document.

3. OBJECTIVES

3.1 The main objective of this policy is to achieve an acceptable standard of good health amongst the general population of the country. The approach would be to increase access to the decentralized public health system by establishing new infrastructure in deficient areas, and by upgrading the infrastructure in the existing institutions. Overriding importance would be given to ensuring a more equitable access to health services across the social and geographical expanse of the country. Emphasis will be given to increasing the aggregate public health investment through a substantially increased contribution by the Central Government. It is expected that this initiative will strengthen the capacity of the public health administration at the State level to render effective service delivery. The contribution of the private sector in providing health services would be much enhanced, particularly for the population group which can afford to pay for services. Primacy will be given to preventive and first-line curative initiatives at the primary health level through increased sectoral share of allocation. Emphasis will be laid on rational use of drugs within the allopathic system. Increased access to tried and tested systems of traditional medicine will be ensured. Within these broad objectives, NHP-2002 will endeavour to achieve the time-bound goals mentioned in Box-IV.

4. NHP-2002—POLICY PRESCRIPTIONS

4.1 Financial Resources

4.1.1 The paucity of public health investment is a stark reality. Given the extremely difficult fiscal position of the State Governments, the Central Government will have to play a key role in augmenting public health investments. Taking into account the gap in health care facilities, it is planned, under the policy to increase health sector expenditure to 6 percent of GDP, with 2 percent of GDP being contributed as public health investment, by the year 2010. The State Governments would also need to increase the commitment to the health sector. In the first phase, by 2005, they would be expected to increase the commitment of their resources to 7 percent of the Budget; and, in the second phase, by 2010, to increase it to 8 percent of the Budget. With the stepping up of the public health

Box IV

Goals to be Achieved by 2000-2015

Goal	Year
Eradicate Polio and Yaws	2005
Eliminate Leprosy	2005
Eliminate Kala Azar	2010
Eliminate Lymphatic Filariasis	2015
Achieve Zero level growth of HIV/AIDS	2007
Reduce Mortality by 50% on account of TB, Malaria and Other Vector and Water Borne diseases	2010
Reduce Prevalence of Blindness to 0.5%	2010
Reduce IMR to 30/1000 and MMR to 100/Lakh	2010
Increase utilization of public health facilities from current level of <20 to >75%	2010
Establish an integrated system of surveillance, National Health Accounts and Health Statistics.	2005
Increase health expenditure by Government as a % of GDP from the existing 0.9% to 2.0%	2010
Increase share of Central grants to Constitute at least 25% of total health spending	2010
Increase State Sector Health spending from 5.5% to 7% of the budget	2005
Further increase to 8%	2010

investment, the Central Government's contribution would rise to 25 percent from the existing 15 percent by 2010. The provisioning of higher public health investments will also be contingent upon the increase in the absorptive capacity of the public health administration so as to utilize the funds gainfully.

4.2 Equity

4.2.1 To meet the objective of reducing various types of inequities and imbalances—inter-regional; across the rural-urban divide; and between economic classes—the most cost-effective method would be to increase the sectoral outlay in the primary health sector. Such outlets afford access to a vast number of individuals, and also facilitate preventive and early stage curative initiative, which are cost effective. In recognition of this public health principle, NHP-2002 sets out an increased allocation of 55 percent of the total public health investment for the primary health sector; the secondary and tertiary health sectors being targeted for 35 percent and 10 percent respectively. The Policy projects that the increased aggregate outlays for the primary health sector will be utilized for strengthening existing facilities and opening additional public health service outlets, consistent with the norms for such facilities.

4.3 Delivery of National Public Health Programmes

4.3.1.1 This policy envisages a key role for the Central Government in designing national programmes with the active participation of the State

Governments. Also, the Policy ensures the provisioning of financial resources, in addition to technical support, monitoring and evaluation at the national level by the Centre. However, to optimize the utilization of the public health infrastructure at the primary level, NHP-2002 envisages the gradual convergence of all health programmes under a single field administration. Vertical programmes for control of major diseases like TB, Malaria, HIV/AIDS, as also the RCH and Universal Immunization Programmes, would need to be continued till moderate levels of prevalence are reached. The integration of the programmes will bring about a desirable optimisation of outcomes through a convergence of all public health inputs. The Policy also envisages that programme implementation be effected through autonomous bodies at State and district levels. The interventions of State Health Departments may be limited to the overall monitoring of the achievement of programme targets and other technical aspects. The relative distancing of the programme implementation from the State Health Departments will give the project team greater operational flexibility. Also, the presence of State Government officials, social activists, private health professionals and MLAs/MPs on the management boards of the autonomous bodies will facilitate well-informed decision-making.

4.3.1.2 The Policy also highlights the need for developing the capacity within the State Public Health administration for scientific designing of public health projects, suited to the local situation.

4.3.2 The Policy envisages that apart from the exclusive staff in a vertical structure for the disease control programmes, all rural health staff should be available for the entire gamut of public health activities at the decentralized level, irrespective of whether these activities relate to national programmes or other public health initiatives. It would be for the Head of the District Health administration to allocate the time of the rural health staff between the various programmes, depending on the local need. NHP-2002 recognizes that to implement such a change, not only would the public health administrators be required to change their mindset, but the rural health staff would need to be trained and reoriented.

4.4 The State of Public Health Infrastructure

4.4.1.1 As has been highlighted in the earlier part of the Policy, the decentralized Public health service outlets have become practically dysfunctional over large parts of the country. On account of resource constraints, the supply of drugs by the State Governments is grossly inadequate. The patients at the decentralized level have little use for diagnostic services, which in any case would still require them to purchase therapeutic drugs privately. In a situation in which the patient is not getting any therapeutic drugs, there is little incentive for the potential beneficiaries to seek the advice of the medical professionals in the public health system. This results in there being no demand for medical services, so medical professionals and paramedics often absent themselves from their place of duty. It is also observed that the functioning of the public health service outlets in some States like the four Southern States—Kerala, Andhra Pradesh, Tamil Nadu and Karnataka—is relatively better, because some quantum of drugs is distributed through the primary health system network, and the patients have a stake in approaching the Public Health facilities. In this backdrop, the Policy envisages kick-starting the revival of the Primary Health System by providing some essential drugs under Central Government funding through the decentralized health system. It is expected that the provisioning of essential drugs at the public health service centres will create a demand for other professional services from the local population, which, in turn, will boost the general revival of activities in these service centres. In sum, this initiative under NHP-2002 is launched in the belief that the creation of a beneficiary interest in the public health system, will ensure a more effective supervision of the public health personnel through community monitoring, than has been achieved through the regular administrative line of control.

4.4.1.2 This Policy recognizes the need for more frequent in-service training of public health medical personnel, at the level of medical officers as well as paramedics. Such training would help to update the personnel on recent advancements in science, and would also equip them for their new assignments, when they are moved from one discipline of public health administration to another.

4.4.1.3 Global experience has shown that the quality of public health services, as reflected in the attainment of improved public health indices, is closely linked to the quantum and quality of investment through public funding in the primary health sector. Box-V gives statistics which clearly show that standards of health are more a function of the accurate targeting of expenditure on the decentralised primary sector (as observed in China and Sri Lanka), than a function of the aggregate health expenditure.

Box V

Public Health Spending in Select Countries

Indicator	*% Population with income of <$1 day*	*Infant Mortality Rate/1000*	*% Health Expenditure to GDP*	*% Public Expenditure on Health to Total Health Expenditure*
India	44.2	70	5.2	17.3
China	18.5	31	2.7	24.9
Sri Lanka	6.6	16	3	45.4
UK	—	6	5.8	96.9
USA	—	7	13.7	44.1

Therefore the Policy, while committing additional aggregate financial resources, places great reliance on the strengthening of the primary health structure for the attaining of improved public health outcomes on an equitable basis. Further, it also recognizes the practical need for levying reasonable user-charges for certain secondary and tertiary public health care services, for those who can afford to pay.

4.5 Extending Public Health Services

4.5.1.1 This policy envisages that, in the context of the availability and spread of allopathic graduates in their jurisdiction, State Governments would consider the need for expanding the pool of medical practitioners to include a cadre of licentiates of medical practice, as also practitioners of Indian Systems of Medicine and Homeopathy. Simple services/procedures can be provided by such practitioners even outside their disciplines, as part of the basic primary health services in under-served areas. Also, NHP-2002 envisages that the scope of the use of paramedical manpower of allopathic disciplines, in a prescribed functional area adjunct to their current functions, would also be examined for meeting simple public health requirements. This would be on the lines of the services rendered by nurse practitioners in several developed countries. These extended areas of functioning of different categories of medical manpower can be permitted, after adequate training, and subject to the monitoring of their performance through professional councils.

4.5.1.2 NHP-2002 also recognizes the need for States to simplify the recruitment procedures and rules for contract employment in order to provide trained medical manpower in under-served areas. State Governments could also rigorously enforce a mandatory two-year rural posting before the awarding of the graduate degree. This would not only make trained medical manpower available in the underserved areas, but would offer valuable clinical experience to the graduating doctors.

4.6 Role of Local Self-Government Institutions

4.6.1 NHP-2002 lays great emphasis upon the implementation of public health programmes through local self-government institutions. The structure of the national disease control programmes will have specific components for implementation through such entities. The Policy urges all State Governments to consider decentralizing the implementation of the programmes to such Institutions by 2005. In order to achieve this, financial incentives, over and above the resources normatively allocated for disease control programmes, will be provided by the Central Government.

4.7 Norms for Health Care Personnel

4.7.1 Minimal statutory norms for the deployment of doctors and nurses in medical institutions need to be introduced urgently under the provisions of the Indian Medical Council Act and Indian Nursing Council Act, respectively. These norms can be progressively reviewed and made more stringent as the medical institutions improve their capacity for meeting better normative standards.

4.8 Education of Health Care Professionals

4.8.1.1 In order to ameliorate the problems being faced on account of the uneven spread of medical and dental colleges in various parts of the country, this policy envisages the setting up of a Medical Grants Commission for funding new Government Medical and Dental Colleges in different parts of the country. Also, it is envisaged that the Medical Grants Commission will fund the upgradation of the infrastructure of the existing Government Medical and Dental Colleges of the country, so as to ensure an improved standard of medical education.

4.8.1.2 To enable fresh graduates to contribute effectively to the providing of primary health services as the physician of first contact, this policy identifies a significant need to modify the existing curriculum. A need-based, skill-oriented syllabus, with a more significant component of practical training, would make fresh doctors useful immediately after graduation. The Policy also recommends a periodic skill-updating of working health professionals through a system of continuing medical education.

4.8.2 The Policy emphasises the need to expose medical students, through the undergraduate syllabus, to the emerging concerns for geriatric disorders, as also to the cutting edge disciplines of contemporary medical research. The policy also envisages that the creation of additional seats for post-graduate courses should reflect the need for more manpower in the deficient specialities.

4.9 Need For Specialists in 'Public Health' And 'Family Medicine'

4.9.1 In order to alleviate the acute shortage of medical personnel with specialization in the disciplines of 'public health' and 'family medicine', the Policy envisages the progressive implementation of mandatory norms to raise the proportion of post-graduate seats in these discipline in medical training institutions, to reach a stage wherein ¼ th of the seats are earmarked for these disciplines. It is envisaged that in the sanctioning of post-graduate seats in future, it shall be insisted upon that a certain reasonable number of seats be allocated to 'public health' and 'family medicine'. Since the 'public health' discipline has an interface with many other developmental sectors, specialization in Public health may be encouraged not only for medical doctors, but also for non-medical graduates from the allied fields of public health engineering, microbiology and other natural sciences.

4.10 Nursing Personnel

4.10.1.1 In the interest of patient care, the policy emphasizes the need for an improvement in the ratio of nurses vis-à-vis doctors/beds. In order to discharge their responsibility as model providers of health services, the public health delivery centres need to make a beginning by increasing the number of nursing personnel. The Policy anticipates that with the increasing aspiration for improved health care amongst the citizens, private health facilities will also improve their ratio of nursing personnel *vis-à-vis* doctors/beds.

4.10.1.2 The Policy lays emphasis on improving the skill-level of nurses, and on increasing the ratio of degree-holding nurses *vis-à-vis* diploma-holding nurses. NHP-2002 recognizes a need for the Central Government to subsidize the setting up, and the running of, training facilities for nurses on a decentralized basis. Also, the Policy recognizes the need for establishing training courses for super-speciality nurses required for tertiary care institutions.

4.11 Use of Generic Drugs and Vaccines

4.11.1.1 This Policy emphasizes the need for basing treatment regimens, in both the public and private domain, on a limited number of essential drugs of a generic nature. This is a pre-requisite for cost-effective public health care. In the public health system, this would be enforced by prohibiting the use of proprietary drugs, except in special circumstances. The list of essential drugs would no doubt have to be reviewed periodically. To encourage the use of only essential drugs in the private sector, the imposition of fiscal disincentives would be resorted to. The production and sale of irrational combinations of drugs would be prohibited through the drug standards statute.

4.11.1.2 The National Programme for Universal Immunization against Preventable Diseases requires to be assured of an uninterrupted supply of vaccines at an affordable price. To minimize the danger arising from the volatility of the global market, and thereby to ensure long-term national health security, NHP-2002 envisages that not less than 50% of the requirement of vaccines/sera be sourced from public sector institutions.

4.12 Urban Health

4.12.1.1 NHP-2002 envisages the setting up of an organised urban primary health care structure. Since the physical features of urban settings are different from those in rural areas, the policy envisages the adoption of appropriate population norms for the urban public health infrastructure. The structure conceived under NHP-2002 is a two-tiered, one, the primary centre is seen as the first-tier, covering a population of one lakh, with a dispensary providing an OPD facility and essential drugs, to enable access to all the national health programmes; and a second-tier of the urban health organisation at the level of the Government general hospital, where reference is made from the primary centre. The Policy envisages that the funding for the urban primary health system will be jointly borne by the local self-government institutions and State and Central Governments.

4.12.1.2 The Policy also envisages the establishment of fully-equipped 'hub-spoke' trauma care networks in large urban agglomerations to reduce accident mortality.

4.13 Mental Health

4.13.1.1. NHP-2002 envisages a network of decentralised mental health services for ameliorating the more common categories of disorders. The programme outline for such a disease would involve the diagnosis of common disorders, and the prescription of common therapeutic drugs, by general duty medical staff.

4.13.1.2 In regard to mental health institutions for in-door treatment of patients, the Policy envisages the upgrading of the physical infrastructure of such institutions at Central Government expense so as to secure the human rights of this vulnerable segment of society.

4.14 Information, Education and Communication

4.14.1 NHP-2002 envisages an IEC policy, which maximizes the dissemination of information to those population groups which cannot be effectively approached by using only the mass media. The focus would therefore be on the inter-personal communication of information and on folk and other traditional media to bring about behavioural change. The IEC programme would set specific targets for the association of PRIs/NGOs/ Trusts in such activities. In several public health programmes, where behavioural change is an essential component, the success of the initiatives is crucially dependent on dispelling myths and misconceptions pertaining to religious and ethical issues. The community leaders, particularly religious leaders, are effective in imparting knowledge which facilitates such behavioural change. The programme will also have the component of an annual evaluation of the performance of the non-Governmental agencies to monitor the impact of the programmes on the targeted groups. The Central/State Government initiative will also focus on the development of modules for information dissemination in such population groups, who do not normally benefit from the more common media forms.

4.14.2 NHP-2002 envisages giving priority to school health programmes which aim at preventive-health education, providing regular health check-ups, and promotion of health-seeking behaviour among children. The school health programmes can gainfully adopt specially designed modules in order to disseminate information relating to 'health' and 'family life'. This is expected to be the most cost-effective intervention as it improves the level of awareness, not only of the extended family, but the future generation as well.

4.15 Health Research

4.15.1 This Policy envisages an increase in Government-funded health research to a level of 1 percent of the total health spending by 2005; and thereafter, up to 2 percent by 2010. Domestic medical research would be focused on new therapeutic drugs and vaccines for tropical diseases, such as TB and Malaria, as also on the sub-types of HIV/AIDS prevalent in the country. Research programmes taken up by the Government in these priority areas would be conducted in a mission mode. Emphasis would also be laid on time-bound applied research for developing operational applications. This would ensure the cost-effective dissemination of existing/future therapeutic drugs/vaccines in the general population. Private entrepreneurship will be encouraged in the field of medical research for new molecules/vaccines, *inter alia*, through fiscal incentives.

4.16 Role of the Private Sector

4.16.1.1 In principle, this Policy welcomes the participation of the private sector in all areas of health activities—primary, secondary or tertiary. However, looking to past experience of the private sector, it can reasonably be expected that its contribution would be substantial in the urban primary sector and the tertiary sector, and moderate in the secondary sector. This Policy envisages the enactment of suitable legislation for regulating minimum infrastructure and quality standards in clinical establishments/medical institutions by 2003. Also, statutory guidelines for the conduct of clinical practice and delivery of medical services are targeted to be developed over the same period. With the acquiring of experience in the setting and enforcing of minimum quality standards, the Policy envisages graduation to a scheme of quality accreditation of clinical establishments/medical institutions, for the information of the citizenry. The regulatory/accreditation mechanisms will no doubt also cover public health institutions. The Policy also encourages the setting up of private insurance instruments for increasing the scope of the coverage of the secondary and tertiary sector under private health insurance packages.

4.16.1.2 In the context of the very large number of poor in the country, it would be difficult to conceive of an exclusive Government mechanism to provide health services to this category. It has sometimes been felt that a social health insurance scheme, funded by the Government, and with service delivery through the private sector, would be the appropriate solution. The administrative and financial implications of such an initiative are still unknown. As a first step, this policy envisages the introduction of a pilot scheme in a limited number of representative districts, to determine the administrative features of such an arrangement, as also the requirement of resources for it. The results obtained from these pilot projects would provide material on which future public health policy can be based.

4.16.2 NHP-2002 envisages the co-option of the non-governmental practitioners in the national disease control programmes so as to ensure that standard treatment protocols are followed in their day-to-day practice.

4.16.3 This Policy recognizes the immense potential of information technology applications in the area of tele-medicine in the tertiary health care sector. The use of this technical aid will greatly enhance the capacity for the professionals to pool their clinical experience.

4.17 The Role of Civil Society

4.17.1 NHP-2002 recognizes the significant contribution made by NGOs and other institutions of the civil society in making available health services to the community. In order to utilize their high motivational skills on an increasing scale, this Policy envisages that the disease control programmes should earmark not less than 10% of the budget in respect of identified programme components, to be exclusively implemented through these institutions. The policy also emphasizes the need to simplify procedures for government – civil society interfacing in order to enhance the involvement of civil society in public health programmes. In principle, the state would encourage the handing over of public health service outlets at any level for management by NGOs and other institutions of civil society, on an 'as-is-where-is' basis, along with the normative funds earmarked for such institutions.

4.18 National Disease Surveillance Network

4.18.1 This Policy envisages the full operationalization of an integrated disease control network from the lowest rung of public health administration to the Central Government, by 2005. The programme for setting up this network will include components relating to the installation of data-base handling hardware; IT inter-connectivity between different tiers of the network; and in-house training for data collection and interpretation for undertaking timely and effective response. This public health surveillance network will also encompass information from private health care institutions and practitioners. It is expected that real-time information from outside the government system will greatly strengthen the capacity of the public health system to counter focal outbreaks of seasonal diseases.

4.19 Health Statistics

4.19.1.1 The Policy envisages the completion of baseline estimates for the incidence of the common diseases—TB, Malaria, Blindness—by 2005. The Policy proposes that statistical methods be put in place to enable the periodic updating of these baseline estimates through representative sampling, under an appropriate statistical methodology. The policy also recognizes the need to establish, in a longer time-frame, baseline estimates for non-communicable diseases, like CVD, Cancer, Diabetes; and accidental injuries, and communicable diseases, like Hepatitis and JE. NHP-2002 envisages that, with access to such reliable data on the incidence of various diseases, the public health system would move closer to the objective of evidence-based policy-making.

4.19.1.2 Planning for the health sector requires a robust information system, *inter-alia,* covering data on service facilities available in the private sector. NHP-2002 emphasises the need for the early completion of an accurate data-base of this kind.

4.19.2 In an attempt at consolidating the data base and graduating from a mere estimation of the annual health expenditure, NHP-2002 emphasises the need to establish national health accounts, conforming to the 'source-to-users' matrix structure. Also, the policy envisages the estimation of health costs on a continuing basis. Improved and comprehensive information through national health accounts and accounting systems would pave the way for decision-makers to focus on relative priorities, keeping in view the limited financial resources in the health sector.

4.20 Women's Health

4.20.1 NHP-2002 envisages the identification of specific programmes targeted at women's health. The Policy notes that women, along with other under-privileged groups, are significantly handicapped due to a disproportionately low access to health care. The various Policy recommendations of NHP-2002, in regard to the expansion of primary health sector infrastructure, will facilitate the increased access of women to basic health care. The Policy commits the highest priority of the Central Government to the funding of the identified programmes relating to woman's health. Also, the policy recognizes the need to review the staffing norms of the public health administration to meet the specific requirements of women in a more comprehensive manner.

4.21 Medical Ethics

4.21.1.1 NHP-2002 envisages that, in order to ensure that the common patient is not subjected to irrational or profit-driven medical regimens, a contemporary code of ethics be notified and rigorously implemented by the Medical Council of India.

4.21.1.2 By and large, medical research within the country in the frontier disciplines, such as gene-manipulation and stem cell research, is limited. However, the policy recognises that a vigilant watch will have to be kept so that the existing guidelines and statutory provisions are constantly reviewed and updated.

4.22 Enforcement of Quality Standards for Food and Drugs

4.22.1 NHP-2002 envisages that the food and drug administration will be progressively strengthened, in terms of both laboratory facilities and technical expertise. Also, the policy envisages that the standards of food items will be progressively tightened up at a pace which will permit domestic food handling/manufacturing facilities to undertake the necessary upgradation of technology so that they are not shut out of this production sector. The Policy envisages that ultimately food standards will be close, if not equivalent, to Codex specifications; and that drug standards will be at par with the most rigorous ones adopted elsewhere.

4.23 Regulation of Standards in Paramedical Disciplines

4.23.1 NHP-2002 recognises the need for the establishment of statutory professional councils for paramedical disciplines to register practitioners, maintain standards of training, and monitor performance.

4.24 Environmental and Occupational Health

4.24.1 This Policy envisages that the independently-stated policies and programmes of the environment-related sectors be smoothly interfaced with the policies and the programmes of the health sector, in order to reduce the health risk to the citizens and the consequential disease burden.

4.24.2 NHP-2002 envisages the periodic screening of the health conditions of the workers, particularly for high-risk health disorders associated with their occupation.

4.25 Providing Medical Facilities to Users from Overseas

4.25.1 To capitalize on the comparative cost advantage enjoyed by domestic health facilities in the secondary and tertiary sectors, NHP-2002 strongly encourages the providing of such health services on a payment basis to service seekers from overseas. The providers of such services to patients from overseas will be encouraged by extending to their earnings in foreign exchange, all fiscal incentives, including the status of "deemed exports", which are available to other exporters of goods and services.

4.26 Impact of Globalisation on the Health Sector

4.26.1 The Policy takes into account the serious apprehension, expressed by several health experts, of the possible threat to health security in the post-TRIPS era, as a result of a sharp increase in the prices of drugs and vaccines. To protect the citizens of the country from such a threat, this policy envisages a national patent regime for the future, which, while being consistent with TRIPS, avails of all opportunities to secure for the country, under its patent laws, affordable access to the latest medical and other therapeutic discoveries. The policy also sets out that the Government will bring to bear its full influence in all international fora—UN, WHO, WTO, etc.—to secure commitments on the part of the Nations of the Globe, to lighten the restrictive features of TRIPS in its application to the health care sector.

5. SUMMATION

5.1 The crafting of a National Health Policy is a rare occasion in public affairs when it would be legitimate, indeed valuable, to allow our dreams to mingle with our understanding of ground realities. Based purely on the clinical facts defining the current status of the health sector, we would have arrived at a certain policy formulation; but, buoyed by our dreams, we have ventured slightly beyond that in the shape of NHP-2002, which, in fact, defines a vision for the future.

5.2 The health needs of the country are enormous and the financial resources and managerial capacity available to meet them, even on the most optimistic projections, fall somewhat short. In this situation, NHP-2002 has had to make hard choices between various priorities and operational options. NHP-2002 does not claim to be a road-map for meeting all the health needs of the populace of the country. Further, it has to be recognized that such health needs are also dynamic, as threats in the area of public health keep changing over time. The Policy, while being holistic, undertakes the necessary risk of recommending differing emphasis on different policy components. Broadly speaking, NHP-2002 focuses on the need for enhanced funding and an organisational restructuring of the national public health initiatives in order to facilitate more equitable access to the health facilities. Also, the Policy is focused on those diseases which are principally contributing to the disease burden—TB, Malaria and Blindness from the category of historical diseases; and HIV/AIDS from the category of 'newly emerging diseases'. This is not to say that other items contributing to the disease burden of the country will be ignored; but only that the resources, as also the principal focus of the public health administration, will recognize certain relative priorities. It is unnecessary to labour the point that under the umbrella of the macro-policy prescriptions in this document, governments and private sector programme planners will have to design separate schemes, tailor-made to the health needs of women, children, geriatrics, tribals and other socio-economically under-served sections. An adequately robust disaster management plan has to be in place to effectively cope with situations arising from natural and man-made calamities.

5.3 One nagging imperative, which has influenced every aspect of this Policy, is the need to ensure that 'equity' in the health sector stands as an independent goal. In any future evaluation of its success or failure, NHP-2002 would wish to be measured against this equity norm, rather than any other aggregated financial norm for the health sector. Consistent with the primacy given to 'equity', a marked emphasis has been provided in the policy for expanding and improving the primary health facilities, including the new concept of the provisioning of essential drugs through Central funding. The Policy also commits the Central Government to an increased under-writing of the resources for meeting the minimum health needs of the people. Thus, the Policy attempts to provide guidance for prioritizing expenditure, thereby facilitating rational resource allocation.

5.4 This Policy broadly envisages a greater contribution from the Central Budget for the delivery of Public Health services at the State level. Adequate appropriations, steadily rising over the years, would need to be ensured. The possibility of ensuring this by imposing an earmarked health cess has been carefully examined. While it is recognized that the annual budget must accommodate the increasing resource needs of the social sectors, particularly in the health sector, this Policy does not specifically recommend an earmarked health cess, as that would have a tendency of reducing the space available to Parliament in making appropriations looking to the circumstances prevailing from time to time.

5.5 The Policy highlights the expected roles of different participating groups in the health sector. Further, it recognizes the fact that, despite all that may be guaranteed by the Central Government for assisting public health programmes, public health services would actually need to be delivered by the State administration, NGOs and other institutions of civil society. The attainment of improved health levels would be significantly dependent on population stabilisation, as also on complementary efforts from other areas of the social sectors—like improved drinking water supply, basic sanitation, minimum nutrition, etc.—to ensure that the exposure of the populace to health risks is minimized.

5.6 Any expectation of a significant improvement in the quality of health services, and the consequential improved health status of the citizenry, would depend not only on increased financial and material inputs, but also on a more empathetic and committed attitude in the service providers, whether in the private or public sectors. In some measure, this optimistic policy document is based on the understanding that the citizenry is increasingly demanding more by way of quality in health services, and the health delivery system, particularly in the public sector, is being pressed to respond. In this backdrop, it needs to be recognized that any policy in the social sector is critically dependent on the service providers treating their responsibility not as a commercial activity, but as a service, albeit a paid one. In the area of public health, an improved standard of governance is a prerequisite for the success of any health policy.

BOOKS BY THE SAME AUTHOR

1. International Administration: WHO South East-Asia Regional Office (New Delhi, 1977), Sterling Publishers
2. Principles, Problems and Prospects of Co-operative Administration (New Delhi, 1979), Sterling Publishers (Co-Author Dr. B.B. Goel)
3. Administration of Personnel in Co-operative (New Delhi, 1979), Sterling Publishers (Co-Author Dr. B.B. Goel)
4. Health Care Administration: Ecology, Principles and Modern Trends (New Delhi, 1980), Sterling Publishers
5. Health Care Administration: Policy-making and Planning (New Delhi, 1980), Sterling Publishers
6. Health Care Administration: Levels and Aspects (New Delhi, 1980), Sterling Publishers
7. International Civil Service: Principles, Problems and Prospects (New Delhi, 1984), Sterling Publishers
8. Public Health Administration (New Delhi, 1984), Sterling Publishers
9. Public Personnel Administration (New Delhi, 1984), Reprint 1987, Sterling Publishers
10. International Civil Services—Principles, Problems and Prospectives (New Delhi, 1984), Sterling Publishers.
11. Social Welfare Administration: Theory and Practice (Vols. I and II) (New Delhi, 1988), Deep & Deep Publications Pvt. Ltd.
12. Hospital Administration and Management (ed.) Co-Author Dr. R. Kumar in 3 volumes (New Delhi, 1989), Deep & Deep Publications Pvt. Ltd.
13. Policy and Administration: Family Planning & Beyond (New Delhi, 1990), Deep & Deep Publications Pvt. Ltd.
14. Modern Management Techniques (Revised and Reprinted) (New Delhi, 1990), Deep & Deep Publications Pvt. Ltd.
15. Development Planning and Administration (ed.) S. Bhatnagar (Co-editor) (New Delhi, 1992), Deep & Deep Publications Pvt. Ltd.
16. Financial Administration and Management (New Delhi, 1993), Sterling Publishers
17. Advanced Public Administration (New Delhi, 1993), Sterling Publishers

18. Personnel Administration and Management
(New Delhi, 1994), Deep & Deep Publications Pvt. Ltd.
19. Educational Policy and Administration
(New Delhi, 1994), Deep & Deep Publications Pvt. Ltd.
20. Slum Improvement Through Participatory Urban Based Community Structures
(New Delhi, 1999), Deep & Deep Publications Pvt. Ltd.
21. Distance Education in 21st Century
(New Delhi, 2000), Deep & Deep Publications Pvt. Ltd.
22. Health Care System and Management: Organization and Structure
(New Delhi, 2000), Deep & Deep Publications Pvt. Ltd.
23. Health Care System and Management: Policies and Programmes
(New Delhi, 2000), Deep & Deep Publications Pvt. Ltd.
24. Health Care System and Management: Management and Administration
(New Delhi, 2000), Deep & Deep Publications Pvt. Ltd.
25. Heath Care System and Management: Primary Health Care Management
(New Delhi, 2000), Deep & Deep Publications Pvt. Ltd.
26. Management Techniques: Principles and Practices
(New Delhi, 2001), Deep & Deep Publications Pvt. Ltd.
27. Encyclopaedia of Disaster Management in 3 Volumes
(New Delhi, 2001), Deep & Deep Publications Pvt. Ltd.
28. Management of Hospitals: Hospital Core Services
(New Delhi, 2002), Deep & Deep Publications Pvt. Ltd.
29. Management of Hospitals: Hospital Supportive Services
(New Delhi, 2002), Deep & Deep Publications Pvt. Ltd.
30. Management of Hospitals: Hospital Preventive and Promotive Services
(New Delhi, 2002), Deep & Deep Publications Pvt. Ltd.
31. Management of Hospitals: Hospital Managerial Services
(New Delhi, 2002), Deep & Deep Publications Pvt. Ltd.
32. Public Personal Administration
(New Delhi, 2002), Deep & Deep Publications Pvt. Ltd.
33. Public Financial Administration
(New Delhi, 2002), Deep & Deep Publications Pvt. Ltd.
34. Urban Development and Management
(New Delhi, 2002), Deep & Deep Publications Pvt. Ltd.
35. Public Administration: Theory and Practices
(New Delhi, 2003), Deep & Deep Publications Pvt. Ltd.
36. Advanced Public Administration (Revised and Enlarged Edition)
(New Delhi, 2003), Deep & Deep Publications Pvt. Ltd.

37. Panchayati Raj in India
(New Delhi, 2003), Deep & Deep Publications Pvt. Ltd.
38. Encyclopedia of Higher Education in 21st Century: Organisation and Structure
(New Delhi, 2004), Deep & Deep Publications Pvt. Ltd.
39. Encyclopaedia of Higher Education in 21st Century: Quality and Excellence
(New Delhi, 2004), Deep & Deep Publications Pvt. Ltd.
40. Encyclopedia of Higher Education in 21st Century, Extension Education Services
(New Delhi, 2004), Deep & Deep Publications Pvt. Ltd.
41. Stress Management and Education: An Indian Perspective
(New Delhi, 2004), Deep & Deep Publications Pvt. Ltd.
42. Human Values and Education:
(New Delhi, 2004), Deep & Deep Publications Pvt. Ltd.
43. Public Health Policy and Administration
(New Delhi, 2004), Deep & Deep Publications Pvt. Ltd.
44. Administration and Management of NGO's: Text and Case Studies
(New Delhi, 2004), Deep & Deep Publications Pvt. Ltd.
45. Nursing Services: Management and Administration
(New Delhi, 2005), Deep & Deep Publications Pvt. Ltd.
46. Population Policy and Family Welfare Administration
(New Delhi, 2005), Deep & Deep Publications Pvt. Ltd.
47. Human Resource Development in 21st Century
(New Delhi, 2005), Deep & Deep Publications Pvt. Ltd.
48. Encyclopaedia of Disaster Management (3 Volumes)
(New Delhi, 2006) Deep & Deep Publications Pvt. Ltd.
49. School Health Education
(New Delhi, 2007), Deep & Deep Publications Pvt. Ltd.
50. Health Education: Theory and Practices
(New Delhi, 2007), Deep & Deep Publications Pvt. Ltd.
51. Good Governance: An Integral Views
(New Delhi, 2007), Deep & Deep Publications Pvt. Ltd.
52. Right to Information and Good Governance
(New Delhi, 2007), Deep & Deep Publications Pvt. Ltd.
53. Disaster Management: Text and Case Studies
(New Delhi, 2007), Deep & Deep Publications Pvt. Ltd.
54. Hospital Administration: Theory and Practices
(New Delhi, 2007), Deep & Deep Publications Pvt. Ltd.
55. Environmental Health Values and Education,
(New Delhi, 2008), Deep & Deep Publications Pvt. Ltd.

56. Administrative and Management Thinkers: Revelvance in New Millennium
(New Delhi, 2008), Deep & Deep Publications Pvt. Ltd.
57. Principles and Practices of Human Values
(New Delhi, 2008), Deep & Deep Publications Pvt. Ltd.
58. Distance Education: Principles, Potentialities and Perspectives
(New Delhi, 2008), Deep & Deep Publications Pvt. Ltd.
59. Educational Administration and Management: An Integral View
(New Delhi, 2008), Deep & Deep Publications Pvt. Ltd.
60. Women Health Education
(New Delhi, 2008), Deep & Deep Publications Pvt. Ltd.
61. Health Care System and Hospital Administration
Vol. 1 (Organizational Structure)
(New Delhi, 2008), Deep & Deep Publications Pvt. Ltd.
62. Health Care System and Hospital Administration
Vol. 2 (Resources: Human, Finance and Material)
(New Delhi, 2008), Deep & Deep Publications Pvt. Ltd.
63. Health Care System and Hospital Administration
Vol. 3 (Policy-making and Programmes)
(New Delhi, 2008), Deep & Deep Publications Pvt. Ltd.
64. Health Care System and Hospital Administration
Vol. 4 (Emerging and Thrust Areas)
(New Delhi, 2008), Deep & Deep Publications Pvt. Ltd.
65. Health Care System and Hospital Administration
Vol. 5 (Primary/Rural Health Care)
(New Delhi, 2008), Deep & Deep Publications Pvt. Ltd.
66. Health Care System and Hospital Administration
Vol. 6 (Secondary and Tertiary Health Care)
(New Delhi, 2008), Deep & Deep Publications Pvt. Ltd.
67. Health Care System and Hospital Administration
Vol. 7 (Management Techniques and Good Governance)
(New Delhi, 2008), Deep & Deep Publications Pvt. Ltd.
68. Education of Lifestyle and Lifetime Diseases
(Deep & Deep Publications Pvt. Ltd.)
69. Health Education Administration—From International Level to Village Level
(Deep & Deep Publications Pvt. Ltd.)
70. Education for Healthy Urban Cities
(Deep & Deep Publications Pvt. Ltd.)
71. Rural Health Education
(Deep & Deep Publications Pvt. Ltd.)

Bibliography

Acton Society Trust, Hospitals and the State: Hospital Organisation and Administration under the National Health Service Series, London: Action Society Trust, 1956, 54p.

Acton Society Trust, Hospitals and the State: Hospital Organisation and Administration under the National Health Service, London: The Trust, 1959, iii, 80p.

Andhra Pradesh, Health and Local Administration Department Panchayats Executive Officers Regulations relating to Recruitment, etc., Hyderabad: The Author, 1956, l6p.

Bannington, B.G., English Public Health Administration, 2nd ed., London: P.S. King, 1929, 325p.

Berkov, Robert, The World Health Organisation: A Study in Decentralized International Administration, Geneva Droz, 1957, 173p.

Better Health by Community Projects Administration, Planning Commission, New Delhi: Community Projects, Planning Commission, n.d., 32p.

Blum, Henrik L., Public Administration: A Public Health Viewpoint, N.Y.: Macmillan, 1963, 532p.

Hugh Flanagan and Peter Spurgeon, Public Sector Managerial Effectiveness: Theory and Practice in the National Health Service, Buckingham: Open Univ. Press, 1996, 128p.

Freeman, Ruth B., Administration of Public Health Services and Edward M. Holmes, Philadelphia: Saunders, 1960, 507p.

Goddard, H.A., Principles of Administration Applied to Nursing Service by H.A. Goddard, Geneva: World Health Organisation, 1958, 106p.

Goel, Rajneesh, Community Health Care, New Delhi: Deep & Deep Publications Pvt. Ltd., 2004, 403p.

Goel, S.L., Health and Care Administration: Policy-making and Planning, Delhi: Sterling, 1980, 288p.

Goel, S.L, Health Care Administration: Ecology, Principles and Modern Trends, Delhi: Sterling, 1980, 233p.

Goel, S.L., Health Care Administration: Levels and Aspects, Delhi: Sterling, 1980, 245p.

Goel, S.L., Health Care System and Management, New Delhi: Deep & Deep Publications Pvt. Ltd., 2004, 4 Vols.

Goel, S.L., International Administration: WHO South-East Asia Regional Office, Delhi: Sterling, 1977, 344p.

Goel, S.L., Population Policy and Family Welfare: Reproductive and Child Health Administration, New Delhi: Deep & Deep Publications Pvt. Ltd., 2005, 526p.

Goel, S.L., Public Health Administration, Delhi: Sterling, 1984, 472p.

Goel, S.L, Public Health Policy and Administration, New Delhi: Deep & Deep Publications Pvt. Ltd., 2005, 651p.

Graduate Study in Public Administration: A Guide to Graduate Programs by Office of Education, Department of Health, Education and Welfare, Washington: United States Government Printing Office, 1961, 158+p.

Greenfield, Margert, State-Local Service for Mental Health, Bureau of Public Administration, Berkeley: The Bureau, 1955, 93p.

Guangde, Sun, Health Care Administration in China, Westport: Greenport, 1993, pp. 53-62.

Handbook on Human Services Administration, edited by Jack Rabin and Marcia B. Steinhauer, New York: Marcel Dekker, 1988, 604p.

Health Policy Research in South Asia: Building Capacity for Reform, edited by Abdo S. Yazbeck and David H. Peters, Washington, D.C.: World Bank, 2003, 428p.

Heaver, Richard, Managing Primary Health Care: Implications of the Health Transition, Washington, D.C.: World Bank, 1995, 41p.

Health Status of the Underprivileged, New Delhi: Centre for Urban Studies, Indian Institute of Public Administration, 1991, 225p.

Indian Institute of Public Administration, Centre for Urban Studies, Urban Health System, edited by P.K. Umashankar and Girish K. Misra, New Delhi: Reliance and IIPA, 1993, 259p.

Institute for Training in Municipal Administration, Administration of Community Health Services, Chicago: ICMA, 1961, 560p.

Johnston, Timothy, Investing in Health: Development Effectiveness in the Health, Nutrition, and Population Sector, Washington, D.C.: World Bank, 1999, 69p.

Khandewale, Shreekant V., Health Administration and the Weaker Sections in an Indian Metropolis, Delhi: Devika, 1996, 231p.

Klinoubol, Kriengkrai, Public Health Development and Administration: A Study of Developing Economy, Delhi: Deep & Deep Publications Pvt. Ltd., 1989. 436p.

Local Self-Government Administration in States of India, 1956, New Delhi: Ministry of Health, 1956, 149p.

Local Self-government Administration in States of India, 1962, Ministry of Health, Delhi: The Manager of Publications, 1962, 161+p.

Legislature Committee on Local Administration by Health, Education and Local Administration Department, Madras, Madras: Health, Education and Local Administration Department, 1958, 5 Parts.

Morden, Margaret Gorsuch, Cooperative Health Administration in Metropolitan, Los Angeles: The Bureau, 1949, 52p.

Panchayat Manual, Madras: Health, Education and Local Administration Department, 1956, 368+p.

Papers in Public Administration, No. 6, Ann Arbor: The Bureau, 1950, 85p.

Public Services M.B.A. Induction Module: India-U.K. context (August-September, 1999: Indian Institute of Public Administration, New Delhi), Gender-related Issues (course material), New Delhi: Indian Institute of Public Administration, 1999, vp.

Report of the Regional Training Seminar on Social Security Administration, New Delhi: Regional Office for Asia and Oceania, 1979, 75p.

Rowbottom, R., Hospital Organisation: A Progress Report on the Brunel Health Services Project, London: Heinemann, 1973, 314p.

Survey of Research in Public Administration, 1980-90, edited by V.A. Pai Panandiker, Delhi: Konark, 1997, 631p.

Tebow, Hilda P., Staff-Development as an Integral Part of Administration, Washington, D.C.: Department of Health, Education and Welfare, 1959, 33+p.

The Indo-US Symposium on Community Mental Health at National Institute of Mental Health and Neuro Sciences, Bangalore: National Institute of Mental Health and Neuro Sciences, 1992, 520p.

Weaver, Jerry L., Conflict and Control in Health Care Administration, Beverly Hills: n.p., 1975, 197p.

Welfare Administration and Social Welfare Around the World, by Department of Health, Education and Welfare, United States, Washington: Government Printing Office, 1963, 9p.

Wishwakarma, R.K., Health Status of the Underprivileged, New Delhi: Centre for Urban Studies, Indian Institute of Public Administration, 1993, 283p.

Index